Sex Differences in Behavior

SEMINARS IN HUMAN REPRODUCTION

Series Editors:

Raymond L. Vande Wiele (M.D.) and
Ralph M. Richart (M.D.)
*International Institute for the Study of
Human Reproduction*
Columbia University, New York

BIORHYTHMS AND HUMAN REPRODUCTION

Edited by Michel Ferin, Franz Halberg,
Ralph M. Richart, and Raymond L. Vande Wiele

SEX DIFFERENCES IN BEHAVIOR

Edited by Richard C. Friedman, Ralph M. Richart,
and Raymond L. Vande Wiele

Sex Differences in Behavior

A Conference Sponsored by the
International Institute
for the Study of Human Reproduction
College of Physicians and Surgeons
of Columbia University

EDITED BY

RICHARD C. FRIEDMAN, M.D.

RALPH M. RICHART, M.D.

RAYMOND L. VANDE WIELE, M.D.

ASSISTANT EDITOR

LENORE O. STERN

A WILEY BIOMEDICAL-HEALTH PUBLICATION

JOHN WILEY & SONS, New York • London • Sydney • Toronto

Library of Congress Cataloging in Publication Data

Main entry under title:
Sex differences in behavior.

(Seminars in human reproduction) (A Wiley biomedical-health publication)
"Sponsored by International Institute for the Study of Human Reproduction."
Includes bibliographical references.
1. Sex differences (Psychology)—Congresses.
I. Friedman, Richard C., 1941-   ed.
II. Richart, Ralph M., ed. III. International Institute for the Study of Human Reproduction.
IV. Series. [DNLM: 1. Behavior.   2. Congresses—Sex characteristics.   2. Congresses. BF692 S515]

BF692.S43   155.3′3   74-9769
ISBN 0-471-28053-4

Printed in the United States of America

10 9 8 7 6 5 4 3 2 1

List of Conference Participants

Susan W. Baker
Assistant in Psychoendocrinology
State University of New York,
    Children's Hospital
Buffalo, New York

Estelle P. Bender, M.D.
Research Associate
New York State Psychiatric Institute
New York, New York

Susan Coates
Clinical Assistant Professor
Division of Child and Adolescent
    Psychiatry
Department of Psychiatry
State University of New York
Downstate Medical Center
Brooklyn, New York

Zira DeFries, M.D.
Assistant Clinical Professor of Psychiatry
College of Physicians and Surgeons
Columbia University
New York, New York

Charles H. Doering, Ph.D.
Research Associate
Department of Psychiatry
Stanford University School of Medicine
Stanford, California

Harlow D. Dunton, M.D.
Professor of Clinical Psychiatry
College of Physicians and Surgeons
Columbia University
New York, New York

Anke A. Ehrhardt, Ph.D.
Clinical Associate Professor of Psychology
Department of Psychiatry
Research Assistant Professor in Pediatrics
State University of New York,
    Children's Hospital
Buffalo, New York

Richard C. Friedman, M.D.
Instructor in Clinical Psychiatry
Director of Medical Education
International Institute for the Study of
    Human Reproduction
College of Physicians and Surgeons
Columbia University
New York, New York

Eleanor Galenson, M.D.
Associate Professor of Psychiatry
Albert Einstein College of Medicine
Bronx, New York

Richard Green, M.D.
Professor of Psychiatry and
    Behavioral Science

Coordinator, Projects in Human Sexuality
Health Sciences Center
State University of New York
  at Stony Brook
Stony Brook, New York

Beatrix A. Hamburg, M.D.
Assistant Professor of Psychiatry
Director, Child Psychiatry Clinic
Stanford University School of Medicine
Stanford, California

Howard F. Hunt, Ph.D.
Professor of Psychology
College of Physicians and Surgeons
Columbia University
New York, New York

Joseph Jaffe, M.D.
Associate Clinical Professor of Psychiatry
College of Physicians and Surgeons
Columbia University
New York, New York

Lawrence Kohlberg, Ph.D.
Professor of Education and
  Social Psychology
Laboratory of Human Development
Harvard University
Cambridge, Massachusetts

Anneliese F. Korner, Ph.D.
Senior Scientist
Department of Psychiatry
Stanford University School of Medicine
Stanford, California

Seymour Levine, Ph.D.
Professor and Director
Laboratory of Developmental
  Psychobiology
Department of Psychiatry
Stanford University School of Medicine
Stanford, California

Michael Lewis, Ph.D.
Professor and Director
Infant Laboratory
Institute for Research in Human
  Development
Educational Testing Service
Princeton, New Jersey

Sidney Malitz, M.D.
Deputy Director
New York State Psychiatric Institute
New York, New York

Elizabeth McCauley, Ph.D.
Fellow in Psychoendocrinology
State University of New York,
  Children's Hospital
Buffalo, New York

Heino F. L. Meyer-Bahlburg, Ph.D.
Research Assistant Professor in Pediatrics
Research Assistant Professor of Psychology
  in the Department of Psychiatry
State University of New York,
  Children's Hospital
Buffalo, New York

**Richard P. Michael, M.D., D.Sc., Ph.D.,
D.P.M., F.R.C. Psy.**
Professor of Psychiatry and Anatomy
Director, Biological Psychiatry Research
  Laboratories
Woodruff Medical Center of
  Emory University
Atlanta, Georgia

Robert Michels, M.D.
Psychiatrist-in-Chief
Cornell University Medical Center
The New York Hospital
New York, New York

Howard A. Moss, Ph.D.
Research Psychologist
Chief, Section on Parent-Infant Behavior
Child Research Branch
National Institute of Mental Health
Bethesda, Maryland

Kenneth E. Moyer, Ph.D.
Professor
Department of Psychology
Carnegie-Mellon University
Pittsburgh, Pennsylvania

John F. O'Connor, M.D.
Associate Clinical Professor of Psychiatry
Director, Behavioral Science Unit
International Institute for the Study of
  Human Reproduction

College of Physicians and Surgeons
Columbia University
New York, New York

Harold Persky, Ph.D.
Professor
Department of Psychiatry
University of Pennsylvania and the
  Philadelphia General Hospital
Philadelphia, Pennsylvania

Ethel S. Person, M.D.
Assistant Clinical Professor of Psychiatry
College of Physicians and Surgeons
Columbia University
New York, New York

Charles H. Phoenix, Ph.D.
Assistant Director
Oregon Regional Primate Research Center
Beaverton, Oregon

Ralph M. Richart, M.D.
Professor of Pathology
Director, Biomedical Division
International Institute for the Study
  of Human Reproduction
College of Physicians and Surgeons
Columbia University

Leonard A. Rosenblum, Ph.D.
Professor of Psychiatry
Director, Primate Behavior Laboratory
State University of New York
Downstate Medical Center
Brooklyn, New York

Edward Sachar, M.D.
Director of Psychiatry
Bronx Municipal Hospital Center
Bronx, New York

Gene P. Sackett, Ph.D.
Professor of Psychology
Regional Primate Research Center
Child Development and Mental
  Retardation Center
University of Washington
Seattle, Washington

Daniel N. Stern, M.D.
Chief, Department of Developmental
  Processes

New York State Psychiatric Institute
Assistant Professor of Psychiatry
College of Physicians and Surgeons
Columbia University
New York, New York

Lenore O. Stern
Staff Associate
Conference Coordinator
International Institute for the Study of
  Human Reproduction
College of Physicians and Surgeons
Columbia University
New York, New York

Ruth Tendler
Associate Clinical Psychologist
New York State Psychiatric Institute
New York, New York

Dorothy Z. Ullian
Research Assistant
Laboratory of Human Development
Harvard University
Cambridge, Massachusetts

Raymond L. Vande Wiele, M.D.
Chairman and Professor
Department of Obstetrics and Gynecology
Director, International Institute for the
  Study of Human Reproduction
College of Physicians and Surgeons
Columbia University
New York, New York

Ingeborg L. Ward, Ph.D.
Associate Professor of Psychology
Villanova University
Villanova, Pennsylvania

Richard E. Whalen, Ph.D.
Professor of Psychobiology
University of California
Irvine, California

Joseph Zubin, Ph.D.
Professor Emeritus of Psychology
College of Physicians and Surgeons
Columbia University
New York, New York

Foreword

The International Institute for the Study of Human Reproduction (IISHR) was organized at Columbia University in 1965, largely through the efforts of Dr. Howard C. Taylor, Jr., with the generous support of the Ford Foundation and other agencies. The IISHR includes three divisions —Biomedical, Reproductive Biology and Biochemistry, and Social and Administrative Sciences—and its research and teaching activities range from basic research in reproductive biology to the evaluation of international family planning programs. This conference was the second in a planned series of meetings dealing with various aspects of human reproduction which are designed to explore new or expanding fields.

Following a chronobiology symposium, it was logical to choose behavior as an area of emphasis. We feel it crucial to understand the influence of physiological systems on behavior and of behavioral symptoms on biologicalihomeostasis.

The conference was organized with the view that the mind and the body are not dichotomous categories but are, rather, the names given to different aspects of an organic unity.

The present is a particularly exciting time in the history of the life and behavioral sciences, since new methods of data collection (such as the development of the radioimmunoassays) are resulting in a massive accumulation of facts which require the creation of new conceptual frameworks in order to be more fully understood.

It is hoped that this book, by clarifying present areas of knowledge and outlining problems for future investigators, will foster the development of models that will have relevance both for the research scientist and the clinician.

RAYMOND L. VANDE WIELE, M.D.

Preface

At the time this conference was planned, sex differences in psychological functioning had received relatively scant attention, possibly because the subject matter was immediately less appealing than other topics such as erotic behavior. One reason for the symposium was to emphasize the importance of an area frequently alluded to, but less often the focus of scientific inquiry.

In order to open new lines of communication, we attempted to bring together specialists who might not otherwise meet. A developmental theme was followed, species similarities and differences were identified, and the connections between multiple levels of behavioral organization were at least partially exposed.

The general approach was to describe the influences of psychological, physiological, and social systems on each other within a sex-difference framework. For example, boys and girls behave differently, and mothers respond to them differently. Are maternal responses primarily induced by congenital differences in children, or do mothers, in compliance with social norms, teach distinct patterns of behavior on the basis of gender? How early in life can behavioral differences between males and females be documented? To what degree do biological determinants influence the induction of behavioral differences, and to what degree are they induced by them? Can positive and negative feedback effects be clarified with regard to sex differences in perception, cognition, unconscious mental mechanisms, physiological homeostasis, responses to stress, social interactions?

As a group, these papers highlight the need to keep an open mind when analyzing sets of behaviors in terms of antecedents and consequences.

Principles do emerge (such as the notion of masculine vulnerability), but mechanistic models based on simple cause-effect relationships are challenged at every turn by the intricacies of the systems under study.

In addition to providing an up-to-date review, the Conference Proceedings may stimulate the reader to expand his perspective by applying unfamiliar models to previously familiar material.

In the sex-difference field, as in so many other areas, new methods of investigation have too often resulted in the accumulation of data within specialized compartments of knowledge. It is hoped that this book will foster the development of points of view that integrate diversity and lead to new directions for research.

In conclusion we would like to express our appreciation to the many individuals, not least the contributors to the meeting, whose unceasing efforts made the conference possible. We are particularly grateful to Ms. Susan Coates for many rich and stimulating discussions that helped shape the organization of the conference. Our thanks are also due to Mrs. Lenore Stern who functioned as conference administrator and hostess, manuscript reviewer and editorial associate. Mrs. Stern's diligence, charm, enthusiasm, and patience were appreciated beyond measure by all who worked with her. Finally, we wish to acknowledge the help and cooperation of the publisher who enabled us to prepare this book in so short a time.

RICHARD C. FRIEDMAN

RALPH M. RICHART

New York, New York
July 1974

Contents

xiii

5 GENDER IDENTITY
Richard C. Friedman, *Moderator*
Ruth Tendler, *Rapporteur*

6 AGGRESSION, ADAPTATION, AND EVOLUTION
Heino F. L. Meyer-Bahlburg, *Moderator*
Daniel N. Stern, *Rapporteur*

1 Effect of Hormones on the Development of Behavior

SEYMOUR LEVINE, *Moderator*

CHARLES H. DOERING, *Rapporteur*

CHAPTER 1

Sexual Behavior Differentiation: Prenatal Hormonal and Environmental Control

INGEBORG L. WARD

Department of Psychology
Villanova University
Villanova, Pennsylvania

We now understand that hormones operating during "critical periods" of perinatal development control the differentiation not only of sexual morphology but of sexual behavior potentials as well. If androgen is present during these very specific periods of early development, masculinization and defeminization of behavior potentials, reproductive physiology, and morphology occur. In the absence of androgen, morphology and behavior are feminized. This chapter reviews recent studies, using subhuman animal species, that have clearly established the critical role of hormones in determining sexual differentiation. The effects of environmental stressors acting during these critical periods are also discussed.

What distinguishes the genetic male from the genetic female at a very early stage of embryonic development is a functioning set of testes. In the rat, the most commonly studied species, testosterone is present at detectable levels by day 14 of gestation (1). This endogenous androgen ensures masculinization of the brain and morphology of male fetuses. The female, differentiating in a hormonal milieu that is relatively free of androgen, is feminized. Obviously, any condition that somehow alters normal titers of gonadal hormones circulating in developing fetuses would induce alterations of both sexual morphology and behavior. A few specific examples, utilizing a variety of experimental strategies, will serve to illustrate this basic principle.

Exposure of genetic females to androgen during prenatal development, and in some species during early neonatal development, results in distinct masculinization of various morphological structures. These changes include increases in body weight and length, differentiation of a penis in place of a clitoris, and suppressed development of mammillary glands and of the vaginal orifice. Internal reproductive structures are also modified. For example, treatment of female rats with the potent synthetic androgen testosterone propionate (TP) during prenatal (day 16 to day 20 of the rat's 22-day gestation period) as well as neonatal (day 1 to day 40 postpartum) ontogeny induces development of such distinct male reproductive structures as the vas deferens, seminal vesicles, coagulating glands, prostates, and scrotal sacs (2). Changes in morphology resulting from perinatal androgenization have been reported in females of a variety of species, including cattle (3), opossums (4), mice (5), guinea pigs (6, 7), rats (8, 9), hamsters (10), beagles (11), rhesus monkeys (12), and humans (13).

Conversely, if effective androgen utilization is blocked in genetic males, external as well as internal structures are feminized. The most striking demonstration of this phenomenon is to be found in the numerous studies in which cyproterone acetate, an antiandrogen believed to block androgen-receptor sites (14, 15), was administered to fetal male rats (16–18). The effects of this treatment include reduced body weight, formation of mammillary glands, and development of a patent vagina. Typically, the penis is hypospadic and reduced in length and diameter.

The nature and extent of morphological alterations depend on the exact stage of ontogeny in which changes in androgen levels occur. For example, in the rat, the critical period for differentiation of the mammillary glands, derivatives of the Wolffian and Müllerian duct systems, and some components of the external genitalia are prenatal (2, 8). Thus, though neonatal manipulations change body weight and length, they have a lesser effect on the development of the vagina and penis, and do not at all influence earlier developing structures, such as the duct system and mammillary glands. Androgen titers altered before or after the specific critical period for any given component of the reproductive morphology are largely without effect. Once structural development or suppression has occurred, it cannot be reversed, at least not by hormonal means.

If one now considers the mechanism underlying the differentiation of sexual behavior potentials, it appears that a similar set of principles hold. The classic study of Phoenix, Goy, Gerall and Young (7) demonstrated that injections of TP to pregnant guinea pigs drastically altered the reproductive behavior of the female offspring. Female sexual response was much impaired in adulthood, even after the administration of exogenous estrogen and progesterone, a hormonal regime that ordinarily induces receptivity in normal females. Conversely, when treated with TP as adults and paired with receptive females, prenatally androgenized females showed high levels of male copulatory behavior. Numerous studies published subsequent to this pioneering report have added the needed detail to document the generality of these behavioral alterations and delineated some of the parameters involved.

Although some investigators have been unable to demonstrate increased male copulatory behavior in prenatally androgenized female rats (19), the most frequent finding (17, 20, 21) is that illustrated in Table 1. Prenatal TP resulted in significant increases, as compared with control females, in both incomplete and complete copulatory responses. Although both incomplete and complete responses are characterized by posterior mounting of the lure female and palpation of her flanks with the forepaws, the pelvic thrusting accompanying the complete response is much more vigorous than in the case of the incomplete response, and the dismount is usually followed by genital self-grooming. Postnatal treatment alone enhanced only complete copulations, a well-documented finding

Table 1   Mean Number of Incomplete (I) and Complete (C) Copulations Engaged in by Females Treated with Oil or Testosterone Propionate (TP) During Prenatal or Neonatal Development[a]

Treatment[b]	N	Mean I+C	Mean C
Control	13	46	8
Postnatal TP	8	43	18
Prenatal TP	8	93	19

[a] Adapted from I. L. Ward and F. J. Renz, *J Comp Physiol Psychol* **78**: 349, 1972.
[b] In adulthood, all groups received daily TP injections during the 24-day period of behavioral testing.

(19, 21–23). Complete copulations are seen infrequently in normal females.

If androgen is administered both prenatally and postnatally to female rats, masculinization is complete. Not only do these females possess many of the morphological structures of males, but, as seen in Table 2, the behavior is so totally masculinized as to include the ejaculatory pattern (2, 24–26). The response is indistinguishable from that of normal males and is followed by a characteristic postejaculatory refractory period. Furthermore, these females emit the ultrasonic vocalization (25), termed "postejaculatory song," characteristic of ejaculating males (27). One female, tested for a total of $2\frac{1}{2}$ hours, ejaculated seven times, a performance typical of vigorous male rats (2). Furthermore, ejaculations were accompanied by deposition of semen into the vagina of the lure female (2). Although this is not surprising, considering that the needed apparatus for fluid production, seminal vesicles, coagulating glands, and prostates was present, it does demonstrate that the ejaculatory response observed in these females is accompanied by actual insertion of the penis into the vagina. The semen, of course, contained no sperm since these females had no testes. Although prenatal TP treatment alone did not induce a potential for ejaculatory behavior in female rats, it does result in total behavioral masculinization of species with longer gestation periods, for example, the guinea pig (28) and the rhesus monkey (29). In the rat, neonatal androgen alone is sufficient to induce a capacity for ejaculation in a small percentage of females (2, 25, 26).

When such perinatally androgenized female rats are treated with estrogen and progesterone in adulthood and tested for female lordotic

Table 2   Percentage of Perinatally Androgenized Females Showing the Ejaculatory Response on at Least One of 15 Tests[a]

Subjects[b]	N	Percentage Ejaculating
Normal females	16	0
Postnatal TP females	23	30
Prenatal TP females	14	0
Prenatal and postnatal TP females	11	73
Normal males	7	100

[a]Adapted from I. L. Ward, *Horm Behav* **1**: 25, 1969.
[b]Testing and daily TP injections were initiated in all groups at 60 days of age.

behavior, there is a sharp reduction in the display of female receptivity (21, 22, 30–33). As illustrated in Table 3, both the number of lordosis responses and the quality of the estrous behavior pattern displayed are much impaired by either prenatal or postnatal TP treatment. Indeed, Barraclough and Gorski (30) were the first to demonstrate that even a single injection of androgen within the first 5 days after birth to female rats will induce sterility—that is, ovulation does not occur, and behavioral receptivity is decreased or eliminated. Thus such females are unable to reproduce because the physiological and behavioral apparatus required to allow fertilization of an ovum is impaired.

If genetic males are deprived of androgen during perinatal development, feminization and demasculinization of behavior result. In rats, postnatal deficiencies induced by castration on the day of birth eliminate the potential for ejaculatory behavior in adulthood, although high levels of incomplete copulatory behavior persist. Such males, however, show high-quality female lordotic patterns if they are treated with estrogen and progesterone (17, 34–37). Similarly, prenatal androgen deficiencies, induced by cyproterone acetate treatment, will impair development of male copulatory behavior while increasing the potential for lordosis (Fig. 1), although the effect is not as great as that observed after neonatal castration (18, 38). For example, soliciting behavior, a distinct component of the female rat's estrous behavior pattern, is routinely observed in males castrated on the day of birth. It is rarely present in males treated prenatally with cyproterone acetate (18).

The conclusion that might be drawn from this series of studies is that

Table 3   Mean Number of Lordosis Responses and Mean Quality of Estrous Behavior Exhibited by Perinatally Androgenized Females[a]

Treatment[b]	N	Mean Number of Lordosis Responses	Mean Quality[c]
Control	13	29	6
Postnatal TP	8	9	3
Prenatal TP	9	10	3

[a]Adapted from I. L. Ward and F. J. Renz, *J Comp Physiol Psychol* **78**: 349, 1972.

[b]Animals were primed with estrogen and progesterone before each of four tests.

[c]Rated on a seven-point scale.

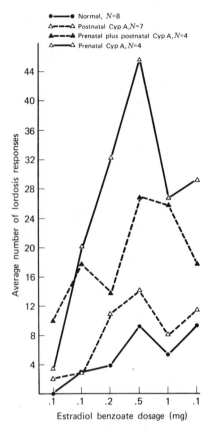

Figure 1 Average number of lordosis responses emitted by normal male rats and males treated with the anti-androgen cyproterone acetate (Cyp A) during prenatal or postnatal development. A different dosage of estradiol benzoate (EB) and a constant dosage of progesterone (1 mg) were injected before each weekly behavioral test. (Adapted from I. L. Ward, Physiol Behav 8: 53, 1972).

differentiation of tissues regulating adult sexual behavior is indeed governed largely by the same mechanism as that determining reproductive morphology. The presence of androgen results in masculinization and defeminization of adult behavior potentials. In the absence of androgen, the reverse occurs. Furthermore, manipulation of androgen titers will affect the course of development of specific components of the reproductive patterns only during their critical period of differentiation. Thus altered androgen titers during early perinatal ontogeny affect the potential for incomplete male copulatory responses. Somewhat later interventions influence the development of complete copulations and ejaculations but have little effect on incomplete patterns. The potential for ejaculation is greatest if androgen levels are high over a relatively long period of perinatal development. In the rat, this spans both prenatal and early neonatal stages. Differentiation of various components of female potentials begins early in development and continues for a relatively prolonged period. Thus prenatal cyproterone acetate induces high levels of lordotic behavior in genetic male rats, but soliciting does not occur. Castration on the day of birth induces high levels of both lordosis and soliciting behavior, but this treatment is too late to render the male equivalent to normal females (35, 37). Once it has been differentiated or suppressed, a behavior potential cannot be altered in adulthood. Even prolonged treatment with estrogen and progesterone is ineffective in activating normal lordotic response in neonatally androgenized female rats (21, 39). Similarly, months of daily TP treatment do not restore ejaculatory capacity to neonatally castrated males (34–36).

Though the release of endogenous androgen at certain stages of development is automatic in normal fetal males, a recent discovery in my laboratory suggests that noxious external environmental events, acting on the pregnant mother, may decrease the output of fetal androgens and thus influence the course of sexual behavior differentiation (40). Pregnant rats were stressed during the period from day 14 to day 21 of gestation. The stressor consisted of restraint in a Plexiglas tube and exposure to 200 foot-candles of light. Treatment was repeated three times daily for 45 minutes. Control mothers were separately housed and not handled. At birth, half of the stress and control litters were exposed daily to postnatal stressors beginning on the day of birth and continuing to day 10 postpartum. This treatment consisted of three daily 30-minute sessions during which the pups were separated from the mother and placed into individual compartments of a vibrating plastic tray. After the male offspring reached adulthood, weekly tests for male copulatory behavior were given with a receptive lure female. As shown in Figure 2, the prenatally stressed groups, for the most part, neither copulated nor ejaculated. The postnatally stressed group was not impaired, and combining prenatal and postnatal treatment did not enhance the effect above that produced by the prenatal treatment alone. This tended to be an all-or-none effect in that few animals, once having initiated copulation, subsequently failed to ejaculate. If copulation or ejaculation occurred, the pattern was normal.

The animals were then castrated and tested with vigorous males for female lordotic behavior, after injections of estrogen and progesterone. A summary of the behavior elicited on five weekly tests is given in Table 4. Prenatally stressed males emitted over three times as many lordosis responses as control males. They also had a higher percentage of positive tests. Again, postnatal treatment was largely ineffective. It should be noted that although the quality of the estrous behavior pattern emitted by prenatally stressed males was high, it was not equal to that of normal females. Such soliciting behaviors as hopping, darting, and

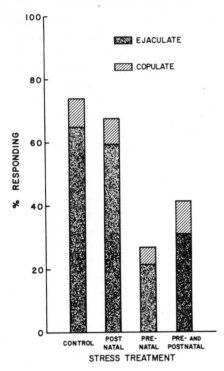

Figure 2 Percentage of control and perinatally-stressed male rats ejaculating or copulating on at least one of six tests. (Adapted from I. L. Ward, Science *175: 82, 1972.)*

ear wiggling were not seen, and the lordotic posture was rarely held after the lure male had dismounted. However, these males were tense, exhibited no resistance to being mounted, and lordosed readily, with good curvature of the neck and rump. The lordosis was held for as long as the stud remained mounted.

The female littermates of these males were also tested for possible modification of sexual behavior potentials. After 5 weeks of daily TP injections and biweekly testing with an estrous female, no differences could be detected in the number of incomplete and complete copulations emitted by responding animals in the various treatment groups. However, prenatal stress reduced the percentage of females capable of showing male copulatory behavior. Similarly, no differences were obtained in the quality or quantity of lordotic behavior displayed on four weekly tests with a vigorous male. Animals had been primed with estrogen and progesterone prior to testing.

In summary, the prenatal stress treatment had little effect on the female fetuses, but it radically altered the course of sexual differentiation

Table 4   Summary of Lordotic Behavior Exhibited by Males Exposed to Stress During Various Perinatal Stages of Development[a,b]

Stress Treatment	N	Mean Lordotic Responses	Mean Times Mounted	Percentage of Tests Receptive
Control	7	2.7	22.1	36
Postnatal	8	4.0	21.1	53
Prenatal	14	8.8	25.8	73
Prenatal plus postnatal	8	8.4	22.6	88

[a]Adapted from I. L. Ward, *Science* **175**: 82, 1972.
[b]All animals were treated with estrogen and progesterone before each behavioral test.

in the males. Males were behaviorally feminized and demasculinized. Using the same type of environmental stressor during pregnancy, this finding has recently been replicated in another laboratory by Gurley (41). Gurley also found that prenatally stressed males were less aggressive than control males but showed no increased potential for maternal behavior.

We have recently completed an additional study that further delineates the degree of modification resulting from prenatal stress. In the original study (40), intact males were tested for male copulatory behavior activated by their endogenous androgen levels. The question therefore arises whether the behavior was attenuated because the animals lacked a potential for copulatory behavior or because the treatment had suppressed testicular release of sufficient androgen in adulthood to activate an existing potential. Control, prenatally, postnatally, and prenatally plus postnatally stressed males were produced. Only the postnatal treatment was changed. In this study, beginning on the day of birth, male pups were removed twice daily from the mother, handled, and placed singly into plastic beakers for 15 minutes. This treatment was repeated for 10 consecutive days. Denenberg and associates (42) had found this procedure to effectively increase corticosterone levels in newborn rat pups. It was hoped that this treatment would influence the later stages of sexual behavior differentiation, which in the rat extend to about day 10 postpartum.

At 60 days of age, males were given seven weekly tests for male copulatory behavior. They were then castrated and injected daily with TP for 5 weeks. Biweekly testing continued. Animals that failed to ejaculate on any of these tests were then exposed to a procedure that Caggiula and

Eibergen (43) and, more recently, Crowley, Popolow, and Ward (44) have used to induce copulatory behavior in sexually inactive male rats. Briefly, in this procedure, arousal was increased by administering mildly painful electric skin shocks. As seen in Figure 3, the basic finding regarding demasculinization was replicated in that only 10% of the prenatally stressed animals exhibited male copulatory behavior prior to injections of androgen. The postnatal stress regime employed in this study, like that in the first experiment (40), had no significant effect on male behavior. However, part of the deficiency seen in the prenatal stress animals may be overcome with exogenous androgen treatment since after TP injections an additional 40% ejaculated. This required a minimum of 3 weeks of daily treatment. Several noncopulating postnatally stressed males also responded to the injections. However, all the control males that failed to mate spontaneously also did not respond with exogenous androgen treatment. The therapeutic application of electric skin shock was most effective in inducing copulatory behavior in previously non-copulating control males. Only one prenatally stressed animal responded to this treatment. In all, 40% of the prenatally stressed males failed to ejaculate, despite numerous opportunities, extensive hormone treatment, and, finally, electric skin shock.

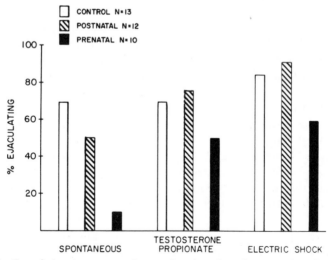

Figure 3   Cumulative percentage of control and perinatally stressed male rats ejaculating under one of the following conditions: (1) spontaneously before castration, (2) after castration and exogenous testosterone propionate (TP) treatment, (3) TP plus mild electric skin shock.

This experiment uncovered one additional modification. After each test for male copulatory behavior, the estrous lure female was removed and replaced with a vigorous stud male. This procedure was designed to ascertain whether the experimental males had the capacity to display female lordotic behavior while under the influence of endogenous or exogenous male gonadal hormones. No female behavior was seen in the initial 7 tests given prior to castration and androgen injections. However, after approximately 3 weeks of daily TP treatment, 80% of the prenatally stressed males showed lordotic behavior. None of the control males and a negligible number of the postnatally stressed animals showed this pattern. Even the control males that had failed to ejaculate did not lordose. It should be pointed out that treatment with exogenous androgen evoked female behavior in a larger percentage of prenatally stressed males than it did male copulatory behavior. After TP treatment, many of the males were truly bisexual. They could assume either masculine or feminine copulatory patterns, depending on the stimulus animal to which they were exposed. They mounted an estrous female and, in turn, lordosed when mounted by a vigorous male. The stimulus animal determined the direction of the behavior emitted. A few males showed exclusively male or exclusively female behavior. Only one showed neither pattern.

In addition to extensive behavioral testing, we have taken a variety of measures to ascertain whether physiological or morphological alterations occurred as a function of any of our perinatal treatments. At the time that males in the above study were castrated, body and testes weights, as well as anal–genital distance were measured. The only significant difference was that the postnatal group had lighter testes. It should be recalled that this treatment had no appreciable behavioral consequences. Histological studies were made of the testes of males in each treatment group that both did and did not spontaneously ejaculate. Spermatogenesis was detectable in every case. We were not able to assess whether the sperm count was normal. In another study, we found that there also were no differences between prenatally stressed and control males in testicular or body weights on the day of birth. Furthermore, both groups at day 10 postpartum showed equal degrees of compensatory testicular hypertrophy induced by hemicastration on the day of birth. It thus appears that prenatally stressed males have a relatively normal pattern of postpartum gonadotrophin release.

From all the data so far gathered it appears that prenatally stressed males are physiologically and morphologically able to reproduce. The impairment is primarily in reproductive behavior. They cannot impregnate a female because they lack the behavioral repertoire needed to do so.

How do the stress findings fit into the generally accepted theory that male behavior automatically results when fetuses develop in an androgenic medium and female potentials evolve in the absence of androgen? There are a number of possible hormonal pathways through which environmentally imposed stressors may be able to directly influence the amount of androgen secreted by the fetal testes. There appears to be a reciprocal relationship between ACTH and gonadotrophin release. When an animal is stressed, ACTH secretion increases and gonadotrophin output is decreased. Decreased gonadotrophin release in turn results in lower gonadal hormone titers. Data gathered in a variety of stress situations have demonstrated decreased testosterone titers in the adult males of several species (45–53). If this basic relationship is also characteristic of fetal males, then it might be expected that stress responses triggered during prenatal development would reduce androgen release by the fetal testes. Such a release would result in demasculinization and feminization of adult behavior potentials. The degree of alteration should depend on the timing, duration, and intensity of the stressor operating during critical periods of perinatal development. Since females require no androgen for normal development, altered gonadotrophin output should not affect them, a prediction that our data bear out. Indeed, in the rat, the small amount of male behavior typically evoked by injecting normal adult females with TP appears to be organized by exposure *in utero* to androgens produced by the male littermates (54). Prenatal treatment of females with cyproterone acetate will practically eliminate all potential for incomplete and complete copulation (21). The finding that male behavior was shown by a lower percentage of prenatally stressed females than control females may be attributed to decreased production of androgen by the prenatally stressed male littermates.

The dissociation between alterations in behavior and morphology is striking. It would appear either that behavior differentiation is more sensitive to moderate fluctuations in endogenous androgen levels than is development of reproductive structures or that differentiation of behavior and morphology is mediated by different androgens. Prenatal stress may selectively attenuate the particular class of testicular secretions primarily responsible for the organization of behavior.

Thus it appears that the process of sexual behavior differentiation is susceptible to modification by extreme external environmental events acting on developing male fetuses through the mother. Exposure to stimuli able to activate the pituitary–adrenal stress response should alter the pattern and amounts of androgen released into the systemic circulation. This, in turn, would have predictable effects on the course of sexual behavior differentiation. Furthermore, since a few prenatally stressed males began to copulate after extensive androgen treatment, it appears either that limited suppression of androgen secretion persists into adulthood or that the threshold for activating male sexual behavior in prenatally stressed males is higher than normal, requiring more androgen than is endogenously available. A large portion of these males are, however, totally unable to display male copulatory behavior, at least under the conditions we have tested. Furthermore, in the vast majority of them, a very high potential for female behavior exists. Unlike in normal male rats (55–57), in prenatally stressed males, female lordotic behavior can even be activated by exogenous treatment with male gonadal hormones.

The similarity between human bisexuality and the behavior observed in animals subjected to specific prenatal hormonal or environmental manipulations is striking. The demasculinization and feminization of behavior in the absence of major structural modification, which have been noted in both human male homosexuals and prenatally stressed male rats, is particularly interesting. In most cases of human homosexuality there are no demonstrable prenatal hormonal deviations induced by either pathology or hormone ingestion that would make this syndrome analogous to animal hormone-injection studies. But the possibly more subtle effects of maternal stress on normal fetal hormone titers organizing human sexual behavior potentials have not been investigated. However, one should beware of science by analogy. Generalizations from one species to another, without a sound data base, are rarely productive. The real value of such speculation lies in emphasizing that animal research has opened some promising new avenues of inquiry that should be vigorously pursued for possible relevance to our understanding of human sexuality.

ACKNOWLEDGMENTS

Personal research reported in this review has been supported at various times by the following: grant HD-00867 (directed by A. A. Gerall) from the National Institute of Child Health and Human Development as well as grants GB-7165 and HD-04688 (directed by I. L. Ward) from the National Science Foundation and the National Institute of Child Health and Human Development, respectively. The assistance of O. B. Ward, Jr., in the writing of this manuscript is gratefully acknowledged.

REFERENCES

1. Price, D. and E. Ortiz, in De'Haan, R. L. and H. Ursprung (eds.), *Organogenesis*, Holt, Rinehart and Winston, New York, 1965, p. 629.

2. Ward, I. L., *Horm Behav* **1**: 25, 1969.
3. Lillie, F. R., *J Exper Zool* **23**: 371, 1917.
4. Burns, R. K., *Proc Soc Exp Biol Med* **41**: 60, 1939.
5. Turner, C. D., *J Morphol* **65**: 353, 1939.
6. Dantchakoff, V., *C R Soc Biol* **127**: 1255, 1938.
7. Phoenix, C. H., R. W. Goy, A. A. Gerall, and W. C. Young, *Endocrinology* **65**: 177, 1959.
8. Hamilton, J. B. and J. M. Wolfe, *Anat Rec* **70**: 433, 1938.
9. Greene, R. R., M. W. Burrill, and A. C. Ivy, *Am J. Anat* **65**: 415, 1939.
10. Bruner, J. A. and E. Witschi, *Am J. Anat* **79**: 293, 1946.
11. Beach, F. A. and R. E. Kuehn, *Horm Behav* **1**: 347, 1970.
12. Phoenix, C. H., R. W. Goy, and J. A. Resko, in Diamond, M. (ed.), *Perspectives in Reproduction and Sexual Behavior*, Indiana University Press, Bloomington, 1968, p. 33.
13. Money, J. and A. A. Ehrhardt, *Man & Woman, Boy & Girl*, Johns Hopkins University Press, Baltimore, 1972.
14. Wollman, A. L. and J. B. Hamilton, *Anat Rec* **161**: 99, 1968.
15. Wollman, A. L. and J. B. Hamilton, *Endocrinology* **82**: 868, 1968.
16. Neuman, F., W. Elger, and M. Kramer, *Endocrinology* **78**: 628, 1966.
17. Nadler, R. D., *Horm Behav* **1**: 53, 1969.
18. Ward, I. L., *Physiol Behav* **8**: 53, 1972.
19. Whalen, R. E., D. A. Edwards, W. G. Luttge, and R. T. Robertson, *Physiol Behav* **4**: 33, 1969.
20. Gerall, A. A. and I. L. Ward, *J Comp Physiol Psychol* **62**: 370, 1966.
21. Ward, I. L. and F. J. Renz, *J Comp Physiol Psychol* **78**: 349, 1972.
22. Harris, G. W. and S. Levine, *J Physiol* **181**: 379, 1965.
23. Whalen, R. E. and D. A. Edwards, *Anat Rec* **157**: 173, 1967.
24. Whalen, R. E. and R. T. Robertson, *Psychon Sci* **9**: 319, 1968.
25. Sachs, B. D., E. I. Pollak, M. S. Krieger, and R. J. Barfield, *Science* **181**: 770, 1973.
26. Pollak, E. I. and B. D. Sachs, personal communication.
27. Barfield, R. J. and L. A. Geyer, *Science* **176**: 1349, 1972.
28. Gerall, A. A., *J Comp Physiol Psychol* **62**: 365, 1966.
29. Eaton, G. G., R. W. Goy, and C. H. Phoenix, *Nature New Biol* **242**: 119, 1973.
30. Barraclough, C. A. and R. A. Gorski, *J Endocrinol* **25**: 175, 1962.
31. Goy, R. W., C. R. Phoenix, and W. C. Young, *Anat Rec* **142**: 307, 1962.
32. Barraclough, C. A., in Martini, L. and W. F. Ganong (eds.), *Neuroendocrinology*, Vol. 2, Academic Press, New York, 1967, p. 62.
33. Gerall, A. A., *Anat Rec* **157**: 97, 1967.
34. Grady, K. L., C. H. Phoenix, and W. C. Young, *J Comp Physiol Psychol* **59**: 176, 1965.
35. Gerall, A. A., S. E. Hendricks, L. L. Johnson, and T. W. Bounds, *J Comp Physiol Psychol* **64**: 206, 1967.

36. Larsson, K., Z *Tierpsychol* **23**: 867, 1966.

37. Hendricks, S. E., *J Comp Physiol Psychol* **69**: 408, 1969.

38. Neuman, F. and W. Elger, *Endokrinologie* **50**: 209, 1966.

39. Whalen, R. E., W. G. Luttge, and B. B. Gorzalka, *Horm Behav* **2**: 83, 1971.

40. Ward, I. L., *Science* **175**: 82, 1972.

41. Gurley, E. I., M. S. thesis, Tufts University, 1973.

42. Denenberg, V. H., J. T. Brumaghim, G. C. Haltmeyer, and M. X. Zarrow, *Endocrinology* **81**: 1047, 1967.

43. Caggiula, A. R. and R. Eibergen, *J Comp Physiol Psychol* **69**: 414, 1969.

44. Crowley, W. R., H. B. Popolow, and O. B. Ward, Jr., *Physiol Behav* **10**: 391, 1973.

45. Christian, J. J., *Am J Physiol* **182**: 292, 1955.

46. Eik-Nes, K. B., *Endocrinology* **71**: 101, 1962.

47. Bardin, C. W. and R. E. Peterson, *Endocrinology* **80**: 38, 1967.

48. Fariss, B. L., T. J. Hurley, S. Hane, and P. H. Forsham, *Endocrinology* **84**: 940, 1969.

49. Charters, A. C., W. D. Odell, and J. C. Thompson, *J Clin Endocrinol* **29**: 63, 1969.

50. Rose, R. M., *Psychosom Med* **31**: 405, 1969.

51. Rose, R. M., P. G. Bourne, R. O. Poe, E. H. Mougey, D. R. Collins, and J. W. Mason, *Psychosom Med* **31**: 418, 1969.

52. Kreuz, L. E., R. M. Rose, and J. R. Jennings, *Arch Gen Psychiatr* **26**: 479, 1972.

53. Matsumoto, K., K. Takeyasu, S. Mizutani, Y. Hamanaka, and T. Uozumi, *Acta Endocrinol* **65**: 11, 1970.

54. Clemens, L. G. and L. Coniglio, *Am Zool* **11**: 617, 1971.

55. Whalen, R. E. and D. A. Edwards, *J Comp Physiol Psychol* **62**: 307, 1966.

56. Pfaff, D., *J Comp Physiol Psychol* **73**: 349, 1970.

57. Pfaff, D. W. and R. E. Zigmond, *Neuroendocrinology* **7**: 129, 1971.

CHAPTER 2

Prenatal Testosterone in the Nonhuman Primate and Its Consequences for Behavior

CHARLES H. PHOENIX

Oregon Regional Primate Research Center
Beaverton, Oregon

As a result of studies on the sexual behavior of adult female guinea pigs treated with testosterone during fetal development, we suggested that prenatal testosterone has an organizing action on the tissues that mediate mating behavior. We contrasted this action with the activating function of the hormone administered in adulthood (1, 2). Although the concepts of organization and activation were not rigorously defined, the experiments on which they were based and the studies they suggested were not limited in scientific rigor by the ambiguity of the concepts themselves. For example, on the basis of the concept of the organizing action of prenatal testosterone, we hypothesized that the genetic male deprived of testosterone during a critical period in development would fail to display the normal pattern of male sexual behavior as an adult (3). To test this hypothesis, we castrated male rats prenatally, on the day of birth, and at various times after birth (4). Only one of the prenatally castrated males

19

survived to be studied as an adult, but several males that had been castrated on the day of birth survived for adult studies. When injected with testosterone as adults and tested with receptive females, they displayed fewer intromissions and ejaculations than males castrated at 5 days of age or later. When injected with estrogen and progesterone, these rats displayed the complete pattern of female receptive behavior. The lordosis response was rarely seen in males castrated after 5 days of age. Our findings are well known and have been replicated in many laboratories. We interpreted these findings as evidence of the organizing action of prenatal testosterone. Obviously, the failure of male rats castrated on day 1 to achieve intromission and ejaculation could have been due not to any central nervous system effects but to inadequate penile development. However, such an interpretation does not account for the readiness of these males to show the female pattern when injected with the appropriate hormones, nor does it account for cyclic ovulation when they bear a transplanted ovary (5).

In short, I view the concept of organization not as dogma but as a useful hypothesis from which to generate other hypotheses that will lead to the experimental investigation of differences between the sexes.

From the earlier work of embryologists and from our work with the guinea pig we concluded that the fetal period is critical for the psychosexual masculinization of the nervous system. However, further work with the rat convinced us that it is not the fetal period *per se* that is critical but rather the period of differentiation, whether prenatal or postnatal. Moreover, not all periods of fetal or neonatal development are equally susceptible to the masculinizing action of testosterone. Unfortunately, we are not yet able to predict which are the specific periods of maximum susceptibility, the dosage levels of hormone, or the amount of treatment that are necessary to achieve masculinization in all species. The critical periods and dosages need to be determined empirically for each species. In addition, when we refer to the organizing action of testosterone in masculinizing an individual of a species, we must bear in mind the pattern of behavior that is characteristic of the male of that species. Such a note of caution may seem redundant if ejaculation happens to be the behavior under consideration; but other behaviors, such as aggression, may not be most characteristic of the male of a given species even though the two are commonly associated.

Indeed it was the prevalence of fighting behavior among adult female hermaphroditic guinea pigs that led, in part, to our initial suggestion that prenatal testosterone affects patterns of behavior beyond those that are primarily sexual. From this lead we eventually studied nonhuman primates to explore whether prenatal testosterone affects patterns of social behavior.

All of our extensive reports about the action of prenatal testosterone in the nonhuman primate have been based on only eight female hermaphroditic rhesus monkeys that were available for postnatal studies. In contrast, our first two studies on this problem used 153 female guinea pigs treated prenatally with testosterone propionate (TP) (1, 6). The length of gestation (for the guinea pig, 68 days; for the rhesus, 168 days) is especially significant from an experimental standpoint because the longer the gestation, the greater the problem in determining the critical period for psychosexual differentiation. We have just begun to identify the critical periods and dosage levels that yield maximum masculinization of the tissues mediating sexual and sex-related social behaviors in the monkey. To my knowledge, no other laboratory has undertaken such work with the primate. Table 1 shows the injection schedule used to treat the eight male and eight female fetal rhesus monkeys so far studied.

It was not by chance that we chose the rhesus monkey as our experimental animal. Rosenblum (7) had described the sexually dimorphic play behavior of young rhesus monkeys, and van Wagenen and Hamilton (8) and Wells and van Wagenen (9) had produced hermaphroditic rhesus monkeys and had described the morphological changes in the genital tract and external genitalia of these animals. In addition, at that time the species was readily available and more was known about its husbandry than about that of most other nonhuman primates.

All of the hermaphrodites we produced were born with a well-developed scrotum and, from gross morphological appearance, a small but normally formed penis. The external vaginal orifice was absent and was replaced by a median raphe. The appearance of the external genitalia at birth was that of a normal genetic male. The genital tract tissues of these animals have not yet been studied.

The hermaphrodites we produced were studied in groups of four to five animals over the first 4 years of life. Details of housing and testing have been given elsewhere and will not be repeated here (10–13). Since the sex composition of these groups was largely determined by the availability of other rhesus monkeys of approximately the same age, we were not able to standardize the sex ratios for the groups. Some groups included here are composed of an untreated male and one untreated female, a male treated prenatally with testosterone, or a male castrated at birth. One group, the first to be studied, contained two hermaphrodites and two untreated females.

Generally, the infants were allowed to remain alone with their mothers

Table 1　Amount and Temporal Distribution of Prenatal Injections of Testosterone Propionate in Rhesus Monkeys

Number of Offspring	Genetic Sex	Gestational Age Started	Gestational Age Ended	Amount and Number of Injections of TP into Mother					Total mg
				Mg×days		Mg×days		Mg×days	
828	♀	40	69	20×30					600
829	♀	40	69	20×30					600
1239	♀	38	66	25×25[a]					625
1656	♀	40	111	10×50	↑	5×22			610
836	♀	40	89	25×10	↑	15×20	↑	10×20	750
1616	♀+♂	39	88	25×10	↑	15×20	↑	10×20	750
1619	♀+♂	39	88	25×10	↑	15×20	↑	10×20	750
1640	♀+♂	39	88	25×10	↑	15×20	↑	10×20	750
1558	♂	42	92	25×10	↑	15×20	↑	10×20	750
1561	♂	39	45	25×7					175
1618	♂	43	92	25×10	↑	15×20	↑	10×20	750
1644	♂	44	113	10×50	↑	5×20			600
1645	♂	39	129	25×10	↑	10×19[b]	↑	5×22[b]	550
1648	♂	39	119	25×3	↑	5×78			465
1653	♂	43	134	25×10	↑	10×17	↑	5×24	540
1966	♂	40	109	15×10	↑	10×40	↑	5×20	650

[a] Injected 6 days per week.
[b] Injected on alternate days.

for 3 months. Other rearing methods might have raised the total level of social interaction in the groups, but we have no evidence that differences betwen the sexes would have been altered. The young were then weaned, caged individually, and brought together for about 30 minutes each day, 5 days per week, for 100 days of observation. The groups were then tested annually for 50 days through the fourth year of life. From 3 months until 4 years of age, four items of social behavior were consistently displayed more frequently by males than by females: rough-and-tumble play, threat, play initiation, and chasing play. These behaviors were displayed significantly more often by the hermaphrodites than by untreated females. When the mean frequency of these behaviors was plotted for all the hermaphrodites and for control males and females, the hermaphrodites were intermediate between the two sexes. Figure 1 shows the differences in the frequency of rough-and-tumble play that is characteristic of the four sexually dimorphic play behaviors we recorded. The behaviors occurred in the absence of any circulating exogenous testosterone. The last injection of testosterone was given to the mother 85 days or more before term. In addition to displaying an increased frequency of male play behavior, the hermaphrodites also mounted more frequently than females (Fig. 2). The data plotted in Figure 2 include both no-foot-clasp and foot-clasp mounts. More significant than the frequency of mounts was the qualitative difference in the mount executed by females and by hermaphrodites. Foot-clasp mounts were virtually never displayed by the control females but were commonly displayed by the hermaphrodites.

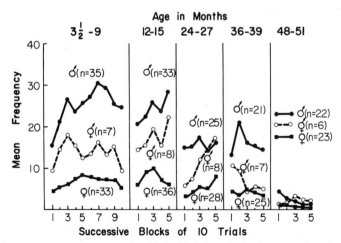

Figure 1   The frequency of rough-and-tumble play shown by control males, control females, and hermaphroditic female monkeys during the first 50 months of life.

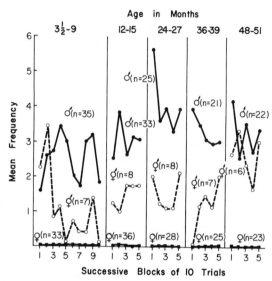

Figure 2 *The frequency of mounting shown by control males, control females, and hermaphroditic female monkeys during the first 50 months of life.*

Foot-clasp mounts involve clasping the calves or lower legs of the partner with the feet and placing the hands on the hips or lower back of the partner, shifting the entire weight to the partner. As might be expected, such mounts require the cooperation of the partner. Goy (14) has pointed out that the hermaphrodite's ability to elicit such cooperation by the partner is not frequently seen in control females and constitutes an important facet of prenatal testosterone action.

We remain uncertain about the relative effectiveness of different treatment schedules. The two hermaphrodites receiving the smallest total amount of testosterone (600 mg) showed a lower frequency of rough-and-tumble play and other play behaviors than hermaphrodites receiving the highest amount (750 mg) of the hormone (Fig. 3). The problem is complicated by the fact that the low-dosage animals did not receive injections after day 69 of fetal life, whereas the higher dosage animals were last treated on day 88 or 89 of fetal life. As an additional complication, the two low-dosage hermaphrodites, whose frequency of rough-and-tumble play is plotted in Figure 3, were tested in a group with two untreated females and did not have males present in the group. In general, total behavior output varies considerably from group to group, and absolute frequencies are meaningful only within the context of the individual group. Within groups of mixed sexes, the frequency of male play behavior is always higher than that of females and the performance level of hermaphrodites is always higher than that of untreated females. Hence the

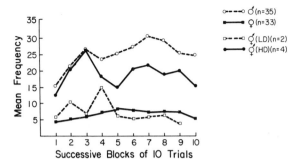

Figure 3   The frequency of rough-and-tumble play shown by control males, control females, and low- and high-dosage hermaphroditic female monkeys during the first year of life.

question of the relative effectiveness of the dosage levels used and the time of treatment remains unanswerd.

Note that in tests at 48 to 51 months of age the frequency of rough-and-tumble play by males and hermaphrodites was near zero (Fig. 1); that is, the age for play had ended. In another environment play behavior by males and hermaphrodites might be prolonged, and in other situations I have seen adult males play with infant and juvenile animals. Under our testing conditions, however, play behavior was seldom observed after 3 years of age. Group tests were terminated in the fifth year because excessive aggression occurred when animals were placed together for observation.

In addition to differences in play and mounting behavior, the age at menarche was greater among the 9 hermaphrodites (mean age 36.8 months) than among the 18 control females (mean age 29.2 months). The differences was statistically reliable. Age at menarche was not related to the dosage of testosterone injected prenatally. Once menstrual cycles were established, the hermaphrodites showed normal cycles except, of course, that bleeding occurred through the penis.

When they were about 5 years old, five of the hermaphrodites were ovariectomized on day 18 of the menstrual cycle. Blood taken at the time of ovariectomy showed normal levels of progesterone and androstenedione. In one hermaphrodite, blood levels were monitored for estradiol and progesterone throughout one menstrual cycle. The hormone levels of this hermaphrodite resembled those of normal females, including an estrogen surge and a rise in luteal progesterone (15). Gonadotropin levels are currently monitored in the hermaphrodites, and changes in gonadotropin output in response to injected steroids are being investigated.

Seven of the adult hermaphrodites and five adult controls were recently tested for the display of male behavior (16). The hermaphrodites and control females were ovariectomized and paired weekly with stimulus females rendered sexually receptive by daily injections of 10 μg of estradiol benzoate for 10 to 18 days before testing. After six tests, the hermaphrodites and control females were injected with 0.5 mg TP/kg daily for 24 weeks and then with 15 mg TP per animal per day for 6 weeks.

Before TP injections, the hermaphrodites differed significantly from the control females on only one of the recorded variables: aggression. After treatment with TP, the hermaphrodites continued to be aggressive, but they also sat next to the stimulus females (proxed) more frequently than did the control females. Moreover, they mounted the stimulus females more frequently than did the control females (.91 and .09 per test, respectively), but because of the great variability among individuals, the differences in mounting were not statistically significant. One of the hermaphrodites achieved intromission and ejaculated in two different tests in which her mean intromission frequency was 5.5 and the latency to ejaculation was 8.5 minutes. The mean latency to ejaculation in adult breeding males that we studied was 5.36 minutes. Although only one hermaphrodite ejaculated during intromission of the female partner, three hermaphrodites were observed to masturbate to ejaculation with emission of seminal fluid. This experimental tour de force tells us little about the usual sexual behavior of the female rhesus; but it does suggest a source of unadaptive sexual behavior. In the guinea pig we found a correlation between the degree of morphological modification and the amount of male behavior displayed, although the correlation was not perfect. In general, it would seem highly appropriate for the reproduction of a species that an individual who is morphologically equipped to penetrate the female be psychologically equipped to do so.

Ten years ago, when we proposed that it was the testosterone in the developing male fetus that organized the characteristic behavioral patterns in the adult male of a species, we had no direct evidence that testosterone was, in fact, present during differentiation or that, if this hormone was present, its levels differed in the two sexes. The hypothesis was based on studies of the effects of injected tetosterone in female guinea pigs and of neonatal castration in the male rat.

Since then Resko (17) has shown, by gas–liquid chromatography, that testosterone is present in the developing male rhesus and that at different times in gestation the amount of testosterone in the pools of umbilical artery plasma is greater in male than in female fetuses. More recently Resko and co-workers (18) have shown by means of radioimmunoassay that the average quantity of testosterone in the male rhesus fetus, when analyzed individually, is higher than in the female from day 59, the earliest time sampled, to day 163 of gestation, or just before birth. One of 23 male fetuses studied had a concentration of testosterone that fell within the female range, and one of 21 female fetuses had a concentration of testosterone that fell within the male range. Whereas the males sampled by Resko varied greatly in the amount of testosterone at each fetal age studied, females showed much less variability. Male fetuses had twice as much testosterone in the umbilical artery as in the umbilical vein, and female fetuses had approximately the same amount in umbilical artery and vein. The suggestion, of course, is that the source of testosterone in the fetal male is the testis. On day 150 of gestation the blood levels of testosterone in three male fetuses that had been castrated on day 100 of gestation were similar to those in females and the blood levels of testosterone in umbilical artery and vein were approximately the same.

These biochemical findings tend to support our hypothesis that in the developing fetus testosterone constitutes the mechanism whereby the psychosexual differences between the sexes are translated from a genetic substrate to the tissues that mediate sexual and sex-related behaviors. The biochemical picture is much more complicated than I have suggested. No one could for a moment conceive that testosterone acts in a hormonal vacuum. For example, there is more progesterone in the fetal circulation of the female rhesus than of the male (19). More progesterone is found in both the umbilical vein and the umbilical artery of the female than of the male, and the female placenta produces more progesterone *in vitro* without added substrate than the male placenta (21). The ratio of testosterone to progesterone with known antiandrogenic action rather than the absolute amount of testosterone in the developing fetus may be the critical factor in determining the degree of masculinization of the nervous system (20). When these and other hormones act to produce their effect remains to be determined.

What may be a very important period for the differentiation of genital tract tissues associated with reproduction may not be critical to psychosexual differentiation, although the two are correlated. In the normal male rhesus monkey, androgen levels drop sharply soon after birth and cells of the epididymis that are differentiated at 150 days of fetal life return to their undifferentiated state, something that would not be expected of tissues of the central nervous system. If a male rhesus is castrated at day 100 of gestation and replaced *in utero* until term (168 days), the cells of the epididymides do not differentiate (22). What happens to the behavior pattern of such a prenatally castrated male?

We studied the early social and sexual behavior of one such male rhesus, Rasputin, beginning at about 7 months of age. He was observed 30 minutes per day, 5 days a week, every other week, until he was 1 year old (series I) and again for 30 minutes each day for a month at 17 months of age (series II).

He was tested in a group of three animals, a control male (Burt) and a control female (Anna). In general, we used the same procedure that had been used to test the pseudohermaphrodites and control subjects reported on earlier.

Table 2 shows the frequency of the sexually dimorphic play behaviors previously mentioned (rough-and-tumble play, threat, play initiation, and chasing play) and a nonsexually dimorphic behavior called "cage exploration." Both Burt and Rasputin showed about the same level of performance for all of the predominantly male play behaviors, and Anna displayed these behaviors with a frequency that was not only low but, more importantly in this context, lower than that of the males. Castration at the end of the second trimester of fetal development did not seriously affect the frequency of play behaviors characteristically engaged in by males. The three animals engaged in nonsexually dimorphic behaviors such as cage exploration with frequencies that were remarkably similar.

A summary of data on mounting frequencies shows that during series I the two males mounted without foot-clasp mounts (NFCM) with about equal frequency. However, Rasputin failed to show any single- or double-foot-clasp mounts (SDFCM), whereas Burt displayed a total of 60 such mounts. The data in Table 3 are arranged in such a way as to indicate not only which animal mounted (actor), but which animal was mounted (partner). In series II, Burt failed to display a no-foot-clasp mount and Rasputin achieved three such mounts, just as he had in series I. In this second series, Rasputin showed foot-clasp mounts for the first time, and although the frequency was much lower than that displayed by Burt, the orientation and qualitative aspects of the mounts were indistinguishable

Table 2   Average Frequency (per Block) of Five Behaviors Displayed by a Control Male (♂) and Female (♀) and a Male Castrated Prenatally (✗)

Series	Animal No.	Cage Exploration	Threat	Play Initiation	Chasing Play	Rough-and-Tumble Play
I[a]	♂ 6269	16.1	3.6	2.9	0.2	3.5
	♀ 6258	10.9	0.3	0.3	0.0	0.4
	✗ 6209	16.2	2.9	2.0	0.3	3.8
II[b]	♂ 6269	10.8	4.8	3.8	0.0	3.8
	♀ 6258	10.8	0.0	0.0	0.0	0.4
	✗ 6209	10.6	9.2	6.2	1.0	6.4

[a] Tests starting at 7 months of age.
[b] Tests at 17 months of age.

Table 3   Behavior Matrices for Burt (B, Control Male) Anna (A, Control Female) and Rasputin (R, Prenatally Castrated Male) as Actors and Partners Showing Frequency of No-Foot-Clasp Mounts (NFCM) and Single- and Double-Foot-Clasp Mounts (SDFCM) During Series I (50 Tests) and Series II (25 tests)

			NFCM					SDFCM		
			Partner					Partner		
			B	A	R			B	A	R
Series I	A c t o r	B	—	8	0		B	—	5	55
		A	0	—	0		A	0	—	0
		R	1	2	—		R	0	0	—
			B	A	R			B	A	R
Series II	A c t o r	B	—	0	0		B	—	11	16
		A	0	—	0		A	0	—	0
		R	2	1	—		R	1	3	—

from those of normal males. Anna failed to display either no-foot-clasp or foot-clasp mounts.

Had Rasputin failed to engage in male play behavior, or had he failed to display any mounting, this research based on one experimental animal would not have been reported. Moreover, since this is a single sample, the differences in mounting frequency may not represent anything but random variation from normal. However, because the behavior displayed by this single animal is positive, it suggests that, although testosterone is normally present at higher levels in the male fetus than in the female fetus from day 108 of gestation (the time at which this male was castrated) to term, the continued higher levels of testosterone in late gestation are not crucial to psychosexual masculinization. However, responsiveness to testosterone as an adult and the frequency of mounting, intromission, and ejaculation in adulthood need to be checked in the prenatally castrated animal.

Fetal male testosterone levels were found at their highest mean concentration (2000 pg/ml) on day 59 of gestation, the earliest time sampled (18). This compares with about 300 pg/ml of testosterone in adult males 1 year after castration (23). To be effective in preventing psychosexual masculinization, prenatal castration would presumably have to be carried out by this time if not earlier. Because of technical problems, use of an antiandrogen during this early time period with castration at day 100 may be the only practical way to achieve in the genetic male rhesus what was accomplished by castrating the male rat on the day of birth.

It is a long way from the rat to the monkey and an even longer way from the monkey to man. Primates may have achieved some emancipation from hormonal control with an increase in cortical determination of the behavior (24). Some of our work with castrated adult male and ovariectomized female rhesus monkeys lends support to such a view (25). However, this evidence relates to the role of the gonadal hormones in regulating adult sexual behavior, and not to the importance of the steroidal hormones (especially testosterone) during prenatal life. How testosterone masculinizes the nervous system is purely conjectural. We have suggested that it does so by modifying the nervous system so that the individual is predisposed to acquire predominantly masculine patterns of behavior (16). Continued and more extensive research in this direction may help define the process of human psychosexual differentiation. In the question of hormonal determination, man remains beyond the experimental approach, but careful clinical studies, such as those pioneered by Money and colleagues (26), have done much to provide information in man that parallels experimental investigations on non-human primates.

It is to be hoped that the concept of the organizing action of prenatal androgen will not give rise to time-worn arguments of heredity versus environment or be conceived of as a fatalistic theory that renders useless the need for studying the effect of the environment on the development of normal sexual behavior. Twenty years ago Valenstein, Riss, and Young (27) demonstrated the importance of early environment for the normal development of sexual behavior in the male guinea pig. Harlow and associates (28) have demonstrated that a male rhesus reared in isolation is emotionally maladjusted and sexually incompetent as an adult. No one could seriously propose that the sexual behavior of the adult male human being, monkey, or even guinea pig is fully determined by a few nanograms of testosterone present during fetal life. On the other hand, no one has seriously questioned the hypothesis that the presence of a Y rather than an X chromosome at fertilization has far-reaching consequences for the sexual behavior that will be displayed by the normal individual of a given species bearing a Y chromosome. What is suggested here is a mechanism whereby the information encoded in genetic material is translated into morphology and, ultimately, behavior.

ACKNOWLEDGMENTS

All of the research on hermaphroditic monkeys was carried out in collaboration with R. W. Goy and since 1965 with the collaboration of J. A. Resko. Thanks to J. N. Jensen for years of animal observation and technical assistance.

This material has been presented as Publication No. 727 of the Oregon Regional Primate Research Center, supported in part by grants (RR–00163 and HD–05969) from the National Institutes of Health, U.S. Public Health Service.

REFERENCES

1. Phoenix, C. H., R. W. Goy, A. A. Gerall, and W. C. Young, *Endocrinology* **65:** 369, 1959.

2. Young, W. C., in Young, W. C. (ed.), *Sex and Internal Secretions*, 3rd ed., Williams & Wilkins, Baltimore, 1961.

3. Young, W. C., R. W. Goy, and C. H. Phoenix, *Science* **143:** 212, 1964.

4. Grady, K. L., C. H. Phoenix, and W. C. Young, *J Comp Physiol Psychol* **57:** 176, 1965.

5. Harris, G. W., *Endocrinology* **75:** 627, 1964.

6. Goy, R. W., W. E. Bridson, and W. C. Young, *J Comp Physiol Psychol* **57:** 166, 1964.

7. Rosenblum, L. A., Ph.D. thesis, University of Wisconsin, Madison, 1961.

8. van Wagenen, G., and J. B. Hamilton, in Cowles, T. (ed.), *Essays in Biology*, University of California Press, Berkeley, 1943, p. 581.

9. Wells, L. J. and G. van Wagenen, *Contrib Embryol* **35:** 93, 1954.

10. Goy, R. W., *J Anim Sci* **25**, Suppl. p. 21, 1966.

11. Goy, R. W., in Michael, R. P. (ed.), *Endocrinology and Human Behavior*, Oxford University Press, London, 1968, p. 12.

12. Phoenix, C. H., R. W. Goy, and W. C. Young, in Martini, L. and W. F. Ganong (eds.), *Neuroendocrinology*, Vol. 2, Academic Press, New York, 1967, p. 163.

13. Phoenix, C. H., R. W. Goy, and J. A. Resko, in Diamond, M. (ed.), *Perspectives in Reproduction and Sexual Behavior*, Indiana University Press, Bloomington, 1968, p. 33.

14. Goy, R. W., in Schmitt, F. O. (ed.), *The Neurosciences: Second Study Program*, Rockefeller University Press, New York, 1970, p. 196.

15. Goy, R. W. and J. A. Resko, in Astwood, E. B. (ed.), *Recent Progress in Hormone Research*, Vol. 28, Academic Press, New York, 1972, p. 707.

16. Eaton, G. G., R. W. Goy, and C. H. Phoenix, *Nature New Biol* **242:** 119, 1973.

17. Resko, J. A., *Endocrinology* **87:** 680, 1970.

18. Resko, J. A., A. Malley, D. E. Begley, and D. L. Hess, *Endocrinology* **93**: 156, 1973.

19. Hagemenas, F. C. and G. W. Kittinger, *Endocrinology* **91**: 253, 1972.

20. Resko, J. A., in press.

21. Hagemenas, F. C. and G. W. Kittinger, *Endocrinology*, **94**: 922, 1974.

22. Alexander, N. J., *Anat Rec* **172**: 260, 1972.

23. Resko, J. A. and C. H. Phoenix, *Endocrinology* **91**: 499, 1972.

24. Beach, F. A., in Roe, A. and G. G. Simpson (eds.), *Behavior and Evolution*, Yale University Press, New Haven, 1958, p. 81.

25. Phoenix, C. H., in Phoenix, C. H. (ed.), *Primate Reproductive Behavior*, Karger, Basel, 1974, p. 99.

26. Money, J. and A. A. Ehrhardt, *Man and Woman, Boy and Girl*, Johns Hopkins University Press, Baltimore, 1972, pp. 1–311.

27. Valenstein, E. S., W. Riss, and W. C. Young, *J Comp Physiol Psychol* **48**: 397, 1955.

28. Harlow, H. F. and M. K. Harlow, *Bull Menninger Clin* **26**: 213, 1962.

CHAPTER 3

Fetal Androgens, Human Central Nervous System Differentiation, and Behavior Sex Differences

ANKE A. EHRHARDT and SUSAN W. BAKER

Departments of Psychiatry and Pediatrics
State University of New York at Buffalo
School of Medicine
Buffalo, New York

The role of prenatal hormones in the central nervous system differentiation that mediates aspects of postnatal behavior of rats and monkeys has already been extensively reviewed. We now continue the discussion on prenatal hormone levels and their possible effects on behavior as relevant for *human* sex differences.

In the area of human behavior, evidence of fetal hormonal influences is much harder to obtain since it is impossible to design careful experiments analogous to planned animal research studies. Instead we are limited to research on spontaneously occurring clinical conditions with a known history of prenatal hormonal aberrations.

One such clinical condition will be the center of the next two chapters: the adrenogenital syndrome.

THE ADRENOGENITAL SYNDROME

The adrenogenital syndrome (AGS) is a condition in which the adrenal glands have a genetically determined defect in their function from fetal life on. The syndrome is transmitted as an autosomal recessive, which implies that both parents have to be carriers to produce one or several children with the illness. The genetic defect prevents the adrenal cortices from synthesizing cortisol. Instead the adrenal cortices release too much of another adrenal hormone that is androgenic in biological action, that is, a male sex hormone.

In the genetic female with AGS, excessive androgen production before birth masculinizes the external genitalia to varying degrees, in some cases only affecting the clitoris (enlargement) and in others also the formation of the labia (labial fusion). The masculinization of the genitalia is restricted to the external sex organs. The internal reproductive organs are differentiated as female. Postnatally, with proper endocrine management, the adrenal androgen output is regulated with life-long cortisone-replacement therapy. With proper treatment, puberty, secondary sex characteristics, and female reproductive function are normal in female AGS patients, although menses tend to be of late onset (1). The masculinized external genitalia can be surgically feminized soon after birth.

The adrenogenital syndrome also occurs in genetic males, usually with no noticeable effect on the genitalia. Boys with AGS also have to be treated with cortisone; otherwise the excessive adrenal output of androgen will induce early male pubertal development. However, if corrected with early and regular cortisone replacement, boys with AGS will grow up looking like normal boys of their age.

Different subtypes of AGS occur, including one with an increased tendency to salt loss and another with hypertension. These additional traits of the clinical condition are not of particular concern here since the matter of interest in this context is the exposure to too much androgen before birth.

Genetic females with AGS are in many respects a human analogue to genetic female rats, guinea pigs, and monkeys who were experimentally exposed to androgens during the prenatal and/or neonatal critical period of central nervous system differentiation. Genetic males with AGS represent a human analogue to genetic male animals who were experimentally treated with additional amounts of androgens before and/or around birth.

Of special importance for the discussion of the effects of prenatal hormones on postnatal human behavior are those children with AGS who are regulated with cortisone at an early age, so that postnatal continuing developmental masculinization is prevented. With early regular cortisone-replacement therapy and, in the case of females, after surgical correction of the external genitalia, children with AGS grow up looking like normal boys and girls.

PURPOSE

The studies concerning the effects of prenatal hormones on behavior in human females were started at The Johns Hopkins Hospital with John Money several years ago. At that time 10 girls with progestin-induced hermaphroditism and 15 girls with early-treated AGS, between 4 and 6 years old, were evaluated and compared with matched normal control girls (2–5).* In brief, the results of these earlier studies suggested that fetally androgenized females were different from normal control girls in that they displayed a higher level of physical energy expenditure in rough outdoor play and a lesser interest in dolls and other typical female childhood rehearsal of adult female roles in fantasy and play; they were also more often identified as long-term tomboys and preferred boys over girls as playmates. The question whether the behavior modifications were related to a group difference in fetal hormone history or to any other postnatal environmental variable is difficult to answer.

The goal of our more recent studies in Buffalo was to evaluate a comparable sample of fetally androgenized genetic females at another hospital to validate or disprove the findings at Johns Hopkins. In addition, we made a change in research design. In order to have both the experimental group and control group from a social environment as similar as possible, we evaluated complete families with one or more children with AGS. We also included not only genetic females but also genetic males with AGS. Females with AGS were compared with female siblings and mothers, and males with AGS were compared with male siblings. The project has two parts: one was aimed at behavior comparisons (the subject of this chapter), the other dealt with intelligence and cognitive abilities, and will be described in Chapter 4.

As to sexually dimorphic behavior, the following group comparisons will be reported: (1) genetic AGS females versus "unaffected" female

---

*Progestin-induced hermaphroditism occurred in genetic daughters of mothers who had been treated with progestinic drugs during pregnancy to prevent miscarriage. The drugs sometimes had an unexpected virilizing effect on the daughters' external genitalia.

siblings (i.e., female siblings who do not manifest AGS) and their mothers; (2) genetic AGS males versus "unaffected" male siblings (i.e., male siblings who do not manifest AGS).

The hypotheses can be formulated as follows:

1. Genetic females with a known history of high levels of prenatal androgen have been shown in previous studies at Johns Hopkins to differ as a group from normal control girls in some aspects of gender-related behavior. If similar differences in behavior can be documented for AGS females compared with unaffected female siblings and mothers who share many aspects of their social environment, this finding is more likely also related to a difference in prenatal history, rather than solely to social environmental factors.

2. Genetic AGS males may be exposed to even higher levels of pre-natal androgen than normal males. If so, they may differ from unaffected male siblings in some aspects of typically masculine behavior. The under-lying (unproved) assumption is that excessive androgen for the male fetus may affect the central nervous system and be related to a pro-nounced pattern of postnatal masculine behavior.

METHODS

Sample Selection and Characteristics

The sample for our family study in Buffalo consists of 27 patients—17 females and 10 males. This is clearly a representative sample of the clin-ical population seen in the Pediatric Endocrine Clinic, considering that at the time of our study only 31 patients with AGS had been seen since the clinic's inception 10 years before. The age range was 4.3 to 19.9 years for females and 4.8 to 26.3 years for males, with most of the children in middle childhood and early adolescence. Several families had more than one child with AGS. The total unaffected sibling sample consists of 11 females and 16 males with comparable age ranges (see Table 1). Eighteen mothers and 14 fathers participated in the study. Not all sib-lings and parents were available for all parts of the study. The respective numbers will be indicated for each comparison. The families came from social classes II to V according to the Hollingshead index (6), with a greater number from lower than from middle and upper classes.

All patients were under corrective treatment with cortisone replace-ment. Fourteen of the females began receiving cortisone treatment during the first year of life, usually shortly after birth. The other three patients

Table 1   Sample Characteristics

	Sex	Patients	Parents	Siblings
N	F	17	18	11
	M	10	14	16
Age range and	F	4.3–19.9	28–49	6.8–24.7
Mean		10.8	37	12.93
	M	4.8–26.3	32–52	6.8–23.7
		11.8	40.5	13.22
Race	F	25 W, 2 B	29 W, 3 B	24 W, 3 B
	M			

were started on cortisone in the second, third, and fourth year of life, respectively. Surgical correction of the external genitalia varied as follows: in six patients within the first year of life, in seven patients between ages 1 and 3 years, and in four patients later in life.

Six of the male patients began receiving cortisone treatment during the first month of life. The other four patients were started on cortisone in their fifth, sixth, seventh, and eighth year of life, respectively. The latter four patients had signs of precocious male puberty at the beginning of treatment. One of these late-treated boys was excluded from the behavior study, because both he and his mother were mentally retarded and detailed interview information could not be obtained.

Behavior Assessment

The methods and, in particular, the problems of getting good measurements of gender-related behavior are still largely the same as in the earlier studies. As in the Johns Hopkins project, we were interested in long-term childhood behavior that we could operationally define and assess in interviews with the mothers and the children themselves. These interviews were conducted with semistructured schedules. The areas included in the schedule were general developmental and play-behavior items intermixed with typical gender-related behavior.

Our interview schedule included items that are related to established sex differences in the normal population. Our choice was not influenced by a particular theory that the specific behavior item was clearly culturally determined or possibly also hormone-dependent. Our primary goal was to examine the kind of gender-related behavior that has been shown to differentiate between normal boys and girls consistently and over a wide age range. Next, we wanted to compare girls and boys with a specific atypical prenatal hormonal history to girls and boys with a presumably normal prenatal history.

One of the most consistent sex differences found in normal boys and girls has to do with rough-and-tumble play and aggression (7). From an early age on, boys tend to exert more energy in rough outdoor pursuits and become more frequently involved in fighting behavior. The results are not only remarkably consistent for our own culture but have also been noted in several cross-cultural comparisons and in nonhuman primate observations (8, 9). Thus we wanted to know whether fetally androgenized females are different from their normal sisters and mothers in this area of gender-related behavior and more similar to normal boys. Concerning boys with AGS, the question is whether, as a group, they show a higher level of intense energy expenditure and aggression than their normal brothers.

Preference of playmates is another gender-related childhood behavior in which girls, and boys typically differ. From about age 4 on, girls consistently prefer girls and boys prefer boys if they have a choice in playmates. At about the same age, sex differences in toy preferences occur. Girls typically like dolls, doll houses, toy stoves, and the like, whereas boys prefer cars, trucks, and guns. In spite of a considerable overlap between the sexes regarding play behavior, the sex differences in typical toy preferences, play activities, and choice of playmates remain fairly consistent throughout childhood (7).

Doll play probably has a very important function in preparation for the maternal role. Actually, we know very little about the response of human children to small infants or whether and when girls and boys differ in handling and care-giving behavior. Most of our evidence comes from animal studies or indirect nurturant behavior, as in response to baby dolls. Observations of free-living nonhuman primates indicate that adolescent females show more interest in infants than do males of the same age (10, 11). Numerous studies on human subjects show that girls play more and show more care-giving behavior with dolls than do boys of the same age. However, it is by no means the case that only girls respond to dolls or infants. Boys not only have the potential but often display care-giving behavior. The difference seems to be that females manifest increased readiness to respond to the young. For example, girls were found to show significantly greater nurturant responses to a baby doll than did boys of comparable ages (12). However, when the same group of children was subdivided by sex and ordinal position in their family, it was found that girls tended to be nurturant to the baby doll irrespective of having younger siblings or not, whereas boys tended to show nurturance only if they had younger siblings at home (13). This study suggests that boys may need more exposure to small infants than do girls in order to display nurturant behavior in the presence of a baby doll. The findings are in agreement with animal studies, which also suggest that males have a longer latency phase or a higher threshold before they respond to the very young of their species.

Since the response to infants is an important area in the study of sex differences, we compared AGS girls with their sisters and mothers in doll play, their attitude toward becoming a mother, and their response to infants. The question under study is whether fetally androgenized females have less interest in any aspect of maternal behavior suggestive of a higher threshold in their response to infants.

We also compared AGS males with their normal brothers on analogous items appropriately modified for boys, to see whether boys with a history of excessive androgen before birth differ in this respect from normal boys and show behavior modification toward an even higher degree of masculinity.

Another cluster of items in our interview schedule concerned gender-role preference and more arbitrary sex differences, such as interest in appearance, clothing, jewelry, and hairdo. Concerning gender-role preference, each subject was asked whether he or she would have preferred to be a boy or a girl if there had been a choice in the beginning of life and if boys or girls had more fun and advantages in our society.

Concerning clothes, jewelry, and cosmetics, we were not interested in the preferred style, which obviously changes rapidly with different fashions, but rather whether the subject showed an interest in being attractive or clearly preferred functional outfits with little or no concern about looks.

The interview schedule also included specific items for adolescents— for example, dating, erotic attractions, love affairs.

Procedure

The families were referred by the Pediatric Endocrine Clinic and were asked to cooperate in our project. We informed them that we were interested in various aspects of child development in AGS patients and their normal siblings. Furthermore, we proposed to do an intelligence study of all family members on the basis of a battery of cognitive-ability tests. The cooperation of the families was unusually good, which probably can be largely explained by their excellent rapport with the staff of the Pediatric Endocrine Division, whom they had often known for many years.

Originally we only collected data on the children. To obtain insight into the mothers' own developmental history and to ensure that we were not dealing with a sample of unusual mothers reinforcing their own attitudes and interests in their children, we asked the mothers to return and administered a standard interview about their own developmental history, comparable to the data we had collected on their children. We were able to collect data from 13 mothers (seven mothers of female, three mothers of male, and three mothers of both male and female patients).

The interview sessions were arranged on an individual basis and were scheduled according to the family's convenience. Data were collected over several sessions for each family. Each session lasted at least 2 to 3 hours.

Every subject and her or his mother was interviewed with the same interview schedule. The items were always consistent, although the sequence was flexible, so as to be unstilted in manner. All interviews were tape-recorded and subsequently transcribed. The transcribed interviews were rated according to coding scales, with a range from two to five verbally anchored points. Agreement between answers from mothers and from children as to the same aspect of the child's behavior has been found in the past to be very high (4), so that the answers can be pooled. Two raters tabulated the data from the transcribed interviews.

Statistical Analysis

Comparison of the patient and the various control groups were statistically tested with appropriate nonparametric tests after the rating scales for each item were dichotomized (for methodological details see ref. 4).

Data on the females are based on a comparison of the 17 patients versus the 10 mothers of females and 11 unaffected female siblings of all families in our study. Ideally we would have liked to use only the sisters of female patients. However, in order to increase sample size, we used all female siblings of AGS female and male patients.

Data were analyzed with a 3×2 chi-square test (14). In case of expected frequencies less than 5, the Freeman–Halton test was applied (15.)

The behavior data on the males are based on 9 patients and 11 unaffected male siblings of all families. Comparisons of the two male groups were tested with the Fisher Exact Test for fourfold tables (14).

RESULTS

Fetally Androgenized Girls versus Unaffected Female Siblings and Mothers

Activity and Aggression. We found that girls with AGS were significantly more often described by mothers, sisters, brothers, fathers, and themselves as having a high level of intense physical energy expenditure in comparison with the two other groups (Fig. 1). This behavior was long-term and specific in the sense of a high degree of rough outdoor play rather than a general elevation of activity level. This kind of energetic play and sport behavior has to be differentiated from hyperactivity, which interferes with the ability to focus attention and to concentrate and which was not typical for AGS females.

Girls with AGS also differed in choice of playmates. About 50% clearly preferred boys over girls most or all of the time when a choice was available. This did not hold true for the other two groups, although some of the unaffected female siblings did play with boys and some of the mothers remembered having done so in their own childhood. However, if there was a choice, it was clearly for members of their own sex.

Our data on fighting behavior were initially quite crude and centered basically only around the question as to which member of the family usually instigated fights. There is a tendency for fetally androgenized girls to start fights more frequently than females in the other two groups, but the difference was not significant. Since fighting behavior appears to be one of the most consistent sex differences cross-culturally and in comparisons between various mammalian species, we studied this behavior again and have in the meantime obtained more detailed data on aggression (as yet unanalyzed). At this point it is not clear whether AGS females are in any way different from their sisters and mothers in respect to childhood fighting behavior.

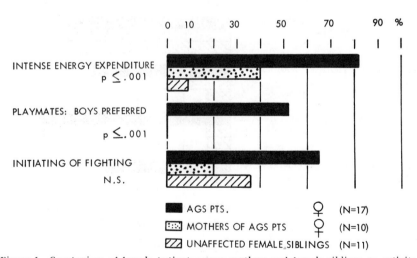

Figure 1 Comparison of female patients versus mothers and female siblings on activity and aggression. The bars represent the percentage of subjects from each group who were reported to exhibit the behavior specified by the category to the bars.

Marriage and Maternalism.   The second cluster of pertinent results centers around toy preferences, response to infants, and rehearsal of adult female roles. As one can see from Figure 2, AGS girls show a conspicuously low interest in dolls. About 80% were rated as having had little or no interest in dolls at any time during their childhood, whereas this was only true for a small number of sisters and mothers. The AGS girls tended to play with cars, trucks, and blocks. They also appeared to care little for future roles as bride and mother, but were much more concerned with future job roles. Female siblings and mothers, on the other hand, were described as being interested in childhood rehearsal of wedding and marriage as well as of various career roles and were in the latter aspect not different from the patients.

Girls with AGS were also more frequently characterized as being indifferent to small infants or expressing aversion to, and dislike of, handling babies. In contrast to their mothers and female siblings, they often avoided caring for a baby at home and preferred not to babysit. They did not exclude the possibility of becoming a mother one day; rather their attitude was noncommittal and matter-of-fact, with little or no

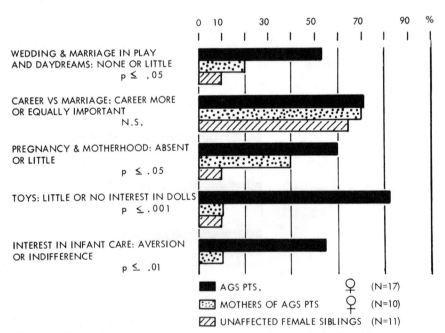

Figure 2   Comparison of female patients versus mothers and female siblings on marriage and maternalism. The bars represent the percentage of subjects from each group who were reported to exhibit the behavior specified by the category adjacent to the bars.

rehearsal in daydreams or role play about motherhood—quite in contrast to the majority of unaffected female siblings and most of their mothers during childhood.

Gender Role, Appearance, and Adolescent Dating Behavior. The next cluster of items has to do with gender-role preference and with more arbitrary sex differences, such as interest in appearance (Fig. 3). If a girl tends toward rough-and-tumble play and prefers boys and boys' toys, then she is traditionally identified as a tomboy. Fifty-nine percent of the patients were identified by themselves and others as having been tomboys during all of their childhood. This was significantly different from the sample of unaffected siblings, none of whom demonstrated this complete and long-term pattern of tomboyism. However, 27% were rated as having manifested a limited episode of some tomboyish traits during their childhood. Girls with AGS were also significantly different from the sample of mothers, only two of whom described themselves as long-term tomboys.

To the question whether it was better to be a girl or a boy, 35% of the patients were undecided or thought that they might have chosen to be a boy if such a choice had been possible. However, it is important to see these results in the proper perspective: none of the AGS girls had a conflict with her female gender identity or was unhappy about being a girl.

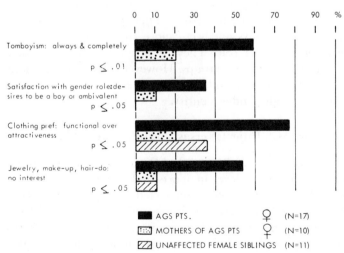

Figure 3   Comparison of female patients versus mothers and female siblings on gender-role and clothing preference. The bars represent the percentage of subjects from each group who were reported to exhibit the behavior specified by the category adjacent to the bars.

They were generally comfortable in the female role and liked to be tomboys.

The last two items relate to clothing and appearance. More girls in the patient sample preferred functional to attractive clothing and in general were not particular about their appearance. Consistently, they were also more frequently rated as having no interest in jewelry, makeup, and hairdo than were the unaffected female siblings and the mothers during their childhood.

Our evidence on adolescent behavior is based on too few cases to make any definitive statement. Preliminary impressions tend to indicate that AGS patients are somewhat late in developing relationships with members of the opposite sex. They seem to be slow in starting to date and having their first crush on a boy. However, there is no evidence that homosexuality is increased in the patient sample. Several of the adolescent girls expressed interest in, and attraction to, boys, but were more reticent, not as eager, and possibly less skilled than the unaffected female siblings in becoming involved in a flirtatious relationship with a boy.

In summary, the comparison of female AGS patients with unaffected female siblings and mothers revealed several differences in childhood behavior. The patients tended to be long-term tomboys with a pattern of intense energy expenditure in rough-and-tumble outdoor activities, demonstrated a preference for boys over girls in peer contact, and showed little interest in clothing, hair-do, and jewelry. The patients were also less interested in playing with dolls, in taking care of small infants, and in playing bride and mother roles. They preferred trucks, cars, and building material as toys and were more concerned with the future in terms of a job or career role. They were significantly different in these respects from the other two groups. However, this behavior pattern was not considered abnormal and did not interfere in any way with the formation of a female gender identity.

Male AGS Patients versus Unaffected Male Siblings

Activity and Aggression. Boys with AGS manifested more frequently a high energy-expenditure level in sports and rough outdoor activities on a long-term basis, whereas more unaffected boys were rated as having a moderate or periodic interest in sports and physical activities (Fig. 4).

There were no significant differences in fighting behavior between the two groups as judged by the criterion of initiating fights in the family and elsewhere in their environment.

Almost all boys in both groups preferred boys over girls as playmates.

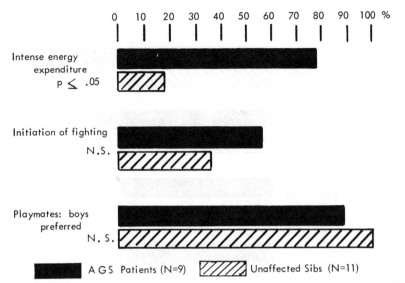

Figure 4   *Comparison of male patients versus male siblings on activity and aggression. The bars represent the percentage of subjects from each group who were reported to exhibit the behavior specified by the category adjacent to the bars.*

Marriage and Fatherhood.   No significant difference was found between AGS boys and unaffected brothers in toy preferences and rehearsal of future roles of husband and father (Fig. 5). In both groups of males, very few boys were interested in dolls and other girls' toys. In both groups, some boys had thoughts and fantasies of becoming a father, although much less so than the unaffected girls who are concerned with becoming a mother. The same was true for the number of boys who liked to handle their little brothers or sisters and other small infants. The frequency was considerably lower than in the group of unaffected females, who scored 100% in the moderate and strong category.

Gender-Role Preference and Adolescent Dating Behavior.   The next cluster concerns satisfaction with the male gender role, which is 100% in both groups (Fig. 6). There was a total absence of effeminacy in both groups, and most of them were rated or rated themselves as extremely masculine rather than average in this regard. All boys preferred boys' clothes; approximately half in each sample had no interest in their appearance, whereas the other half had a moderate or strong interest in clothes and looking attractive. Interest in appearance *per se* is thus not specifically feminine but also a noticeable part of boys' behavior in childhood and adolescence.

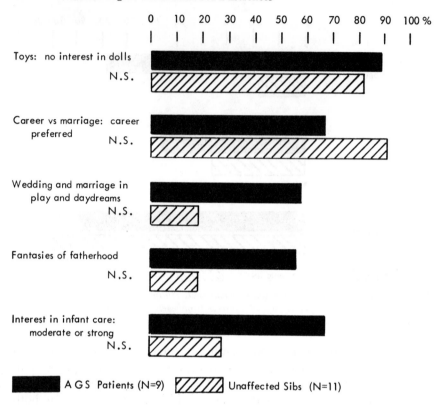

Figure 5   Comparison of male patients versus male siblings on marriage and fatherhood. The bars represent the percentage of subjects from each group who were reported to exhibit the behavior specified by the category adjacent to the bars.

The number of adolescents was too small to make a definitive statement concerning erotic attraction and dating behavior. In both groups, some boys had begun dating and had become involved in adolescent love affairs—in all cases heterosexual and with no evidence of any conflict with the male sex role.

In summary, AGS males differed from the group of unaffected male siblings in only one aspect of gender-related behavior: intense energy expenditure in outdoor play and sports activities. Otherwise, both male groups followed the typical masculine behavior pattern of our culture, with no interest in dolls, preference for boys over girls in peer contacts, some interest in the future role of husband and father, and a clear-cut preference for the masculine role.

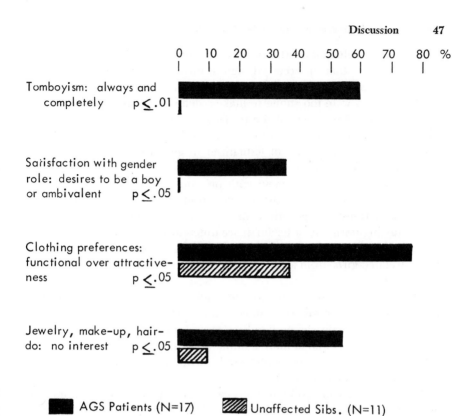

Figure 6 *Comparison of male patients versus male siblings on gender-role and clothing preference. The bars represent the percentage of subjects from each group who were reported to exhibit the behavior specified by the category adjacent to the bars.*

DISCUSSION

We found that girls with AGS differed from a sample of unaffected female siblings and their mothers in certain aspects of their sexually dimorphic behavior in childhood. They were significantly more often long-term tomboys with a profile of a high energy-expenditure level in rough outdoor play, showed a preference for boys over girls in peer contact, a low interest in playing with dolls and taking care of small infants, little rehearsal of the maternal adult role as wife and mother, and little concern about the attractiveness of their appearance in clothing, hairdo, and jewelry. However, AGS girls were clearly identified in the female role, and their behavior was not considered abnormal by them, by their parents, or by their peers. Rather, they presented an acceptable pattern of tomboyish behavior in this society, not unlike tomboyism in normal females except that it occurred significantly more often in the AGS sample than in either the sibling or the mother sample.

The patients were too young to make a definitive statement concerning homosexuality. Since most of the teenage girls were already romantically interested in boys, however, it seems unlikely that we shall find a significantly higher frequency of lesbianism in girls with a history of fetal hormonal androgenization.

Our findings are in agreement with previous studies on early- and late-treated AGS females (5). Thus we have confirmed in two different hospital populations that genetic females with an exposure to endogenous masculinizing hormones after birth are different in several aspects of their sexually dimorphic behavior in childhood from a matched group of normal unrelated girls, from a sample of unaffected female siblings, and from their mothers.

The results are also comparable to findings on subhuman female primates exposed to testosterone during intrauterine development. Fetally androgenized female rhesus monkeys were found to show more rough-and-tumble play as well as more dominance behavior; they were also more similar in some other aspects of their behavior to male monkeys than to normal female monkeys (16, 17).

The consistency of results in both earlier and more recent studies suggests strongly that it is the fetal exposure to androgens that contributes to the typical profile of behavior exhibited by AGS females. This conclusion is corroborated by the fact that girls with exogenous fetal androgenization by progestinic drugs showed a very similar behavior to that of AGS girls. In the progestin-treated group the hormonal abnormality was clearly limited to the prenatal phase. In the case of AGS, however, one cannot completely rule out the possibility that postnatal hormonal abnormalities may still affect behavior development in some way, although all girls in our sample were generally well regulated on cortisone, and, in most cases, treatment was initiated shortly after birth.

Girls with the progestin-induced condition and those with the early-treated AGS have abnormalities in their external genitalia. In spite of the fact that surgical correction to normal-looking sex organs usually took place early in infancy in our previous and present studies on children with either of the two conditions, one cannot completely exclude the genital abnormality as a factor that in some way might influence subsequent behavior. One way this effect could be transmitted would be by parental attitudes toward the affected child. It is undoubtedly a traumatic experience for parents to have a baby girl born with a genital abnormality. We interviewed the parents in great depth about their reactions and any possible lurking fears. Most parents had little persistent concern about the genital abnormality at birth, especially since the appearance of their daughter's genitalia had been normal for so many years. The tomboyish behavior was not seen as related to the genital abnormality. There was usually very little parental pressure toward more femininity, which is not surprising, since the behavior in the girls with AGS was not viewed as being abnormal or masculine.

The patients typically knew that their child's medical condition was one that was affected by cortisone levels. The older girls were informed about the clitoral enlargement at birth, which usually was accepted as a minor birth defect that had been corrected. As far as the behavior was concerned, girls with AGS typically enjoyed being tomboys without any fears of being different.

In summary, from our data it is unlikely that parental or patient attitude is a significant factor modifying the particular temperamental set of behavior toward tomboyism in either sample of girls with the progestin-induced or the adrenogenital condition.

The data on AGS males suggest no difference between the patient and male sibling sample in any area assessed, except for an increase in energy level in the patient group. The even higher level of physical strength and energy in sports and play activities in the AGS sample may be related to their prenatal history of a possibly even higher level of androgens compared with normal males; in three boys it may have also been due to postnatal androgen levels before treatment was initiated. The finding in the male sample also suggests that most aspects of masculine behavior development in male childhood are not affected by the prenatal hormone abnormality in the adrenogenital condition. This result is in agreement with earlier findings by Money and Alexander (18).

If prenatal exposure to androgens modifies behavior in genetic females as in the described clinical conditions, one may assume that similar hormonal factors contribute to the development of temperamental differences between males and females in general, and finer variations of fetal hormones may also possibly influence behavior differences within the sexes. We are obviously on speculative grounds with this theory at present, but let us assume for the sake of discussion that this was a proved fact. What implications and social consequences would such a finding have? We are aware that all sex differences in human behavior are much influenced by social-environmental reinforcement of appropriate behavior for girls and boys. Thus we are not suggesting that sexually dimorphic play, toy, and peer behavior is solely determined by prenatal and/or postnatal hormone levels. We rather suggest that prenatal androgen is one of the factors contributing to the development of temperamental differences between and within the sexes. Undoubtedly it will depend to a large extent on the interaction between prenatal hormone levels and the particular environment of the child as to what quality the specific behavior will have.

We would like to close with one other point. If prenatal hormone levels contribute to sex differences in behavior, the effects in human beings are subtle and can in no way be taken as a basis for prescribing social roles. In fact, we rather like to make an argument from the opposite point of view. If it can be documented that prenatal hormone levels are among the factors that account for the wide range of temperamental differences and role aspirations within the female, and possibly also within the male, sex, a great variety of adult roles should be available and can be adequately fulfilled by both women and men, and they should be equally acceptable and respectable for either sex.

ACKNOWLEDGMENTS

The study was supported by a grant (Cl-10-CH-71) from the United Health Foundation of Western New York, the Human Growth Foundation, and the Variety Club of Buffalo, Tent No. 7.

The patients in this sample were diagnosed and managed by Drs. Thomas Aceto, Jr., and Margaret MacGillivray of the Pediatric Endocrine Clinic at Children's Hospital of Buffalo, New York. Their clinical cooperation is greatly appreciated.

The data graphs were designed by the Department of Medical Illustrations, State University of New York at Buffalo.

REFERENCES

1. Jones, H. W., Jr. and B. S. Verkauf, *Am J Obstet Gynecol* **109**: 292, 1971.
2. Ehrhardt, A. A. and J. Money, *J Sex Res* **3**: 83, 1967.
3. Ehrhardt, A. A., R. Epstein, and J. Money, *Johns Hopkins Med J* **122**: 160, 1968.
4. Ehrhardt, A. A., in Duhm, E. (ed.), *Praxis der Klinischen Psychologie II*, Verlag für Psychologie, Dr. C. J. Hogrefe, Göttingen, 1971, p. 94.
5. Money, J. and A. A. Ehrhardt, *Man & Woman, Boy & Girl*, Johns Hopkins University Press, Baltimore, 1972.
6. Hollingshead, A. B., *Two Factor Index of Social Position*, privately printed, New Haven, Conn., 1957.
7. Maccoby, E. E. and C. N. Jacklin, *The Psychology of Sex Differences*, Stanford University Press, Palo Alto, Calif., 1974.

8. Harlow, H., *Am Psychol* **17**: 1, 1962.

9. Harris, G. W., *Endocrinology* **75**: 627, 1964.

10. DeVore, I., in Rheingold, H. L. (ed.), *Maternal Behavior in Mammals*, Wiley, New York, 1963.

11. Jay, P., in Rheingold, H. L. (ed.), *Maternal Behavior in Mammals*, Wiley, New York, 1963.

12. Sears, R. R., L. Rau, and R. Alpert, *Identification and Child Rearing*, Stanford University Press, Stanford, Calif., 1965.

13. Maccoby, E. E. and C. N. Jacklin, *Scientific American*, in press.

14. Lienert, G. A., *Verteilungsfreie Methoden*, Anton Hain, Meisenheim am Glan, 1962, p. 88.

15. Freeman, G. H. and J. H. Halton, *Biometrika* **38**: 41, 1951.

16. Goy, R. W., *Phil Trans Roy Soc London* **259**: 149, 1970.

17. Eaton, G. G., R. W. Goy, and C. H. Phoenix, *Nature New Biol* **242**: 119, 1973.

18. Money, J. and D. Alexander, *J Nerv Ment Dis* **148**: 111, 1969.

CHAPTER 4

Prenatal Androgen, Intelligence, And Cognitive Sex Differences

SUSAN W. BAKER and ANKE A. EHRHARDT

Departments of Psychiatry and Pediatrics
State University of New York at Buffalo
School of Medicine
Buffalo, New York

This chapter discusses the possible relationship of hormones and their implications for sex differences in cognitive functioning.

Although it has been documented and accepted that normal males and females do not differ in Full IQ, the question of the effects of sex hormones on intellectual functioning was raised when studies on clinical populations with unusual hormonal histories showed that elevation of IQ values might be associated with prenatal exposure to excessive progesterone and/or androgen. These findings have given rise to speculation that there may be, after all, a constitutionally linked sex difference in intellectual development.

In this chapter, we first review the major publications reporting a relationship between exposure to prenatal androgens or progesterone and an elevation in intellectual functioning. We then report the results of our own family study and discuss how they relate to previous findings.

REVIEW OF PREVIOUS STUDIES

The study that opened discussion in this country on prenatal androgen levels and elevation of IQ was one by Money and Lewis (1) on the adrenogenital syndrome (AGS). All individuals with this condition have a history of high prenatal androgen levels, and in the late-treated condition, of high postnatal androgen levels also. For details on aspects of the adrenogenital syndrome see Chapter 3.

The question under study is whether the central nervous system that is exposed to abnormally high levels of androgen favors advanced intellectual development.

The purpose of the Money and Lewis paper (1) was to assess the level and distribution of IQ in a sample of 70 AGS patients. A second purpose was to examine subsamples to determine if any of four relevant variables were related to IQ. The four variables were (1) residential distance from the hospital as an indirect indicator of social class, the assumption being that patients who are able to afford long-distance travel to a medical center can be expected to be of higher socioeconomic status than local patients; (2) age at therapy; (3) sex; and (4) secondary features associated with the condition (e.g., salt loss or hypertension).

The Money and Lewis sample consisted of both males and females, some of whom were treated with cortisone at an early age whereas others had gone for several years without treatment. The late-treated females had shown various signs of postnatal virilization, and the late-treated males had experienced early male puberty.

Money and Lewis (1) used one of the age-appropriate Wechsler tests as an intelligence measure. They found a mean Full IQ of 109.9 (SD 19.3) as opposed to the expected norm of 100. Sixty percent of the sample had Full IQs of 110 or above, clearly an elevated frequency of high IQs compared with the expected 25% in a normal distribution. The skewness of the distribution toward the upper end was statistically significant at the 1% level.

Of the four variables previously mentioned, none of the comparisons showed statistically significant differences between subsamples. Money and Lewis concluded that there was no known biasing factor that could account for the raised IQ.

The elevation of IQ in AGS patients was clear-cut. Since none of the various comparisons of subgroups explained this finding, the authors concluded that it might be related to the syndrome itself. One possible explanation mentioned was that increased adrenal androgen production in fetal life might in some way be responsible for the postnatal enhancement of IQ. They also discussed the possibility that an elevation in IQ might be related to the same genetic trait that is responsible for the condition.

In further studies by Ehrhardt, Epstein, and Money (2, 3) of 15 early-treated AGS girls (some of whom had also been included in the previous sample of 70), Hollingshead socioeconomic indices (4) were reported. All possible socioeconomic classes were represented, from unskilled laborers to high-level executives and professionals. The mean Full IQ of 111.53 was above the expected norm, as it had been in the previous study.

Money and co-workers have since been involved in a series of intelligence studies on various endocrine subsamples. They reported a summary of their findings in 1967 (5). While most endocrine syndromes did not differ from the norm in intellectual functioning, a few were associated with overall impairment or specific deficits. The only endocrine syndromes associated with IQ elevation were AGS and idiopathic precocious puberty.

The hypothesis that fetal exposure to high levels of androgenic hormones may be related to elevation in intelligence was strengthened by a study of Ehrhardt and Money (6). They tested 10 girls whose mothers had taken synthetic progestinic drugs (17-ethinyltestosterone or 19-nor-17-ethinyltestosterone, trade names Progestoral, Pranone, and Norlutin) during pregnancy. These drugs had been administered to prevent threatened miscarriages. (The progestin-exposed group differs from the adrenogenital group in that after birth there is no additional excess of masculinizing hormone present in the body.) At the time of testing the sample ranged in age from 3 years and 9 months to 14 years and 3 months. The drugs had an unexpected virilizing effect on the external genitalia of some of the daughters.

In the 10-patient sample studied by Ehrhardt and Money (6) the mean Wechsler Full IQ was 125, with a standard deviation of 11.8. None of the patients had a Full IQ below 100, and six patients had a Full IQ above 130. Thus 60% were in the "very superior" range compared with the 2.2% one would expect from the population norms. It is, admittedly, not very meaningful to speak of percentages in such a small sample. The illustration is primarily useful to elucidate the peculiar distribution, with an unusually high frequency of superior IQs, particularly beyond two standard deviations above the mean. The difference between Verbal and Performance IQs was not significant. Both means were 125.

The authors showed a relationship between the IQs of patients and the educational level of their parents. There was one patient with a Full IQ in the 100 to 109 range and two with IQs in the 110 to 119 range. These three patients came from the three families whose parents were high school graduates or lower. The other seven patients, one with an IQ above 120 and six with IQs above 130, came from families whose parents were college graduates or higher. The authors considered the possibility that the elevation in IQ was due to a selective factor toward upper socio-economic level that may be characteristic for this syndrome. On the other hand, the elevation in IQ is still unusually high even for the socioeconomic level of the sample and thus may also have had some relationship to the prenatal treatment with progestin, in particular, in light of the previous findings by Money and Lewis on the adrenogenital patients (1).

At about the same time Dalton (7) reported an educational follow-up study of children (both male and female) whose mothers had been given progesterone in pregnancy with no resultant masculinizing effects on the offspring. The progesterone was administered daily by intramuscular injection in dosages varying from 50 to 300 mg for the relief of toxemic symptoms. These were defined as headache, nausea and vomiting, lethargy, backache, vertigo, fainting, cramps or paresthesia, depression or irritability.

The children used in the educational follow-up study were those whose mothers had been included in a previous study on toxemia in pregnancy treated with progesterone (8). Dalton (7) matched 44 progesterone children with two control groups. One group, "normal controls," consisted of next-born children listed in the labor-ward register whose mothers had a normal pregnancy and delivery. The "toxemia control" group were children delivered from mothers who had toxemia during pregnancy without hormonal treatment. The educational follow-up was done on these children 9 to 10 years later. School teachers filled out a form stating whether the child was above or below average in verbal reasoning, English, arithmetic, craftwork, and physical education. Educational ratings were received on 79 children: 29 progesterone, 21 normal controls, and 29 toxemic controls. The study was on a blind basis; that is, the teachers who rated the children did not know which group the child belonged to. The results showed that progesterone children received significantly more "above average" grades than those of either control group. These results were significant for all academic subjects. Dalton also demonstrated a positive correlation between "high dosage" and "early treatment" on one hand and above-average school achievement on the other hand. Dalton did not divide her samples by sex in any of the school-performance results, so it is not possible to determine whether this was a relevant factor.

In some respects the Dalton study is a model for research on clinical samples. It is rare to find such good control groups. Taking the next-born infants from the hospital register probably is a good match for social class factors, age factors, and other unforeseeable biases. There were, however, still some tendencies for group characteristics to differ. The mothers of progesterone children tended to be older and of higher parity. They had experienced a significantly greater number of previous abortions than the combined control groups. The group characteristics for the children themselves differed in only one respect: progesterone children tended to be heavier than those in the control groups. However, this difference was not significant. Thus one cannot completely exclude the possibility that factors other than prenatal hormonal history may have affected achievement in school. On the other hand, there seems to be a strong suggestion that prenatal exposure to exogenous progesterone may have a (direct or secondary) effect on parts of the developing brain, enhancing postnatal intellectual development.

One other recent study by Perlman (9, 10) should be mentioned. Although this research effort had several goals that are not relevant to the present discussion, Perlman's experimental groups included AGS children, tested with the Wechsler Intelligence Scale for Children and specific abilities tests oriented toward the diagnosis of specific learning disabilities. Perlman used normal control groups matched on the basis of age and socioeconomic status. In her results on the Full IQs of AGS boys and girls, she reaffirmed the elevation of IQ in the patients with this syndrome. Although the Full IQs of these patients were not significantly different from those of the control group, this finding is not surprising in light of the fact that there was a socioeconomic bias in her sample of patients and controls toward the upper end. The bias appeared slightly more extreme in the control group.

From the evidence presented in this review of previous studies, there would seem to be a definite possibility that abnormally high prenatal androgen levels, exposure to exogenous synthetic progestins masculinizing the fetus, or exposure to exogenous progesterone with no virilizing effect on the fetus may be associated with an enhancing influence on postnatal intellectual development.

PURPOSE OF FAMILY STUDY

The purpose of the present study was threefold. First, we wanted to repeat the original study of AGS by Money and Lewis (1) on a different hospital population and compare our findings with those of previously tested populations. The second goal was to compare the AGS patients with a relevant control group that would meet several theoretical requirements. We needed to control not only for family socioeconomic status but also for genetic background. A critical question in determining the etiology of IQ elevation in AGS patients is whether it might be explained by some genetic factor related or unrelated to the hormonal differences. The only control group that would be able to shed light on this question is "unaffected" family members (i.e., parents and siblings who do not have AGS). Both parents and some siblings have to be carriers, since AGS is genetically transmitted as an autosomal recessive trait. If prenatal androgenization plays an important role in the elevation of IQ in this syndrome, one would expect that the patient sample should be significantly different from their parents and siblings.

The third purpose of our study was to look at differential abilities. Normal females and males differ in certain cognitive abilities. In extensive reviews of the literature on differences in intellectual abilities, Maccoby and Jacklin (11, 12) summarize the data as follows: From about age 10 or 11, through high school and college years, girls do better on a variety of verbal skills than do boys. Sex differences in verbal skills, usually favoring girls, are also found between the ages of 3 and 11 years. However, they have not been as consistently reported as for adolescents and adults. In quantitative-analytical abilities, sex differences develop only after age 9, generally favoring boys. No consistent pattern of sex differences for computational abilities alone has been demonstrated. The most clear-cut and consistent sex differences have been reported for spatial abilities throughout most ages. In this area, however, sex differences also remain small and are inconsistent until the age of 10 or 11, when the superiority of boys emerges more consistently than in earlier years.

If fetal hormones are involved in the development of normal sex differences in the cognitive abilities of humans, we would expect that females exposed to high levels of male hormones (thus probably having a prenatal hormonal history closer to that of normal males than to that of normal females) would show a pattern of strengths and weaknesses on cognitive abilities more similar to that of normal males than that of normal females. One might speculate that AGS males may be exposed to even higher prenatal androgen levels than normal males and thus may presumably demonstrate a pronounced male pattern of differential cognitive abilities.

METHODS

Sample Selection and Characteristics

Thirty-one AGS patients had been seen in the Buffalo Pediatric Endocrine Clinic at the time of our study. Of this sample, we were able to test 27 patients, who came from 21 families.

Five families had more than one AGS child. All together, 32 parents and 27 siblings were tested. Three mothers refused to cooperate or were inaccessible because they moved away. Seven fathers were missing, due either to divorce or refusal to participate. Twelve siblings were missing from the sample; eight came from one family where only one sibling was available for testing. Of the remaining four siblings not included, two were too young and two did not live in the Buffalo area. (For more details of sample characteristics see Chapter 3.)

Money and Lewis (1) did not report socioeconomic indices on their sample of 70 patients. Thus we chose the previously mentioned Hopkins subgroup of 15 AGS patients (2), for which Hollingshead indices were available, and compared them with the Hollingshead indices of our 21 families.

As is obvious from Figure 1, our sample in Buffalo tended to come from a slightly lower socioeconomic background. No one was in the highest socioeconomic class (I), and most families came from classes IV and V. Thus we were clearly not dealing with a sample biased toward the upper socioeconomic level.

Selection of Tests

General Intelligence. We administered a widely used standard intelligence measure—one of the three Wechsler intelligence scales: the Wechsler Preschool and Primary Scale of Intelligence (WPPSI), for children below 5 years of age (13); the Wechsler Intelligence Scale for Children (WISC) for children from 5 years to 15 years, 11 months (14); or the

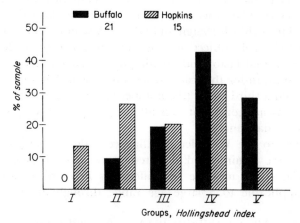

Figure 1 Socioeconomic indices of 21 Buffalo AGS families and a Johns Hopkins (2, 33) subsample of 15 AGS families on the Hollingshead scale. The highest index is represented by I, *the lowest by* V.

Wechsler Adult Intelligence Scale (WAIS) for everyone 16 years or older (15). On all three tests, the subject obtains a Full IQ (mean 100; SD 15), which is our measure of general intelligence.

Differential Abilities.   To test some of our hypotheses on differential abilities, we also analyzed the results on the Wechsler tests in terms of Verbal and Performance IQs and Cohen factors.

The Wechsler intelligence tests are divided into two sections of subtests referred to as the verbal part and the performance part. Four of the six tests of the verbal part rely more heavily on verbal abilities, information queries, vocabulary, and so forth. The other two tests in the verbal part relate to number and memory abilities. The six verbal subtests (including the optional Digit Span subtest on the WISC) are pooled to give a Verbal IQ (mean 100; SD 15). The performance subtests include various visual-motor tasks that are pooled to give a Performance IQ (mean 100; SD 15).

The division into verbal and performance parts was done by Wechsler on an intuitive basis, not by statistical factor analysis, as in some other abilities tests. The verbal part contains several tests in which females are expected to excel, and the performance part contains several perceptual tests in which males often excel.

Closer to a statistical model of differential measures of cognitive abilities are the clusters of subtests found by Cohen (16, 17) on the basis of factor analysis. There are two such factors consistent over age groups for the WISC and the WAIS. One of them is a verbal-comprehension factor, loaded by four verbal subtests (Information, Comprehension, Similarities, and Vocabulary). The other is a perceptual factor, loaded by two performance subtests (Block Design and Object Assembly). The factor scores are obtained for each subject by summing the scaled scores for the subtests loading on that factor and dividing by the same number of subtests. The expected mean for the scaled scores (and factors) is 10.

Cohen found a third factor (the number or "freedom of distractability" factor) that was not consistent over all age groups and was therefore not included in our data analysis.

In addition to the Wechsler intelligence scales, a battery of special ability tests were administered. The tests were selected according to two main criteria: (1) to measure sex differences in cognitive abilities and (2) to be applicable to a large age range throughout childhood and adulthood.

The Primary Mental Abilities (PMA) tests fulfilled these requirements relatively well (18). The PMA is a test measuring specific abilities based on a factor-analysis model. There are five differential abilities test scores and one total score applicable to various PMA school-grade ranges. Norms are given in deviation quotients (DQ) with a population mean of 100 and a standard deviation of 16. Of the five differential abilities tests, there are only three that are consistently given from kindergarten throughout high school. These three are the verbal, number, and spatial tests.

Since the choice of tests on the basis of our criteria was limited, we compromised and selected additional methods to look at some specific variables within limited age ranges, so that at least a comparison between patients and siblings (excluding the parents) would be possible. The Embedded Figures Test (19), the Differential Aptitude Tests (20), and the Conservation Kit (21) were appropriate tests for these comparisons.

As of now, only the findings on the Wechsler scales and the PMA tests have been analyzed and will be reported in this chapter.

Procedures

The patients' parents were asked for their cooperation in a research study of the intelligence and abilities of AGS patients and their families. As described in Chapter 3, the cooperation of the subjects was high. Rapport was excellent in nearly every case. Testing was scheduled at the family's convenience: during the day, on holidays, evenings, or weekends.

Testing usually required two individual sessions. The PMA was occasionally given in small groups, with two or three people in the same family screened from each other by large dividers.

Analysis of Data

There are obviously many different ways of comparing the data of a family study on the various measures. We are dealing with three main subject groups (patients, siblings, parents) that could be subdivided into male and female. Our data analysis was performed with the three main groups and, if appropriate, with the six subdivided groups. We refer to the different types of comparisons as three- and six-group analyses (see Fig. 2).

We also make the distinction of between- and within-group comparisons. In between-group comparison, we compare the various groups with each other regarding the results on the same tests. In within-group comparison, we compare the results on various tests within the same group.

Depending on the specific hypothesis for our data, we applied different

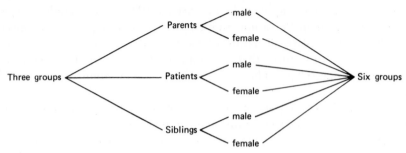

Figure 2   Types of group comparisons.

types of sample comparisons, including different types of family constellations. We refer to the complete sample, the mean sample, and the
matched sample. The definitions are as follows:

Complete-sample analysis: everyone for whom data are available unless
specific exceptions are made and noted specifically.

Mean-sample analysis: whenever multiple members of a group are
available within a family (i.e., two parents, more than one sibling, more
than one patient), the average score per group within family is used.

Matched-sample analysis: this comparison is only possible if there is at
least one member in each group in one family for the specified data
analysis. Whenever there is more than one member, the average score
per group within family is used again. Table 1 gives illustrative examples.

We were basically interested in three types of statistical analysis:

1. To test our sample results against the norm, as in mean Full IQ
group results against the population mean. For this type of comparison
we chose the z-test using the population variance.

2. To test the hypothesis that an obtained distribution of test scores is
different from an expected distribution, as in a sample IQ distribution
compared with the population distribution. We applied the Kolmogorov–
Smirnov test (22).

3. Most statistical analyses concerned the significance of various differences of group results. We used the appropriate matched or unmatched
t-tests.

RESULTS

General Intelligence (Full IQ)

Patients versus Norm.   The mean Full IQ of our complete sample of
patients (N 27) is 112.74 (SD 16.52) and is significantly elevated from the
norm (z-test; $p \leq .01$; one-tailed).

Table 1 Types of Sample Comparisons and Types of Families[a]

	Complete Sample			Mean Sample			Matched Sample		
	P	AGS	S	P	AGS	S	P	AGS	S
Parents missing; several siblings	—	x	xxx	—	x	x	—	—	—
Siblings missing; several patients	xx	xx	—	x	x	—	—	—	—
Parents missing; siblings missing	—	x	—	—	x	—	—	—	—
Both parents; multiple patients and siblings	xx	xx	xxx	x	x	x	x	x	x
One parent; one patient; one sibling	x	x	x	x	x	x	x	x	x

[a]Abbreviations: P, parents; S, siblings.

63

The elevation of mean IQ is mainly due to an usually high number of IQs above 110 (59% instead of the expected 25%). Thus the distribution of Full IQs of the complete patient sample is significantly different from the norm distribution (Kolmogorov–Smirnov test; $p \leq .01$; two-tailed).

If one subdivides the complete sample into female and male patients, and compares AGS females (N 17) against the norm and AGS males (N 10) against the norm, the finding is similar. The mean Full IQ of AGS females is 113 (SD 14) and is significantly elevated from the norm (z-test; $p \leq .01$; one-tailed). The mean Full IQ of AGS males is 111 (SD 21) and is significantly elevated from the norm (z-test; $p \leq .05$; one-tailed). Thus both female and male AGS patients have an elevated Full IQ in comparison with the population norm.

Buffalo Sample versus Other Hospital Samples. Our finding of IQ elevation in the patient sample is remarkably similar to previous findings (Fig. 3). Money and Lewis (1) and Perlman (9) found a similarly elevated mean Full IQ in their samples of AGS patients with very similar frequency distributions. The frequencies of observed above-average Full IQs are strikingly close in all three studies. In the Johns Hopkins study, there were 60% and in the Perlman study 53%, instead of the expected 25% IQs above 110.

Patients versus Parents and Siblings. We compared the mean Full IQ (112.74; SD 16.52) in the complete sample of patients (N 27) versus the mean Full IQ (107.06; SD 14.75) in the complete sample of parents (N 32) and also versus the mean Full IQ (110.59; SD 17.40) in the complete sample of siblings (N 27). All three means were significantly elevated from the norm (z-test; $p \leq .01$; two-tailed), but not significantly different from each other (t-test) by complete-, mean-, and matched-sample analysis.

The three distributions (Fig. 4) are not as similar as the three different hospital distributions already described, but they are not significantly different from each other (Kolmogorov–Smirnov test). Both the patients' and the parents' distributions (but not the siblings' distribution) are significantly different from the norm distribution (Kolmogorov–Smirnov test; $p \leq .01$; two-tailed).

In addition to three-group analyses, we did six-group analyses (see Fig. 2) to see whether all subgroups were similarly elevated from the norm. As Table 2 shows, five of the six groups were significantly elevated (z-test; $p \leq .05$). The mothers' mean Full IQ was not significantly elevated, although 50% of the mothers had IQs of 110 or above versus the expected 25%.

We looked at various factors that might have inadvertently biased the

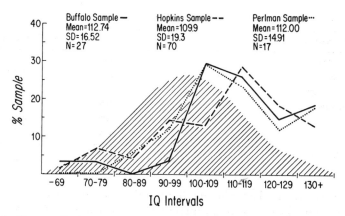

Figure 3 Mean Full IQs and frequency distributions of three independent samples of
AGS patients tested at different hospitals (1, 9) compared with the normal distribution.

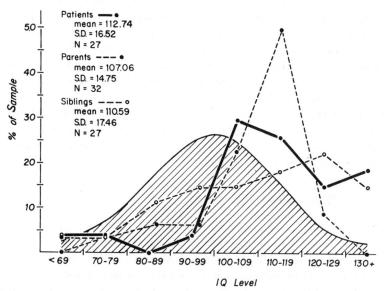

Figure 4 Mean Full IQs and frequency distributions of AGS patients, parents, and
siblings in the Buffalo complete sample. The shaded area represents the expected normal
distribution.

65

Table 2   Patients and Siblings: Mean Full IQ

Complete Sample	N	Mean IQ	Significance Level
AGS Females	17	113	.001*
AGS Males	10	111	.05*
Female siblings	11	113	.01
Male siblings	16	109	.05
Mothers	18	103	N.S.
Fathers	14	112	.01

* One-tailed test.

results. First, we checked whether the number of patients or siblings per family was homogeneous over different levels of parents' IQs. We found that the bright parents did not differ in this respect from the parents with lower IQs.

Next, we looked at the socioeconomic indices and Full IQs of family members. As mentioned, our sample does not have a known socioeconomic class bias toward the upper end. An interesting side finding is the relationship between intelligence and socioeconomic class in our three groups. Only four of the possible Hollingshead socioeconomic indices are represented on Figure 5, because there were no families with index I. The sibling scores show a steady decrease in mean IQ from the highest (II) to the lowest (V) socioeconomic index, with a significant relationship between IQ and socioeconomic index [reduction to fourfold table; Fisher Exact Probability Test (23); $p \leq .05$; one-tailed]. No similar relationship appeared for the two other samples, suggesting that the elevation of Full IQ was relatively unrelated to socioeconomic class in case of the patients and parents.

In summary, our patient population is elevated in Full IQ, with a distribution remarkably similar to the distributions described in previous studies. However, the patients were *not* different either in mean Full IQ or in distribution from their parents and siblings.

Differential Abilities

Verbal and Performance IQ.   On the Verbal IQ, the mean scores of all six groups cluster closely together in a complete-sample analysis (Fig. 6). Female siblings scored highest and mothers scored lowest. None of the six between-group differences on Verbal IQ was significant.

On the Performance IQ, the range of mean scores of the six groups (complete-sample analysis) was wider, with a significant difference between the highest score (AGS males) and the lowest score (mothers)

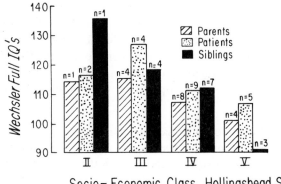

Figure 5   *Relationship between mean Full IQ of parents, patients, and siblings with the socioeconomic indices of the various families. Here n represents the number of families who have members in the group specified by the bar within each socioeconomic class. For example, four families in socioeconomic class V have IQ scores for parents, five families in that class have scores for patients, and three families have scores for siblings. Although sometimes data on parents or siblings were missing, in every case we had data for patients. The one retarded family in our sample was excluded from this comparison.*

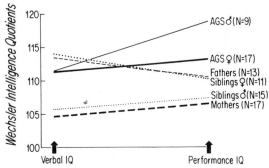

Figure 6   *Mean Verbal and Performance IQs for six groups of the complete Buffalo sample (20 families). The retarded family was excluded.*

(unmatched t-test; $p \leq .05$; two-tailed). However, when only the subgroup of mothers of AGS males (instead of the complete sample of mothers) was compared with the sample of AGS males (mean-sample analysis), the difference had decreased and was not significant. No other between-group comparison of performance scores was significant.

As to Verbal versus Performance IQs, a within-sample comparison for AGS males did not show a significant difference, nor did any other within-group comparison.

Several of the trends in these results are interesting, although the differences are not significant. For example, female siblings did the best on Verbal IQ, consistent with the theory that females normally excel on verbal tasks. The AGS males were the top group on the Performance IQ, also consistent with the theory that males excel on visual-motor tasks. Other trends were sometimes supportive of our hypotheses, but frequently not.

Cohen Factors.   In the complete-sample analysis, surprisingly, the fathers had the highest scores on the verbal factor and the mothers had the lowest (Fig. 7). The comparison between mothers and fathers reflected the only significant difference in all complete-sample analyses for the verbal factor.

On the perceptual factor, AGS males scored highest and male siblings lowest, but none of the complete-sample analyses was significant in this case.

There were several interesting observations in group trends in matched-sample analyses. As can be seen in Table 3, there are several trends that seem to support our hypotheses and a few that do not. Arbitrarily taking one scaled score as a cutoff point, we find 12 differences of one or more than one scaled score point in between- or within-group comparisons. Of these differences, nine were consistent with expectations for normal sex differences and our hypotheses regarding AGS patients. For example, consistent with the hypothesis that females usually do better on verbal than on perceptual tasks, female siblings of female patients excelled on verbal subtests represented on the verbal factor, compared to their own performance on the perceptual factor. The hypothesis that AGS females

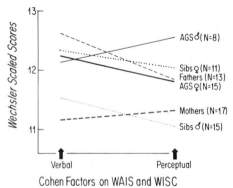

Figure 7   Mean verbal and perceptual Cohen factors for six groups of the complete Buffalo sample (20 families). The retarded family was excluded.

*Table 3   Matched Family Comparisons: Mean Cohen Verbal
and Perceptual Factor Scores*

(N=4)	Parents	Female AGS	Female Siblings
Verbal	12.5	12.8	12.4
Perceptual	11.8	12.6	11.4

(N=5)	Parents	Female AGS	Male Siblings
Verbal	11.7	12.1	11.6
Perceptual	10.7	11.3	11.0

(N=3)	Parents	Male AGS	Male Siblings
Verbal	11.7	10.9	12.5
Perceptual	10.4	12.5	10.2

(N=4)	Parents	Male AGS	Female Siblings
Verbal	11.9	11.4	11.5
Perceptual	12.2	13.6	11.8

should do better on the perceptual factor score than their unaffected
female siblings was supported. We expected the AGS males to do better
on the perceptual factor than any other group in between-group comparisons and better on the perceptual factor than on the verbal factor in
within-group comparisons. This hypothesis was supported by all comparisons.

One difference of one or more scaled scores was against our expectations for normal sex differences: the brothers of male patients did better
on the verbal factor score than on the perceptual factor in a within-
group comparison.

In two cases a difference of at least one point was found not to be
related to any hypothesis on sex differences: parents did better on verbal
than on perceptual factor scores in two within-group comparisons.

In summary, no significant differences were found on the two Cohen
factors between AGS patients and other groups. Several trends were in
the expected direction, but did not reach statistical significance.

Primary Mental Abilities.   As already mentioned, the data analysis on
the PMA is only concerned with the scores of patients and siblings
(parents excluded) on three tests (verbal, number, and spatial).

We looked first at within- and between-group comparisons in complete-
sample analyses for four groups (Fig. 8). The most striking finding is the
decline for both AGS males and females on the number deviation quo-
tient. Within-group comparisons resulted in a significant difference for

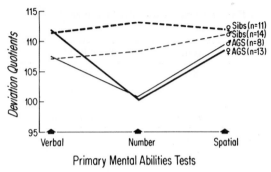

Figure 8   *Mean PMA deviation quotients on three tests for four groups of the complete Buffalo sample (20 families). The retarded family was excluded.*

both groups between their own scores on the verbal and spatial tests, and their scores on the number test. Neither sibling group showed a similar decline.

On the verbal test alone no between-group analysis was significant. The trend of the data is in the expected direction for normal sex differences: both female groups do slightly better than both male groups. Fetally androgenized females did not perform less well than female siblings on the PMA verbal test.

On the number test between-group comparisons showed that all AGS patients scored significantly lower than all siblings (unmatched t-test; $p \leq .05$; two-tailed). The difference is also significant for AGS females alone compared to all female siblings (unmatched t-test; $p \leq .05$; two-tailed) and remains significant in a matched-sample analysis of AGS females versus their sisters (matched t-test; $p \leq .05$; two-tailed). The AGS males are not significantly different from male siblings (complete-sample analysis, unmatched t-test). There were only three families for which a matched-sample analysis was possible; the AGS males were not different from their male siblings.

On the spatial test none of the between-group comparisons was significant.

Thus our data clearly show that AGS patients tend to score lower than their siblings on the number test and also score lower on this test than on the other two PMA tests.

Concerning trends, our hypothesis was that female siblings do best on the verbal test and poorest on the spatial test. Male siblings should perform in a reverse pattern: better on the spatial test than on the verbal one. The AGS females should resemble normal males more than normal females in their performance on verbal and spatial tests, and the

AGS males should do better on spatial tests than all other groups and poorer on the verbal test than all other groups. We had no specific hypothesis about the performance on the PMA number test since normal males and females do not differ consistently in computational ability.

The table of trends (Table 4) is arranged like Table 3 (Cohen factors). The trends were not consistent and were less indicative of any tendencies supportive of sex differences than the trends on the Cohen factors.

We found 15 trend differences on the basis of at least an 8-deviation-quotient cutoff point. Nine of these 15 trends were related to the significantly lower performance of AGS females and males on the number test. The other six trends were divided into one for, two against, and three unrelated to any of our hypotheses on sex differences. None of these group differences was significant, except those regarding the lower performance on the number test for AGS patients in between- and within-group comparisons.

In summary, analysis of our data on the PMA revealed a pattern of relative inferiority on the number test for the AGS patients versus their performance on the verbal and spatial tests and versus their siblings. The group differences in the verbal and spatial scores alone did not support any of our hypotheses.

Table 4   *Matched Family Comparisons: Mean PMA Deviation Quotients, Verbal, Number and Spatial Tests*

(N = 4)	Female AGS	Female Siblings
Verbal	110.25	117.88
Number	100.75	111.75
Spatial	113.50	109.50

(N = 4)	Female AGS	Male Siblings
Verbal	112.25	115.38
Number	100.75	115.63
Spatial	106.75	108.25

(N = 3)	Male AGS	Male Siblings
Verbal	98.00	105.17
Number	93.00	92.00
Spatial	101.30	105.67

(N = 3)	Male AGS	Female Siblings
Verbal	111.75	97.63
Number	98.00	111.75
Spatial	118.25	116.00

DISCUSSION

General Intelligence

Our findings are in some respects clear-cut and answer several questions concerning the hypothesis that abnormally high prenatal androgen levels may enhance postnatal intellectual development. In other respects they are puzzling and raise new issues. The main results can be summarized as follows:

1. The previous finding that AGS patients tend to have an above-average Full IQ more frequently than expected in the normal population was confirmed. This cannot be attributed to social class bias since the socioeconomic background of our sample was clearly representative. If anything, it was possibly a little biased toward the lower end. This finding also cannot be explained by a theory that all patients who come to pediatric endocrine clinics tend to have higher IQs since studies on other endocrine samples do not support this assumption (5, 24, 25). In line with the same reasoning, it is also unlikely that the finding of IQ elevation in AGS patients is solely due to possibly outdated norms of the Wechsler scale.

2. To elucidate some of the factors that may contribute to the enhancement of intellectual development in AGS patients, we tested a relatively large number of parents and unaffected siblings. We found in both samples of parents and siblings a significantly elevated Full IQ compared with the norm. In this respect, parents and unaffected siblings were not different from the patients.

This finding agrees with the study by Money and Lewis (1), which included a very small unaffected-sibling sample that also did not differ in Full IQ from the affected patients.

Thus it appears that families with one or more AGS children tend to have a higher IQ. The enhancement of intellectual development cannot be attributed specifically to the prenatal and/or postnatal hormonal aspects of the adrenogenital syndrome, since patients did not differ in IQ from unaffected siblings and parents.

Several alternative hypotheses should be considered to explain the elevated IQ in families with AGS children. First, AGS is a genetically transmitted autosomal recessive condition. Both parents have to be carriers to produce an AGS child. The majority of the unaffected siblings can also expect to be carriers. Statistically it is expected that, of four children born to two heterozygote carriers, one will have AGS, two will be heterozygote carriers, and one will be genetically unaffected. It is conceivable that the recessive genetic trait may be somehow linked to another trait favoring postnatal intellectual development. This theory would be compatible with the finding of an elevated IQ in the patient sample, the parent sample, and the sibling sample.

Two side findings may be seen to support the genetic theory. In comparing the three frequency distributions in Full IQ we observed that the patients and parents had distributions that differed significantly from the norm, largely due to an unexpected high number of IQs in the above-average and superior range. The sibling distribution was not different from the norm distribution, although their sample also had an elevated Full IQ. Since the sibling sample probably consists of both heterozygote carriers and genetically unaffected individuals, one may expect their IQ elevation to be less uniform than for the patients and parents, who are known to be homozygote or heterozygote carriers in all cases. The other side finding supporting this theory is the fact that only in the sibling sample could a significant relationship between Full IQ and family socioeconomic index be demonstrated, as one would usually expect in the normal population. The same relationship was not found for the patient and parent sample, possibly suggesting that their intellectual level is less dependent on socioeconomic class.

Obviously the suggested genetic theory, previously also mentioned by Money and Lewis (1), is on very speculative grounds. Once heterozygote carriers can be determined, this question can be investigated more fully.

An alternative to the question of genetics is the possibility of an as yet unknown selection process of families who bring their AGS children to pediatric endocrine clinics. If such a process does exist, it seems to be unrelated to social class, since our social data did not suggest a bias toward the upper end.

Finally, let us return to the question of prenatal hormone levels and intelligence. Our findings do not support the theory that excessive prenatal androgens, as in AGS subjects, are responsible for the elevation of IQ. However, the possibility that other prenatal hormones may sometimes have a positive effect on postnatal intellectual development cannot be completely eliminated. There remains the study by Dalton (7) showing that girls and boys who were exposed to additional amounts of progesterone during fetal development excelled in school performance as compared to control groups. We know that AGS itself affects not only androgen levels but also several other hormonal interactions, which may conceivably be linked to the enhancement of intellectual development. Also one cannot ignore the possibility that heterozygote AGS carriers have variations in prenatal hormone levels compared to normal individuals. If this is so, these hormonal aberrations obviously do not masculinize the external genitalia. In any case, neither the Dalton study on progesterone effects (7) nor our data on IQ elevation in unaffected siblings and parents as well as in the AGS patients themselves support the claim that masculinizing prenatal hormones favor postnatal intellectual development.

Differential Abilities

Summarizing our results on differential abilities, we did not find any significant differences between Verbal and Performance IQ for the patient sample, which is consistent with previous findings (9, 26). The patients were also not significantly different from their siblings and parents in performance on the Wechsler parts. The same held true for analysis of Cohen factors on the Wechsler subtests.

The results of the PMA rendered the only significant findings involving patients, and these were unexpected and inconsistent with any hypothesis on sex differences. Both male and female patients performed significantly below male and female siblings on the number test. The patients had significantly lower scores on the number test than on either the verbal or the spatial test in within-group comparisons. This relative decline in number-test scores did not exist for the siblings. This finding is puzzling. One may argue that out of a multitude of statistical analyses, one may come out significant, as a chance finding. However, the difference is too clear-cut and consistent in within- and between-group comparisons to support this assumption. Furthermore, Perlman (9) also reported that her sample of AGS patients scored significantly lower on an arithmetic computation test than did the control group. Since no consistent sex differences have been found in computational abilities in the normal population, it is difficult to venture a guess as to why AGS patients may be less elevated in number abilities than in other areas and be different in that respect from their normal siblings. Future research has to clarify whether the finding is reliable and whether it is syndrome specific or perhaps prevalent in various pediatric clinical samples. If it is characteristic of AGS patients, it should be investigated further whether a particular aspect of the endocrine problem may selectively affect computational abilities relative to other enhanced intellectual abilities.

Although our results on differential abilities generally did not show any differences between patients, siblings, and parents, we hesitate to conclude that fetal androgen levels do not affect the development of cognitive sex differences in AGS. The whole area of differential abilities in females and males is very complicated. Sex differences reported in the literature are frequently small and differ with different methods, different ages, and different cultural groups; some studies have reported no differences at all. Maccoby and Jacklin (11, 12) report that age is very important. Recent studies indicate that differences in verbal and spatial abilities may not appear consistently before the ages 10 or 11. Our family study included subjects with a wide age range and small numbers in each group. Existing differences may have diminished and not become apparent merely because we had to combine different age groups. Ideally, one would like to study large numbers of AGS patients in one age group and to compare them with large numbers of siblings and unrelated control groups of the same age—an almost impossible goal considering the relatively rare occurrence of the clinical entity.

The question of the role of prenatal androgen in the development of differential abilities has yet to be resolved. We hope to shed more light on this issue with the analysis of the remaining test data on differential abilities, controlling as much as possible for the age factor.

CONCLUSION

The study confirms previous findings of elevated IQ in groups of AGS patients. This elevation is not due to patient history of prenatal androgenization because parents and siblings show a comparable IQ elevation. Furthermore, AGS patients did not differ from their families with regard to those mental abilities in which sex differences have been typically reported. These findings are in marked contrast to the behavioral findings reported in the preceding chapter. Clearly, prenatal exposure to male hormones affects temperamental differences in sexually dimorphic behavior, but it does not appear to influence intelligence and differential abilities.

ACKNOWLEDGMENTS

The study was supported by a grant (Cl-10-CH-71) from the United Health Foundation of Western New York, the Human Growth Foundation, and the Variety Club of Buffalo, Tent No. 7.

The patients in this sample were diagnosed and managed by Drs. Thomas Aceto, Jr., and Margaret MacGillivray of the Pediatric Endocrine Clinic at Children's Hospital, Buffalo, New York. Their clinical cooperation is greatly appreciated.

The data graphs were designed by the Department of Medical Illustrations, State University of New York at Buffalo. We thank Dr. Heino F. L. Meyer-Bahlburg for his assistance in the statistical data analysis.

REFERENCES

1. Money, J. and V. G. Lewis, *Bull Johns Hopkins Hosp* 118: 365, 1966.
2. Ehrhardt, A. A., in Duhm, E. (ed.), *Praxis der Klinischen Psychologie II*, Verlag für Psychologie, Dr. C. J. Hogrefe, Göttingen, 1971, p. 94.

3. Ehrhardt, A. A., R. Epstein, and J. Money, *Johns Hopkins Med J* **122**: 160, 1968.

4. Hollingshead, A. B., *Two Factor Index of Social Position*, privately printed, New Haven, Conn., 1957.

5. Money, J., V. G. Lewis, A. A. Ehrhardt, and P. W. Drash, in Zubin, J. (ed.), *Psychopathology of Mental Development*, Grune & Stratton, New York, 1967, p. 22.

6. Ehrhardt, A. A. and J. Money, *J Sex Res* **3**: 83, 1967.

7. Dalton, K., *Br J Psychiatr* **114**: 1377, 1968.

8. Dalton, K., *Br Med J* **2**: 378, 1957.

9. Perlman, S. M., unpublished Ph.D. thesis, Northwestern University, 1971.

10. Perlman, S. M., *J Learning Disab* **6**: 26, 1973.

11. Maccoby, E. E. and C. N. Jacklin, in *Proceedings of the 1972 Invitational Conference on Testing Problems—Assessment in a Pluralistic Society*, Educational Testing Service, 1973.

12. Jacklin, C. N. and E. E. Maccoby, paper presented to the American Educational Research Association, Chicago, 1972.

13. Wechsler, D., *Manual for the Wechsler Preschool and Primary Scale of Intelligence*, the Psychological Corporation, New York, 1963.

14. Wechsler, D., *Wechsler Intelligence Scale for Children, Manual*, the Psychological Corporation, New York, 1949.

15. Wechsler, D., *Manual for the Wechsler Adult Intelligence Scale*, the Psychological Corporation, New York, 1955.

16. Cohen, J., *J Consult Psychol* **21**: 451, 1957.

17. Cohen, J., *J Consult Psychol* **23**: 285, 1959.

18. Thurstone, T. G., *Primary Mental Abilities* (revised 1962), Science Research Associates, Chicago, 1963.

19. Witkin, H. A., P. K. Oltman, E. Raskin, and S. A. Karp, *A Manual for the Embedded Figures Tests*, Consulting Psychologist Press, Inc., Palo Alto, Calif., 1971.

20. Bennett, G. K., H. G. Seashore, and A. G. Wesman, *Differential Aptitude Tests*, 4th ed. manual, the Psychological Corporation, New York, 1966.

21. Goldschmid, M. L. and P. M. Bentler, *Manual: Concept Assessment Kit-Conservation*, Educational and Industrial Testing Service, San Diego, Calif., 1968.

22. Siegel, S., *Nonparametric Statistics for the Behavioral Sciences*, McGraw-Hill, New York, 1956.

23. J. R. Geigy, A. G. (ed.), *Wissenschaftliche Tabellen*, 7th ed., Geigy, Basel, 1968, p. 109.

24. Ehrhardt, A. A., C. Cotton, and T. Aceto, paper presented at annual meeting of the Midwestern Society for Pediatric Research, Pittsburgh, 1973.

25. Meyer-Bahlburg, H. F. L., E. McCauley, C. Schenck, T. Aceto, Jr., and L. Pinch, this volume, Chapter 15.

26. Lewis, V. G., J. Money, and R. Epstein, *Johns Hopkins Med J* **122**: 192, 1968.

Discussion: Effect of Hormones on the Development of Behavior

SEYMOUR LEVINE, Moderator

CHARLES H. DOERING, Rapporteur

Dr. Sackett opened the discussion on Dr. Ward's paper concerning prenatal control of sex-behavior differentiation. After eliciting the fact that increased fetal and newborn death occurred as a result of maternal stress, he observed that this introduced a sample bias. Dr. Ward agreed that her study compared normals to animals that survived a procedure associated with considerable mortality. Stress during pregnancy is inherently associated with increased fetal and newborn death. This, however, should not be viewed as producing a sample bias. Rather, the population of subjects from which the stress sample was drawn for purposes of behavioral testing naturally only includes animals that survived the early effects of the treatment.

Dr. Whalen asked what significance attached to the fact that the prenatal plus postnatal treatments were less effective than the prenatal treatment alone, in both the cyproterone acetate and the stress studies. Dr. Ward replied that the reason for this effect is currently unknown and pointed out that this phenomenon seemed to be present in a number of prenatal–postnatal experiments, including those that involved prenatal and postnatal testosterone propionate treatment in females.

Dr. Whalen commented that the spines of the phallus are an extremely sensitive index of androgen activity and wanted to know if they had been looked at. Dr. Ward said that they had not.

Dr. Meyer-Bahlburg suggested that the experiments might lead to a model for homosexuality and for the influence of prenatal or postnatal treatment on sexual behavior. He noted that in a series of tests (males with males, females with estrous females) one could study the effect of postnatal stress on behavior after puberty.

Dr. Green emphasized that the sexual behavior of rats could not be equated with the highly complex sexual behavior of human beings.

Dr. Hunt asked why the rats were tested at 60 days of age rather than later; for example, at 100 days, when they would have had the opportunity for more life experience. Dr. Ward replied that rats have ample opportunity to get complete sexual experience by the time they are 60 days old. Responding to another question of Dr. Hunt's regarding the influence of rearing experience on the test situation, she stated that this had been little studied by her group. Rats are caged in same-sex pairs at weaning and remain so until adulthood.

Dr. Vande Wiele commented that a single injection of testosterone propionate, prenatally or postnatally, will usually permanently alter an animal's metabolism of testosterone, androstenedione, and cortisol. Altered steroid metabolism, then, persists for the entire lifetime of the animal. If testosterone is administered to such an animal when it has become an adult, one cannot conclude that the amount that reaches the target organ is the same as in a control animal. If a testosterone-sterilized animal is given estrogens, the increase in uterine weight is less than that in controls. In addition, there is some evidence that the conversion of androgen to estrogen also changes. These data suggest that effects of sex steroids attributed to differential central nervous system sensitivities, presumed to reflect dimorphic brain differentiation, might really reflect peripheral metabolic differences. Since the relationship between differential central nervous system responsivity and peripheral metabolic differences is not yet clear, Dr. Vande Wiele stated that dimorphic hypothalamic differentiation should be viewed as a hypothesis, rather than a fact.

The discussion then turned to Dr. Phoenix's findings on prenatal testosterone and its consequences for behavior. In response to a question by Dr. Vande Wiele as to the length of the menstrual cycle in monkeys whose mothers had received testosterone, Dr. Phoenix explained that these data are currently being collected for publication. Preliminary analysis fails to reveal any menstrual irregularity, but menarche is delayed.

Dr. Vande Wiele asked whether this implied a species difference between the rat and the monkey with regard to the organism's response to testosterone given early in life. Dr. Phoenix responded that, although the effects of testosterone on the differentiation of the centers regulating ovulation and mating behavior have not been demonstrated for the monkey in a fashion similar to the rat, in his opinion that was because the optimum dosage and schedule had not yet been identified in the monkey. He predicted that the rat data might well be replicated in the monkey in the near future.

Dr. Ehrhardt requested Dr. Phoenix to comment on the manner in which the altered genitals of the female hermaphrodites might have affected maternal behavior, since differential maternal response to the sexes probably exists in monkeys. Dr. Phoenix agreed that maternal behavior might have been influenced by the presence of male genitalia in these female monkeys. He emphasized the fact that androgenized females were typical neither of normal males nor of normal females, and that no matter what the nature of mother–infant interaction was like, it might not be relevant for understanding interactions between mothers and normal offspring. He suggested that maternal response may be particularly important for the development of male monkeys and that this relationship is presently being investigated in many laboratories.

Dr. Rosenblum stated that differential maternal responsiveness to male and female infants has been observed in the rhesus and other monkey species. Recently accumulated data would indicate that the setting in which rearing takes place should be considered when attempts are made to account for this phenomenon. For example, it has been reported that male infants are rejected earlier and more vigorously than female infants. Dr. Rosenblum hypothesized that this might be related to the differential response of males to a restricted rearing environment, in which males are not stimulated to explore. Under more enriched environmental circumstances, males might spontaneously leave their mothers and thus elicit less rejection.

Dr. Rosenblum then answered a question raised earlier by Dr. Ehrhardt regarding maternal interest in the genitals of the offspring. He noted that mothers tend to be more preoccupied with the genitalia of male, rather than female, infants. In his laboratory, newborns are sexed simply by noting whether their mothers turn them over and handle their genitalia frequently. The mothers of females usually do this only once or twice, whereas the mothers of males do this often.

Regarding sexual behavior patterns, Dr. Rosenblum commented that both sexes may manifest the same behaviors, including mounting, foot clasp, and pelvic thrust. These behaviors can be observed in interactions between males, between females, or between males and females. Since various parameters—including social circumstances, dominance rank, novelty and stressfullness of the test situation—may influence the form of behavior elicited in a given animal, he asked Dr. Phoenix to discuss the environmental stimuli that might facilitate the expression of different types of sexual behavior in monkeys.

Dr. Phoenix replied that, in his view, the *frequency* of the observed behavior was a function of the sex of the animal. For example, although females occasionally mount, males do so far more habitually, and this is true regardless of the age of the animal, or whether the behavior occurs in the laboratory or in a more natural setting, such as a large outside enclosure containing 200 monkeys.

Dr. Michael then showed a slide that illustrated how the sexual behavior of an animal may be influenced by the hormonal condition of the partner. He pointed out that castrated males decline in their ejaculatory capacity and that after the castration of the male mounting behavior by the female partner increases. When testosterone is given to the castrate, the female's mounting behavior decreases. Dr. Phoenix replied that he had not found this to be true in 10 males castrated for 5 years and tested 500 times, some for 10 minutes and some for 60 minutes. Dr. Michael responded that the contradictory data might be explained by the fact that Dr. Phoenix's laboratory routinely tested only for 10 minutes, whereas his laboratory routinely tested for 60 minutes.

Dr. Sachar then directed the conversation to the presentations of Dr. Ehrhardt and Ms. Baker concerning the effects of fetal and prenatal androgen on behavioral and cognitive sex differences. He remarked that Ms. Baker reported on observed behavior, while Dr. Ehrhardt discussed either the parents' or child's perception of the child's behavior. These two sets of data are not directly comparable. He suggested that, had Ms. Baker interviewed parents to determine which child they thought was more intelligent, she might have obtained findings at variance with the actual behavior of the child. Although direct observation would not provide definitive data, since children frequently conform to roles expected of them in a family, it would be the logical next step in methodological refinement. Dr. Ehrhardt responded that most adrenogenital children attend the Clinical Research Study Center of Buffalo for several days once or twice a year. Nurses who are unaware of the hypotheses of the investigators fill out a behavioral checklist based on the children's interactive styles and on their preference for boys' or girls' playthings. Correlation between nurses' ratings of children and the information obtained in interviews was high. Dr. Ehrhardt agreed that an observational study is indicated.

Dr. Zubin commented that the meaning of intelligence tests is not entirely clear. He questioned whether the increased aggressivity of the adrenogenital group might not have produced greater motivation to perform on the intelligence tests.

Dr. Lewis asked whether the comparison siblings in Dr. Ehrhardt's study were sometimes younger and sometimes older. When Dr. Ehrhardt answered affirmatively, he noted that it would be important to determine if differences are more marked when adrenogenital patients are compared with older siblings than they are when the patients are compared with younger siblings. A cohort effect might exist that would be uncovered by the analysis of such data.

Dr. Lewis also observed that the patients had experienced various types of stress related to the treatment of their illness. Rather than comparing them with well children, it might have been interesting to compare them with children who had been subjected to different kinds of trauma early in life. Since stress can alter many developmental parameters, including even the growth of the child, it is particularly critical to control for this variable. Dr. Ehrhardt replied that the children in her sample demonstrated normal growth. In her studies of children with other endocrine abnormalities, such as the androgen insensitivity syndrome and sexual precocity, she did not find a behavior pattern similar to that reported for adrenogenital children.

Dr. Michels commented that the *well* siblings are possibly more heavily stressed because they have a sick sibling than are the adrenogenital patients themselves. The results could be interpreted as showing that the siblings of sick children are less assertive and aggressive than normal. The illness might, in fact, encourage the patient to develop a sense of being "special" later in life. He emphasized the need for a control group of children who had been subjected to a stress in early years that made them feel special, but not one associated with neuroendocrine developmental differences.

Dr. Stern observed that clinically, in families containing daughters but no sons, parental pressures are exerted for one of the girls to be more aggressive and "boyish" than the other(s). In families that contain a son, this type of parental influence is not applied. Dr. Stern also inquired whether the data for girls with the adrenogenital syndrome indicated the same behavioral trends regardless of whether the siblings were male or female. Dr. Ehrhardt said that data have been analyzed for these variables and reveal that the sex of the sibling does not alter the trend of expected behavior in these patients.

Drs. Galenson and Moss wanted to know about the children's understanding of the basis for their treatment. Dr. Ehrhardt explained that they are taught they were born with faulty adrenals that do not make enough cortisone, and if they take replacement medicine, they will be well.

Dr. Galenson emphasized the importance of understanding the child's view of her illness and treatment in order to more fully comprehend he development.

Dr. Moss questioned whether parents relate differently to the defective child than to the siblings. Was it possible that, as a method of coping with their own anxiety, they covertly communicated a sense of being different on a sexual basis to the sick children? Could the mothers have structured the children's play activity in a way that resulted in the observed differences? Dr. Ehrhardt replied that, when interviewed about these matters, parents of children with the adrenogenital syndrome do not usually appear anxious. She acknowledged, however, that some parental anxiety might go undetected and that this factor could probably never be completely excluded.

Dr. Lewis asked for the ages at which hormonal and surgical interventions were initiated. Dr. Ehrhardt answered that cortisone treatment in females was initiated within the first year of life in 14 girls and during the second, third, and fourth year of life, respectively, in 3 girls. In six cases, marked anatomical deformities were corrected shortly after birth; in seven patients, clitoral enlargement was corrected in the second or third year; and a few patients underwent surgery later in life. There appeared to be no differences in the parameters discussed in the paper between children who had medical or surgical intervention at the earlier or later ages.

Dr. Hamburg noted that hypospadia is a condition affecting the genitals, but not the hormones, and suggested that parental attitudes toward children with this deformity might be useful to study and compare with parents' attitudes toward children with the adrenogenital syndrome. Dr. Ehrhardt agreed and stated that Dr. Meyer-Bahlburg is presently doing this study.

Dr. Phoenix commented that maternal behavior toward hermaphroditic monkeys did not seem to be critically important with regard to the variables under consideration. His group had observed two such monkeys who were removed from their mothers at birth and reared in a nursery and who, nonetheless, developed increased male patterns of behavior.

Dr. Friedman asked if an attempt had been made to assess the sibling pecking order within the families studied. Dr. Ehrhardt responded that these data have been collected, but not yet analyzed.

Dr. Friedman also wondered whether rough-and-tumble play had been evaluated in detail, particularly with regard to preference for body-contact play versus non-body-contact play. Dr. Ehrhardt said that this type of analysis had not been done.

Dr. Vande Wiele commented on some endocrinological issues. In congenital adrenal hyperplasia, androstenedione, *not* testosterone is the main steroid produced. In addition, large amounts of 17-hydroxyprogesterone and estrogens are excreted, as well as various other steroids. The secretion of ACTH and probably that of the corticotrophin-releasing factor are increased, each of which might directly affect the central nervous system. Therefore one has to be cautious in inferring that the behavior of children with this condition is simply a result of androgen excess.

Dr. Green raised the issue of the effects of prenatal androgen on postnatal aggressivity in humans. He discussed a study of his and Dr. Yalom's at the Joslyn Clinic where large doses of estrogen were given to pregnant diabetics in an effort to reduce fetal mortality. Both 6- and 16-year-old males who had been exposed to higher than normal amounts of estrogen *in utero* manifested diminished assertiveness, aggressiveness, and rough-and-tumble play when compared with normal controls and with sons of diabetic mothers who were not exposed to high levels of estrogen. This study on the human male complements the data presented by Dr. Ehrhardt on the human female.

Dr. Doering wanted to know if cortisone replacement is completely effective in suppressing excessive androgen production in adrenogenital children. Had plasma testosterone levels, for example, been measured? Dr. Ehrhardt replied that, as judged by endocrinologists, these children generally appeared to be well regulated.

Dr. Vande Wiele remarked that notwithstanding large doses of cortisone, suppression is frequently *not* adequate in children with congenital adrenal hyperplasia. Usually, 10 to 20% of patients are difficult to regulate and are allowed to have slightly higher than normal levels of androgens, since administration of higher doses of cortisone would result in the cessation of growth.

Regarding the relationship of the hypothalamus to endocrine rhythmicity, Dr. Ehrhardt observed that fetally androgenized females on cortisone-replacement therapy frequently have delayed menarche. Once menstruation begins, however, it is usually normal, although often irregular. There have been a number of adrenogenital patients who have given birth to children.

Dr. Galenson wondered whether the increased activity of the androgenized females did not reflect anxiety rather than aggressivity. Dr. Ehrhardt responded that the children appeared to have a higher than normal energy level, but not to be unusually anxious when observed at the Research Center or in their daily lives, as reported by themselves and parents.

With respect to the development of self-perception in adrenogenital children, Dr. Galenson asked whether data had been obtained from children below the age of 4 years. Dr. Ehrhardt said that a small amount of data had been collected, but had not been systematically analyzed.

Dr. Hunt commented that Ms. Baker's study suggested that the adrenogenital syndrome produced a mild deficit in the number subtest. Ms. Baker agreed that, relative to the other abilities, there might be a weakness in computation performance.

Ms. Ullian inquired whether cognitive functioning was analyzed in depth in the adrenogenital children who did *not* show the expected differences in activity level. Dr. Ehrhardt stated that, although several aspects of developmental interactions of these children have been studied, their cognitive abilities have not been analyzed in relationship to activity level. She commented that this would be a fruitful area for future data analysis.

Dr. Vande Wiele concluded the discussion by observing, in response to a comment of Ms. Baker's, that since men make as much progesterone as women do, at least for most of the month, progesterone should not be considered a female hormone.

2 Stress and Early Life Experience in Nonhumans

CHARLES H. PHOENIX, *Moderator*

ELIZABETH McCAULEY, *Rapporteur*

CHAPTER 5

Differential Response to Early Experience as a Function of Sex Difference

SEYMOUR LEVINE

Department of Psychiatry
Stanford University School of Medicine
Stanford, California

It has been repeatedly observed that normal male and female organisms exhibit a number of behavioral differences. These differences often persist even after gonadectomy. However, recent findings have revealed another and very intriguing sex difference in behavior: the effect of certain kinds of early experience on adult behavior varies as a function of the sex of the neonate.

The most elaborate data are those reported by Sackett (1), which reveal that, in the rhesus monkey, the effect of isolation during infancy is much more severe in the male than it is in the female. Sackett's data have prompted us to reexamine some of our own studies on the effects of a variety of treatments during both prenatal and postnatal periods of development in the rat with reference to sex differences. It is both surprising and somewhat bewildering that these differences have not been examined more closely.

As early as 1968 Meier and Schutzman (2) pointed out that in many studies related to the influence of early experience on later behavior a significant sex treatment interaction was present. They state that under the usual test procedures constituting the criterion of early-experience sex effects, the sexes were differentiated in the experimental or manipulated group, but not in the control group. However, none of these interactions was elaborated on. An attempt to review this literature in order to come up with a consistent relationship between sex and early experience proved to be a frustrating exercise, since a variety of procedures were used during both the neonatal manipulations and the adult testing procedures. Consequently, the scope of this chapter is limited to examining in detail some recent evidence from our own laboratory. These studies demonstrate how the sexes differ in response to widely different experimental manipulations, both prenatal and postnatal. The experiments presented are not intended, by any means, to be exhaustive but to exemplify the complexities of the problem and to emphasize the need for systematic investigations in this area. It should be noted that the primary focus of these studies was not the sex difference in the responses of the organisms to the experimental treatment.

PRENATAL INFLUENCES

Our study, carried on in collaboration with Drs. Karmela Milkovic and Justin Joffe, was concerned with obtaining further information on how a lack or excess of maternal corticoids during gestation affects the development and function of the adult pituitary–adrenocortical system. The effect of lack of maternal corticosteroids and the consequent increase in fetal pituitary ACTH and accelerated fetal adrenal growth were studied in the offspring of female rats adrenalectomized prior to mating. The influence of elevated levels of maternal corticosterone in the fetal blood was studied by implanting an ACTH-producing pituitary tumor ($MtTF_4$) on the first day of pregnancy (3). This tumor markedly stimulates the production of corticosterone by the maternal adrenals, thus raising circulating corticosterone levels in the fetus. Since ACTH does not itself cross the placenta, fetal growth is inhibited by maternal corticosterone rather than stimulated by ACTH. After these prenatal treatments, all animals were cross-fostered onto normal mothers and reared until adulthood. At approximately 2 months of age, two males and two females were selected from each litter. Each group (i.e., animals derived from adrenalectomized mothers, from mothers with MtT tumors, or control mothers) consisted of 20 animals—10 males and 10 females. These animals were then subjected to a procedure routinely used in our laboratory to evaluate the role of a variety of experimental procedures on pituitary–adrenal activity in the adult. This procedure consists of taking two samples of blood, each approximately 0.3 to 0.4 ml, from the jugular vein. The jugular vein is exposed under ether anesthesia, and an initial sample is obtained within 45 to 50 seconds after removal from the cage. This sample is used to determine the basal levels of corticosterone (4). Stress levels are determined from another sample obtained from the same animal 15 minutes later. Plasma corticosterone levels are determined in all the experiments described here by the method of Glick, von Redlich, and Levine (5).

The results of this study (see Fig. 1) showed that animals whose mothers secreted excessively high amounts of corticoids as a consequence of the presence of an ACTH-producing tumor showed a significant suppression of adrenal corticoids in response to ether in adulthood. This was true of both sexes in this group. However, though the males of the adrenalec-tomized mothers showed an equivalent suppression of adrenocortical activity in response to ether, the females did not.

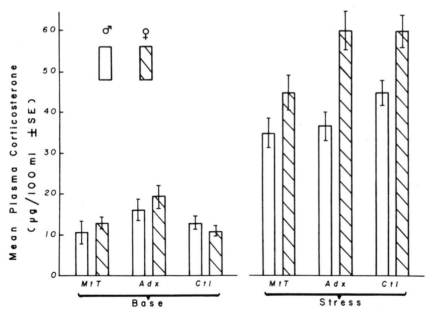

Figure 1 Plasma corticosterone concentrations in basal and stress conditions in adult offspring of tumor implanted (MtT), adrenalectomized (Adx), and control (Ctl) mothers.

In a previous experiment we demonstrated that plasma levels of corticosterone are elevated in the fetuses of both adrenalectomized mothers and mothers implanted with an MtT tumor. This elevation has different origins in the two cases. In the adrenalectomized mother, the lack of feedback inhibition of the fetal pituitary by maternal corticoids results in increased fetal ACTH secretion and a concomitant rise in both plasma and adrenal corticosterone levels. In contrast, the offspring of the MtT-tumor mothers have decreased adrenal weight, presumably due to inordinately high levels of maternal corticoids crossing the placenta and inhibiting fetal secretion of ACTH. However, these elevated levels of maternal corticoids also result in very high circulating levels of corticosterone in the fetus. Thus, where fetal corticoid titers were highest, in the offspring of mothers implanted with MtT tumors, the stress response of both males and females was suppressed in adulthood. In the progeny of the adrenalectomized mothers, where fetal corticoid levels were also increased, though not to the same extent as in the MtT-tumor group, the stress response of the adult male was still suppressed while the response of the female was spared.

POSTNATAL EFFECTS

It has been demonstrated in many studies that a variety of treatments imposed on the neonatal rat have profound and permanent effects on subsequent behavioral and physiological processes (6, 7). One such study, which we have recently completed, examined the influence of early experience on shock-induced fighting. In particular, we were interested in the influence of early experience on ACTH secretion after either shock or shock plus fighting. This study was prompted by a recent finding that fighting animals had lower pituitary–adrenal activity (less ACTH secretion) than the shock control animals (8). These data were interpreted as indicating that engaging in fighting behavior represents a coping response. According to this interpretation, an animal engaging in an organized pattern of behavior is coping even though the actual execution of, or persistence in, that behavior does nothing to alleviate the intensity or duration of the aversive stimulation. Due to our recent interest in certain aspects of coping and coping behavior, we questioned whether early experience would have any influence on the ACTH secretion induced by fighting. Animals were either treated by being handled on days 1 through 10 or days 21 through 30 postpartum or remained undisturbed (non-handled controls). In adulthood, both males and females of each of these early-experience groups were tested in the shock-induced fighting procedure reported by Ulrich and Azrin (9), which consists of fighting animals in pairs. Fighting behavior was studied at several shock intensities during each experimental session. The session began with a presentation of a train of 10 shocks at a fixed intensity. The duration of each shock was 0.5 second, and there was a 1.5-second interval between the onset of successive shocks in the train. Trains of 10 shocks at a given intensity were separated by a 15-second interval of no shock. In such sequences trains of three different shock intensities were presented three times, making a total of 90 shock trials in each 4.5-minute session. In order to monitor pituitary–adrenal activity, at the end of the fighting session, animals in both the fight and shock groups were decapitated and blood samples from the trunk were collected into heparinized tubes for ACTH determination by a radioimmunoassay. The results of these studies, presented in Figure 2, indicate that females show essentially few differences among the various early-experience groups with respect to their response to the shock, fighting, and control situations. In all instances, once again, the response to fighting reduces ACTH secretion. The males, however, do significantly differ in that while both the early- and late-handled groups show a significant reduction of ACTH after fighting, no such reduction is observed in the nonhandled males. This is due principally to the failure of the nonhandled males to show as significant an increase in aftershock ACTH secretion as that observed in the two other groups.

Our observation of low ACTH secretion in response to shock in nonhandled animals is consistent with an earlier finding (10) of a differential time course to acute electric shock. The handled animals in that experiment all showed a very marked significant elevation of plasma corticoid levels within a few minutes after shock, whereas in the nonhandled animals the elevation was significantly retarded. These data were interpreted at that time as indicating that there was a differential release of ACTH. This hypothesis is verified by this experiment—but only in the male, not in the female.

These data are inconsistent with what Meier and Schutzman (2) claimed to be a general observation: that the sexes were differentiated in the experimental, or manipulated, group, but not in the control group. In this case sexual differences were clearly distinguishable in the control group, but not in the experimental group. It is important, however, to state that these results are not completely representative of general findings in the field. There are experiments that clearly do report that males and females are equally susceptible to some types of infantile stimulation.

Thoman and Levine (11) studied temperature and maternal variables as possible mediating factors in infantile treatment effects. Groups of infant rats were handled with and without temperature reduction on

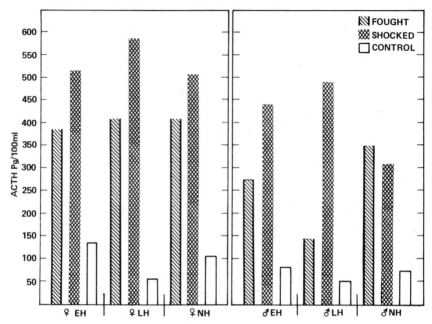

Figure 2   Plasma values of ACTH in early-handled (EH), late-handled (LH), and non-handled (NH) male and female adult rats after electric shock and electric shock plus fighting.

days 2 through 7 after birth. Additional groups were handled with temperature reduction, but one group was returned to the mother cool and the other was returned to the mother warm. Still another group of pups was untreated, but their mothers were disturbed in the same way as the mothers of the handled animals. As adults, all animals were tested in an open field, and after the final testing session blood samples were obtained for an assay of plasma corticosterone levels. As can be seen in Figure 3, regardless of whether or not treatment in infancy involved a reduction in temperature and regardless of whether or not the pups had been returned to the mother cool or warm, all handled groups except one had significantly lower corticosterone levels than did the like-sex controls. However, inspection of these data shows that even here there are indications of a differential response in males and females to the same infantile conditions. The male animals, regardless of the infantile treatment, all show essentially the same reduction in plasma corticosterone levels after the last testing session. Females, however, tend to be more variable and in some conditions do indeed show a significant reduction in plasma corticosterone levels, but in others—in this case the condition of being re-

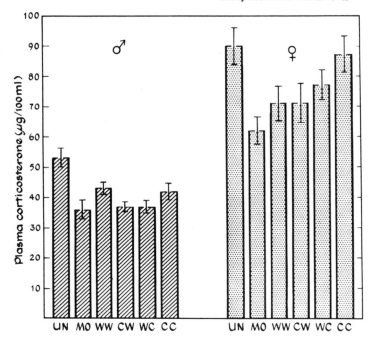

Figure 3   Mean plasma corticosterone levels of females and males in the six experimental groups after open-field testing.

turned to the mother cold—did not differ in response from the untreated controls.

POSTNATAL EFFECTS–DIFFERENTIAL RESPONSE TO EARLY HORMONE TREATMENTS

Sex dimorphism in response to gonadal hormones is now a well-established phenomenon and clearly differentiates sexes in postpubertal organisms. Thus the response to estrogen and progesterone is markedly different in the female than it is in the male, and, conversely, the response to testosterone is equally sex differentiated. It has been determined to some extent that the nature of this differential response to gonadal steroid hormones is partly due to the hormonal milieu of the neonatal organism. These data have been so well documented as to make unnecessary any extensive review at this time. However, the hormonal environment of the neonate is not the sole determinant of adult sex behavior. The findings to be discussed strongly suggest that even neonatal males and females can respond differently to the same hormonal treatment.

When female rats receive low doses of testosterone in infancy, the quantity and quality of female sex behavior they display on being treated with estrogen and progesterone as adults depend on the amount of testosterone administered neonatally. Female rats treated approximately 5 days after birth with high doses of testosterone propionate (TP) fail to exhibit the female lordosis response as adults, even though the vaginal epithelium is in a constantly cornified state (12). Furthermore, large doses of estrogen and progesterone given after castration in adulthood fail to increase the receptivity of these females, which indicates that a change in the sensitivity of the neural mechanisms controlling female sex behavior is involved in the lack of receptivity, and not just a deficiency in peripheral hormone levels (12). However, Barraclough and Gorski (13) reported that female rats given a single 10-μg injection of TP at 5 days of age were receptive to males for several successive days in adulthood, although these animals showed the same anovulatory physiological condition as seen in those receiving higher doses in infancy.

We treated female rats with 5 to 1000 μg of TP at approximately 120 hours after birth (14). When tested in adulthood for 5 consecutive days with a sexually vigorous male, the females demonstrated a degree of receptivity (as measured by the ratio of lordosis to mounts) that varied inversely with the size of the neonatal dose (Fig. 4). When these animals were castrated and given doses of estrogen and progesterone more than sufficient to produce receptivity in untreated females, the amount of receptivity for the various groups did not increase above that seen on the first day of testing before castration, and the same inverse relationship between the amount of hormone administered in infancy and the degree of receptivity was maintained.

The male rat, when neonatally castrated and injected with a low dose of testosterone, is less responsive as an adult to estrogen and progesterone than the neonatally androgenized genetic female. Castration of the newborn male leads to the retention of the cyclic female pattern of gonadotrophin release in adulthood. Such animals also show normal female sexual receptivity when given small doses of estrogen and progesterone, despite the fact that males castrated in adulthood will not show the lordosis response except to very large repeated doses of these hormones.

We injected 4-day-old male rats, castrated on the day of birth, with 10, 100, or 1000 μg of TP (15). Control animals received an oil-vehicle injection. When given in adulthood doses of estrogen and progesterone that were larger than those needed to bring normal females into heat, the animals given the two larger doses of testosterone neonatally failed to show female sexual behavior and those receiving a 10-μg dose showed a very low (0.25) ratio of lordosis to mounts, similar to that seen in

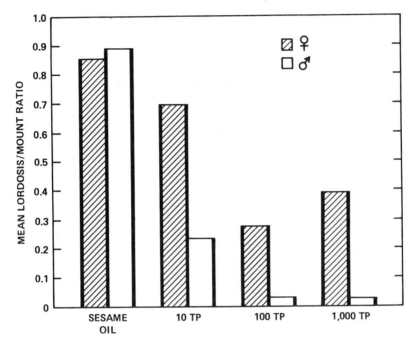

Figure 4   Female sex behavior in female and neonatally castrated male rats injected with androgen 96 to 120 hours after birth and given estrogen and progesterone in adulthood.

female rats that had received 500 or 1000 μg of TP at 4 days of age. The control animals, both male and female, showed good female receptivity.

When the same doses of estrogen and progesterone were administered to female rats given low doses of testosterone in infancy and to neonatally castrated males, it was found that the males show a much lower lordosis-to-mount ratio. It does appear that the brain of the newborn male is more sensitive to testosterone than the brain of the newborn female.

Further evidence of the differential response of the neonatal rat to hormonal manipulation comes from a series of studies on sex dimorphism and sexual differentiation in adrenocortical activity. It has been repeatedly observed that there are marked differences between normal male and female rats in both base and stress levels of corticosterone, with females having significantly higher plasma levels. Several papers have described the effects of early androgen treatment on both male and female rats with regard to the adult response to stress. Proulx and Gorski (16) reported no difference in compensatory adrenal hypertrophy after uni-lateral adrenalectomy in normal as compared with neonatally androgen-treated females. Schapiro (17) investigated plasma corticosterone response in androgen-treated males and females as compared with control animals 15 minutes after ether anesthesia. Again, no differences were found as a function of neonatal androgen treatment. However, in an experiment conducted in our laboratory (18) it was determined that whereas neonatally androgenized and normal females do not differ in their adrenocortical response to stress, neonatally castrated males do indeed differ from normal males and that an injection of androgen to the neonatal male reestablishes the normal male pattern. In this experiment all animals were castrated: a group of females and males were castrated at weaning, and two additional groups of animals were castrated within 24 hours after birth. One of the neonatally castrated animals received a single 100-μg injection of TP. At approximately 50 days of age all animals were treated with either testosterone or estrogen, or a control injection of oil. These treatments continued for 10 days, and on the eleventh day the animals were subjected to a severe stress consisting of exposure to ether and laparotomy. A blood sample was taken 15 minutes after the onset of the stress to determine the pituitary–adrenal response. The data presented in Figure 5 indicate marked differences between male and female weanling castrates in their response to the stress used in this experiment. The females showed a much greater elevation than the males, even though

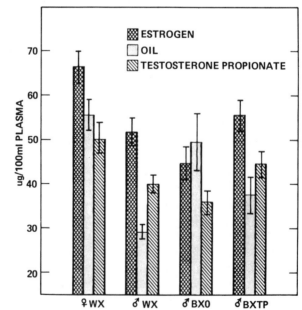

Figure 5   Plasma corticosterone concentrations after stress in female and male adult animals castrated at weaning (WX) and at birth (BX).

both had been without the gonads for a considerable length of time. Response to estrogen augments the stress response both in the male and in the female, whereas the response to testosterone increases the response only in the male, actually suppressing it to some extent in the female.

When the neonatal castrate is treated with oil rather than testosterone at the time of castration, the response to stress is clearly different even in the absence of any hormone administration in adulthood. The oil-treated neonatal castrate's response is significantly higher than that of the neonatal castrate given testosterone. The response of the neonatal castrate given testosterone is in fact almost identical with that of the animal that was castrated after weaning. In contrast, the neonatal castrate given no treatment does not show the estrogen facilitation of the pituitary–adrenal activity but does show the suppression that results from testosterone treatment in adulthood. Thus the neonatal castrate shows a significant response to testosterone treatment at the time of castration and clearly resembles a normal male, whereas, as already stated, androgenization of the female does not in any way influence the pituitary–adrenal activity.

DISCUSSION

It is difficult to fit all of these disparate pieces of evidence into a single conceptual framework. In the case of the differential sensitivity to neonatal hormonal treatments of the male and female rat and, in particular, the differential response to androgen, the hypothesis has been advanced that the process of behavioral masculinization must start before birth. Thus some of the differentiation of central nervous system mechanisms has already taken place before the testes in these males are removed. The evidence does indicate that the fetal testes late in gestation are actively producing testosterone, which may be acting on the central nervous system of the fetal organism to render it more sensitive to these hormones in the immediate postnatal period.

With regard to the data concerning early handling, it could be that the sexes respond differently to experimental treatment and hence present different stimuli to the mother, who also responds differentially. However, other mechanisms can be suggested for these effects (2, 19). Although we have been able to arrive at some tentative hypotheses concerning the differential response by sex to early hormone treatment and early experience, at present there seems to be no very plausible explanation for prenatal effects. Thus the possibility that the sexual differentiation of the central nervous system is at least partially genetically determined cannot easily be dismissed.

The major problem is that this area has not been systematically investigated, so that the evidence comes from disparate sources—different kinds of experiments using a multiplicity of treatments and variables. The data do, however, indicate very clearly that there is a broad spectrum of sex differences in response to neonatal environmental conditions and the time has come for these observations to be brought under systematic experimental analysis.

ACKNOWLEDGMENTS

This study was supported by a research grant (NICH&HD 02881) from the National Institutes of Health and by the Leslie Fund, Chicago. The author is supported by USPHS Research Scientist Award K5-MH-19936 from the National Institute of Mental Health.

REFERENCES

1. Sackett, G. P., this volume, Chapter 6.
2. Meier, G. W. and L. H. Schutzman, *Dev Psychobiol* **1**: 141, 1968.
3. Milkovic, K., S. Efendic, J. Paunovic, J. Ronkulin, V. Dulibic, and S. Milkovic, *Bull Sci Conseil Acad RSF Yougoslavie, Section A,* **11**: 107, 1966.
4. Davidson, J. M., L. E. Jones, and S. Levine, *Endocrinology* **82**: 655, 1968.
5. Glick, D., D. von Redlich, and S. Levine, *Endocrinology* **74**: 653, 1964.
6. Denenberg, V. H., in Hafez, E. S. E. (ed.), *The Behaviour of Domestic Animals,* Bailliere, Tindall, and Cox, London, 1962, p. 109.
7. Levine, S., in Levine, R. (ed.), *Endocrines and the Central Nervous System,* Williams & Wilkins, Baltimore, 1966, p. 280.
8. Conner, R. L., J. Vernikos-Danellis, and S. Levine, *Nature* **234**: 564, 1971.
9. Ulrich, R. E. and N. H. Azrin, *J Exp Anal Behav* **5**: 511, 1962.
10. Levine, S., *Science* **135**: 795, 1962.
11. Thoman, E. B. and S. Levine, *Physiol Behav* **4**: 143, 1969.
12. Harris, G. W. and S. Levine, *J Physiol* **163**: 42, 1962.
13. Barraclough, C. A. and R. A. Gorski, *Anat Rec* **139**: 205, 1961.
14. Mullins, R. F., Jr. and S. Levine, *Physiol Behav* **3**: 333, 1968.
15. Mullins, R. F., Jr. and S. Levine, *Physiol Behav* **3**: 339, 1968.
16. Proulx, R. P. and R. Gorski, *Endocrinology* **77**: 406, 1965.
17. Schapiro, S., *Endocrinology* **77**: 585, 1965.
18. Levine, S. and Mullins, R. F., Jr., *Endocrinology* **80**: 1177, 1967.
19. Levine, S. and R. F. Mullins, Jr., *Science* **152**: 1585, 1966.

CHAPTER 6

Sex Differences in Rhesus Monkeys Following Varied Rearing Experiences

GENE P. SACKETT

Department of Psychology,
Regional Primate Research Center, and
Child Development and Mental Retardation Center
University of Washington
Seattle, Washington

Infant rhesus monkeys reared under social deprivation conditions are usually devastated in their development of many adaptive behaviors. These effects are among the best established facts in animal behavior and developmental psychology. Reviews by Harlow and by Mason (1–3) clearly show that rhesus monkeys raised in total or partial isolation have persisting abnormalities in personal, exploratory, social, maternal, and sexual behavior. Other work has revealed abnormalities in reactions to painful stimulation, adrenocortical response to stress, and operant conditioning (4–6).

Some of the more dramatic effects of social deprivation occur in personal behavior. Animals raised in isolation spend much of their time during a typical day in stereotyped repetitive motor behaviors, in self-clasping huddled postures, and in sucking and manipulating various body parts. In addition, these animals often are hyperaggressive, directing inappropriate explosive physical attacks against their own bodies, against younger monkeys, or against older, much stronger, animals (7). Monkeys reared with access to mothers and/or agemates rarely display any such behavior.

Less well known, however, are findings that many of the qualitative and quantitative effects of total and partial isolation depend on the sex of the monkey subject. The purpose of this chapter is to describe these studies.

REARING CONDITIONS

The studies reviewed here concern six basic rearing conditions, five of which are illustrated in Figure 1. Rank-ordered from the greatest to the least amount of social–sensory deprivation in infancy, these conditions include (1) total social isolation, (2 and 3) partial social isolation and surrogate mothering, (4) peer contact but no mothering, (5) mothering and peer contact, and (6) rearing in a natural environment (feral).

Wild-reared rhesus monkeys come from India and other parts of Southeast Asia. Their "natural habitats" include forests, mountains, plains, small towns, and cities. Most of the feral monkeys discussed here were captured and brought to the laboratory before or shortly after attaining reproductive maturity at 3 to 4 years of age. In the laboratory they lived individually in small cages or were grouped together in indoor enclosures.

The mother–peer subjects (Fig. 1f) discussed here were usually raised in a "playpen" apparatus (1). The monkey mother and her baby lived together in one of four outer living cages. The baby, but not the mother, could enter a central play area through a small hole in the wire-mesh wall of the living cage. Interaction with toys and other infants was available in the play cage.

Animals in the peer-only, surrogate-mother, and partial isolation groups were usually separated from their mothers shortly after birth. The first month of life was spent in a nursery, where the neonate received feeding and intimate physical contact from humans (Fig. 1b). After self-feeding was achieved, usually 2 to 3 weeks after birth, the neonates were placed into environments appropriate for their rearing group. They usually remained there for a significant portion of infancy (year 1 of life). Peer-only subjects (Fig. 1e) lived in wire cages with one to five other animals in their group. Surrogate-mothered subjects (Fig. 1c) lived in partially or totally enclosed cages containing a device that provided food and sometimes provided warmth and "contact comfort" from a cloth that covered

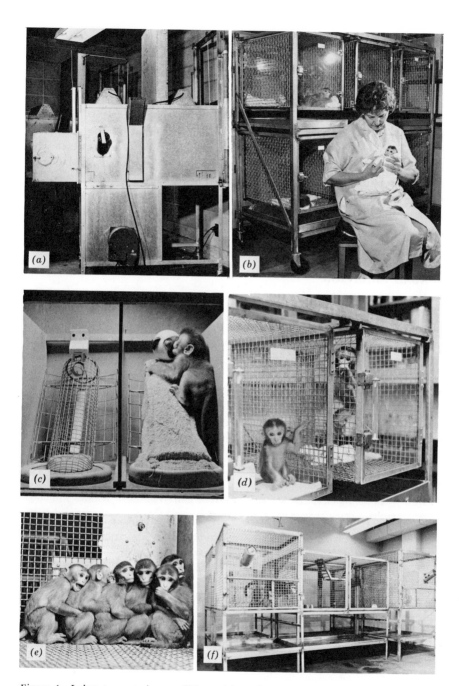

Figure 1 Laboratory rearing conditions: (a) total social isolation chamber; (b) Hand feeding in the nursery; (c) cloth and wire surrogate mothers; (d) partial isolation cages; (e) peer-only group of six infants; (f) playpen unit with outer living cages containing a mother and her baby and central play area.

the device. Partial isolates (Fig. 1d) lived in wire-mesh cages from which they could see, hear, and smell other infants. Physical contact with other monkeys was not available to partial isolates.

Total social isolates (Fig. 1a) lived in completely enclosed metal or wood cages. These cages were lighted, so the monkey could see the walls, food, and parts of its body. Physical, visual, and auditory contact with other animals was completely eliminated, and the monkey lived in a situation containing almost no varying stimulus changes. The sole source of temporally varied input came from the total isolate's own movements. Even physical contact with humans was minimized, as total isolate neonates were usually fed through portholes in the side of their cages.

SEXUAL BEHAVIOR

One behavioral dimension of critical importance for species survival is, of course, sexual behavior. A number of studies have documented differences in the extent of sexual abnormalities between males and females reared under deprivation conditions (8–10). Aspects of data from one such report (8), presented in Table 1, illustrate this sex-of-subject interaction with rearing conditions.

In this study experimental subjects were given a number of 30-minute sex testing sessions. Partners were sexually sophisticated, born in the wild, male and female breeders. Twelve of the subjects were wild-reared controls. The other 32 subjects had been raised under partial isola-

Table 1   Sexual Behavior of Socially Deprived and Wild-Born Rhesus Monkeys

Sex	Rearing Condition	N	Number of Sessions	Normal Copulation[a] %	Insemination[b] %
Females	Feral	8	256	85	70
	Socially deprived	16	512	30	20
Males	Feral	4	128	60	23
	Socially deprived	16	512	0	0

[a]Percentages of total test sessions on which normal copulation postures and movements occurred.
[b]Percentages of total test sessions on which insemination occurred.

tion or surrogate-mother conditions. Socially deprived females differed markedly from feral females in the amount of sexual activity (measured by the presence of normal copulation postures, gestures, and movements and by occurrence of insemination). However, these deprived females did show some normal sexual behavior. Socially deprived males had no normal sexual activity. These data show that adult heterosexual performance in social isolates is more deficient for males than for females.

Although certainly not a trite observation with respect to species survival, this outcome may be explained on the basis of the relatively simple role in the sex act normally taken by female rhesus monkeys. However, analysis of specific behaviors during these tests suggests that this explanation may be too simple. Socially deprived females usually display violent aggression toward their much larger partners during initial sex test sessions. Although the males often attempt to position the female for mounting, the female generally resists these attempts at initiating and maintaining physical contact. With repeated experiences, however, many females inhibit these behaviors that are incompatible with normal sexual activities, allowing the male to perform at will. On the other hand, socially deprived males usually begin the test series by showing a great deal of arousal. As excitement mounts, they usually either masturbate, bite themselves in violent bouts of self-aggression, or mount their female partner's head, shoulders, or hips. Unfortunately, these behaviors are incompatible with copulation and fail to adapt over months of testing. This leads to eventual withdrawal and disinterest on the part of the once-receptive female partner. Thus one possible explanation of this sex difference in sexual adequacy may lie in the deprived female's ability to inhibit behaviors that compete with normal sexual reaction, whereas deprived males will not, or cannot, come to do this.

MATERNAL BEHAVIOR

Adult females reared under social deprivation conditions have been called "motherless mothers" by Harlow (1). When these females give birth to offspring, their maternal behavior is usually inadequate. Although some do hold and nurse their babies, most are either (1) indifferent to the baby, offering little contact comfort and failing to nurse, or (2) brutal to the baby, attacking it and sometimes causing mortal wounds. Although not directly related to the question of sex interactions with rearing experiences, the data in Table 2 (11) show an important difference in reaction toward male and female newborn by motherless mothers ($\chi^2 = 7.80$; $df = 2$; $p < .025$). Although the difference is small, a higher percentage of females

Table 2   Motherless Mothering as a Function of Infant Sex: Numbers and Percentages of Male and Female Offspring Receiving Adequate, Indifferent, and Brutal Maternal Care

Sex of Infant	Quality of Maternal Behavior		
	Adequate	Indifferent	Abusive
Male	3 (12%)	10 (42%)	11 (46%)
Female	7 (39%)	9 (50%)	2 (11%)

receive adequate treatment, whereas proportionately more males are treated brutally. Three different explanations can be offered: (1) motherless mothers who are prone to brutalizing babies give birth to more male offspring, whereas those that will adequately care for babies give birth to females; (2) motherless mothers react differently to male and female offspring as stimuli; (3) the behaviors of newborn males and females differ, thereby eliciting different reactions from motherless mothers.

SELF-AGGRESSION

Among the dramatic products of social deprivation are juveniles and adults who attack parts of their own bodies, often producing serious wounds and broken bones (12). These self-destructive behaviors sometimes occur spontaneously, in the absence of any obvious environmental stimulus. More often, bouts of self-aggression are elicited by the same types of stimulus that produce object-directed attacks in normal monkeys: unfamiliar or fear-provoking people, monkeys, and objects.

Gluck and Sackett (13) studied self-aggressive behavior in partial isolate and mother–peer raised adult (5–6 years old) rhesus monkeys. Each subject was placed in an unfamiliar wire-mesh operant-conditioning cage. An observer sat near the cage during 10 adaptation days and recorded the number of self-directed attacks during the first 5 minutes of each 30-minute trial. Examples of self-directed aggression in this situation are shown in Figure 2. The mean numbers of self-directed aggression bouts per trial are shown in Figure 3.

Mother–peer controls exhibited no self-aggressive behavior. Partial isolates, as expected, had many more bouts of these attacks. However, males averaged twice the number of self-directed attacks as did females ($p<.01$). Thus in this situation and in the home-cage setting studied by Cross and Harlow (12), socially deprived males exhibited much more self-aggression than did deprived females.

The reputed aggressiveness of normal rhesus monkey males may appear to make this sex-difference observation somewhat trivial. Although it is

Figure 2   Top: two examples of self-aggression. Bottom: two examples of self-clutching withdrawn behavior.

true that the rhesus male is more dangerous than the female because of his larger size and much larger canine teeth, it is not obvious that the frequency of actual physical aggression in a well-adapted social group is higher for males. In fact, frequency counts of physical attack in laboratory groups show that biting, hair pulling, and gouging behaviors occur more frequently among females than among males or between males and females (14). Thus the assumption of more frequent physical aggression on the part of males may not be true, and the finding of more self-aggression in socially deprived males may be less trivial than it seems on the surface.

EXPLORATORY BEHAVIOR AND RESPONSE IN A NOVEL ENVIRONMENT

Monkeys are said to be a very curious lot. When presented with a novel object, they may completely destroy it in a matter of seconds. Exploratory

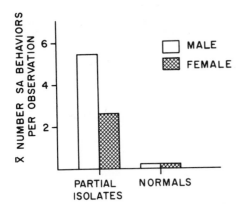

Figure 3   Self-aggressive (SA) behaviors by partial isolate and mother-peer adults in a novel environment.

behaviors and curiosity were studied in juvenile and subadult rhesus monkeys to assess rearing and sex effects. In the first experiment (15) the 2- to 3-year-old subjects had been reared in total-social isolation, peer-only, or mother–peer conditions during the first 9 months of life. Subsequently the four males and four females in each group received a variety of experiences during social and nonsocial behavior tests and group housing for 1 year prior to testing.

Five-minute daily tests were conducted on 4 consecutive days. The apparatus was a $3 \times 3 \times 3$-ft wire cage, containing a $1 \times 1 \times 1$-ft wire stimulus box attached to one wall. Access to the stimulus box was available when a sliding door was raised. On trial 1, the door of the stimulus box was closed. On trial 2, the door was opened after the subject was placed into the cage, but no stimulus was put into the box. On trial 3, a small straw-stuffed Goldilocks doll (6 inches long) was suspended by a wire from the ceiling of the box. On trial 4, a red balloon (diameter 6-in.) was suspended from the ceiling. Locomotor behavior (time spent moving about on the cage floor, walls, or ceiling) and duration of clutching, self-directed rocking, and huddling behaviors (see Fig. 3) were recorded for all four trials. Latency to touch the stimulus objects when the stimulus-box door was opened and time spent exploring and/or destroying the Goldilocks doll and the balloon were recorded on trials 3 and 4. These data are summarized in Figures 4 through 7.

Analyses of variance revealed significant group and group $\times$ sex interaction effects on all four measures (all $p < .001$). On all measures total isolates were deficient in comparison with the other groups. However, as shown in Figure 4, total isolate females were significantly more active than their counterpart males ($p < .01$). These females also spent less time in self-directed activities ($p < .001$; Fig. 5), had shortened latencies to touch the stimulus objects ($p < .001$), and explored the stimuli for longer

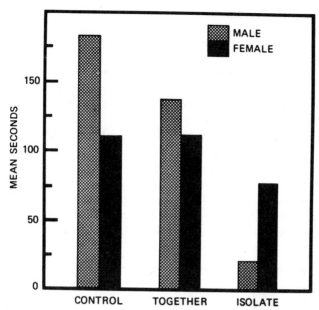

Figure 4 Locomotion duration of 2- to 3-year old animals when placed in a novel environment.

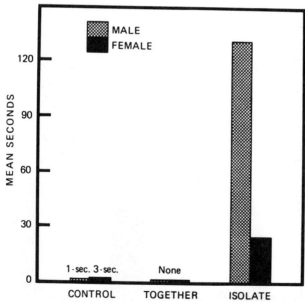

Figure 5 Self-directed clutching, rocking, and huddling behaviors by 2- to 3-year-old animals tested in a novel environment.

periods ($p<.05$). Thus, although isolation *per se* had large effects on these behaviors, these effects were more extreme for male than for female total isolates. In addition, total isolate females did not differ significantly from peer-only females on the latency and exploration-duration measures, whereas total isolate males differed reliably from all other rearing group–sex combinations on all measures.

Sex differences were also found within and between the two socialized groups. Mother–peer control males were more active than any other group ($p<.025$). Although both male and female peer-only subjects had longer latencies to touch the novel object than either male or female mother–peer subjects ($p<.025$), female peer-only subjects took even longer than peer-only males ($p<.01$). Finally, males in both socialized groups explored the stimulus objects a longer time than did females.

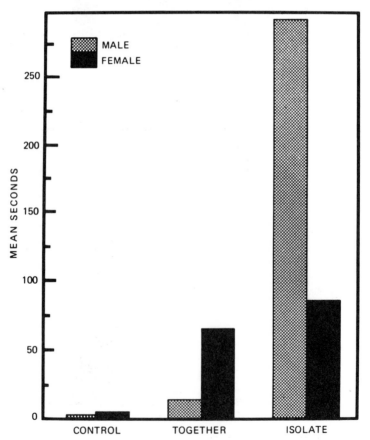

Figure 6   Latency to touch Goldilocks doll and the red balloon during novel-object tests.

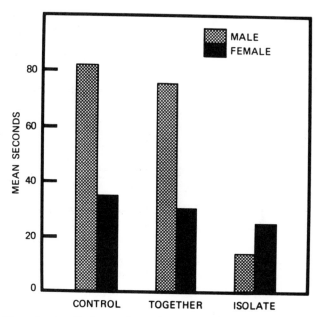

Figure 7   Time spent exploring or destroying the Goldilocks doll and the red balloon.

Thus even among socialized animals sex differences appeared in exploratory behavior, and the sex of subject interacted with rearing groups on some measures. The potency of this interaction is shown by the finding that (1) no total isolate ever destroyed Goldilocks or the balloon; (2) all four male peer-only subjects destroyed at least one of the stimuli, but no female peer-only monkey performed an act of destruction; (3) every male and female mother–peer subject either killed Goldilocks or broke the balloon or destroyed both.

A similar pattern of results was observed in the exploratory behavior of older (3.5–5 years old) animals (16). On seven daily 10-minute trials, subjects were placed into the dual cage apparatus illustrated in Figure 8. Each trial was conducted by placing the subject into one side (start compartment) of the cage, allowing 5 minutes to elapse, and then raising the guillotine door separating the two sides of the cage. Ten minutes were then allowed for the subject to enter the other side (stimulus compartment), cross back and forth at will, and explore a gray 1 × 1-ft patch projected onto the rear wall of the stimulus compartment. The gray patch was changed in intensity from trial to trial to provide a minimally novel stimulus. Male and female subjects from each of the following rearing conditions were studied: (1) feral, four males and four females; (2) mother–peer, nine males and eight females; (3) partially isolated and surrogate-mother, thirteen males and seven females; (4) totally isolated

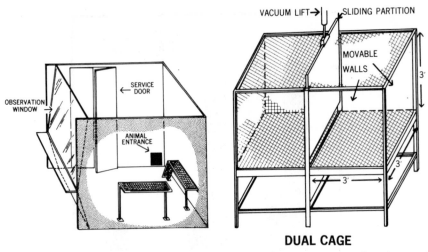

DUAL CAGE

Figure 8   Dual cage unit used to study exploratory behavior in a novel environment and playroom used to study the development of socially interactive behaviors.

from birth through 6 months of age, five males and five females; and (5) totally isolated from birth through 9 to 12 months of age, six males and six females. Measures taken included latency to leave the start compartment when the door was opened, duration of locomotion, and time spent visually or physically exploring the visual stimulus wall. These data are summarized in Figures 9, 10, and 11.

Start Latency

Feral males and females left the start compartment quicker than any other group. Male and female mother–peer subjects took only slightly

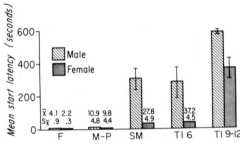

Figure 9   Latency to leave the starting compartment and enter the other side of the dual cage during tests for exploration in a novel environment in feral (F), mother–peer (M–P), wire-cage surrogate-mother (SM), totally isolated for 6 months (TI 6), and totally isolated for 9 to 12 months (TI 9–12) monkeys.

longer ($p<.025$) as a group. Partially isolated monkeys and those who had been totally isolated from birth through 6 months of age took longer to leave the start side ($p<.001$), with the males in each group taking much longer than did the females (both $p<.001$). Although the subjects who had been totally isolated from birth through 9 to 12 months of age had the longest starting latency ($p<.001$), even after this extreme social-sensory deprivation experience during infancy females were not as impaired as males ($p<.001$).

Motor Activity

Locomotion did not differ reliably between groups or sexes in the feral and mother–peer groups. Partial isolate females were reliably higher in motor activity than either sex of the mother–peer group and feral females ($p<.05$). Partial isolate males, on the other hand, had much less motor activity than did socialized animals or partial isolate females ($p<.001$).

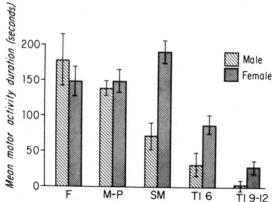

Figure 10 Motor activity duration during exploratory behavior tests in feral (F), mother–peer (M–P), wire-cage surrogate-mother (SM), 6-month total isolate (TI 6), and 9- to 12-month total isolate (TI 9–12) monkeys.

The 6-month total isolates had less motor activity ($p<.01$), and the 9- to 12-month total isolates were the least active ($p<.001$). However, even in these two total isolate groups, females were more active than males ($p<.001$ in both cases).

Exploration

The rearing groups were ordered in exploration time from feral monkeys at the high end, through mother–peer, to partial isolate and 6-month

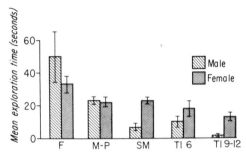

Figure 11 Time spent exploring the cage wall containing the projected visual stimulus patch during exploratory behavior tests in feral (F), mother–peer (MP), wire-cage surrogate-mother (SM), 6-month total isolate (TI 6), and 9- to 12-month total isolate (TI 9–12) monkeys.

total isolate, and last 9- to 12-month total isolate. Within groups, feral males had somewhat higher exploration times than females ($p < .05$), no sex differences occurred between mother–peer subjects, while females explored more than males in the three socially deprived groups (all $p < .01$).

Taken together, these two studies suggest the following conclusions about the persistence of rearing-condition effects on locomotion in a novel environment, self-directed withdrawal and disturbance behaviors, willingness of the animal to expose itself to novel objects (indexed by the latency measures), and time spent exploring novel objects:

1. Socialized animals move about in a novel environment and approach novel objects with relatively little hesitation. Some minor sex differences appear in exploratory behavior, but these sex differences do not alter overall rearing-condition differences.

2. Socially deprived animals are withdrawn in a novel environment, generally unwilling to approach novel objects, and relatively inactive. However, these conclusions hold only for males. On many exploration measures socially deprived females differ only slightly from socialized females, and on some measures partial and total isolate females do not differ from socialized females.

SOCIAL BEHAVIOR

The social development of rhesus monkeys receiving different types of peer contact during infancy was studied extensively by Pratt (17). The subjects in his study were reared in (1) total social isolation from birth through 9 months, (2) partial isolation for the same period, or (3) peer-only groups from birth through 7 to 9 months of age. Each group contained six males and six females. From months 12 to 18 all subjects were given a battery of tests designed to gradually pace their introduction to novel and complex stimuli. Beginning at month 18, a series of social behavior tests were conducted in the playroom illustrated in Figure 8.

Two types of playroom tests were given. Between-group tests grouped together same-sex subjects from all three rearing conditions. Groupings contained three or four animals. Within-group tests placed together same-sex sets of four animals from the same rearing group. All sessions were 30 minutes long. Two observers used a pencil–paper checklist to record the frequency of a mutually exclusive, exhaustive categorization of all behaviors occurring for a given subject during 5-minute continuous sampling periods. The original 19 behavioral categories were condensed into 7 units.

Three nonsocial behavior units were (1) *disturbance* reactions, including self-directed clasping and mouthing, rocking, huddling, and bouts of stereotyped locomotor responses; (2) *exploratory* behaviors directed toward inanimate parts of the test environment; and (3) *passive* behaviors, in which the subject simply sat or stood in one place, performing none of the other behaviors defined under the nonsocial and social units. Four social behavior units included (4) passively *orienting* toward another animal or animals while they were engaged in an interaction or were interacting with the subject; (5) play, approach, and sexual behavior with one or more monkeys; (6) socially elicited *fear*, disturbance, or withdrawal reactions; and (7) threat and *aggression* directed toward a group member or, infrequently, toward the observer. Although several other behavior types were defined, the units described here include all scorable behaviors that actually occurred during the 6-month testing period of this study.

Behavior Changes

Figure 12 presents the mean number of changes in scorable behaviors per 5-minute sampling period during 3 months of between-group tests. Total isolates (I) had fewer changes in behavior than did partial isolates (WC) ($p<.025$), who in turn changed behavior less often than peer-only (TT) subjects ($p<.01$). Sex differences appeared within both socially deprived groups. Total isolate ($p<.05$) and partial isolate ($p<.01$) females changed behavior more often than did their male counterparts.

Between-Group Social Behavior Profiles

Figure 13 presents behavior profiles summarizing the social and nonsocial behavior of each rearing condition during 3 months of between-group

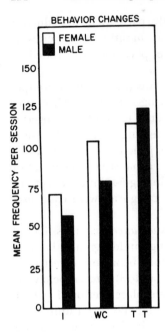

Figure 12 Number of behavior changes by total isolates (I), partial isolates (WC), and peer-only (TT) monkeys during between-group social tests in the playroom.

social tests. To adjust for the individual and group differences in total behavioral output revealed by the behavior-change analysis, the probability of occurrence of each behavior unit was computed for each subject and analyzed by a repeated-measures ANOVA. Probability was calculated as the number of times the behavior unit occurred on a trial divided by the total number of behavior changes. Figure 13 cumulates these probability averages for each rearing condition on the three nonsocial behavior units (below the heavy bar) and the four social behavior units. This gives a representation of the probability contribution of each behavior unit to the total behavior repertoire within each condition, and of differences on each unit between rearing conditions.

Analysis of variance for each unit revealed significant group differences (all $p < .001$) on every behavior unit except social orienting:

1. Total isolates were reliably less passive than the other two groups; ($p < .05$).
2. Disturbance was higher for total than for partial isolates ($p < .01$), whereas peer-only subjects had a very low probability of this unit (peer-only versus partial isolates, $p < .001$).
3. Peer-only monkeys explored more than did partial isolates ($p < .01$), who in turn explored more than did total isolates ($p < .01$).
4. The same relationship as in item 3 occurred on the play and aggression units (all $p < .01$).

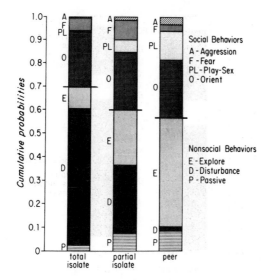

Figure 13 Behavior profiles showing the cumulative probabilities of the seven behavior units scored during 3 months of between-group social development tests.

5. Social fear was higher for partial than for total isolates ($p<.05$) and higher for total isolates than for peer-only subjects ($p<.01$).

These profiles reflect the basic outcomes that have been described for socially deprived animals over the last 15 years of research. However, as shown in Figures 14 and 15, these outcomes vary quantitatively, and in some instances qualitatively, with the sex of the socially deprived monkey.

Sex Differences in Social Group Behaviors

Figure 14 presents behavior-probability profiles for male and female total isolates during 3 months of between-group and 3 months of within-group playroom tests. The following data were obtained:

1. Passive behavior did not differ by sex in either test.

2. Disturbance behavior was lower for females during between-group tests ($p<.01$), with no difference occurring in within-group tests.

3. Exploration of the environment was higher for females on both types of test (both $p<.01$).

4. The same situation held for social orienting, with females reliably higher in looking at other monkeys in between-group ($p<.01$) and within-group ($p<.05$) tests.

5. Play behavior never occurred for either sex, and social fear was higher for males than for females in both tests (both $p<.05$).

6. Aggression was very low and did not differ by sex.

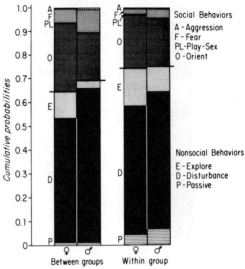

Figure 14 Behavior profiles of male and female total isolates during between- and within-group social playroom tests.

These data show that total isolate females, although markedly affected by their rearing experience, were less affected than their male counterparts. Furthermore, in the between-group tests when more socially competent animals were present in the playroom, female–male differences were larger than in within-group pairings involving only total isolates, thereby showing that interaction with relatively normal animals has a more detrimental effect on male than on female total isolates.

Figure 15 presents behavior-probability profiles for partial isolates. These profiles reveal qualitative differences between females and males, with the male profile looking very much like that of total isolates (Fig. 14), whereas the female profile bears more resemblance to that of peer-only females (Fig. 16):

1. Male partial isolates had higher passive probabilities than did females on both types of test (both $p<.05$).

2. In disturbance behavior male scores were almost triple the value of female scores on both types of test (both $p<.001$). Monkeys of both sexes reliably showed decreased disturbance in within-group tests (both $p<.05$).

3. Exploratory behavior mirrored effects on disturbance responses, with females exploring at almost triple the probability of males (both $p<.001$).

4. Passive behavior did not differ between males and females on either test, but females had much more social play behavior than did males (both $p<.001$). Females showed less fear during between-group

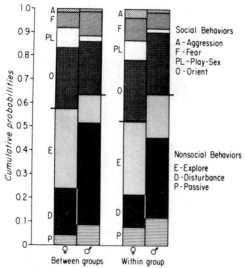

Figure 15   Behavior profiles for male and female partial isolates during between- and within-group social playroom tests.

tests, and females tended to show more aggression than did males during within-group sessions ($p < .07$).

These data show that female partial isolates—as opposed to some common understandings about partial isolates as a group—are not severely disturbed in social groups, explore the environment at relatively high levels, and show a high probability of positive social behaviors such as play, approach, and sex. Male partial isolates, on the other hand, perform much more like the typical conception of socially deprived monkeys.

Figure 16 presents behavior-probability profiles for peer-only subjects during between- and within-group tests. These profiles are very similar and contain only a few statistically reliable sex differences:

1. Males were more disturbed than females on both types of test (both $p < .01$), and males reliably showed increased disturbance level during within-group sessions ($p < .025$), whereas females did not.

2. Females had higher probabilities of exploration than did males on both types of test (both $p < .025$).

3. Males showed more threat and aggression on both types of test (both $p < .01$), and males increased their fear and aggression levels during within-group tests (both $p < .025$), whereas females did not.

These data reveal only minor sex differences between the most normally reared subjects in this study. Thus, although females were more exploratory and males were more aggressive and fearful, these differences were

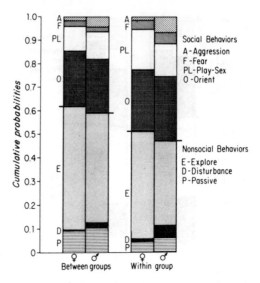

Figure 16   Behavior profiles for male and female peer-only monkeys during between- and within-group social playroom tests.

very small compared with the sex differences observed between male and female total and partial isolates. Also, it appears that peer-only males were more affected than females in their socially interactive behavior when interacting with similarly reared animals. This is suggested by the reciprocal and not surprising increases in both aggression and in fear–disturbance behaviors for males.

SURVIVAL IN A FREE-RANGING ENVIRONMENT

A final experiment concerns the ability of differently raised male and female rhesus monkeys to survive under free-range conditions (18). In this study fully adult (6 to 8 years old) rhesus monkeys were released onto Guayacon Island, a rugged 80-acre semi-arid area off the southwest coast of Puerto Rico. Approximately 80 wild-born rhesus monkeys, arranged into three social groups, were residents of this island belonging to the Caribbean Primate Center. The subjects had had the following experiences in early life: (1) wild-born and brought to the laboratory at ages estimated between 1.5 and 3 years, (2) mother–peer during the first 9 months of life, (3) partial isolation during the first year of life, and (4) total isolation during the first 6 to 12 months of life. The sample sizes for each group of released subjects are shown in Table 3, as are the numbers of survivors in each group.

Of the six released males, only two survived. Of special importance, these two came from the three socially raised original subjects. The three socially deprived males all died or have disappeared for over 3 years. Of the nine released females, seven have survived—and two of the four socially deprived females are among this survivor group. Although the sample sizes are not overwhelming, these data suggest that (1) laboratory behaviors are predictive of ability to survive in a free-ranging situation, and 2) females appear to be better able to survive than males. Several anecdotes taken from observations of these animals during their first year of freedom illustrate these conclusions.

The mother–peer male who survived was the dominant animal in the laboratory group released onto the island. This animal was attacked by native males from the largest group on the island at the time and finally became solitary—living alone in a mangrove area near a feeding station. For about 9 months animals from this largest group were trapped off the island in preparation for the release of a South American monkey group. After 9 solitary months, this mother–peer male reappeared and challenged the new male leaders of this group. After winning a fight, the mother–peer male became dominant in this native group until he was trapped off the island.

A partial and a total isolate male were observed, several days after release, slowly walking toward the dominant males of the large native group. They were picking and eating flowers off bushes and cacti, apparently oblivious to the presence of these large, alert, and mean native males. By the next day, both of these males had disappeared and have not been seen in the intervening 3-year period.

The surviving total isolate female joined a small (eight-monkey) group as a peripheral animal. Although she was rarely observed to interact physically with these residents, she did travel, eat, rest, and sleep near them. While the other monkeys rested and groomed during the day and in the evening, the total isolate female was often observed on the ground or in a tree engaged in self-clasping, rocking, huddling behaviors or in

Table 3   Survival of Laboratory Groups in a Free-Ranging Seminatural Environment

Rearing Condition	Original Subjects		Survivors	
	Male	Female	Male	Female
Feral	1	3	1	3
Mother–peer	2	2	1	2
Partial isolate	1	2	0	1
Total isolate	2	2	0	1
Total	6	9	2	7

stereotyped locomotor activities. Thus a female could apparently adapt to, and survive in, a natural environment while carrying on the types of abnormal behaviors associated with the total isolation syndrome.

FEMALES—THE BUFFERED SEX

The studies reviewed here involved a variety of experiments on behavior development in rhesus monkeys. I could have cited many other experiments that show neither sex differences nor interactions of sex with rearing variables. For example, studies on discrimination learning, visual perception, diurnal cycles of behavior, and preference for differentially complex visual stimuli fail to show any important sex effects (16, 19, 20). However, the admittedly selected set of studies discussed in this chapter do represent a wide range of behavioral dimensions generally thought to be important in adaptive-response repertoires.

The overall conclusions from these studies can be stated in a few sentences:

1. Under socialized conditions of rearing, few important sex differences appear on any behaviors not directly related to sexually dimorphic anatomical or physiological variables.

2. Males reared under social-sensory deprivation are susceptible to the development of grossly abnormal behaviors and generally fail to modify these abnormalities over years of postrearing experiences.

3. Females reared under social–sensory deprivation appear to be buffered against the development of many abnormal behaviors. Of major importance is the finding that isolate females are able to modify the extent and quality of these behaviors with postrearing experience, often approaching or attaining a species-typical response repertoire.

An explanation of these sex-differential reactions to deprivation rearing is not obvious. A theorist with an evolutionary bent might say that these effects are adaptive because only a few males are necessary for species survival, whereas many females must live to reproduce their kind. However, this explanation says little about the physical, physiological, or behavioral mechanisms and functions responsible for differential susceptibility. Also, the socially deprived male and female monkeys probably give little thought to their mission of perpetuating their species.

One possible behavioral mechanism that could have specific physiological correlates concerns my proposal (21) that deprivation-rearing effects are due to a developmental failure of inhibitory response mechanisms. In brief, this theory suggests that (1) the species-atypical behaviors that develop in isolation rearing are adaptive responses forming the best possible repertoires that can develop under stimulus impoverishment and (2) failure to modify these behaviors later in life does not result directly from perceptual deficits or an inability to learn new behaviors, but rather from a deficiency in inhibiting those responses that are inappropriate and maladaptive in postrearing situations. In essence, then, this theory suggests that the isolate repertoire of responses competes with those behaviors that are necessary for adapting to the changed behavioral demands of new social and nonsocial situations. The isolate cannot or will not inhibit these incompatible, competing behaviors that developed during infancy.

If this inhibitory mechanism has any validity, it suggests several possible explanations for the sex differences described in this chapter:

1. Females may develop the physiological bases for response inhibition prenatally and therefore are not as adversely and persistently affected by abnormal rearing environments as are males.

2. Alternatively, because of biochemical differences in prenatal and early postnatal life (e.g., hormones), females may not require the variation, quantity, or quality of sensory input during infancy that is needed by males to develop the anatomy and physiology of effective inhibitory response systems. (Also, perhaps, to control excessive levels of physiological arousal in the presence of novel or intense stimulus changes.)

The suggestion has been made that some sex differences in humans and animals are produced by different levels of androgen (22). We could readily test this possible mechanism in monkeys, using the types of rearing conditions and behavioral tests described here. Females could be androgenized at birth by implanting chemical pellets, and males could be castrated at birth. After being reared in a socially deprived environment, androgenized females should behave abnormally, like intact males; castrated males should behave more normally, like "androgenless" females. Such a study would test the effects of postnatal androgen levels. However, if prenatal levels of androgen or other biochemicals were critical in producing sex-differential reactions, the efforts of scientists like Drs. Phoenix and Levine will be required to attack the problem of the "buffered female."

ACKNOWLEDGMENTS

Many of the studies reviewed here were supported by grants (RR-0167 and MH-11894) from the U.S. Public Health Service to the University of Wisconsin Regional Primate Research Center. Other work was supported by a grant (R-00166) from the U.S. Public Health Service to the Regional Primate Research Center at the University of Washington. I wish to express my thanks to Richard Holm and Gerald Ruppenthal for their help in preparing this manuscript.

REFERENCES

1. Harlow, H. F. and M. K. Harlow, *Am Scientist* **54**: 244, 1966.
2. Harlow, H. F. and M. K. Harlow, in Schrier, A. M., Harlow, H. F. and F. Stollnitz (eds.), *Behavior of Nonhuman Primates*, Vol. 2, Academic Press, New York, 1965, p. 287.
3. Mason, W. A., in Glass, D. C. (ed.), *Biology and Behavior: Environmental Influences*, Rockefeller University Press, New York, 1968, p. 70.
4. Lichstein, L. and G. P. Sackett, *Dev. Psychobiol* **4**: 339, 1971.
5. Sackett, G. P., R. E. Bowman, G. Meyer, R. Tripp, and S. Grady. *Physiol Psychol* **1**: 209, 1973.
6. Gluck, J., unpublished Ph.D. thesis, University of Wisconsin, 1970.
7. Mitchell, G. D., *Folia Primatol* **8**: 132, 1968.
8. Harlow, H. F., in Beach, F. A. (ed.), *Sex and Behavior*, Wiley, New York, 1965, p. 234.
9. Harlow, H. F., W. D. Joslyn, M. G. Senko, and A. J. Dopp, *Anim Sci* **25**: 49, 1966.
10. Harlow, H. F., *Am. Psychol* **17**: 1, 1962.
11. Ruppenthal, G. C., G. Arling, and H. F. Harlow, manuscript in preparation, 1973.
12. Cross, H. A. and H. F. Harlow, *J Exp Res Person* **1**: 57, 1965.
13. Gluck, J. and G. P. Sackett, *J Abn Psychol*, in press, 1973.
14. Sackett, G. P., manuscript in preparation, 1973.
15. Sackett, G. P., manuscript submitted for publication, 1973.
16. Sackett, G. P., *Dev Psychol* **6**: 260, 1972.
17. Pratt, C. L., unpublished Ph.D. thesis, University of Wisconsin, 1969.
18. Sackett, G. P., J. T. Westcott and R. Westcott, manuscript in preparation, 1973.
19. Harlow, H. F., K. A. Schiltz and M. K. Harlow, in Carpenter, C. R. (ed.), *Proceedings of the Second International Congress of Primatology*, Vol. 1, 1969, p. 178.
20. Sackett, G. P., manuscript in preparation, 1973.
21. Sackett, G. P., in Jones, M. R. (ed.), *Miami Symposium on Prediction of Behavior: Early Experience*, University of Miami Press, Coral Gables, Fla., 1970, p. 11.
22. Broverman, D. H., E. L. Klaiber, W. Kobayashi and W. Vogel, *Psychol Rev* **75**: 23, 1968.

CHAPTER 7

Sex Differences in Mother-Infant Attachment in Monkeys

LEONARD A. ROSENBLUM

Department of Psychiatry and
Primate Behavior Laboratory
State University of New York
Downstate Medical Center
Brooklyn, New York

In the nonhuman primates, as in man, infants are born quite helpless and are dependent for prolonged periods on a care-giving figure—in general, the biological mother. In most nonhuman primates such dependence is manifest in almost continuous contact and close orientation in the first days of life, which then gradually wane to very low levels or complete absence during the next 6 months to 2 years, depending on the species. Most information on monkeys suggests that the decay in close attachment to the mother follows generally parallel but not identical time courses in male and female infants. Unlike the findings in humans, which generally suggest relatively minimal sex differences in the degree of attachment early in life (1, 2), studies in both the laboratory and the field have uncovered indications that, at least in macaques, by the end of the first 6 months of life males begin to show a more rapid decay in contact and orientation toward the mother than do females (3–5). In fact, for troop-living species it is a common observation that under wild conditions, as most males mature, they move out of the central portions of the troop, which contain the mothers and younger infants, and remain either peripherally associated with their natal group or break free completely. As females mature, on the other hand, they frequently maintain their position in the central core of the group and often are reported to sustain prolonged relationships with mothers and female siblings well into maturity.

Despite the obvious significance in primates of the early infant bond to the mother, we actually know quite little about the initial formation of the infant's attachment to a specific maternal figure. The work of Harlow's group on artificial mother surrogates, of course, provides a rich store of information regarding the role of specific stimulus factors—including "contact comfort," feeding, heat, and related variables—in facilitating the growth of the "affectional bond" (6). However, the critical question of how the infant comes to respond to a single, specific mothering figure and to avoid filial responsiveness to nonmothers has actually received little systematic attention. Harlow and Harlow (7) have none-theless suggested that "the infant learns attachments to a specific mother *(the mother)* . . . well before 15–20 days of life," a position apparently supported by both Bowlby and Hinde (8). Unfortunately these somewhat incidental observations and conclusions fail to distinguish between differ-ential responsiveness to a specific individual (i.e., the mother) and the possibility that the infant tends to respond initially not to a specific indi-vidual but to a class of eliciting behaviors. When an infant monkey is confronted with several individuals, only one of whom is emitting a set of "appropriate" (i.e. "maternal") behaviors, it would be a mistake to interpret the infant's response to that individual as specific to *her*, rather than to the behaviors that she alone may be directing toward it. It is also the case that none of the existing literature on early mother–infant rela-tions in nonhuman primates offers any clear indication of early sex differences in either the pace or process involved in the development of specific attachments.

RESPONSES TO MOTHER AND STRANGERS

In an attempt to obtain more systematic information on the development of discrimination of the mother and the changing response to strangers in male and female infants early in life, we have tested a total of 20 bonnet macaque (*Macaca radiata*) infants ranging in age from 2 to 60 weeks. These infants have been observed in a new situation specifically designed to assess preferential responsiveness, including approach and avoidance to both mother and conspecific strangers (9). The infants used in this study were conceived and born in the Primate Behavior Laboratory of the State University of New York Downstate Medical Center. All were reared in group settings containing a number of mothers and other infants, all living in relatively large pens of approximately 600 ft^3 (10). In order to assess responsiveness to mother and strangers across the widest possible age range, all infants born in the laboratory during the last 18 months have been tested, at least once and as many as five times. Different infants have been tested beginning at different ages, with repetitions of testing at least 3 weeks apart. Four to six male and female infants have been tested within each of the 8-week age blocks presented in the accompanying figures, except for the 19- to 26-week period in which at present only two males and two females have each been tested twice.

Testing was carried out in a chamber 2.5 m long and 0.5 m wide. The interior of the chamber was painted flat black, and the floor was covered with shaggy carpeting to facilitate locomotion in young infants. Infants were placed in a center 0.6-m area and restrained there for 30 seconds by two clear Plexiglas guillotine doors. At either end of the chamber, behind *one-way glass screens*, one or another of three stimuli could be seen: (1) the mother, (2) a strange, conspecific female, or (3) an empty stimulus chamber. Illumination was provided only in the stimulus chambers, and thus, because of the one-way glass, the infant was easily able to see either the mother or the stranger, but the stimulus animals could not see the infant or respond to it differentially. Except for the use of the one-way vision screens, which ensured that the infant was responding to the visual appearance of mother and stranger rather than to specific behaviors directed toward it by either animal, this apparatus was essentially similar in design to that utilized by Sackett (11) and subsequently by Kaplan and Schusterman (12). In our experience, after an initial period of upset, both the mothers and the strangers generally sat quietly and behaved quite similarly while awaiting the conclusion of testing.

Each test day, the infant was given seven 180-second trials. Several minutes elapsed between trials, during which time the infant was restrained once again in the center start area. Each set of test trials was preceded by an adaption trial in which each of the two stimulus chambers was empty. Then, on each test day, in balanced order for sequence and side, infants received two trials for each of three conditions: (1) mother versus empty; (2) stranger versus empty; and (3) mother versus stranger.

After the infant had 30 seconds of exposure to the stimuli of a given trial, the Plexiglas doors were raised. Using a clock-counter device, a record was made of the frequency and duration the infant spent in each 1-ft segment of the test chamber. Although a wide variety of emotional and exploratory behaviors were also recorded, the primary measure to be considered here is the amount of time the infant spent within 2 ft of each stimulus compartment. These scores are expressed as a percentage of the total test period (180 seconds). Figure 1 displays the development of preferential response to the mother as compared to the stranger in the mother–stranger trials. In the first age block, weeks 3 through 10, although there were no statistically significant differences in overall response to mother and stranger between males and females, females did show a barely significant preference for mother ($p < .05$; Wilcoxen test, one-tailed), whereas males did not. Whereas females during this first age block spent approximately twice as much time with the mother as with the stranger, males showed virtually equivalent mean scores for both stimulus choices. In the 11- to 18-week age block unequivocal levels of preferential response to the mother as opposed to the stranger emerged for both sexes. Nonetheless, preference for the mother emerged more rapidly and dramatically in female infants than in males. Considering the ages from 11 through 26 weeks, females spent approximately 75% of the mother–stranger trials at the mother's end of

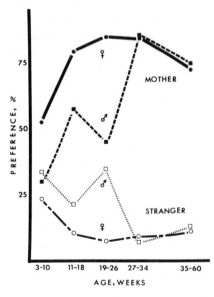

Figure 1   The percentage of each trial spent in choice of either the mother or a strange conspecific female by male and female bonnet macaque infants at varying ages.

the chamber, whereas males spent only about half of each trial engaged in such a choice. This significantly greater preference for response to mother in females (Mann–Whitney U-test; $p < .02$; two-tailed) gave way to virtually equivalent male and female preference for mother in the second 6 months of life.

An examination of the trials in which mother and stranger were each paired against the empty stimulus chamber reveals several additional dimensions of male and female response to mothers and strangers in this situation. It should be noted that both male and female infants responded quite strongly to both mother and stranger when each was presented alone. For both sexes and in all ages, for the great majority of trials, infants spent most of the test period in close proximity to whichever stimulus animal, either mother or stranger, was present. In male infants this relatively equivalent readiness to move toward both mothers and strangers on empty trials remained exceedingly stable across the age range tested, with the ratio of scores to mother versus those to stranger rarely exceeding 1.1:1. In female infants, on the other hand, there was a gradual increment in preferential response to mother as compared to strangers, and the ratio of scores to mother versus to stranger on empty trials averaged approximately 1.5:1 after about 4 months of age. Even more striking, however, is the fact that although, as indicated, female infants would generally move toward strangers when the latter were presented alone, females when compared to males showed strikingly greater levels of intermittent avoidance of strangers. As depicted in Figure 2, the ratio of time spent at the empty end of the chamber when stranger was present as compared to trials when the mother was present rose to markedly high levels in female infants, particularly in the 11- to 34-week age range. Male infants, on the other hand, throughout the age span tested, showed only a slightly greater tendency to move to the empty end of the chamber when the stranger was present as compared to those trials in which the mother was available. Thus, whereas males spent about twice as much time at the empty end on stranger trials than on mother trials, females moved away from the stranger 10 times more than they moved away from mother. Again, this significant sex difference in the relative avoidance of strangers ($p < .05$; Mann-Whitney U-test; two-tailed) disappeared by the end of the first year of life, as females no longer showed any pronounced avoidance of stranger, and their ratio scores dropped to the lower male levels. It should be noted that this mixture of both positive and negative responses to strangers shown in all these infants is quite in keeping with the most recent findings on human infants (13).

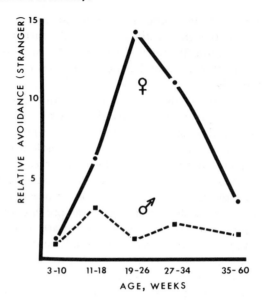

Figure 2 The relative avoidance of strange females by male and female bonnet macaque infants of varying ages. The measure used is the ratio of time spent at the empty end of the apparatus when mother was present compared with similar scores when a stranger was present.

This first study suggests that in the very early stages of life, in bonnet macaques at least, female infants more rapidly develop the capacity to differentiate the mother from other conspecific adult females and show more pronounced and clear-cut preferences for response to her. In general it may be suggested that this development of preferential response in females is completed by about the beginning of the third month of life. It seems likely, however, that in males it is not until approximately a month later that similarly high levels of preferential discrimination and response to the mother are obtained. Second, these results indicate that the relatively early development of preferential response to the mother in female infants in the fourth and fifth months of life, although accompanied by a generally positive response to strange females when the mother is absent, leads to rather pronounced tendencies toward some degree of intermittent wariness and avoidance of the proximity of strange conspecific adult females. Male infants, on the other hand, even after attainment of high levels of preferential response to the mother, continue to respond positively to strangers in the mother's absence, at least throughout the first year of life.

ENVIRONMENTAL COMPLEXITY AND ATTACHMENT

Although there are relatively few publications on the onset of infant attachment in monkeys and possible sexual differences in its establishment, a considerable amount of research has been reported regarding the effects of different rearing environments on the nature of the early infant–mother bond. Several studies have compared the development of infant–mother relations when the dyad was isolated with dyads observed in social settings. They include observations of rhesus monkeys (14), pigtail macaques (15, 16), and squirrel monkeys (17). In essence, all of these studies suggest that, in comparison with isolate dyads, group-reared infants show higher levels of attachment behavior in terms of various forms of contact and proximity with the mother during early development. Unfortunately, in these earlier studies no attempt was made to balance infant groups for sex, and often the social as well as physical setting within which dyads were observed was manipulated simultaneously. Indeed, in each of the studies on macaques, the majority, and in some cases all, of the infants were females, and when males were available, no analysis of sex differences was presented. It should be noted, however, that in his study of isolation- and group-reared squirrel monkey dyads, Kaplan (17) indicated that, although sex was not completely balanced, there was no evidence that the sex of the infant played a significant role in the behavioral differences observed.

It seems reasonable to suggest, however, that the sex of the developing infant may play a significant role in the nature of the mother–infant relationship as a function of the environment within which the dyad was observed. Sackett (18) has assessed the impact on male and female infants of early rearing in environments of varying complexity. After testing young rhesus monkeys (3½ to 4½ years old) that had been reared in circumstances ranging from 6 to 12 months of almost total isolation to laboratory or jungle rearing with their mothers and a social group, Sackett concluded: "These data suggest that deprivation rearing is much more devastating on the exploratory reaction of male monkeys. Thus, generalizations concerning rearing condition effects must be tested on, and qualified by, sex differences" (ref. 18, p. 265).

The current study was designed to assess in more precise terms, early-development differences between male and female infants raised with their mothers over a range of environments varying in physical and social stimulus complexity. The basic theoretical framework of this study was derived from a detailed analysis of the available controlled and quantitative studies of mother–infant relations in a number of macaque species

(19). On the basis of available data the author proposed a sexually homogeneous model of the relationship between environmental complexity and the development of attachment-independence in the infant. The model utilized data from four species observed in settings ranging from dyads housed within soundproof rooms to semi-free-ranging Japanese macaques, and used the time spent in contact with the mother and the time spent maximally separated from her as the counterposed measures reflecting the level of attachment-independence. It was suggested that in the first days of life the degree of environmental complexity or danger does not markedly influence the dyadic relationship; that is, regardless of environmental conditions, the pair remains closely attached. Thereafter, if an infant matures under conditions of relatively low complexity (i.e., arousal), the increase in the independent functioning of the infant, although initially somewhat accelerated, ultimately proceeds relatively slowly. If, on the other hand, the infant matures under conditions of "moderate" complexity, there is an enhancement of independent functioning. At very high levels of complexity (e.g., complex groups or natural settings), however, it was suggested that there initially may well be a relative inhibition of the infant's independent functioning, perhaps largely due to its hesitancy to move out and explore the highly stimulating field. It was hypothesized further, however, that with increasing age this U-shaped relationship between environmental complexity and infant attachment becomes more linear, with even high degrees of complexity facilitating the ultimate attainment of considerably greater levels of independent functioning than might occur under more deprived conditions.

Inasmuch as the basic age parameters of development in squirrel monkeys parallel those in macaques and because a wide variety of manipulations both in the social and physical environment may be carried out in squirrel monkeys with relative impunity, the first major test of this model was carried out with this small South American species (*Saimiri sciureus*).

A total of 37 squirrel monkey dyads were used in this study. All mothers were wild-born and brought to the laboratory as adults. Breeding and birth of the infants occurred in the laboratory. These dyads consisted of four groupings:

1. Simple environment (SE): this group was composed of eight dyads, four containing male and four containing female infants.

2. Normative controls (NC): this group was composed of 13 dyads, seven with male infants and 6 with female infants.

3. Complex environment (CE): this group contained eight dyads, four with male and four with female infants.

4. Extra-complex environment (XC): this group also contained eight dyads, four with male and four with female infants.

All pens utilized in the study were approximately 1×1 m and 2.5 m high. The walls were covered with clear anodized-aluminum sheet, the ceiling was a large mesh, and the floor was covered with bedding material. Each pen contained three shelves, 12.5 cm wide, set as steps along the back wall of the pen. The front door contained a 0.75×1.2 m one-way observation screen through which all observations were made.

For the CE groups, four standard pens were altered to enhance their physical complexity. Each pen, otherwise identical with those just described, was wallpapered in different wildly patterned and colored plastic material in a band, approximately 60 cm wide, running across both sides and the back wall, and centered around the shelves of the pen. These wall coverings were removed and replaced with different patterns every 5 or 6 weeks of the study. In addition, the CE pens contained a variety of complex manipulanda.

PROCEDURE

Breeding and Group Formation

All females were bred in the large breeding groups maintained in the laboratory and removed when pregnancy was first detected. Females were assigned to their respective groups in such a fashion as to keep infants very close in age within given treatment conditions while maintaining the appropriate sex balance. Dyads were assigned to the simple environment regardless of birth intervals since cohesive group formation was unnecessary. The completion of all cells in the study represented portions of the births in the laboratory across 4 years of breeding.

Rearing Environments

The SE dyads were each placed alone on the day of the infant's birth into a single pen of the type already described. A dyad continued to occupy the same pen throughout the course of the study. Similarly the NC groups, each initially containing four dyads (several infants did not survive), were housed as stable groups in single standard pens throughout the course of the observations. Thus, for both SE and NC subjects, neither the social nor the physical environment was manipulated during the course of the infants' development.

For CE subjects, two groups of four dyads were formed simultaneously, each containing two male and two female infants. Each such group was initially housed in one of the wallpapered pens. Thereafter, at the beginning of each week of the study, the composition of these two groups was rearranged so as to maximize unfamiliarity of group members, although the two-male, two-female composition of each group was maintained. In addition, the newly restructured groups were each moved to a new wallpapered pen each week.

For the XC group, the eight subject dyads were included as part of a total group containing 24 adult animals. Of these additional subjects, nine were mothers with infants of their own of varying ages, and seven were adult females without babies. These 24 adults, including the eight dyads under study, were arranged into three groups of eight animals, each occupying its own pen. Every Monday, Wednesday, and Friday during the course of the study, all 24 animals were rearranged randomly to form three new groups of eight in the three pens. Thus, for both the CE and XC groups, in varying degrees, both the social and physical environment was manipulated throughout the course of the study in order to markedly enhance total environmental complexity.

Observation

Every dyad in the study was observed four times a week for the first 18 weeks of the infants' life, using a 30-second cumulative time-sample method. The observer used a check sheet containing a list of behavior items. The occurrence or nonoccurrence of each behavior during successive 30-second intervals was recorded. Each check sheet was used to sample 10 successive 30-second intervals, and two to three sheets were used for each dyad on each observation day. The original check sheet included a total of 21 behaviors used to sample a large array of mother–infant, general social, and nonsocial activities. Of these, the following items, defined in more detail previously (20) were deemed pertinent to the current report:

1. Dyadic contact. This category was composed of three major elements, each recorded separately on the check sheet and combined after the conclusion of the study. These elements were *ventral–dorsal contact*, the most common posture in which the infant clings to the back of the mother; *ventral–ventral contact*, in which the infant clings to the mother's ventral surface with or without the nipple in the mouth or active nursing; and *other contact*, which includes several different patterns but primarily

the occurrence of the infant sitting next to, and pressed against, the mother.

2. Maternal protection. This category was composed of two basic elements originally recorded separately. These behaviors were *prevent departure*, in which the mother prevents the infant from leaving her back or breaking contact with her; and *retrieval*, in which the mother moves against the infant with her chest pressed close to the floor and her head down, usually nudging the infant with her head and shoulders until the infant grasps her and climbs onto her back.

3. Rejection. This category includes several behaviors of the mother, such as physical removal of the infant from her back or ventrum, or repetitive, vigorous grabbing of the infant's arm, leg, body, and head while the infant attempts to maintain its clinging to the mother's back.

It is perhaps most appropriate to begin a consideration of this study by examining the results obtained under the normative control conditions—that is, when dyads were raised in a physical and social environment that remained stable throughout. In general, this is the type of situation used for most laboratory observations of social groups and mother–infant dyads within them. As indicated in Figure 3, observations of both male and female infants in these normative groups revealed quite similar decreases in infant contact with mother over the course of the first 5 months of life. In virtually all dyads, in the first month or so of life, infant and mother maintained close contact during almost every 30-second observation interval. By the fifth month of life, however, both male and female infants were spending less than half the observation periods in contact with their mothers. Most of this decline in contact involved sharp decreases in ventral–dorsal and ventral–ventral contact after about the fourth week of life. Other contacts, however, rose slightly between the fifth and tenth week, and then gradually stabilized, only slowly thereafter approaching a low asymptotic level. Under these normative conditions there were no statistically significant differences between male and female infants on any of these measures during any selected period.

As one might have anticipated from prior work (20), during the course of the first 5 months of life, mothers in the normative condition shifted their behavior from being primarily protective to being primarily rejecting. As indicated in Figure 4, the ratio of the frequency of protecting and rejecting behaviors shifted to a negative value during the second to third month of the infant's life. Under these stable environmental conditions, there were no significant differences in the amount of protection or rejec-

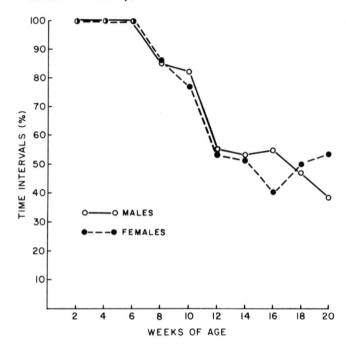

Figure 3   The development of dyadic contact in male and female infant squirrel monkeys reared in the normative environment.

tion directed at male or female infants during any phase of early development.

Using these normative data as a base, we may now consider the three other conditions under which dyads were observed. For all three experimental conditions (i.e., SE, CE, and XC) male and female infant contact with the mother was virtually continuous during the first 3 to 4 neonatal weeks. Similarly, during the next 6 weeks of life, when infants began to make regular excursions from the mother, male and female infants in each of the environments showed decreases in total contact with the mother quite similar to those that had been observed under normative conditions. With regard to maternal response to infants during this period of 5 to 10 weeks of age, however, some tentative differences began to emerge. In the simple environment, both male and female infants received somewhat higher levels of maternal *protection* as well as unusually high levels of maternal *rejection* in some cases. Thus, whereas male infants in the normative condition were rejected by their mothers on the average in 0.1% of the 30-second periods, in the simple environment they received rejection in 2.75% of the periods. Rejection of female infants similarly rose from 0.6% in the normative to 2.1% in the simple environment. It

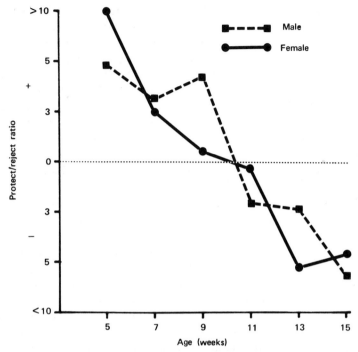

Figure 4   The ratio of maternal protecting and rejecting behaviors toward male and female infants reared in the normative environment.

is striking, however, that this rise in rejection behavior was accompanied by a parallel increase in maternal protective behavior. Male and female protection scores in the normative environment during weeks 5 to 10 of life were 1.9 and 2.0%, respectively, whereas scores of 3.6 and 3.9%, respectively, were recorded in the simple environment. Hence, although the protection-to-rejection ratio in the simple environment was somewhat less positive than in the normative condition, the two ratios did not differ significantly during this age period for either sex. There were instead significantly higher levels of *total maternal interaction* with infants in the simple environment ($p<.05$; Mann–Whitney U-test) versus the normative condition. Mothers engaged in nearly three times as much protection and rejection combined in the simple environment as in the normative condition (6.1 versus 3.2% of observation periods).

An examination of CE and XC groups for the 5- to 10-week age range showed no significant differences from normative conditions on any of the measures taken for either male or female infants. Several suggestive and somewhat unexpected findings did emerge, however, in the extra-complex environment. Although we had anticipated that mothers might be extremely protective of their infants in the frequently changing extra-complex environment, this did not appear to be the case. Although it is possible that in the extra-complex environment infants were hesitant to leave the mother early in life, this possibility alone would not account for the mothers' failure to show relatively high levels of protection. Indeed, there is some indication that if infants at this age were hesitant to leave their mothers, the mothers appear to have responded with increased levels of rejection. Male and female infants combined received significantly more maternal rejection during weeks 5 to 10 in the extra-complex environment ($p < .02$; Mann–Whitney U-test) than did the normative infants. Only 3 of the 13 normative infants had median scores above zero for rejection during weeks 5 to 10, but 7 of the 8 infants raised in the extra-complex environment had appreciable levels of rejection during this early period.

It is in the period after the tenth week of life that the major effects of the different rearing environments could be discerned. For male infants, scores for contact with mother were significantly higher ($p < .02$) in the simple environment than in the normative conditions after the tenth week of life. Female infants showed similarly high levels of contact with mother in the simple environment. It is noteworthy that these relatively high levels of contact with the mother in the simple environment occurred despite the fact that during this age period male and female infants in the simple environment received significantly greater amounts of rejection ($p < .02$) than did the normative infants. No systematic shifts in protective behavior emerged in the simple environment.

Perhaps the most interesting comparisons to emerge in this study, with regard to the interaction of sex of infant with environmental setting, appeared in the complex environment. Whereas male and female infants did not differ in the level of contact with mother in either the simple or in the normative environment, males did show significantly lower levels of contact with mother after the eleventh week when raised in conditions of moderate environmental complexity (weekly changes in group structure and physical environment). As indicated in Figure 5, after the third neonatal month, male infants in the complex environment manifested sharply lower levels of contact with mother ($p < .02$) than those observed in infants under normative conditions, whereas female infants showed just the opposite effect. This difference between the sexes was apparent in both components of dyadic contact. Males in the complex environment sharply decreased their levels of dorsal and ventral contact with the mother as compared with the normative males, whereas females markedly increased their other-contact scores and maintained about the same level

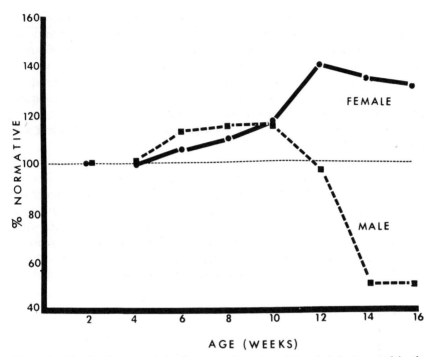

Figure 5   The development of dyadic contact in male and female infants reared in the complex environment compared with the development of this behavior in the normative environment.

of ventral–ventral and ventral–dorsal contact. It is noteworthy that the lower levels of male contact in the complex environment were not the result of increased levels of maternal rejection. For the female infants, the protection-to-rejection ratio was essentially the same in both the complex and the normative environments. For males, on the other hand, the mean protection-to-rejection ratio during weeks 10 to 15, when the values in the normative condition shifted most dramatically toward the negative side, reached $+1.36$ in the complex environment. This is in contrast to a mean value of -2.27 in the normative condition. While maternal rejection of infant males in the complex environment was not different from that observed in the normative conditions, the positive increase in the ratio was due to the significant increase in the maternal protection of male infants from 0.6 to 1.9% $(p < .02)$ during this critical age period.

In the extra-complex environment, after the eleventh week of life, males spent significantly more time in contact with the mother than they did in our comparatively moderate complex environment. In the most paradoxical finding of all, male contact levels with the mother during this age period were not different in the extra-complex environment from the relatively high levels observed in the simple environment (see Figure 6). Female infants in the extra-complex condition also showed significantly greater dyadic contact levels than had been obtained under normative conditions. In fact, for females, compared with normative conditions, all three experimental conditions (simple environment, complex environment, and extra-complex environment) resulted in female infants maintaining significantly higher levels of contact with mother in this late age period ($p<.01$).

Because of the higher levels of contact with infants of both sexes in the extra-complex environment, no significant difference between dyads containing male or female infants was obtained. An examination of maternal behavior with regard to male and female infants in the extra-complex environment once more revealed that heightened levels of contact with the mother occurred despite the fact that in this environment the mother showed significantly greater levels of rejection of male and female infants ($p<.01$) than those observed in the normative condition. Again, despite

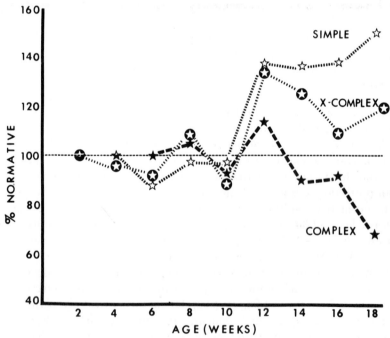

Figure 6 *The development of dyadic contact in male infants in the simple, complex, and extra-complex environments, each compared with the same behavior in the normative condition.*

the instability of the extra-complex environment, there were no apparent changes in the maternal protection of infants of either sex after the eleventh week of life.

CONCLUSIONS

What do these studies suggest regarding differences in early mother–infant relations when male and female infants are involved? First, it seems likely that within 1 to 2 months after the age at which infants begin excursions from the mother and experience more overt contact with the outside environment (in macaques and squirrel monkeys at about 8 to 12 weeks of age), male infants show a greater readiness to move toward moderately novel, complex, or arousing stimuli than do females. If one views the response to increasing levels of external stimulation as shifting from boredom (i.e., nonapproach), through orientation, interest and exploration (i.e., approach), and then on to wariness or fear (i.e., withdrawal), it might be speculated that males have a higher threshold for the evocation of these behavioral transitions than do females, at least during the first year of life. Thus a level of stimulation that provokes interest and approach in males (e.g., a stranger sitting quietly or a moderately complex, changing environment) may provoke wariness or withdrawal in similar age females. Obviously, at levels of extremely high stimulation both may withdraw or be unwilling to approach despite considerable orientation (the extra-complex environment; perhaps a stranger who threatens or is able to approach an infant). At extremely low levels of stimulation, males may suffer more "deprivation" effects as a result of this same threshold phenomenon. This speculation is in keeping with the findings of severe-deprivation studies in monkeys, which show that males are much more debilitated by such experience than are females (18). Certainly one might expect that these behavioral transition thresholds are increasing with age for both sexes, and thus, after a given age, markedly less withdrawal may be manifest toward a given highly complex stimulus in both sexes.

In any event, it is clear that we are as yet at a stage where no more than this type of descriptive modeling is possible. It is also apparent that if we are to move toward more general theoretical structures, we must markedly expand our knowledge of the response of both male and female infants to a variety of stimuli under a broad range of environmental rearing circumstances. Just as a recognition of the striking differences between primate species has required explicit control and designation of species-specific functions, we can no longer be content with the use of "infants" as subjects in our work, but must recognize the need to study and understand the role of sexual dimorphism from the very first days of life onward.

ACKNOWLEDGMENTS

This research was supported by grants (MH 15965 and MH 22640) from the National Institute of Mental Health, U.S. Public Health Service. I wish to thank Edna Lowe, Barbara Turner, and Stephanie Alpert for their assistance in carrying out these studies.

REFERENCES

1. Schaffer, H. R. and P. E. Emerson, *Monogr Soc Res* 3, Serial No. 94, 29, 1964.
2. Morgan, G. A. and H. N. Ricciuti, in Foss, B. M. (ed.), *Determinants of Infant Behavior*, Vol. 4, Methuen, London, and Barnes and Noble, New York, 1969.
3. Jensen, G. D., R. A. Bobbitt, and B. N. Gordon, in Altmann, S. A. (ed.), *Social Communication Among Primates*, University of Chicago, Chicago, 1967.
4. Itoigawa, N., in Carpenter, C. R. (ed.), *Social Regulatory Mechanisms of Primates*, University of Pennsylvania Press, Philadelphia, 1973.
5. Mitchell, G., *Primates* 9: 85, 1968.
6. Harlow, H. F. and R. R. Zimmerman, *Science* 130: 421, 1959.
7. Harlow, H. F. and M. K. Harlow, in Schrier, A. M., H. F. Harlow and F. Stollnitz (eds.), *Behavior of Non-human Primates*, Vol. 2. Academic Press, New York, 1965.
8. Bowlby, J., *Attachment and Loss: Attachment*, Basic Books, New York, 1969.
9. Rosenblum, L. A. and S. Alpert, in Lewis, M. and L. A. Rosenblum (eds.), *The Origins of Behavior: Fear*, Wiley, New York, 1974.
10. Rosenblum, L. A. and K. P. Youngstein, in Lewis, M. and L. A. Rosenblum (eds.), *The Origins of Behavior: The Influence of the Infant on Its Caregiver*, New York, 1974, pp. 141–161.
11. Sackett, G. P., in Rosenblum, L. A. (ed.), *Primate Behavior: Developments in Field and Laboratory Research*, Vol. I, Academic Press, New York, 1971, pp. 112–140.
12. Kaplan, J. and R. J. Schusterman, *Dev Psychobiol* 5: 53, 1972.
13. Lewis, M. and L. A. Rosenblum (eds.), *The Origins of Behavior: Fear*, Wiley, New York, 1974.
14. Hinde, R. A. and Y. Spencer-Booth, in Morris, D. (ed.), *Primate Ethology*, Morrison & Gibb, London, 1967, pp. 267–286.
15. Wolfheim, J. H., G. D. Jensen, and R. A. Bobbitt, *Primates* 11: 119, 1970.
16. Castell, R. and C. Wilson, *Behavior* 39: 202, 1971.

17. Kaplan, J., *Dev Psychobiol* **5**: 43, 1972.
18. Sackett, G. P., *Dev Psychol* **6**: 260, 1972.
19. Rosenblum, L. A., in Moltz, H. (ed.), *Ontogeny of Vertebrate Behavior*, Academic Press, New York, 1971, pp. 315–366.
20. Rosenblum, L. A., in Rosenblum, L. A. and R. W. Cooper (eds.), *The Squirrel Monkey*, Academic Press, New York, 1968, pp. 207–233.

Discussion: Stress and Early Life Experience in Nonhumans

CHARLES H. PHOENIX, Moderator

ELIZABETH McCAULEY, Rapporteur

The discussion began with a series of questions directed toward Dr. Rosenblum concerning the maternal behavior of squirrel monkeys.

Dr. Ehrhardt asked if Dr. Rosenblum had any developmental data that indicated when each component of adult maternal behavior first appears in the young animal and when sex differences first became observable. Dr. Rosenblum replied that he had no longitudinal data, only cross-sectional sampling of his laboratory animals. His observations have revealed no marked differences among young monkeys ranging in age from 14 to 31 months and therefore no developmental trend in this age period. There was a tendency for younger males to be more responsive to infants than older males who were closer to puberty. The components of maternal behavior were present in both immature males and females; however, although immature males showed interest and responsiveness to infants, only the immature females showed retrieval behavior. After puberty, more clear-cut sex differences emerge in maternal behavior.

Dr. Stern asked if immature females showed the same maternal behavior in call and in movements as adult females. Dr. Rosenblum responded that the same motor elements were present, although they seemed more frenetic in the immature animals. Information on the vocal component was less certain because limitations of the observation system made it difficult to tell which of the monkeys was emitting a certain cry. However, he had observed some of the immature females emitting the same call as the mature females, so he would conclude that all the components of adult maternal behavior are present in at least some of the immature female monkeys.

Dr. Vande Wiele commented that the data presented by Dr. Rosenblum showed a significant increase in retrieval behavior in females in late pregnancy. He pointed out that in human beings there is not much difference in levels of progesterone between middle and late pregnancy, and suggested that prolactin increase at that time might be related to the increase in retrieval behavior. Dr. Rosenblum agreed that something happens in late pregnancy that seems to sensitize the female to respond to the infant and that prolactin might play an important role.

A second group of questions related to Dr. Rosenblum's work on mother–stranger reactions in young macaque monkeys. Dr. O'Connor asked if Dr. Rosenblum thought that the animals in his mother–stranger experiments discriminated on the basis of visual or olfactory cues. Dr. Rosenblum's impression was that the discriminations were visual. He had not controlled for smell but had given a series of reversal trials each day so that the olfactory cues would be confused. In a recent study using surrogate-raised squirrel monkeys, J. Kaplan found that they did not discriminate on the basis of visual cues in the first 8 weeks of life, but did discriminate after 2 weeks on the basis of urine and fecal odors. Dr. Rosenblum has not investigated this in bonnet macaques.

Regarding the mothers and strangers in Dr. Rosenblum's experiments, Dr. Lewis wondered whether the mother might be acting differently because of the recent removal of her infant. Could something in her behavior account for the sex differences Dr. Rosenblum found? Dr. Rosenblum responded that they had used as strangers other mothers who had just been separated from their infants, as well as strangers with no separation, and they found no differences.

The discussion then moved on to the question of the greater vulnerability of the male, an issue that had been raised several times in terms of stress and early life experience. Dr. Galenson commented that among human beings the incidence of autistic disturbances is far greater in males than in females, at least during the first few years of life. Dr. Phoenix added that in his observations on rhesus monkeys, masturbation, taken as an indication of anxiety, was always more frequent in males, even in males who have been raised with their mothers until 3 months of age. Dr. Rosenblum mentioned that, among the males he studied, those who showed less overt attachment to their mothers also showed a more disturbed reaction to separation from mother. Dr. Person pointed out that there is a much greater number of cross-dressing men with low sex drive than in women with the same deviant behavior.

Dr. Sackett asked why females seem to be less detrimentally affected by deprivation. Referring to work previously done by himself and H. F. Harlow, he noted that early deprivation does not seem to produce deficits in the ability to later acquire new information. He argued that the deprivation effect may mainly be in the ability to inhibit inappropriate responses. In isolation, both male and female animals develop a set of behaviors adaptive to their deprived condition. Females, however, seem more able than males to evolve new responses and suppress old ones when placed in a new situation requiring new adaptations. Males rigidly repeat old behaviors that might have been useful in a deprived setting but are inappropriate in a more enriched environment.

Dr. Sackett said that he was particularly interested in the neurophysiological and biochemical mechanisms that underlie this type of behavior inhibition. He went on to suggest that perhaps the differences in prenatal hormone levels enable females to develop these inhibitory mechanisms more adequately than do males.

Dr. Levine pointed out that his data also indicate that females are buffered in some way. In his work he looked at physiologically different systems that could not be explained by a theory specific to rhesus macaques. Dr. Sackett argued that the brain mechanisms discussed by Dr. Levine might be organizing these differential inhibitory mechanisms.

Dr. Michels observed that deviant males are less able to be socially appropriate than deviant females and are more likely to be rejected by societal groups. Dr. Sackett agreed and suggested that the reason for this could be the developmental lack of the inhibitory mechanisms he had described.

Dr. Levine interjected that Dr. Sackett's theory would be easy to test by doing a simple set of experiments based on habituation. Dr. Sackett replied that they had tested this point and found that females habituated more rapidly. Dr. Levine suggested that any number of inhibitory tasks could be performed with animals to further test this hypothesis—for example, passive avoidance tasks.

Dr. Korner noted that the greater vulnerability of the male throughout life may be related to his more complicated prenatal development as compared with the female.

Dr. Sackett responded that in this context he would like to experiment with a monkey group consisting of neonatally androgenized females and neonatally castrated males who would be raised in isolation. It would be interesting to see whether the males would behave like females and the females like males on some of the simple tasks he discussed in his presentation. He concluded that the results of such a study would probably lead to further research on prenatal differences between males and females.

3 Early Mother-Child Interaction in Humans

RICHARD GREEN, *Moderator*

SUSAN COATES, *Rapporteur*

CHAPTER 8

Early Sex Differences
and Mother-Infant Interaction

HOWARD A. MOSS

Child Research Branch
National Institute of Mental Health
Bethesda, Maryland

In the last several years we have conducted a number of studies on mother–infant behavior at the Child Research Branch of the National Institute of Mental Health. These studies were aimed at describing the course of early development and, where possible, delineating the factors that seemed to have a major part in determining and shaping early behavior. Moreover, the studies we conducted on mother–infant behaviors were part of a longitudinal research program in which four different teams of investigators independently studied different stages of development.* One team studied early marriage, prior to the birth of the first

* This longitudinal program, in addition to the mother–infant study, includes the study of early marriage directed by Robert Ryder, the analysis of newborn behavior carried out by Thomas Douthitt and Raymond Yang, and a preschool assessment supervised by Charles Halverson. Each project studied the same sample, at different developmental stages, so that a longitudinal assessment could be generated by interrelating the data among each of these independent cross-sectional studies. Richard Bell directed the overall longitudinal program.

child; another group studied newborn behavior; and a third group investigated early preschool behavior in a 4- to 5-week experimental nursery school.

Our research on mother–infant behavior involved pregnancy studies of the mother as well as studies of the mother and infant over the early months of life. Thus the longitudinal projects carried out consisted of the four teams of investigators independently studying subjects from the same sample, but at different stages of development. The general strategy of this longitudinal program was to assess both parental and newborn characteristics prior to experience with, or knowledge of, one another, so as to be better able to ascertain the basis or origin of subsequent behaviors and social interactions. In addition to the longitudinal cohorts that were studied, each section carried out preparatory studies on separate samples. By and large, most of our studies were influenced, in both the selection of variables and in their conceptual focus, by the longitudinal objectives of the program.

In this chapter I summarize findings on sex differences from four studies we have carried out on mother–infant behavior. In one of these studies, father data were also obtained. Although two of these studies were parts of longitudinal cohorts, the results to be discussed are primarily cross sectional in nature. To begin with, our research, as a rule, was not designed in order to study sex differences. Instead, we have been interested primarily in identifying the salient dimensions of mother–infant functioning and in determining the reciprocal effect within dyads. However, we have routinely analyzed our results separately for male and female subjects. We have followed this practice because other research often has shown different patterns of findings for males and females, and, furthermore, when data for the sexes are pooled, there is the possibility of some findings being masked. In addition, for all of our studies we have compared males and females for different behaviors as well as for differences in maternal treatment. These cross-sex comparisons were initiated more in order to shed light on developmental phenomena than to elucidate the nature of sex differences per se.

The task of gaining some understanding of early behavior in the context of the mother–infant relationship is a difficult one. However, we found that by comparing male and female infants on many of our measures we were able to obtain information that enabled us to better understand certain developmental transactions that were of more central interest to us. Thus the study of sex differences constituted a secondary but highly useful aspect of our work. It is quite likely that we would have proceeded differently if our principal interest had been to assess the extent and basis for early sex differences.

Nonetheless, in the course of our studies, sufficient information on sex differences has emerged to suggest fairly cohesive and distinct trends in infant behavior and parental treatment for the respective sexes. In general, the findings indicate that male infants tend to function at a less well organized and less efficient level than do female infants. The males were more irritable and seemed less facile than females in responding to learning contingencies, particularly in regard to social stimuli. This difference in the rate of learning between the sexes may be partly attributable to the males being more prone to physical distress at this stage of development and thus less frequently at an optimal state for monitoring and assimilating environmental events than are females. There is also some evidence that females mature at a more rapid rate than males, which may partly account for some of the difference in learning behavior that we observed.

We also have observed differential treatment by parents toward males and females. The mothers in our studies, and also the fathers where we have the information, seemed to show greater investment in the social behavior of their daughters than that of their sons. These differences in parental behaviors may have been influenced by the females being more often at an optimal state, where they were receptive to social stimulation. On the other hand, the stereotyped sex-role attitudes of the parents may have contributed to their greater emphasis in producing and shaping social behavior in their daughters. We have some evidence that these stereotyped sex-role attitudes are expressed by parents very early in the infant's life. In addition, the optimal physical functioning of the female infants for responding to social stimulation may have facilitated and reinforced parental expectations and behavior related to their differential value of social behavior in male and female infants.

This general pattern concerning early sex differences is gleaned from the series of studies we have conducted on mother–infant behavior. However, before presenting more detailed information concerning our specific findings, it should be pointed out that not all the results were completely in keeping with this picture. There were some inconsistencies or lack of replications. What has been attempted here is to summarize male and female differences in terms of the general themes or trends that were suggested by our findings. It would be helpful to bear in mind that over the approximately 10-year period in which we conducted our studies there were changes in the cultural climate, new ideas concerning child-rearing practices were introduced through the mass media, there was the likelihood of vicissitudes in pediatric practices, and there were variations in the socioeconomic composition of the respective samples we studied. All of these factors may have interfered with our successfully obtaining consistently replicated findings. Moreover, it should be made clear that we are dealing with fairly fragile phenomena. Many of the sex differences we have observed were of marginal statistical significance, and there was a great deal of overlap in the male and female distributions. Thus, it should not be surprising that certain of our results on sex differences were somewhat unstable. With regard to this caveat, one should not take our reported sex differences as findings that clearly characterize males or females.

The first study we conducted on mother–infant behavior was based on a sample of 30 primiparous mothers and their infants (1). The primary data for this study consisted of direct coding of behaviors during home observations that were carried out over the first 3 months of life. For this sample, a cluster of three observations was made at weekly intervals during the first month of life, and a second cluster of three observations was made at about 3 months of age. Each cluster included two 3-hour observations and one 8-hour observation. The 3-hour observations were made with the use of a keyboard that operated in conjunction with a 20-channel Esterline-Angus event recorder. Each of 30 keys represented a maternal or infant behavior. When a key was depressed, one or a combination of pens on the recorder was activated, leaving a trace that showed the total duration of the observed behavior. This technique allowed for a continuous record showing the total time and the sequence of each behavior. For the 8-hour observation the same behaviors were studied, but with a modified time-sampling technique. The time-sampled units were 1 minute long. The observer, using a stenciled form, marked the occurrence of the appropriate behaviors for the time unit in which it occurred. The same behaviors were coded for the observations based on the 3-hour event recorder as for the 8-hour time-sampling procedure.

Examples of maternal behaviors that were coded during the home observations are holding, feeding, rocking, talking to, imitating vocalizations, stimulating/arousing, and stressing the musculature of the infant. For this study, the infant variables mainly consisted of codings of the state or arousal level of the infant; that is, codings were made of the amount of time spent crying, fussing, sleeping, or awake. The time-sample data were used to describe general characteristics of the mother–infant dyad, whereas the continuous event-recorder data were aimed at providing information concerning the sequencing and context of events.

For the two 8-hour time-sampled observations, carried out at 3 weeks and 3 months of age, respectively, the male infants fussed and cried more than the female infants. These differences, however, were statistically significant at both ages only for the scores on fussing. In turn, the mothers had much more interaction with the male infants. The mothers of sons held, attended, stimulated, and looked at their infants more than did the mothers of daughters. These differences were statistically significant only at 3 weeks, but the same trends were noted for the 3-month observation. The possibility that these sex differences in maternal behavior may have been a function of the greater irritability observed among the male infants was tested by comparing the mean scores for the sexes on these maternal variables after statistically controlling for the variance associated with fussing and crying. When infant protesting was controlled for, most of the maternal sex differences disappeared. The exceptions were that the t-values became greater, after this analysis, for the variables *mother imitates infant and stimulates/arouses*. The higher score for *stimulates/arouses* was obtained for the males and was statistically significant at both ages (3 weeks; $t = 2.43$, $p < .05$ level; 3 months; $t = 2.31$, $p < .05$ level). The higher score for imitates was obtained for the females and was significant only for the 3-month observation ($t = 2.14$, $p < .05$).

The 3-hour home observations, for which continuous event-recorder data were obtained, also yielded information concerning sex differences in infant and maternal behaviors. These data were studied in regard to infant protesting (combination of fussing and crying behavior). For this analysis, the protest episodes (duration of fussing and crying behavior) were classified as to the physical location and behavior of the mother (with relationship to the infant) prior to and during the course of the protesting. This resulted in three classes of protest episode: (1) those episodes in which the mother was present at the time the protesting began (mother present, or MP, episodes); (2) those episodes where the mother was not present at the onset of the protesting, but in which she responded to the infant during the course of the protesting (maternal response, or MR, episodes); and (3) those episodes in which the mother was not present when the protesting began and did not respond to the infant during the course of the episode (nonmaternal response, or NMR, episodes). Thus the protest episodes were divided into the three-way classification of *mother present, mother responds,* and *mother does not respond.* To obtain scores for the younger and older age periods comparable to the time-sampled observations, the two 3-hour observations that occurred within the first month were pooled, as were the two that took place at 3 months.

Comparisons of these protest episodes showed that the MP episodes were more frequent at the younger age period and also occurred more often for male than for female infants at both ages. All these differences were statistically significant and suggest that the mothers were more likely to hover over the younger male and female infants and the older males, anticipating, but not effectively intercepting, the cry before it actually occurred. This seems plausible, since infants often exhibit premonitory signs of approaching fussiness or irritability before they actually begin protesting. We also found from these data that mothers took significantly longer to quiet females at 1 month and males at both 1 and 3 months of age. Thus the greater difficulty the mothers apparently experienced in terminating protest behavior in these infants may, in part, account for the greater vigilance shown toward them.

On the other hand, the NMR episodes occurred much more often for the female than the male subjects during the earlier observations. An additional finding that helps to clarify this sex difference is that the NMR episodes proved to be of much shorter duration than the MR episodes. Thus the female infants had more of the short protest episodes to which the mother was less likely to respond. This finding indicates that one of the criteria mothers evidently use in determining whether or not to respond is the length of time the infant is protesting.

Thus, to summarize the findings on sex differences from this study, males tended to show more irritable behavior in which they were fussier and also more difficult to calm than were the females. This sex difference seemed to result in more activities on the part of the mother to interact with the males in an effort to quiet them or to modulate their state. In addition, these data seem to suggest that mothers were more vigilant in attempting to anticipate and control irritable behavior in the male infants. On the other hand, brief, transitory episodes of protesting occurred with greater frequency among the females, and for these episodes, the female infants became quieted and restored themselves to a state of equilibrium without maternal intervention more often than did the males. The one instance of a sex difference in social behavior from these data consisted of mothers imitating, or, if you will, reinforcing, the vocalizations of the females more often than of the males.

Both naturalistic and structured situations yield useful information concerning parent–infant interaction. Each of these situations has its advantages and limitations concerning the type of data it makes available. The ideal approach would be to obtain data utilizing both naturalistic and structured observations. One advantage of the structured procedure is that it is more possible to schedule the data collection so that fathers can be included in the assessment. Another advantage of the structured approach is that it enables the investigator to design procedures so as to maximize the occurrence of information concerning the phenomenon one wishes to study. Most of our studies involved naturalistic observations. However, we did study one sample in which we had parents respond to their infants in a structured situation.

For this investigation, a sample of 44 cases consisting of mothers, fathers, and their 7-week-old infants were studied in our laboratory. The subjects in this sample were selected so as to provide dichotomous groups as to the educational level of the parents, sex of the infant, and whether the infant was the first or the second child. This study was planned with the thought of developing a possible standardized procedure for assessing parent–infant behaviors. Thus we selected a sample composed of specific criterion groups (SES, sex, and ordinal position) in order to assess the validity of our procedure. We felt that if this procedure were to prove useful (valid) for determining individual differences among parents, it should be sufficiently sensitive to discriminate among these criterion groups. Therefore this sample consisted roughly of equal numbers of males and females, first and second children, and low- and middle-class subjects.

The structured situation that was used consisted of asking the parents to work together, in whatever way they chose, in administering a series of nine tests to their infant. At the start of this procedure the infant was placed in a supine position in a crib beside which the parents and the experimenter stood while an observer coded data through a one-way glass window from an observation booth adjacent to the crib. The tasks the parents were asked to administer to the infant involved trying to get the infant to visually follow objects, to exhibit physical strength and coordination, to smile, and to vocalize. The parents were instructed to continue with a task until they judged that their infant had either successfully completed or would be unable to succeed at that task. No time limit was set, and the parents indicated when they were finished with one test and ready for the instructions for the subsequent test.

The observer coded the amount of time that both parents, either separately or jointly, spent in actively participating with their infant on each of the tasks. Also coded were the performance levels and irritability (state) of the infant during each of these tasks. The tests the parents were asked to administer involved behaviors that are generally associated with either social or motor development. For the test that requested "get the infant to smile," mothers and fathers spent significantly more time participating with female than with male infants (Mann–Whitney U-test; $p < .002$ and .005, respectively; one-tailed). Similarly, when the parents were asked to "get their child to vocalize," both mothers and fathers exhibited greater participation time with the females (Mann–Whitney U-test; $p < .04$ and .06; one-tailed). There were no differences in judged performance levels for males and females on these tasks—or for any of the other tasks for that matter. Thus we can rule out sex differences in developmental skill as a reinforcing factor in determining differences for the sexes in parental participation time. For both the "smile" and "vocalization" test, mothers' participation time was significantly longer than fathers' (Mann–Whitney U-test; $p<.001$ for both one-tailed tests). The tests relating to motor development did not reveal much in regard to sex differences. However, on the task where the parents were required to "get the baby to grab for a bell" fathers did participate significantly longer than mothers for both sexes (Mann–Whitney U-test; $p<.005$; one-tailed).

There was a trend for females to be at a more optimal state than male infants during this procedure. Although the sex differences on this measure were not statistically significant, the females were judged to be in a more attentive or less irritable state than the males during each of the nine subtests administered. Infant state also was associated with birth order and social class: the firstborn infants were more irritable than the secondborn ones, and the lower-class infants were more irritable than those of the middle-class group. These group differences contributed to an interaction in which the most irritable behavior occurred among the lower-class firstborn males. This finding agrees with a recent result reported by Bell and Ainsworth (2) in their study of infant crying behavior. They found no sex differences in infant crying behavior when they pooled their data for firstborn and later-born infants. However, when they took birth order into consideration, they did find a sex difference showing more crying for a subgroup of firstborn males.

These results suggest that the greater irritability we generally have observed among males is probably not a necessary or intrinsic characteristic of these infants, but instead may reflect their greater vulnerability to environmental stress; that is, the male's greater vulnerability may only become manifest in disrupted functioning when additional circumstances are unfavorable. When supporting environmental conditions are optimal —such as being born to an experienced, physically fit mother and into a family with sufficient resources for providing preferred care for the infant—this vulnerability is not exposed. Female infants, on the other hand, may be physically better equipped to withstand adverse conditions and thus less likely to show signs of disruption when such conditions are present.

The structured procedure also yielded some information concerning the early expression of stereotyped sex-role attitudes by parents in their verbal behavior toward their infants. The entire procedure was tape recorded, and a frequency count was made of the number of affectionate terms of address the parents used in talking to their infants during the test proper. These terms included common words of endearment, such as "honey," "precious," "angel," "my little girl or boy" (whichever might be the case). Both mothers and fathers used significantly more affectionate terms when addressing the girls than the boys ($t = 2.20$, $p < .05$ level for mothers; $t = 1.81$, $p < .10$ level for fathers). Thus these parents showed evidence of using stereotyped sex-role attitudes in relating to their 7-week-old infants.

In general the findings on sex differences from the structured procedure seem consistent with the results reported from the first home observation study we conducted: there was evidence of greater irritability among males, and parents exhibited more marked investment in producing social responses in their daughters. It is of interest that there was no direct evidence of any infant behavior that might have influenced differential parental behavior between the sexes for these social behaviors. The most parsimonious explanation would be that stereotyped sex-role attitudes in this case shaped the parental behavior.

In addition, we conducted two more studies that involved naturalistic home observations of mothers with their infants. A primary reason for these three separate studies on mother–infant interaction was to enable us progressively to develop and to sharpen our concepts as well as to refine our methodology. Thus, although there is a great deal of overlap in variables and methods used among these three studies, there are also a number of distinct differences. Changes in the research design also were influenced by considerations associated with the larger longitudinal design of our research program. Most of the changes that occurred across studies were in the direction of employing more efficient and economical methods, obtaining larger samples, redefining variables, substituting dyadic for individual variables wherever possible, and adding experimental procedures in order to cross-validate some of the findings obtained from the home observations. This series of studies allowed us both to replicate some of our previous findings and to perform new analyses that built on the results of preceding studies.

The second home observation sample that we studied consisted of 54 primiparous mother–infant pairs who were assessed by means of the modified time-sampling procedure previously described. For this sample, three 6-hour observations were made, two at 1 month of age and one at 3 months. The scores from the two 1-month observations were pooled, resulting in one set of scores for each age period. At approximately 3½ months of age the infants from this sample were studied in our laboratory while the mothers were being interviewed elsewhere in the building. The laboratory procedure consisted of presenting series of social (faces) and geometric (checkerboards) visual stimuli and recording the infant's fixation times (3, 4). The social stimuli consisted of photographs of faces, and the geometric stimuli were pictures of checkerboards of varying degrees of complexity. The visual study was carried out in order to determine whether the frequency of contingent visual interactions between mother and infant, as observed from the home observations, was related to the infant's visual behavior under laboratory conditions.

The sex differences for the home observation data on this sample were minimal. The only instance where a finding obtained from the first sample studied was replicated was for *infant fusses* for the 3-month observation. Once again males had significantly higher scores than females on fussing behavior ($Z = 1.86$, $p < .05$). The scores on crying did not significantly differ for the sexes, although there was a trend, at 3 months, for males to exhibit more of this behavior. Thus, for both home observation studies discussed so far, *infant fusses* was a more sensitive variable than *infant cries* for differentiating the sexes. Fussing is composed largely of "cranky" or "whiney" behaviors, whereas crying is a direct, unequivocal reaction. The full cry might be regarded as a clear, biologically functional response, which is designed to signal distress and evoke comforting treatment from caretakers. The fuss, on the other hand, is an in-between response reflecting a lack of homeostasis and a quality of being unsettled. If one accepts this evaluation of fussing and crying behavior, one might in turn interpret the similarity in the amount of crying for the sexes as indicating that both males and females make comparable usage of this biologically appropriate signaling system. On the other hand, the greater amount of fussing observed for the male infants suggests that males tend to have more difficulty in settling down and achieving a sense of equilibrium.

There was a trend at 3 months for the fussing scores to be related to different maternal responses for the sexes (5). For the females, fussing was apparently responded to through social stimulation (e.g., talking to the infant, imitating her vocalizations, engaging in mutual visual regard) and through the use of distant care-giving activities (attending the infant and using a pacifier). For the male infants, at 3 months of age, fussing was related to stimulation of the distance receptors (auditory and visual) and to close physical contact with the mother. There is some evidence that female infants at 3 months are more socially responsive than males (3), which could account for the mothers in this sample being more inclined to use social stimulation in attempting to quiet their daughters.

Mutual visual regard is one of the earliest channels of communication available to the mother–infant dyad and provides the basis for most of the social interchanges between this pair. We have labeled mutual visual regard as *vis-à-vis* and coded for the occurrence of this interaction from our home observations. Our rationale for conducting the previously mentioned visual study was to determine whether there was a relation between *vis-à-vis* under naturalistic conditions and an infant's visual behavior assessed in the laboratory. The fixation times to the social and geometric stimuli were correlated with the 1- and 3-month *vis-à-vis* scores for males and females. The males' fixation times were unrelated to the antecedent *vis-à-vis* scores. However, for the females, fixation time to the social stimuli and *vis-à-vis* were significantly correlated $(r=.61, p<.01)$. Thus the frequency of *vis-à-vis*, which from the infant's perspective involves looking at the mother's face appears to transfer for female infants to greater visual attentiveness to two-dimensional facial stimuli (3). For the male infants, the state they tended to be in during the home observations was related to their visual behavior in the laboratory study (4). Specifically, the amount of time male infants spent in a quiet, awake state during the 1-month observations and in a nonirritable state during the 3-month observations was associated with their attention time to the visual stimuli, both geometric and social. Thus the male infants who spent more time at activity levels that are optimal for visually observing the environment also were more inclined to look longer at the experimentally presented visual stimuli. The state variables were not predictive of the visual behavior of the female infants.

These data suggest that endogenous attributes of the organism, as manifested by state variables, may be more relevant determinants of visual behavior for males, whereas social learning contributes more heavily to the visual performance of the females. These results should not be regarded as sex differences per se, because some of the actual correlations for males and females did not significantly differ from one another. The results, however, suggest that different factors are salient for each of the sexes in organizing and shaping their visual behavior at the stages of development for which these data were collected.

The data on this sample provided moderate evidence concerning infant sex differences, both from the home observations and from the visual study. The evidence here certainly was not as clear-cut or unequivocal as the findings on sex differences previously summarized from our first home observation study and from the structured procedure we conducted. In particular, direct evidence was lacking in the present results on maternal differences in the treatment of the sexes. However, the fact that those sex differences that did appear were consistent with our earlier findings provides the basis for further considering, or solidifying, a view that there is the potential for different behavioral patterns to be manifest among male and female infants. These differences are not great, but continue to suggest more irritability among male infants and greater channelization or responsiveness toward social stimuli for female infants.

The most recent study we have conducted on mother–infant interaction involved the main longitudinal cohort studied by the Child Research

Branch. This was a large-scale study including other teams of investigators who assessed the same cases we did, but at other stages of development. The scope of this longitudinal project and the necessity to interdigitate with the plans and schedules of the other investigators placed both conceptual and methodological constraints on how we conducted this study. We repeated our practice of time sampling mother–infant behaviors from home observations, but limited this data collection on these cases to two 6-hour visits at the 3-month period. Changes also were made in the variables that were used, although there was still considerable overlap, at least conceptually, with the behaviors that were coded in the previously mentioned studies. Many of the changes that were made were in the direction of trying to code directly for sequences and interactions through the use of dyadic variables or variables that described contingent responses from the mother. In addition, for this study we no longer coded *fuss* and *cries* as separate variables, but pooled these behaviors into a single variable described as *protesting*.

This sample consisted of 121 mothers and their firstborn infants. In addition to the home observations, these infants were studied in our laboratory when they were approximately $3\frac{1}{2}$ months of age. The laboratory studies consisted of a variation of the previously described visual procedure as well as a vocal conditioning experiment. For the visual study we used only a series of facial stimuli, since our primary interest was in studying the effects of learning associated with prior social interactions with the mother. The vocal conditioning experiment also was carried out in order to determine whether there were any observable effects of social learning in the infant that were related to the manner in which a mother responded to her infant during the home observations.

Several experiments (6–8) have shown that the frequency of infant vocalizations can be increased through the use of contingent reinforcement of vocal responses. Nonetheless, these studies still do not account for individual differences among infants in their conditionability; that is, infants vary in the extent to which their vocalizations increase when reinforced in an experimental situation. It seems reasonable to assume that if reinforcements, under natural life conditions, have an appreciable effect in shaping behavior, there should be evidence that differences in the maternal use of contingent reinforcement in the homes should be reflected in differences among infants in their responsiveness to social reinforcements in the laboratory. Our vocal conditioning experiment was designed to test this assumption.

The results for this cohort showed little in the way of sex differences. The finding that males exhibited more irritable behavior than did females was not replicated with this sample. There are a few possible explanations for the failure of this sex difference to replicate. First, our measure of irritability for this study combined fussing and crying behavior, and, in our earlier studies, fussing alone proved to be a more powerful variable for differentiating the sexes. Also, well after this study was under way, we received indications that pediatricians seemed to be more inclined to diagnose colic and prescribe medication more readily when mothers complained of irritable behavior in their infants than seemed to be the case for previous samples we studied. Such a change in pediatric practice certainly could have the effect of attenuating sex differences in irritable behavior. This explanation, of course, is based on impressions on our part that were culled from remarks made by the mothers in the study.

Infants, in progressing from a quiet to an irritable or aroused state, will frequently show a transition from vocalizing, to fussing, to crying behaviors. The male infants in this sample did vocalize significantly more than the females during both the home observations and the vocal conditioning procedure. Perhaps this difference in the frequency of vocal behavior between the sexes for this sample reflected the same endogenous tendencies that produced the sex differences in fussing behavior noted in our other studies. Differences in threshold discrimination among observers as to what constituted a vocalization or a fuss could have produced this shift in the composition of these results.

Using the visual procedure, the relations between the home visit variables and the visual stimuli for this sample generally paralleled the findings reported for the first study we discussed: for the female infants the home observation scores on *vis-à-vis* were positively related to visual attentiveness, whereas for males the amount of *protesting* observed in the home was negatively associated with measures reflecting interest in visual stimuli. These findings were of marginal significance, but did support the results from the previous study. Thus there was continued evidence in this study that social experiences for the females and temperamental physiological predisposition, as indicated through state variables, in the males seemed to influence their respective visual behavior.

For the vocal conditioning procedure the infant was placed in an infant seat in a crib while an experimenter stood by the cribside. Infant vocalizations were counted during a base-line, reinforcement, and extinction phase in this experiment. The base-line phase consisted of the experimenter standing passively by the cribside; for the reinforcement stage the experimenter touched, smiled, and talked to the infant following each vocalization, and for the extinction phase the experimenter once again became nonresponsive. The vocalization scores of the infant for each of the three stages of this experiment were correlated with two of the home observation variables to determine whether behavior and interaction during these observations transferred to vocal behavior under laboratory conditions. The observation variables that were used in this analysis were the amount the infant vocalized in the home and the extent to which the mother contingently reacted to a vocalization from her infant by vocalizing in return (*maternal vocalization to infant vocalization*). This maternal behavior is analogous to the reinforcement behavior provided by the experimenter during the vocal conditioning procedure.

Analyses of these data in general showed that the amount male infant vocalized during the home observations was significantly correlated with the frequency of vocalizations during the experimental procedure for the base-line and reinforcement conditions ($r = .45$, $p < .01$ and $r = .35$, $p < .05$, respectively). On the other hand, for the female infants, maternal reinforcement of vocalizations during the home observations was the strongest predictor of vocal behavior in the conditioning procedure. In this case, the maternal reinforcement scores for the females were significantly correlated with the infant vocalization scores for the reinforcement and extinction conditions ($r = .29$, $p < .05$ and $r = .33$, $p < .05$, respectively).

These results again are consistent with the trends we had noted from our other data, which suggested that general temperamental characteristics of the male infants emerged as their most pervasive behaviors across situations, whereas manifestations of the social learning process were more salient for the female infants. It should be reemphasized that there were not significant differences between the sexes for most of these variables, but merely different correlational trends for the male and female infants.

We have attempted to trace sex differences in mother–infant behaviors from data collected over the last several years. In summary, the sex differences that we found were moderate, but not sufficient to characterize male and female infants in any categorical way. The magnitude and even the presence of these differences varied from sample to sample. Nonetheless, those sex differences that were present were consistent both as to the class of behaviors involved and the direction of the differences. Thus it seems reasonable to regard these sex differences as reflecting an existing phenomenon that may be evident only when certain external conditions occur. For instance, the tendency for greater irritability or aroused behaviors in males may depend on whether or not external conditions are favorable for insulating male infants with regard to their greater vulnerability. When differences occur, they are probably amplified over time through the stereotyped sex-role attitudes of parents, which evidently are present and functioning when the infant is very young.

REFERENCES

1. Moss, H. A., *Merrill-Palmer Quart* 13: 19, 1967.
2. Bell, S. M. and M. D. Ainsworth, *Child Dev* 43: 1171, 1972.
3. Moss, H. A. and K. S. Robson, *Child Dev* 39: 401, 1968.
4. Moss, H. A. and K. S. Robson, *Child Dev* 41: 509, 1970.
5. Moss, H. A., in book to be printed from a symposium on communication and affect, Plenum Press, New York, in press.
6. Rheingold, H. L., Gewirtz, J. L., and H. W. Ross, *J Comp Physiol Psychol* 52: 68, 1959.
7. Todd, G. A. and B. Palmer, *Child Dev* 39: 590, 1968.
8. Weisberg, P., *Child Dev* 34: 377, 1963.

CHAPTER 9

Sex of Parent x Sex of Child: Socioemotional Development

MICHAEL LEWIS and MARSHA WEINRAUB

Institute for Research in Human Development
Educational Testing Service
Princeton, New Jersey

We discuss in this chapter the general issue of the relationship between the infant and its parents as a function of gender. In this discussion we shall hold in abeyance the consideration as to the causes of these differential behaviors until after we have explored some of the data available. However, it would be worth keeping in mind the three major theoretical positions used to account for the observations: (1) the biological—genetic view of sex differences; (2) the social learning view—usually based on some differential learning-through-reinforcement paradigm; and (3) the cognitive view.

Ainsworth's (1) definition of attachment is useful as a starting point in our discussion: "Attachment behavior is behavior through which a discriminatory differential affectional relationship is established with a person or object. . . ." Observe that this is the standard definition; for example, Schaffer and Emerson (2) state that attachment is "the tendency of the young to seek the proximity of certain other members of the species."

These definitions have much in common and suggest several important problem areas. First, the behaviors that lead to this attachment effect are not described, although it has been suggested that both parental and infant behaviors act on one another; that is, both infant and parent become attached. Second, which specific behaviors are characteristics of an attachment are not made clear. This is especially important in light of the belief that, whatever these behaviors may be, they have to describe a *differential* relationship for the infant or parent. Under this definition such social behavior as smiling becomes impossible to classify as an index of attachment until one can demonstrate its differential use. In this case it is not a measure of attachment until the infant does not smile at everyone. This should alert us to part of the measurement problem in the study of attachment. Behaviors in themselves will not serve our purpose until we know their differential use; moreover, the same behavior at different times in the course of development will be subject to different interpretation.

These considerations are obviously germane to any discussion concerning both the measurement of individual differences in attachment and the stability of attachment over time. Before proceeding with the discussion it must be clear that the term "attachment" hereafter will refer to some underlying structure—let us call it a motive—whereas "attachment behavior" refers to some phenotypic behavior.

SITUATIONS

Situations that give rise to the measurement of attachment behavior between parent and child have characteristically grown out of the clinical tradition in which the child was separated from its parents (3, 4). It is no wonder then that the first and most prevalent method of studying attachment has been to observe infants' reactions to parents' absence. In the clinical situation, separation was observed in parentless children or in infants who spent time away from their parents because of hospital care. In the experimental situation, the mother leaves the infant alone in a strange setting. Observation of the degree of the infant's distress is a measure of its attachment to its parent. Experimental situations in which the child separates himself from its mother is an alternative method of observing its attachment (5, 6).

In any analysis of attachment behavior the distinction of the mother separating herself from the infant and the infant's separating itself from its mother must be kept in mind. These situations are quite dissimilar since they involve different degrees of control for the infant. While the infant can control the amount of separation from its mother (both in time and space) when it instigates the separation, it has little or no control when its mother instigates the separation. This distinction may have important consequences.

The separation of the infant from its mother under either situation—its moving from her or her from it—is not the only type of situation in which the attachment of the infant to its mother can be observed. It can be reasonably argued that attachment behaviors can be observed in a realistic setting in which the mother and infant are together. In this type of situation, attachment behavior is no longer measured by the infant's distress as a consequence of its mother's leaving but by its proximity to her or the amount of time it engages her in play. In fact, the degree of distress over its mother's departure may not be a true indicator of the child's attachment at all. It may instead be a measure of distress at the process of separation. This is an important distinction since many parents report the distress their child exhibits when the parent leaves and yet the perfectly wonderful time the child subsequently has with the baby-sitter. Separation can evoke a multitude of behavioral states, only one of them related to attachment. This distinction is more evident in a laboratory experiment, where the infant is often placed in an unfamiliar environment (it is not its home or that of someone it knows) devoid of most objects found in its home (toys, furnishings, etc.). The infant's reaction to the departure of the only familiar element may be extreme distress, but this might be more a measure of its response to novelty/threat than a measure of its attachment.

Distress to departure may be less representative of attachment than responses to return, especially after the child learns that distress will not prevent its mother's leaving. Eventually there is little attachment behavior (distress) when 2-year-olds are left by their mothers at a nursery, but a great deal of response when she returns. A child's response to its mother's leaving is subject to learning, whereas its response to her return seems less affected. If we recall that a necessary condition in the definition of attachment behavior is its differential occurrence, we might argue that the infant would show distress to anyone's leaving it in a novel situation. Thus its response to being left or to being in a new situation may not be a display of attachment behavior as much as exaggerated affiliative behavior derived simply from fear or anxiety.

We have found this to be the case (5). In a room unfamiliar to a sample of 1-year-old infants we observed such attachment behaviors as proximity to mother. Individual differences in attachment behavior were least in the opening minutes, with almost all of the infants spending similar amounts of time in proximity. Over time, individual differences emerged. Our explanation for this was that the anxiety caused by the novelty of the room produced initial affiliation, and not specific attachment. Because the observation period was relatively prolonged, it became possible to note individual differences in proximity as the anxiety diminished and attachment emerged. Even in this example, individual differences might not have been attributable to attachment differences exclusively, but to differential anxiety over novelty. Even the results showing more infant separation when toys were present in the room as compared to when none were available may be more a consequence of the diminution of novelty and subsequent anxiety than attachment; it is less novel for a room to contain some objects than for it to be empty (6).

This raises the additional problem that the nature of the situation may affect attachment behavior in another way. A rich-stimulus environment may elicit in the infant other motives that are sufficient to draw it from its mother. Without such an environment, the mother may be the most interesting object in its environment. Thus there are various and possibly conflicting motives within the infant: the desire to explore, experience, and assimilate new things—and the desire to stay near the mother. Depending on the situation, one could facilitate or inhibit any one of the motives or even induce the child to use its mother to satisfy several. The strangeness of an empty room increases the likelihood that the infant will stay with its mother. Is this proximity a function of attachment, lack of interesting stimuli, or anxiety to novelty?

The discussion so far has been concerned with how a given situation may be instrumental in affecting the observed results on attachment behaviors and attachment. It seems reasonable to conclude that attachment may be measured more directly in situations other than those in which the mother separates herself from her infant. Moreover, we have suggested that naturalistic situations—or as naturalistic as possible—may allow for a more accurate measure of attachment by reducing the occurrences of other sets of motives.

MEASUREMENT

The second issue in the study of individual differences in attachment and the stability of these differences over time is the nature of the measurement of attachment behaviors. We have already touched on this issue in our discussion of situations and recognize that any particular situation will limit the possible number of attachment behaviors to be measured. When the mother separates herself from her child, the measure of attachment may be the amount of protest or crying. Eye contact and regard also may be measured. Moreover, if the child is at all mobile, one may measure its attempts physically to follow its mother or place itself in proximity to her point of exit. A form of verbal communication, visual regard, and physical proximity therefore might all be examples of attachment behavior. Likewise, in situations other than maternal separation the same type of measure is available. The category "seeking the proximity of certain others" (2) can include a rather extensive list of behaviors, from protest or crying in an attempt to recall the mother to trailing the mother as she moves away.

It is clear that proximity to one's mother can take many forms and that to measure a single aspect of behavior may be misleading. Any single behavioral response can be used in the service of more than one structure (or motive), and multiple behaviors can be used in the service of the same motive. For this reason it would appear appropriate to measure a variety of infant responses in order to obtain a wide range of possible attachment behaviors. Although this would seem a reasonable approach, there are few experimental data on the relationship of multiple responses. Although a variety of infant behaviors have been recorded, few studies have examined relationships across measures (7, 8).

This lack of concern for relating multiple response measures is surprising since it would be unlikely that the same behaviors would have the same meaning—that is, be in the service of the same motive—over relatively long periods, especially when the period is one of rapid change. It would be naive to expect the infant, young child, and preschooler all to show the same attachment behavior, even assuming that the attachment motive remained unaltered. Yet insistence on observing a single measure may result in the erroneous conclusion that attachment falls off with increased socialization. For example, physical proximity decreases over age, but does this mean that attachment itself declines? One might be forced to this conclusion, having recorded physical proximity as the only measure of attachment behavior. In any experimental design, then, one should realize that multiple responses or differential response patterns at different ages are under the service of the same structure (or motive). This, of course, requires a more complex model of attachment, but one that is necessary for observing individual stability and change.

In a recent paper we argued for a transformational analysis of attachment behavior (9). Proximal behaviors (touching and staying in proximity) tended to be negatively correlated from one year to the next, whereas distal behaviors (looking and vocalizing) were positively correlated. Moreover, children who touched a great deal at 1 year of age tended to look a great deal at 2 years of age, suggesting that proximal attachment at 1 year is transformed into distal behavior at age 2. Thus it is obvious that different behaviors can be used to express the same needs and emotions at different ages. An infant who is hungry cries to signal its hunger. However, with age, crying decreases. Does this mean hunger, too, is decreasing? No, the child merely begins using other, more socially acceptable, means of expressing its hunger. Thus, like hunger, attachment may persist throughout life, but the behaviors used to express attachment may change. As it matures, the child develops greater competence in communication and mobility, and its desire for exploration increases. These changes and changes in the social demands from the environment may cause the child to relinquish proximal modes of behavior and to rely instead on more distal forms of behavior to maintain attachment relations.

INDIVIDUAL DIFFERENCES AS A FUNCTION OF SEX OF CHILD

It may be naive to expect that the transformation of attachment behaviors (i.e., from proximal to distal) over age follows the same pattern for all children. There may be important individual differences in the patterns of behaviors, depending, for example, on the sex of the child. Though males and females may form attachments of equal intensity, early sex differences in response to stimulation (10–13), differential mothering patterns (5, 14, 15), and divergent personality types in later childhood all suggest that the sexes may demonstrate attachment in different ways.

In the first few months of life boys receive more proximal stimulation, such as rocking and handling, and girls receive more distal stimulation, such as talking and looking from their mothers (14, 15). However, by 6 months of age, proximal stimulation toward boys has decreased (5). In our culture, adult communication between persons is limited to the distal modes of expression, proximal modes of expression being discouraged. In addition, there is even less tolerance of proximal expression for men than there is for women. Such behaviors expressed by men not only are viewed as incompatible with masculine independence but are also seen as connoting sexual interest if expressed toward a female or homosexual tendencies if expressed toward another male. Although all children are socialized to move from proximal to distal modes of relating to others, this socialization may occur earlier and more vigorously for boys than for girls. Thus girls would more likely be permitted to persist in their use of proximal behaviors, whereas boys would be pushed to rely more on the use of distal behaviors in their relationships with the parent.

In several recent studies (16, 17) we were able to replicate the finding, first reported by Goldberg and Lewis (5), that at 1 year of age girls show significantly more attachment behavior toward their mothers than boys in a low-stress free-play situation. These sex differences are found in both a middle-class (5) and a lower-class sample (17). In the Brooks and Lewis study of 1-year-old, opposite-sex twins (i.e., boys and girls with the *same* parents) girls again showed more attachment behavior. In addition, Bronson (18) and Maccoby and Jacklin (19) have reported similar results.

It is important to note that others—for example, Rheingold and Eckerman (6, 20), Ainsworth et al. (21–23), and Coates et al. (7)—have failed to find sex differences. This discrepancy is puzzling, and we recently have been trying to unravel its possible cause. We have centered our attention on four areas: time in the situation, size of the room in which the study took place, the furnishings of the room, and social class.

Time

In most of the studies conducted in our laboratory, the mother and infant are observed for 15 minutes. In many other studies, the observations lasted 3 to 10 minutes. Time in the room may affect sex difference attachment scores. We have recently analyzed the effects of time on attachment behavior exhibited to the mother (24). The data on over 80 infants indicate that, though there were no sex differences in attachment in the first 3 minutes, over a period of 15 minutes the characteristic differences appeared!

Size of Room

Many aspects of the room may be critical. Although it has not yet been explored, it seems quite reasonable to assume that rooms of different sizes and shapes can produce different attachment behaviors and account for the presence or absence of individual and group differences. If the sizes and shapes of tables either retard or facilitate communication (25, 26), might it not be the same for room size and shape? For example, a small room may reduce the need for proximal behavior and thus increase distal behavior. In addition, it may be that room size plays an important role in the interrelationship between the proximal and distal measures. In particular, it appears that large rooms may facilitate the distinctive feature of proximal and distal contact (result in stronger negative correlations) whereas smaller rooms may blur the distinction.

Toys in the Room

It is obvious that the objects in the room will exert an effect. Compare a room that is carpeted, full of toys, and has pictures on the walls with an empty room that has few or no toys and nothing on the walls. Such differences obviously might affect the results of an attachment study.

Under the latter condition, the infant's cognitive concern or even fear of the room's strangeness (i.e., compared with what it is used to) might seriously alter the attachment behavior. One might postulate that, under any strange or unusual condition, the child's *affiliative*, rather than *attachment*, behavior is elicited by its anxiety (see ref. 27 for a discussion of the relationship between anxiety and affiliation). Attachment and affiliation-like behaviors may appear the same, especially for proximity behaviors. A requirement of true attachment behavior is that it be unique between parent and child, and not be elicited between "others" and child. Proximity seeking in a threatening environment may occur with any adult figure, not just the infant's mother. Therefore it is not sufficient to observe behavior independent of the context in which it occurs. Proximity is not always a measure of attachment, especially in a threatening or stressful situation.

Social Class

The final dimension that might affect the results of a study on attachment is family social class background (itself a carrier of the parental attitudes toward the display of attachment behavior). In most studies the background of the subjects has not been mentioned. Coates (7, 28) indicated that his subjects were mainly from the upper middle class, professional, and we suspect that this may be true of many studies conducted in university communities. Thus another possible reason for the failure to observe consistent sex differences is comparison of samples from different social classes.

DEVELOPMENT OF ATTACHMENT IN THE FIRST 2 YEARS OF LIFE

Though sex differences of children in the expression of attachment have been studied, the issue of sex differences in the *object* of attachment has not. The mother is usually assumed to be the child's *first* object of attachment, but she is by no means the only one. Certainly the father plays a significant role in the socialization of the child; nevertheless, his role in the attachment process has been largely ignored in the literature. The study that we report here in some detail is an attempt to study the development of attachment from year 1 to year 2. In this longitudinal study, we examined the interrelationship between the sex of the child and the sex of the parent in the expression of attachment behaviors in the first 2 years of life.

Experimental Procedure

Ten male and ten female Caucasian, middle-class, 1-year-old infants (± 2 weeks) made two visits, a week apart, to the laboratory. On one visit the mother accompanied the child, and on the other, the father. The sample was so split that for half the subjects the mother accompanied the child on the first visit, and for the other half the father did. When the children were 2 years old (± 8 weeks, except for one male who was 2 years and 3 months old), all of the males and eight of the females returned to the laboratory. The children who came with their mother or father on the first visit at age 1 came with the same parent on the first visit at age 2. (Two exceptions were made for parental convenience.)

The play situations at 1 and 2 years of age were identical. The play-room was carpeted, approximately 3.3×4.0 m, and was divided into 12 squares (a 3×4 grid) by thin lines on the floor. A chair in one corner of the room was provided for the parent. Toys were placed in each of the squares except the three in the immediate vicinity of the parent.

Each subject, accompanied by its parent, entered the room. The parent sat on the chair and held the child on his or her lap. On signal (a tap on the observation window) the child was placed on the floor by the parent and was free to move about the room at will. The parent was instructed to watch the child's play and to respond as naturally as possible. However, the parent was told not to *initiate* any interaction. The child's play was observed for 15 minutes from behind a one-way mirror. Different observers at each year recorded on an event recorder four of the child's attachment behaviors: amount of time touching the parent, looking at the parent, vocalizing to the parent, and in the proximity of the parent. Proximity was scored when the child was within any of the four squares surrounding the parent's chair.

Each child was given a score for the cumulative number of seconds it spent touching, in the proximity of, looking at, and vocalizing to each parent at each age. To normalize the scores and stabilize the variance, $\log(x + 1)$ transformations of the four attachment-behavior scores were used in the statistical computations. Nonparametric tests also were performed and in most cases paralleled the parametric results.

Mean Frequency Data

Table 1 presents the mean amounts of time 1-year-old boys and girls touched, stayed in the proximity of, looked at, and vocalized to each parent. In the mean data there were no infant sex differences in the amount of expression of any of the four behaviors; rather, the difference

*Table 1   Mean Scores (in Seconds) of Attachment Behaviors Directed by
1-Year-Old Infants to Their Mothers and Fathers*

Mother-Directed Behavior	Boys (N=10)		Girls (N=10)	
	$\overline{X}$	SD	$\overline{X}$	SD
Touching	213.2	146.8	145.8	118.7
Proximity	595.6	191.3	597.6	205.9
Looking	57.9	23.9	62.6	30.4
Vocalizing	84.2	38.9	75.2	35.0
Father-Directed Behavior	Boys (N=10)		Girls (N=10)	
	$\overline{X}$	SD	$\overline{X}$	SD
Touching	105.4	118.8	58.6	65.4
Proximity	455.4	205.8	472.9	237.7
Looking	94.6	40.8	53.7	34.5
Vocalizing	62.8	56.4	48.6	35.5

occurred in the amounts of these behaviors directed to the mother or father. There was almost twice as much proximal behavior directed toward the mothers as toward the fathers ($F=8.53$, $df=\frac{1}{16}$, $p<.01$ for touching; $F=24.34$, $df=\frac{1}{16}$, $p<.001$ for proximity). In the distal mode, the differences between attachment scores as a function of sex of parent were less conspicuous. More vocalizing was directed toward the mothers ($F=5.57$, $df=\frac{1}{16}$, $p<.05$) by both boys and girls, but for looking there was an interesting interaction between sex of child and sex of parent ($F=9.93$, $df=\frac{1}{16}$, $p<.01$). Boys looked at their fathers significantly more than they looked at their mothers, whereas girls looked more at their mothers than fathers, although this was not significant. Thus, for girls, both proximal and distal behaviors favor mothers over fathers. For boys this is more complex: proximal behavior favors mothers, whereas looking, a distal behavior, favors fathers.

Table 2 lists the mean amounts of time boys and girls touched, stayed in the proximity of, looked at, and vocalized to each parent when the children were 2 years old. There were no significant sex-of-child differences in the mean amounts of behaviors expressed toward the parents. Nonparametric analyses also failed to show significant differences.

By age 2 the mean differences found at age 1 in the expression of attachment behaviors as a function of sex of the parent are no longer apparent. Indeed, there was a tendency for 2-year-old children to spend more time in the proximity of their fathers than their mothers ($F=3.55$, $df=\frac{1}{14}$, $p<.08$).

Figure 1 shows the change from age 1 to age 2 in the attachment

Table 2   Mean Scores (in Seconds) of Attachment Behaviors Directed by 2-Year-Old Infants to Their Mothers and Fathers

Mother-Directed Behavior	Boys (N=10)		Girls (N=8)	
	$\overline{X}$	SD	$\overline{X}$	SD
Touching	151.8	145.2	47.5	25.2
Proximity	488.2	163.7	497.3	139.3
Looking	112.7	42.0	113.8	40.3
Vocalizing	162.0	79.6	111.3	57.2
Father-Directed Behavior	Boys (N=10)		Girls (N=8)	
	$\overline{X}$	SD	$\overline{X}$	SD
Touching	135.9	156.0	47.9	17.9
Proximity	594.2	167.1	568.0	145.3
Looking	119.2	79.2	94.5	49.6
Vocalizing	152.9	112.7	84.1	25.6

behaviors expressed toward each parent. The total amount of proximal behavior—touching and proximity—decreased during the interval, although these differences are not significant ($F = 2.49$, $df = \frac{1}{17}$, $p < .13$; $F = 2.07$, $df = \frac{1}{17}$, $p < .17$, respectively). This was due to the different patterns as a function of the sex of the parent. Touching the mother tended to decrease (from a mean of 177.0 seconds spent touching the mother at 1 year to 99.6 seconds at 2 years of age; $F = 3.30$, $df = \frac{1}{17}$, $p < .09$), whereas touching the father tended to increase (from a mean of 82.0 seconds spent touching to 91.9 seconds; $F = 2.62$, $df = \frac{1}{17}$, $p < .12$). There was a significant interaction between sex of parent and age of child for the proximity scores ($F = 18.16$, $df = \frac{1}{17}$, $p < .001$). Proximity to the father increased (from a mean of 464.1 to 581.1 seconds; $F = 5.50$, $df = \frac{1}{17}$, $p < .03$), but proximity to the mother decreased, although not significantly (from a mean of 596.6 to 492.7 seconds; $F = 1.30$, $df = \frac{1}{17}$, $p < .27$). Although both distal behaviors expressed toward both parents increased significantly over age ($F = 10.55$, $df = \frac{1}{17}$, $p < .005$ for vocalizing; $F = 7.47$, $df = \frac{1}{17}$, $p < .01$ for looking), vocalizing increased more to the fathers than to the mothers ($F = 6.13$, $df = \frac{1}{17}$, $p < .02$).

Observation of touching and looking behaviors toward each parent over the two ages shows a rather interesting pattern. Proximal attachment behaviors expressed toward mothers decreased over age, whereas distal behaviors expressed toward mothers increased. This is consistent with the data of transformational analysis proposed in the Lewis and Ban (9) study. On the other hand, both proximal and distal behaviors expressed toward fathers increased over age. Although touching the father increased

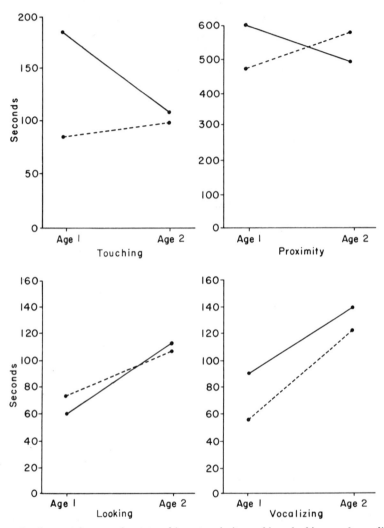

Figure 1 Amount in seconds of touching, proximity seeking, looking, and vocalizing directed toward mothers (solid lines) and fathers (broken lines) by their 1- and 2-year-old infants.

from age 1 to age 2, the levels at age 2 were about the same for both parents.

A Transformational Analysis: Across-Age Correlations

Table 3 presents the correlations between the four attachment behaviors for boys and girls expressed in the presence of each parent at 1 year of

Table 3 Across-Age Correlation Matrices for the Four Attachment Behaviors

A. Mother-Directed Behaviors

			Age 2			
			Touch	Proximity	Look	Vocalize
Touching	Boys[a]		−.29	−.22	.69**	−.04
		Total	−.09	.07	.54*	.09
	Girls[b]		.51	.81**	.28	.50
Proximity	Boys		−.32	−.19	.68**	−.09
		Total	−.08	.07	.44*	.01
	Girls		.37	.65*	.14	−.19
Looking	Boys		−.45	−.23	.69**	.09
		Total	−.35	−.23	.50**	−.07
	Girls		.15	−.34	.16	.54
Vocalizing	Boys		−.50	.02	.58*	.35
		Total	−.35	−.05	.58*	.31
	Girls		.27	−.28	.59	.25

B. Father-Directed Behaviors

			Age 2			
			Touch	Proximity	Look	Vocalize
Touching	Boys[a]		−.26	−.29	.48	.22
		Total	−.26	−.19	.42*	.25
	Girls[b]		−.45	−.01	.31	.35
Proximity	Boys		−.59*	−.32	.44	.42
		Total	−.31	−.27	.30	.47**
	Girls		−.02	−.24	.09	.65**
Looking	Girls		−.38	−.15	.49	.26
		Total	−.17	−.10	.38	.22
	Boys		−.35	.09	.24	−.10
Vocalizing	Boys		−.41	−.28	.19	.17
		Total	−.20	−.13	.13	.02
	Girls		.22	.13	−.02	−.59

*$p < .10$ (two-tailed).
**$p < .05$.
[a] Boys: $N = 10$.
[b] Girls: $N = 8$.

age and the same behaviors expressed by boys and girls at 2 years of age as well as the sexes combined.

In our use of the transformational analysis model we hypothesized that children would decrease their expression of proximal behavior (touching and proximity) but increase their expression of distal behavior (looking and vocalizing). The mean data showed some support for our predictions; namely, that there is a change from proximal to distal forms of behavior in the service of the attachment motive, and not necessarily a change in the strength of the motive itself. Of the four attachment behaviors measured in this study, touching and looking were probably the best measures of the attachment motive. Proximity behaviors may be affected by the position of the parents' chair near the exit of the room and the placement of the toys; vocalization may be affected by the child's developing language abilities independent of attachment. Hence we focus on touching and looking scores to find support for the transformational model.

Table 4 summarizes the data from Table 3 that most directly bear on this issue. If there is a transformation from proximal (i.e., touching) to distal (i.e., looking) modes of behavior in the expression of attachment, then this transformation should be indicated not only by the mean data but also by individual data in the form of correlations. Touching at 1 year of age should be unrelated to touching at age 2, but positively

Table 4   Transformations of Touching to Looking from Age 1 to Age 2

		A. Mother-Directed Behaviors		
Age 1	Age 2	Boys ($N=10$)	Girls ($N=8$)	Total ($N=18$)
Touch → Touch		−.29	.51	−.09
Touch → Look		.69**	.28	.54**
Look → Touch		−.45	.15	−.35
Look → Look		.69**	.16	.50**

		B. Father-Directed Behaviors		
Age 1	Age 2	Boys ($N=10$)	Girls ($N=8$)	Total ($N=18$)
Touch → Touch		−.26	−.45	−.26
Touch → Look		.48	.31	.42*
Look → Touch		−.38	−.35	−.17
Look → Look		.49	.24	.38

*$p<.10$ (two-tailed).
**$p<.05$.

related to looking at age 2. Indeed, for boys with their mothers, boys with their fathers, and for girls with their fathers, touching behavior at age 1 was negatively, though insignificantly, correlated with touching behavior at age 2 ($r = -.29$, $-.26$, and $-.45$, respectively), but positively correlated with looking behavior at age 2 ($r = .69$, $.48$, and $.31$, respectively). Moreover, in order to show that the transformation is unidirectional, we would expect looking at age 1 not to be related, or perhaps to be even negatively related, to touching at age 2. In fact, the correlations were in a negative direction. For the boys for both parents and girls for fathers, the correlation between touching at age 2 and looking at age 1 was $-.45$, $-.38$, $-.35$, respectively. Thus those groups of children who were high touchers at age 1 tended to become relatively low touchers but high lookers at age 2.

Our interpretation is that children who touched a great deal at age 1 were sufficiently attached to their parents to venture out securely into the environment when mobility increased. To maintain contact with the parent, distal forms of behavior were used. Though frequent touching may be indicative of attachment to the parent at 1 year of age, at age 2 frequent touching may be indicative of an insecure attachment and an inability to explore the environment in safety. Indeed, one 2-year-old boy in our sample clung to each of his parents nearly the entire time he was in the playroom with them. He was one of four children in the family and apparently had difficulty functioning independently. Another boy, who appeared very self-sufficient, had very low touching scores in the presence of his parents but very high looking scores. That children who look a great deal at age 1 continued to look a great deal relative to other children at age 2 (for children with their mothers $r = .50$, $p < .05$, and for children with their fathers $r = .38$), despite the overall increase in looking scores for all children, suggests that looking is a developmentally higher level of attachment expression and, as such, is relatively stable over age.

Although similar results were found for boys toward both parents and girls toward their fathers, the pattern of the girls' behavior toward their mothers was somewhat different. While touch at 1 year was positively correlated with look at age 2, touch at 1 year was more predictive of touch at 2 years. Thus the transformation of behaviors that took place for girls toward their fathers was not observed with girls toward their mothers. We strongly suspect that this lack of transformation involves the special attachment relationship that exists in this culture between a girl and her mother.

Further support for the transformation hypothesis is given in Table 3. For boys with both parents, eight out of eight correlations between touching at age 2 with all of the attachment behaviors at age 1 were negative, and eight out of eight of the correlations between looking at age 2 with the attachment behaviors at age 1 were positive. As already mentioned, girls with their mothers did not provide support for the transformational analysis. Touching at age 2, as well as looking, correlated positively with the four attachment behaviors at age 1. On the other hand, for girls with their fathers, three out of four correlations between touching at age 2 and the attachment behaviors at age 1 were negative, whereas three out of four correlations between looking and the attachment behaviors at age 1 were positive.

IMPLICATIONS FOR ATTACHMENT

The developmental pattern of attachment seems to be affected by the sex of both the parent and the child. Nevertheless, some broad statements concerning the overall pattern of the data will be made first, followed by qualifications depending on the sex of the child and sex of parent. It seems likely that there are at least two modes of behavior children use to express attachment: a proximal mode, which includes touching and maintaining proximity; and a distal mode, which includes looking and vocalizing. It seems likely that modes of behavior become increasingly differentiated with age (7, 9).

More important, the results provide strong support for the transformational analysis of attachment behavior suggested by Lewis and Ban (9). As they grow older, children change the behaviors they use to maintain contact with the parent. The mean data indicate that touching, a proximal behavior, tends to decrease from 1 to 2 years of age, whereas looking, a distal behavior, increases with age. Lewis and Ban (9) and Rheingold and Eckerman (20) have found similar results within the first two years of life; Maccoby and Feldman (8) found further decreases in proximity behavior and increases in distal behaviors (smiling, showing toys, and vocalizing) in the third year of life. We might suggest that distal behaviors like looking eventually undergo a further transformation; looking behavior gives way to thinking about the parents. Thus "what would my mother think of what I'm doing" may be the final transformation of an attachment expression that started with the infant and mother in a frontal–frontal full-body contact.

Two factors may be responsible for the transformation from proximal to distal expressions of attachment. With maturity and increasing mobility other motives, such as curiosity and exploration, begin to compete with attachment expression and force the child to use behaviors that will allow it to satisfy more than one strong motive. Hence the child "gives up," or sacrifices, touching its mother and substitutes looking at her, which more efficiently satisfies both its need to explore and its need to maintain contact. Thus, as it matures, the child begins to rely increasingly on distal behaviors to maintain attachment to its parent. In addition, the transformation from proximal to distal forms of behavior is consistent with changing social demands on the child. In our culture most parents wish to make their children as "independent" of them as possible and become impatient with, and embarrassed by, the child's clinging behavior. They then differentially reward different types of attachment behavior, pushing their children from them and encouraging distal forms of contact.

IMPLICATIONS FOR SEX DIFFERENCES

In contrast with earlier studies (5, 16, 17), we were unable to find mean differences attributable to the sex of child in the expression of attachment at either year 1 or year 2. Thus these data do not lend support to our earlier findings. The failure to replicate these sex differences is confusing. This has led us to speculate that the difference may be due to the social class composition of the present sample. In order to obtain fathers as well as mothers, it was necessary to use fathers who could take time off from work. This usually meant fathers who held professional or managerial positions. It appears that this may be a meaningful explanation since almost all of the studies that have not found mean sex differences have included primarily middle to upper-middle class, college-educated families in a university community.

The sex difference that does emerge from this study is related to important sex of child–sex of parent interactions in attachment behavior. Boys' attachment behavior shows similar patterns toward each of the parents. Proximal behavior at 1 year of age is transformed into distal behavior at 2 years of age. Thus at age 1 proximal behavior is an expression of attachment undifferentiated from distal behavior, but by age 2 proximal behavior is transformed into distal behavior, and distal behavior is increasingly relied on to express attachment toward both parents. This, we suggest, is a result of the fact that males in our society are discouraged from using proximal forms of behavior because these behaviors are incompatible with our emphasis on male independence and have come to have possible sexual or homosexual overtones.

Girls, however, show a very different developmental sequence of attachment behavior. Girls show a transformation from proximal to distal expression of attachment behavior with their fathers, but they do not show the same transformation of behaviors expressed toward their mothers. We believe that the reason girls do not change their mode of attachment toward their mothers is that females, unlike males in our society, are relatively free to express proximal behaviors toward other females. It is only with males, beginning early in life with their fathers, that girls must inhibit the expression of proximal behavior for fear of possible societal censure. This female–female proximal relationship may be maintained throughout life, from two girls dancing together on a teenage rock show, to women kissing one another, to old women holding onto each other. Men in our society must give up these proximal relationships. Thus the transformation of proximal relationships takes place in all conditions except female–female, where it is first seen in the mother–daughter relationship.

The general transformational model of attachment behavior must be modified to take into account the individual child's changing relationship with each of its parents. Proximal behaviors toward the mother tend to decrease, whereas distal behaviors increase. The child's relationship to the father is not as clear-cut. Although proximal attachment behavior to the mother seems to be decreasing, proximal attachment behavior to the father either increases or stays the same. In addition, distal behaviors to the father are increasing to a larger extent than these same behaviors are increasing to the mother. Nevertheless, by the second year there are no differences in the amount of behaviors directed toward mothers or fathers. We consider these findings evidence of the fact that the attachment bond to the father in the first year of life is weaker than the attachment bond to the mother. Though attachment in general is undergoing changes in the mode of expression, the attachment behavior to the father is increasing, so that by age 2 the child is equally attached to both parents.

The child's weaker attachment bond to the father than to the mother in the first year of life is understandable in light of the fact that the father's contact with the child is much less frequent and of a different nature than the mother's. The fathers in our study estimated that they spent approximately 15 to 20 minutes of play a day with their children. Since it is socially acceptable to spend time with your child, we assume that this may be an overestimation. In another study (29), fathers spent only 37 seconds a day talking to their infants. Though no estimate of time spent with the child was obtained from the mothers in our study, all of the mothers assumed major care-taking responsibility for the children. The length of time of parental involvement reflects what processes may be at work. In the first year of life most parent–child relationships center around the care-giving functions. These functions—feedings, changing, and the like—have been associated with traditionally female activities (as well as being proximal in nature), and hence fathers are reluctant to participate. However, as the child becomes older, certainly by the second year, more of the parent–child relationship centers around other than care-giving activities—for example, play. Fathers are then less reluctant to participate, and their interaction with their children increases. The expression of distal behaviors toward the father, especially looking, appears to be less affected by the reduced contact of fathers versus mothers in the first year. The fact that fathers may be more novel may contribute to looking-but-not-approaching behavior. By the second year attachment behaviors, at least those proximal ones that were initially weak, become stronger and approach the level found for the mother.

The sex of child × sex of parent differences in attachment behavior that we have found would appear to be culturally specific and seem to herald the kind of interpersonal behaviors that we observe in adults. There is no reason to suspect that these are universal interpersonal characteristics, or, for that matter, that they would hold for different ethnic groups. Rather, they seem to reflect the socialization processes wherein the young are initiated into the particular value of the subculture.

SEX OF CHILD × SEX OF SOCIAL OBJECT

At year 1, we observed a sex of child–sex of parent interaction such that infant boys looked more at their fathers than at their mothers, and girls looked more at their mothers than at their fathers. An analysis of the 2-year-old data reveals a similar pattern of sex of child–sex of parent interaction. There were three findings related to the child's play and attachment behavior (30):

1. The mean amount of time the child spends playing in the presence of a parent depends on the sex of the parent and the sex of the child. For example, an analysis of variance on time spent in sustained play indicated that girls showed more sustained play in the presence of their mothers than of their fathers, whereas boys showed no effect ($F = 5.16$, $df = \frac{1}{16}$, $p < .05$).

2. Boys seem to play independently of proximal contact with parents, whereas girls simultaneously play and maintain proximal contact. For example, the correlations between play behavior and touch and proximity for boys were $-.41$, $-.38$ toward mother and $-.34$, $-.53$ toward father; for girls they were $+.26$, $+.08$, $+.44$, and $.00$, respectively.

3. Distal behavior (eye regard) is related to play, but only when the child is with the like-sexed parent. The correlation between play and eye

regard for boys toward their fathers and mothers was .87 and .17, respectively; for girls it was −.07 toward their fathers and +.60 toward their mothers. This last interaction again centers around eye regard (this time during play) as a function of the sex of child and the sex of parent. Spelke and co-workers (31) have also found a similar interaction. Examining the vocalizations of 1-year-old infants to their mothers and fathers over a series of play and separation sessions, they found that infant boys vocalized significantly more to their fathers than to their mothers, whereas girls did the reverse.

The differential eye regard as a function of the sex of the infant and the sex of the social object being observed has been seen in two other studies. In the first (32) we showed a total of 54 infants, ranging in age from 10 to 18 months, pictures of the same-age infants of both sexes. Fixation time was obtained, and Figure 2 presents the results. The male infants look more at pictures of male infants than of female infants, but just the reverse is true for females ($F = 2.22$, $df = 22$, $p < .05$).

In another study eight sets of four 1-year-old infants and eight sets of four 1½-year-old infants, two male and two female, along with their mothers, were observed in a play situation. The data reveal that the infant boys look more at infant boys than at infant girls, whereas the reverse is true for girls.

Preferences for same-sex playmates have also been reported in the preschool literature (33–36). Muste and Sharpe (36) found that preschoolers display more aggressive behaviors in unisexual groups than they do in heterosexual groups. Langlois, Gottfried, and Seay (34), who observed 3- and 5-year-old children in same- and opposite-sex dyads, found that the 5-year-olds and the 3-year-old females exhibited more social behavior (smiling, touching, and talking as well as hitting) in the unisexual pairs. Preschool children also prefer to play with same-sex peers (33, 35).

Thus there is a growing body of data to indicate that the proximal and distal forms of contact with infants and their parents, and other social contacts are a function of the sex of the infant as well as the sex of the other.

THEORETICAL PERSPECTIVES AS EXPLANATIONS

Recall that we mentioned three theoretical positions that have been used in discussing the etiology of sex differences: social learning and reinforcement, biological, and cognitive.

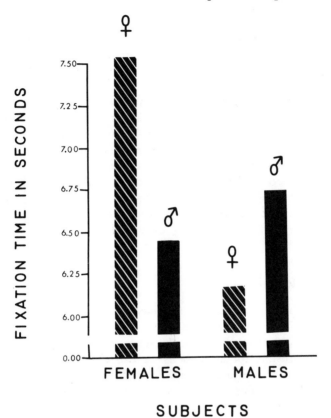

Figure 2   Mean fixation time in seconds as a function of the sex of the infant and the sex of infant pictured in the slide.

Social Learning

The social learning position most widely advocated in infancy is that of differential reinforcement. Under this schema the infant's behavior is shaped by the parent through the use of positive and negative reinforcement. Data to support this position usually come from general observations and studies that report how the mother and father act toward their child; for example, Goldberg and Lewis (5) reported that there was a significant relationship between how much the mother touched her child at 6 months and how much the infants touched their mothers when they were 1 year old. Implicit in the use of these data is the belief that the child's behavior is shaped through differential reinforcement patterns. Since girls receive more distal contact at all ages (14, 15) and more proximal contact after the age of 3 months (14)—the girls may receive more proximal contact before the age of 3 if proximal contact due to the child's upset is controlled—it is not unreasonable to attribute their greater display of proximal and distal contact as having to do with this differential early treatment.

Moreover, there is a great deal of casual as well as documented evidence that parents treat their children in very different ways as a function of their sex. For example, we (16) observed the dress of 17 pairs of opposite-sex twins brought into our laboratory. Of these, only one pair was dressed in identical outfits. Nine sets were wearing overalls, but sex could be identified by the color of the clothing: the girls wore pink, red, or yellow; the boys wore blue, green, or brown. The other seven pairs had been dressed so that the boys wore pants and the girls wore dresses. This differential parental behavior may explain the differences seen in the children.

Biological

Many other chapters in this volume have made the argument that the major source of variance between the sexes can be explained in terms of the biological differences between the sexes. However, for us the issue is still quite confusing, for as early as we can observe differential infant behavior, we can at the same time observe differential parental behavior. Let us look at an example. We have reported that infant girls as young as 12 weeks of age show greater attention to auditory stimulus than do the same-age boys, although there are no sex differences in visual attention (37). However, parent–infant interaction data on the same-age infants show that (1) girls are talked to more than boys by their mothers, and (2) when a girl vocalizes, her mother is more apt to respond with a vocalization than when a boy vocalizes (14). This being so, are girls more attentive because of some biological difference or is the biological difference influencing the mother's behavior, *or* is it affecting the infant differentially?

Is there any evidence that might suggest a more direct link between differences in biology and differences in the display of attachment? One factor leading the infant toward altering its mode of attachment expression may be the increased activity level of the developing infant. Motor development and the need to explore are in conflict with the proximity need, a conflict resolved by developing distal forms of contact. If we could find some relation between activity level and attachment expression, perhaps we could use this to argue for some biological bases of the reported sex differences. The data completely fail to support this hypothesis. We have not found any sex differences in activity nor any relationship within sex between activity level and attachment expression (5, 17, 24).

Surely we will not find the origins or cause of sex differences by observing the age of onset. If this is a question that is of scientific importance, we must look for other ways to deal with the issue. Individual differences should never be reduced to questions of either learning or biology. Rather, it seems that the question we need to ask is: Are there particular attributes we wish the child to have, and are there experimental conditions that will produce those attributes? Phrasing the argument in this fashion makes it possible both to look for these conditions and at the same time to get at the problem of the source and degree of variance.

Cognitive View

The third position is a view of the infant's cognitive capacities. The infant is not only acted on either by its biology or the differential reinforcement patterns of its caregivers; rather, the child itself, through its own cognitive structure, plans and executes its action. In dealing with sex-role-appropriate behavior, the cognitive position states that the child recognizes its gender and acts accordingly. In taking this position we must propose that the child can (1) differentiate the genders, (2) associate the cultural or familial behaviors that are deemed appropriate for the particular genders, and (3) recognize its own gender and therefore act appropriately. We have recently argued that such a position can be used for infants—children less than 2 years old (32, 38). Let us observe the three points necessary for the utilization of this theoretical approach.

Gender Differentiation. The study we have briefly reported concerning fixation differences indicates clearly that infants, at least by 9 months of age, can differentiate others on the basis of gender. Infants show differential fixation time as a function of the sex of the stimulus. In addition, 22-month-old infants tend to label pictures of male and female children with sex-appropriate terms.

Gender Identity. Gender identity also receives support from this study as well as others. The fact that the infants not only differentiated the sexes but showed a preference as a function of their own gender attribute lends some support to this view. In addition, the eye-regard data from the attachment study again show parental differentiation by the infants as a function of their gender. In the general case we would argue that every occurrence of a sex of infant–sex of social object interaction demonstrates the existence of a gender identity. Finally, additional support comes from Money's work (39) on hermaphrodites. If sexual identity is altered, children as young as 2 years are reluctant to alter their gender identity. Thus gender identity seems to be established within the first 2 years of life.

Gender-Role Patterns. The association of gender with appropriate role occurs so frequently within the culture that it would seem no surprise that the young child should be capable of this association. Moreover, given the infant's ability to label its own and other's gender, the child might well be actively seeking information about the gender-role associations.

We feel that the cognitive view of sex differences in infancy has, in fact, some support. At least the notion of gender saliency should be carefully considered. We are discovering that the infant is a more sophisticated information-seeking and information-processing organism than we have imagined. We should not be misled into believing that its intellectual capacities all await the display of language.

As we had anticipated, the data cannot be used to either confirm or refute the etiology of sex-role behavior. However, the data do indicate that, whatever the cause, the infant's socioemotional behavior early in life reflects its own gender as well as that of others.

ACKNOWLEDGMENTS

Our work was supported by grants from the Spencer Foundation and the Office of Child Development. We thank Jeanne Brooks for help with data collection and analysis.

REFERENCES

1. Ainsworth, M. D. S., *Merrill-Palmer Quart* 10: 51, 1964.
2. Schaffer, H. R. and P. E. Emerson, *Monogr Soc Res Child Dev* 29, No. 94, 1964.
3. Bowlby, J., *Int J Psycho-Anal* 39: 350, 1958.
4. Spitz, R., *Psychoanal Rev Child* 1: 53, 1945.
5. Goldberg, S. and M. Lewis, *Child Dev* 40: 21, 1969.
6. Rheingold, H. L. and C. O. Eckerman, *Science* 168: 78, 1970.
7. Coates, B., E. Anderson and W. W. Hartup, *Dev Psychol* 6: 218, 1972.
8. Maccoby, E. E. and S. S. Feldman, *Monogr Soc Res Child Dev* 37 (1, Serial No. 146), 1972.
9. Lewis, M. and P. Ban, paper presented at the Society for Research in Child

Development meeting, Minneapolis, April 1971, *Merrill-Palmer Quart,* in press.

10. Bardwick, J., *Psychology of Women,* Harper & Row, New York, 1971.

11. Kagan, J. and M. Lewis, *Merrill-Palmer Quart* **11:** 95, 1965.

12. Lewis, M., *Dev Psychol* **1**(2): 75, 1969.

13. Moss, H. A. and K. S. Robson, *Child Dev* **39:** 401, 1968.

14. Lewis, M., *Merrill-Palmer Quart* **18:** 95, 1972.

15. Moss, H. A., *Merrill-Palmer Quart* **13:** 19, 1967.

16. Brooks, J. and M. Lewis, paper presented at the Society for Research in Child Development meeting, Philadelphia, March 1973; *Child Dev.* **45:** 243, 1974.

17. Messer, S. B. and M. Lewis, *Merrill-Palmer Quart* **18:** 295, 1972.

18. Bronson, W. C., paper presented at the Society for Research in Child Development meeting, Minneapolis, April 1971.

19. Maccoby, E. E. and C. N. Jacklin, *Child Dev* **44:** 34, 1973.

20. Rheingold, H. L. and C. O. Eckerman, *J Exp Child Psychol* **8:** 271, 1969.

21. Ainsworth, M. D. S., in Foss, B. M. (ed.), *Determinants of Infant Behavior,* Vol. II, Methuen, London, 1963, pp. 67–112.

22. Ainsworth, M. D. S. and S. M. Bell, *Child Dev* **41:** 49, 1970.

23. Ainsworth, M. D. S., S. M. Bell, and D. J. Stayton, in Schaffer, H. R. (ed.), *The Origins of Human Social Relations,* Academic Press, London, 1971, pp. 17–57.

24. Brooks, J. and M. Lewis, Research Bulletin 73–55, Educational Testing Service, Princeton, N.J., 1973.

25. Altman, I. and W. W. Haythorn, *Behav Sci* **12:** 169, 1967.

26. Bass, B. and S. Klubeck, *J Abnorm Soc Psychol* **47:** 724, 1952.

27. Schachter, S., *The Psychology of Affiliation: Experimental Studies of the Sources of Gregariousness,* Stanford University Press, Stanford, Calif., 1959.

28. Coates, B., unpublished Ph.D. thesis, University of Minnesota, 1970.

29. Rebelsky, F. and C. Hanks, *Child Dev* **42:** 63, 1971.

30. Weinraub, M. and M. Lewis, unpublished manuscript, 1973.

31. Spelke, E., P. Zelazo, J. Kagan, and M. Kotelchuck, *Dev Psychol* **9:** 83, 1973.

32. Lewis, M. and J. Brooks, in Cohen, L. and P. Salapatek (eds.), *Perception in Infancy.* Academic Press, New York, in press.

33. Abel, H. and R. Sahinkaya, *Child Dev* **33:** 939, 1962.

34. Langlois, J. H., N. W. Gottfried and B. Seay, *Dev Psychol* **8:** 93, 1973.

35. McCandless, B. and J. Hoyt, *J Abnorm Soc Psychol* **62:** 683, 1961.

36. Muste, J. and D. Sharpe, *Child Dev* **18:** 11, 1947.

37. Lewis, M., H. McGurk, E. Scott and A. Groch, paper presented at the Eastern Psychological Association meeting, New York, April 1971.

38. Lewis, M. and J. Brooks, in Lewis, M. and L. Rosenblum (eds.), *The Origins of Fear,* Wiley, New York, in press.

39. Money, J., J. G. Hampson and J. L. Hampson, *A.M.A. Arch Neurol Psychol* **77:** 333, 1957.

Discussion: Early Mother-Child Interaction in Humans

RICHARD GREEN, Moderator

SUSAN COATES, Rapporteur

Dr. Hamburg expressed disappointment that Dr. Lewis had not presented examples of the pictures shown to the infants he had studied. Dr. Lewis described them as including only the head and the shoulders. Adults were unable to determine the sex of the infant in these pictures at a better-than-chance level. He suggested that infants may be aware of cues that adults do not perceive.

Dr. Zubin stressed the need for precise definitions of sex, commenting that none had so far been offered, despite the fact that sex-related behavior was the central focus of the conference. To emphasize methodological problems in the sex-difference field, he cited two commonly practiced errors in data analysis, one ecological and one clinical. The ecological fallacy is propagated by sociologists who infer differences on the basis of comparisons between the means of large groups. The clinical fallacy is propagated by those who infer differences by comparing small series or individuals. He underscored the need for definitive studies focused on sex differences based on large random samples rather than observations of differences culled indirectly from research primarily directed at other goals.

Dr. Galenson then asked Dr. Moss how he dealt with the conscious or unconscious effects of the infant's sex on the mother. Were maternal responses, either positive or negative, analyzed? Dr. Moss replied that he interviewed mothers to elicit their attitudes toward development, but he was not sure that the methods he used were effective in obtaining the type of data she referred to.

Dr. Michels questioned Dr. Lewis regarding the ages at which infant boys and girls are able to differentiate gender when looking at pictures. Dr. Lewis responded that girls appear to differentiate the sexes about 3 months earlier than boys do. Furthermore, females show the effect more strongly: the difference between females looking more at females than at males is greater than the difference between males looking more at males than at females.

Dr. Michels then referred to the cognitive model proposed by Dr. Lewis and suggested that, to be used most effectively, it would have to demonstrate a link in the infant's mind between boys and men, and between girls and women. He wondered if there were any data indicating that this was, in fact, the case. Dr. Lewis did not know. He then returned to an earlier remark of Dr. Zubin's, stating that he could find nothing untoward in analyzing data that had been collected for reasons other than to discover sex differences in behavior. He proposed that in the history of science this was probably a frequent procedure used to check hypotheses and generate new ones.

Dr. Zubin said he was referring to the possibility that only certain mothers would bring in their children for investigation, which might produce a bias. He commented that the the proposed cognitive model seemed Chomskian and suggested that Dr. Lewis utilized a cognitive factor in much the same way as Chomsky invokes a built-in mechanism for linguistic development. Dr. Lewis responded that his was not a nativist approach. The fact that a phenomenon occurs very early does not necessarily imply that it does not have a developmental course. He felt that the data could be considered from a developmental point of view and need not rely on a nativistic position.

Dr. Kohlberg asked if Dr. Lewis could be more specific as to what he meant by gender identity. He wondered if the finding that children seem to recognize people similar to themselves had the same connotation as an adult's concept of gender identity. He noted that if children preferred other children or adults with brown hair, one would not say they had "brown hair" identity. One would say they recognize some physical similarity between them. Dr. Lewis admitted that he might have to retreat from the concept of gender and agreed that there may be some specific attribute that children use to make the comparison.

Dr. Kohlberg then suggested that they might be making a self–other distinction. Dr. Lewis conceded that he was unable to study perception of gender directly except in his 20-month-old children, at which time he asked them to label according to gender. By this age he could obtain very significant and accurate differentiation of the gender of both young children and adults. He argued that if differentiation of gender was expressed in their early language, the perception was probably there prior to the capacity for speech.

Dr. Green wondered if Dr. Lewis ever showed children pictures of themselves. Dr. Lewis said he had and found that infants do not differentiate same-sex pictures from themselves, but only opposite-sex pictures.

Dr. Green reiterated that children might be making a self–other distinction rather than labeling male and female gender. Dr. Lewis agreed that the attribute by which the distinction was being made was still unidentified.

Ms. Ullian suggested that it might be interesting to present some pictures with diversified attributes. She described the observations of one of her colleagues, who, when varying dress style and length of hair, found that the ability to conserve gender identity fluctuated prior to age 5 or 6.

4 Development of Sex Differences in Behavioral Functioning

MICHAEL LEWIS, *Moderator*

ZIRA DeFRIES, *Rapporteur*

CHAPTER 10

Methodological Considerations in Studying Sex Differences in the Behavioral Functioning of Newborns

ANNELIESE F. KORNER

Department of Psychiatry
Stanford University School of Medicine
Stanford, California

The preceding chapters have clearly shown that the development of behavioral sex differences has both biological and experiential roots. Although we know, in general terms, that genetic, hormonal, and experiential factors all contribute to the development of behavioral sex differences and the formation of gender identity, we know little about the relative contribution of each to any given sex-linked trait. We also have very little knowledge of when behavioral sex differences begin to emerge and under what influences.

The literature amply documents that environmental influences on gender-identity formation begin early, are strong, and are persistent. Perhaps the only time one can study behavioral sex differences that are relatively uncontaminated by sex-related differential experience is right after birth, when differing maternal treatment will not as yet have had

197

much chance to have an impact. It is during the newborn period that behavioral sex differences can more safely be attributed to genetic and/or hormonal factors than at any later time.

In this chapter I summarize what behavioral sex differences we and other investigators have found among newborns. I also discuss some of the methodological and intrinsic problems involved in studying behavioral sex differences in newborns and why these differences are so elusive and difficult to replicate. I conclude by outlining some of the areas that may be fruitful for consolidating what little knowledge we have about behavioral sex differences in newborns and some totally untapped areas where we might possibly find such differences in the future.

BEHAVIORAL SEX DIFFERENCES IN NEWBORNS

I recently reviewed the literature on behavioral sex differences in newborns and found the evidence to be quite sparse (1). One remarkable finding of this survey was the fact that, whenever sex differences were found in behavioral studies, they repetitively occurred in certain target areas. It is the cumulative evidence of these studies, rather than the results of any single study, that makes me think that the differences found are really valid.

Judging from this cumulative evidence, the female tentatively emerges as more receptive to certain types of stimuli and as orally more sensitized. There is also suggestive evidence that the male may be endowed from birth with greater muscular vigor and physical strength. Let me review the evidence.

The results of several studies suggest that the female may have greater tactile sensitivity. For example, Bell and Costello (2) found females to be more responsive to the removal of a covering blanket and to an air-jet applied to the abdomen. Wolff (3), in a longitudinal study of a small sample of infants, observed that 2-week-old girls were more sensitive to skin contact than boys. Lipsitt and Levy (4) found significantly lower electrotactual thresholds in females than in males.

No sex differences have been noted either in auditory receptivity or hearing (5–7). By contrast, the female's response to photic stimulation appears to be significantly faster than the male's. Engel, Crowell, and Nishijima (7) tested the mean photic latency of Oriental, Caucasian, and Black neonates and found significantly shorter latencies in females in each of the three races. These data are of course psychophysiological rather than behavioral in character. We have found no behavioral sex differences in the more active visual behaviors, such as the tracking of a

moving stimulus, the frequency and duration of the state of visual alert-
ness, or in the visual responsiveness evoked by maternal types of min-
istrations (6, 8).

Female newborns appear to be more responsive to sweet taste, which is
the first of several examples that they are what I called orally more
sensitized. Nisbett and Gurwitz (9) found that, when females were given
sweetened formula, they increased their consumption of milk significantly
more than did males. Females were more responsive to the taste of the
formula at each body-weight level tested. This finding, by the way, has
striking parallels with findings in the animal literature. Consistently,
female rats consume more saccharin and glucose solutions than do males
(10, 11).

Balint (12), who also studied feeding behavior, found that during
bottle feeding females showed a quivering, rhythmical clonus of the
tongue much more frequently than did males. In one of our studies (1)
we analyzed 32,000 ft of film taken for purposes of data collection. The
film consisted of 16 time samples that were identical in length and in the
interval since the last feeding for each infant. Our film analysis included
counts and sequences of a large number of oral and activity measures.
In looking at the film we were struck by the fact that infants differed in
their approach behavior in coordinating hand and mouth in attempts at
finger sucking. Some infants coordinated the hand to the mouth, and the
mouth opened only on contact with the hand. In others, the mouth
approached the hand, with the head straining forward to meet the hand.
A systematic analysis of these behaviors showed that females engaged in
significantly more mouth searching than did males ($F = 8.01$, df 1, 90,
$p < .01$).

We also studied the spontaneous discharge behaviors that occurred
during various sleep states in these infants. We found highly consistent
sex-related trends in the types of discharges, but these were, at best, of
only marginal statistical significance (13). Wolff (14), who was the first to
monitor these spontaneous behaviors, postulated that since no known
stimulus evokes them, they may represent the discharge of a neural energy
potential, which occurs in inverse proportion to the degree of afferent
input. In our study (13), spontaneous startles, erections, reflex smiles, and
episodes of rhythmical mouthing were monitored during 2 hours and 20
minutes, divided into six observation periods. The mean hourly rate for
each of these spontaneous behaviors was calculated for each of three
sleep states: regular sleep, irregular sleep, and drowsing. In each state the
mean hourly rate of startles by males exceeded that of females ($p < .10$).
By contrast, females exceeded in reflex smiles and rhythmical mouthing
in each of the states in which these behaviors occur. Since the overall rate

of spontaneous discharge behavior was almost identical for males and females when erections were excluded, it appears that females make up in smiles and rhythmical mouthing what they lack in startles. If indeed these behaviors represent the discharges of a neural energy potential, it would seem that females tend to discharge this potential more frequently via the facial musculature, particularly of the mouth region, whereas males tend to discharge it more frequently through total and vigorous body activation.

Our finding that females engage in more frequent reflex smiles than do males finds confirmation in observations by Freedman (15). In our sample, the rate of reflex smiles during irregular sleep was almost triple that of males ($p < .06$). Even though the hourly rate of rhythmical mouthing was almost twice as large in females as in males, this difference was not statistically significant.

Observations made by Bell and Darling (16) suggest that males may be endowed from birth with greater muscular strength. They found that boys, when put in the prone position, were able to lift their heads higher than girls. This ties in well with the fact that males are on the average larger and heavier than females from birth on (17). Possibly, our finding that the male tends to startle more frequently with the total body activation that this entails, may also be interpreted as an indication of greater muscular vigor.

This sums up the number of behavioral sex differences I could find reported for neonates. I should like to discuss next some of the methodological problems involved in studying behavioral sex differences in newborns. As we shall see, a few of these difficulties could be avoided, whereas others are very much intrinsic to the substantive aspects of the problem.

METHODOLOGICAL AND INTRINSIC PROBLEMS

One problem that may obscure sex differences that might exist or create the appearance of sex differences that are not genuine is the fact that in North America, where most of the behavioral research with neonates is done, male infants are usually circumcised during the first 4 postnatal days. To avoid possible confounding of the results due to circumcision, some investigators of neonatal behavior use only female subjects in their studies, which automatically precludes their finding any sex differences. In the past, it has been our practice to include only those males in our studies who either were uncircumcised at the time or who were circumcised at least 24 hours prior to observation. We do not know whether this interval is sufficient, but hopefully we shall know soon, as I shall outline. There are two published studies on the effects of circumcision on the behavior of the infant. The effects were markedly different in the two studies, but so were the techniques of circumcision. Emde et al. (18) found both through behavioral and polygraph observations that during the 24 hours following a Plastibel type of circumcision, a large majority of the subjects showed increases in quiet, non-REM sleep. These increases ranged between 41 and 121%. The Plastibel type of circumcision is done by chronic ligature, resulting in a progressive necrosis of the foreskin that takes several days. Emde et al. (18) interpreted their results as consistent with a theory of conservation-withdrawal in response to stressful stimulation. Chalemian and Anders (19), by contrast, noted shifts only in the waking states following a Gomco bell type of circumcision. During an hour after circumcision, significant increases in fussing and crying were noted, and during an hour after the next feeding, significant increases in wakeful activity occurred. The differences in the results of these two studies undoubtedly are partly a function of differences in observation periods and procedures, and partly a function of the differences in circumcision technique. In contrast to the Plastibel type of circumcision, the Gomco bell type of circumcision is an acute procedure lasting no more than 10 minutes. Even though the results of these studies differ, it is clear from both of them that any study of sex differences in neonates dealing with differences in state behavior and arousal will need to control for the effects of circumcision.

We are currently starting a study of circumcision effects in connection with a large program of assessing the ontogeny of motility and crying patterns in premature and full-term infants. This will be done with the help of a monitor, developed in our laboratory, that provides for an indefinite period of time activity counts, the distribution of rest–activity cycles, cumulative crying time, and the durations the infant is attended by a caregiver (20). There are several unique features about this apparatus as compared with monitors developed by others. For one, it discriminates between large-, medium-, and small-amplitude motions and thus provides data regarding the vigor or the style of an infant's movements. It is also the only monitor that, in addition to providing counts of the infant's total motions, gives separate counts of movements that are not confounded by the infant's crying. We felt it was important to get a measure of noncrying activity because heretofore the measures of activity obtained were, in part at least, a function of the infant's relative irritability and therefore not highly predictive and very much subject to the differential promptness of maternal care. The latter was well documented in a study by Sander et al. (21), which demonstrated that infants in a rooming-in situation moved significantly less than infants given routine nursery care. In our first monitor study (22), we found that an infant's crying is indeed highly contributory to its total activity scores. Thus we hope, by measuring noncrying activity in addition to total activity, to obtain a stabler, more predictive measure than has been traditionally obtained.

We are doing a study of circumcision effects on the activity and crying patterns of newborns not only because we are intrinsically interested in the problem but also because such a study is an absolute methodological necessity if we are to study sex differences in activity and crying and if we are to compare infants in general. At Stanford, only the acute Gomco bell type of circumcision is practiced. We shall be interested in finding out whether there is an effect of the circumcision on our measures, and if so, what the wear-off time is.

Another problem in the study of sex differences that is minimal in the case of newborns but is nevertheless present is the differential treatment of males and females right from the start. We not only know from the work of Lewis (23), Moss (24), and others that parents interact with their offspring differently depending on the infant's sex, but we are beginning to learn that this process begins immediately after birth. Thoman, Leiderman, and Olson (25) found that primiparous mothers, at least, talk to and smile at their baby girls significantly more during hospital feedings than they do with boys. Parke, O'Leary, and West (26), who observed the interaction of both parents with their firstborn before the infant was 48 hours old, found that both parents touched male babies significantly more than female infants. Although I do not believe that much learning takes place in the first 2 or 3 days of life, it is nevertheless noteworthy that a sex-related trend of parent–infant interaction, similar to that prevailing in later months, begins as soon as the baby is born. Why is this the case? Certainly stereotyped sex-role expectations on the part of the parents cannot fully account for this. Is it possible that behavioral sex differences within the infants exert a subtle influence on the parents, evoking differences in response? This seems quite plausible.

Another problem in studying behavioral sex differences in newborns is more conceptual in nature and therefore more avoidable. When sex differences are found in one behavior and not in another that seems to be in the same area as the first, the conclusion is often reached that the significant finding is spurious and therefore probably not valid. For example, the fact that male newborns are larger, can lift their heads higher, and rely heavily on total body activation in the form of spontaneous startles leads to the expectation that males are generally more active. This is not the case, at least during the newborn period. Numerous studies, some of which have used large samples of neonates, have failed to show significant differences in spontaneous activity between males and females (22, 27–30). In one of our film studies (29) we analyzed separately small, small multiple, global, and diffuse motions, and none of these was more relied on by either sex. Also, our recent monitor study (22) revealed no differences between the sexes in the frequency or the median amplitude of movements.

Similarly, just because females engage in more rhythmical mouthing during sleep (which is probably of neural origin), seek more frequently to establish hand-to-mouth contact with the mouth searching for the hand rather than coordinating the hand to the mouth, and consume significantly more sweet formula when given a chance, this does not mean that they excel in every other behavior with oral connotation. For example, there are no significant sex differences in the frequency, rate, or amplitude of ordinary, nonrhythmical spontaneous sucking, in sucking on pacifiers or for food (29, 31, 32). This type of sucking is strongly influenced by the overriding and sex-unrelated biological function of hunger (29, 31) and by high arousal (33). Also, there appear to be no sex differences in any of the oral behaviors that rely heavily on the activity level of infants since the frequency of movements is not related to sex. Thus we found no significant differences in the frequency of hand-to-mouth contacts, of finger sucking, nor in the efficiency or perseverance of these behaviors (29, 34).

From these examples it is clear that one should not expect morphologically similar behaviors to have the same relation to gender. Totally different principles may be underlying what superficially may seem to be very similar behaviors.

Another problem in studying behavioral sex differences is that they emerge at different stages of development and that their presence at one stage does not guarantee that they are manifest throughout ontogeny. Frequency of crying is a good case in point. For example, Moss (24) found that males cried a great deal more at 3 weeks and 3 months of age than did females. Yet a host of studies failed to find such differences at birth (see, for example, refs. 29, 35, 36). Also, the literature both on animals and humans amply testifies to the male's greater activity level, and yet this has not been documented for newborns. Similarly, with visual behavior, although almost all studies fail to show a significant sex difference in attentiveness for newborns, Moss and Robson (37) found males to have significantly longer visual fixation times at age 3 weeks and 3 months, and Kagan et al. (38) found this to be the case in 4-month-old infants. A variety of factors, singly and in combination, may be responsible for this phenomenon. In the case of activity, circumcision effects may be one such factor. The cumulative effects of differences in mother–infant interaction according to sex undoubtedly is another heavily contributing factor. Purely speculatively, one factor that may also contribute to sex differences becoming manifest at different stages of development may have to do with the hormonal influences responsible for sexual differentiation *in utero*. As Hamburg and Lunde (39) have pointed out, these hormones may sensitize the organism's central nervous system in such a way that sex-linked behaviors will emerge even at a later time when the circulation of these hormones is no longer detectable within the system. It is conceivable that the behaviors so affected may have different time tables when they become more strongly expressed in one sex than in the other.

FURTHER RESEARCH STRATEGIES

One of the simplest ways of expanding our knowledge of behavioral sex differences in neonates is by routinely analyzing all data on newborns for sex differences. It is surprising how frequently this is not done. This omission is difficult to understand, other than perhaps in the light of bias to the effect that all behavioral sex differences are the product of differential cultural expectations and experience, and therefore could not possibly exist in newborns. Such a bias not only makes for missed opportunities for increasing knowledge about innate sex differences but leads to the methodological error of automatically pooling data on males and females whether warranted or not.

In addition to routinely analyzing for sex differences, replication studies should be done of those studies that reveal behavioral sex differences in newborns. From past studies we are alerted to certain target areas in which we may find such differences. They are primarily in the areas of cutaneous sensitivity, muscular vigor, and oral sensitization. Such replication studies should of course use the same or very similar methodolgy. We recently completed data collection in a study of sleep–wake cycles of newborns in which we hope to replicate some of our previous findings regarding the sex differences in startles, rhythmical mouthing, and reflex smiles. One finding that replicates our previous observations is very clear even without statistical data analysis: males startle more during various sleep states than do females. One of the most important studies needing replication is Nisbett and Gurwitz's study (9), which showed that females, when given sweetened formula, increase their milk consumption significantly more than do males. If the reasons for this are similar to those responsible for female rats consuming significantly more glucose and saccharin solutions, then we may have an example where the hormones responsible for the sexual differentiation *in utero* may have sensitized the organism in such a way as to bring about postnatal behavioral effects.

Although the hormones responsible for the female rats' higher consumption of glucose are primarily estrogens, Zucker (40) and Wade and Zucker (11) found that secondarily there is a suppressive effect from testicular secretions on male consumption.

One reason the study of sex differences frequently does not yield significant results is the considerable overlap between males and females with regard to most behaviors. In fact, I cannot think of any behaviors that are exclusively male or female other than those directly associated with the reproductive function. Since the means of the two populations are similar with regard to the majority of neonatal variables, it might be fruitful to assess routinely whether there are differences in the distribution curves of various behavior scores between the sexes. If the patterns of behavioral variables bear any resemblance to the patterns of a number of biological growth parameters, one would expect significantly more variability among males than among females (41). It seems conceivable that in the study of activity, for example, males may be overrepresented in the top frequencies even when the mean differences are not statistically significant. The routine assessment of differences in variability and spread of scores may thus be a very rewarding approach to the study of behavioral sex differences in newborns.

Another important dimension that may reflect behavioral sex differences not yet investigated in the newborn is the stability of behavior. Behavioral stability can be expressed either in day-to-day self-consistency or in long-range developmental terms. Again, if behavioral development parallels physical development, one would expect greater long-range predictability for females. Acheson (41), who reported on skeletal maturation, stated that in almost every respect the physical development of the female is more stable than that of the male. With regard to day-to-day stability of behavior, if females were found to be more self-consistent, this would not only be an interesting finding by itself but would also have important implications for the way the infant may experience itself and its environment and for the beginning mother–infant relationship. Self-consistency and predictability in the experience of internal events such as hunger, elimination, sleepiness, and restlessness should enhance the development of internal sets of expectations and of the anticipatory functions. Likewise, predictability and the expression of regularity of behavior greatly facilitate communication between mother and child. Predictable infants are probably much easier to raise in that the caregiver can more easily identify and anticipate the infant's needs. The clinical and research literature amply documents that unpredictability in the basic biological functions and the behavioral expression of these can have a very disorganizing effect on the mother, her care-giving efforts, and her self-confidence. Behavioral unpredictability in infancy is also associated with developmental deviations in later life; for example, Thomas, Chess, and Birch (42) found in a longitudinal study that children who developed behavior disorders were infants who, among other early deviations, were highly unpredictable and irregular in their functioning. The study of self-consistency and predictability of behavior in the newborn and a comparison of the sexes in this dimension may thus be a very fruitful avenue for studying behavioral sex differences. If males were found to be less stable in their behavior, this would help explain the well-known fact that, later in childhood, males strongly predominate in the incidence of behavior disorder and other developmental deviations.

Finally, there is yet another untapped avenue through which behavioral sex differences in newborns can and should be studied. Kagan (43) observed from two longitudinal studies that much of the time males and females have similar mean scores and standard deviations, but that the patterns of intercorrelations among the variables are different. Kagan suggests that the sexes may have different response patterns even though the characteristics of males and females taken singly may not differ much. Very little is known about sex differences in the organization of responses or, for that matter, in the clustering of behaviors. For example, low sensory thresholds may be associated with hyperactivity more frequently in males and with motor inhibition in females. With sex differences in the patterning of the neonate's characteristics, differences in subjective experience will ensue. When one adds to this the effects of differing parental reinforcement of the infant's behavior, or clusters of behavior, in line with traditional sex-role expectations, plus the effect of the infant's response to these expectations, one can catch a glimpse of the infinite diversity of influences that feed into the development of later behavioral sex differences.

ACKNOWLEDGMENT

The preparation of this manuscript and the author's research reported here were supported by a grant (HD-03591) from the National Institute of Child Health and Human Development, U.S. Public Health Service.

REFERENCES

1. Korner, A. F., *J Child Psychol Psychiatr* **14:** 19, 1973.
2. Bell, R. Q. and N. Costello, *Biol. Neonatorum* **7:** 335, 1964.
3. Wolff, P. H., in Foss, B. M. (ed.), *Determinants of Infant Behavior*, Methuen, London, 1969, p. 113.

4. Lipsitt, L. P. and N. Levy, *Child Dev* **30:** 547, 1959.

5. Eisenberg, R., personal communication, January 6, 1972.

6. Korner, A. F., *Percept Mot Skills* **31:** 499, 1970.

7. Engel, R., D. Crowell, and S. Nishijima, in *Felicitation Volume in Honour of C. C. DeSilva*, Kularatne and Company, Ceylon, 1968, p. 1.

8. Korner, A. F. and E. B. Thoman, *J Exp Child Psychol* **10:** 67, 1970.

9. Nisbett, R. E. and S. B. Gurwitz, *J Comp Physiol Psychol* **73:** 245, 1970.

10. Valenstein, E. S., J. W. Kakolewski, and V. C. Cox, *Science* **156:** 942, 1967.

11. Wade, G. N. and I. Zucker, *Physiol Behav* **4:** 935, 1969.

12. Balint, M., *J Genet Psychol* **73:** 57, 1948.

13. Korner, A. F., *Child Dev* **40:** 1039, 1969.

14. Wolff, P. H., *Psychol Issues* **5:** Monograph 17, 1966.

15. Freedman, D. G., in Monks, F. J., W. W. Hartup, and J. DeWit (eds.), *Determinants of Behavioral Development*, Academic Press, New York–London, 1972, p. 121.

16. Bell, R. Q. and J. F. Darling, *Child Dev* **36:** 943, 1965.

17. Garai, J. E. and A. Scheinfeld, *Genet Psychol Monogr* **77:** 169, 1968.

18. Emde, R. N., R. J. Harmon, D. Metcalf, K. L. Koenig, and S. Wagonfeld, *Psychosom Med* **33:** 491, 1971.

19. Chalemian, R. J. and T. Anders, *APSS Abstr*, 1972.

20. Korner, A. F., E. B. Thoman, and J. H. Glick, *Child Dev*, in press. December 1974.

21. Sander, L. W., G. Stechler, P. Burns, and H. Julia, *J Child Psychiatr* **9:** 103, 1970.

22. Korner, A. F., H. C. Kraemer, M. E. Haffner, and E. B. Thoman, *Child Dev*, in press. December 1974.

23. Lewis, M., *Merrill-Palmer Quar* **18:** 95, 1972.

24. Moss, H. A., *Merrill-Palmer Quar* **13:** 19, 1967.

25. Thoman, E. B., P. H. Leiderman, and J. P. Olson, *Dev Psychol* **6:** 110, 1972.

26. Parke, R. D., S. E. O'Leary, and S. West, *Proc 80th Ann Convention APA*, 1972, p. 85.

27. Brownfield, E. D., *Dissertation Abstr* **16:** 1288, 1956.

28. Campbell, D., *Biol Neonatorum* **13:** 257, 1968.

29. Korner, A. F., B. Chuck, and S. Dontchos, *Child Dev* **39:** 1145, 1968.

30. Pratt, K. C., *J Soc Psychol* **3:** 118, 1932.

31. Hendry, L. S. and W. Kessen, *Child Dev* **35:** 201, 1964.

32. Dubignon, J., D. Campbell, M. Curtis, and M. W. Partington, *Child Dev* **40:** 1107, 1969.

33. Bridger, W. H., *Rec Adv Biol Psychiatr* **4:** 95, 1962.

34. Korner, A. F. and H. C. Kraemer, in Bosma, J. F. (ed.), *Third Symposium on Oral Sensation and Perception: The Mouth of the Infant*, Charles C Thomas, Springfield, Ill., 1972, p. 335.

35. Korner, A. F. and E. B. Thoman, *Child Dev* **43:** 443, 1972.

36. Fisichelli, V. C. and S. Karelitz, *J Pediatr* **62**: 724, 1963.
37. Moss, H. A. and K. S. Robson, *Child Dev* **39**: 401, 1968.
38. Kagan, J., B. A. Henker, A. Hen-Tov, J. Levine, and M. Lewis, *Child Dev* **37**: 519, 1966.
39. Hamburg, D. A. and D. T. Lunde, in Maccoby, E. E. (ed.), *The Development of Sex Differences*, Stanford University Press, Stanford, Calif., 1966, p. 1.
40. Zucker, I., *Physiol Behav* **4**: 595, 1969.
41. Acheson, R. N., in Falkner, F. (ed.), *Human Development*, Saunders, Philadelphia, 1966, p. 465.
42. Thomas, A., S. Chess, and H. C. Birch, *Temperament and Behavior Disorders in Children*, New York University Press, New York, 1968.
43. Kagan, J., *Change and Continuity in Infancy*, Wiley, New York, 1971.

CHAPTER 11

Stages in the Development of Psychosexual Concepts and Attitudes

LAWRENCE KOHLBERG

Laboratory of Human Development
Harvard University
Cambridge, Massachusetts

DOROTHY ZELNICKER ULLIAN

Laboratory of Human Development
Harvard University
Cambridge, Massachusetts

In 1966, a cognitive-developmental analysis of children's sex-role concepts and attitudes was reported (1). The first part of this chapter essentially summarizes that theory and data. The first real study based on this approach since that time is reported in the second part of this chapter.

Basically, the original approach was simple: to study the development of sex-role concepts at face value rather than as indicators of something underlying them, such as identification, masculinity, or personality characteristics. Concepts of sex roles, whatever else they may be, are concepts, and so should undergo the transformations with development that Piaget (2) found in the development of conceptualizing physical objects.

As concepts change in development, so do the attitudes associated with them. Most research on children's psychosexuality formerly focused on either sex differences in behavior, on attitudes, or on measures of masculinity/femininity.The significance of these parameters is not clear. In some cultural settings or for some individuals, a given sex difference might be extremely significant, but for others, it is not. Much research utilized an implicit value that needed questioning: that it was good or mentally healthy for boys to be masculine and for girls to be feminine. This seemed to be a cultural stereotype rather than a scientific notion. Data, except in extreme circumstances, showed no empirical relationship between objective measures of masculinity/femininity and measures of mental health and adjustment.

To search for something meaningful in this area, it would seem that one should start with what was important to the child itself. Not all elements of sex differences or masculinity/femininity are significant for the child; however, one factor clearly is: its gender identity—the sheer fact that it is a boy or a girl. If you doubt that, imagine your reaction if your gender were suddenly transformed. Actually such a transformation has happened to children against their will. The subjects studied by Money and Hampson (3) were hermaphrodites, hormonally of one sex but with some or all of the external genital characteristics of the opposite sex. At various points in childhood, gender was reassigned. One would imagine that this was traumatic and damaging, but if reassignment occurred before age 2 to 4, it had little effect on later sexual adjustment. For gender reassignment to have psychological meaning, the child must have cognitively developed a conception of its own gender identity, an identity that can be at variance with its biological gender. These findings suggest that the growing cognitive constancy or irreversibility of gender identity in early childhood is the bedrock of later sexual and sex-role attitudes. Although the significance of gender identity is not solely its influence on the child's later life, it is the most salient category to which the child assigns itself. In fact, it is the only basic general category or role to which it does assign itself. The other basic category of self-identity for the child is that of child as opposed to adult. Unlike gender, however, age identity is not fixed; children know they will become adults. Perhaps only race can be considered a comparable category to children and then only under some conditions.

Because gender is the only fixed general category into which the child can sort itself and others, it takes on tremendous importance in organizing the child's social perceptions and actions. Therefore the first question we studied was that of the actual development of basic gender identity. Absent in the first year or two of life, by age 6, children's gender identities were found to be fixed and were organizing foci for their social inter-actions. It seemed to me that the development of the child's physical gender-identity category must coincide in time with the development of the other basic physical categories studied by Piaget. If this were the case, gender identity would not become a perceptually or logically unshakeable category until the child reached concrete operations and conservation. This was easy to demonstrate: we simply asked with appropriate illustra-tions whether a girl could turn into a boy if she wished to, by wearing a boy's haircut or a boy's clothes. Not until age 6 to 7 were most children quite certain that a girl could not be a boy regardless of changes in appearance or behavior. Long before, by age 3, a child will label itself correctly and will label the gender of others with partial accuracy. By age 4, children label gender correctly and show some awareness that gender cannot change. For example, Johnny, who is 4½ years old, points out gender constancy to younger Jimmy, who is just reaching age 4. Here is the conversation:

OLDER JOHNNY: I'm going to be an airplane builder when I grow up.
YOUNGER JIMMY: When I grow up, I'll be a mommy.
OLDER JOHNNY: No, you can't be a mommy, you have to be a daddy.
YOUNGER JIMMY: No, I'm going to be a mommy.
OLDER JOHNNY: No, you're not a girl; you can't be a mommy.

Although constancy of gender identity starts to appear at age 4, it does not have a clear logical basis, nor is it linked to genital differences until about age 6 to 7.

So far we have talked about the growth of a single concept, gender and gender identity. We believed that developmental changes in the cog-nitive structure of this concept will be reflected in developmental changes in the attitudes more usually studied in young children. The first was the so-called attitude of masculinity/femininity assessed by various tests of preference for sex-typed objects and activities. Not surprisingly, as a boy becomes sure he is immutably a boy and that boys like certain activities and girls like others, he will come to prefer boy-things. By age 6 to 7, when children reach the ceiling on gender identity, they also reach a ceiling on these tests, making 80 to 100% same-sex choices on them. This is not a response to cultural training or reward any more than the devel-opment of constancy of gender identity is. Rather, it is to be explained in terms of two tendencies. The first is the belief that the child has little choice about sex-typed activities and roles. When our 4-year-old Jimmy abandons the belief that he can be a mother, he also abandons the belief that he can be a nurse or a secretary, or can wear girls' clothes or play with feminine dolls. At age 6 to 7 a child equates the "is" of its sex identity with social value: "You can't be a girl, so you don't want to, you can't be a nurse, so you don't want to, and it's no good to be a nurse." The second tendency is the natural tendency to like oneself, think well of oneself and of that which is connected to the self or is like the self. If other boys are like the self, you like them more than you like girls. A 4-year-old boy expressed a preference for a male babysitter. Asked why, his 7-year-old brother intervened to say, "because he's a boy himself." Actually this consistent or categorical tendency to prefer males because one is a male requires the conceptual growth reflected in the ability to perform concrete operations and to maintain fixed logical classes. For boys less than 5 years old it only applies to peers. By age 6 to 7 it applies to both fathers and strange adults. Doll-play measures of preference and imitation for the father over the mother cross over to same-sex preference at age 6. So do measures of preferential dependency toward strange adult males over females. Thus what is often called father identification, as well as what is called masculinity of values, grows with and out of the cognitive growth of the child's gender identity.

Now that the child has organized its identity and its attitudes and values around its gender identity, we must ask what these attitudes and values are. We enter into the attributes children assign to male and female roles, and the issues of the superiority of one to the other. Here we find almost as much cognitive-developmental regularity as we did for gender identity. By age 6 almost all boys see males as more powerful, aggressive, authoritative, and smarter than females. In part, this is also the old tendency of the boy to attribute value to what is like himself. This is not all, however, because most girls of the same age agree with him. Cross-cultural studies suggest that these stereotypes are universal. In our work, we found that father-absent black boys developed the same stereotypes of a father at the same age as did father-present black and white boys. How do we explain this? By returning to the notion that for the young child sex-linked roles and attributes are linked to body attributes. Because males are perceived as physically bigger, stronger, and more active than females, they are also thought to have certain psychological rather than physical attributes (e.g., aggressiveness, fearlessness, smartness, and dominance). The child does not distinguish physical and psychological attributes; physical strength and energy are equated with intelligence, aggression, and dominance. This tendency to derive psychological attributes and values from physical attributes is compounded by the child's categorical view of sex-role assignments. Boys cannot be nurses, girls cannot be soldiers. Roles we believe that both sexes can play, but are more commonly played by males, are categorically assigned to the male sex; roles from doctor to policeman to President.

In summary, we see that the 6-year-old boy is a full-fledged male chauvinist, much more so than his parents, and he is that way regardless of how he is brought up in a society that fosters role differentiation. Fortunately, later phases of cognitive growth qualify, moderate, or undo this male chauvinism.

At age 6, the physical concepts of sex role have completed their course of cognitive growth. The next phase of cognitive growth in sex-role concepts takes place because the child redefines roles in terms of their place in a moral order called society, rather than in terms of their physical characteristics. It would seem that there are definite stages in sex-role cognitions, stages to be found in any culture and occurring because of general cognitive transformations in the child's perception of its social world. These stages are not biologically innate, like libidinal stages, nor are they cultural age grades. Rather, they are the result of interaction between universal cognitive and social tendencies in the child with the universals in its social world; the universals that, in any culture, involve body differences between the categories of males and females. These categories constitute a pivotal focus of social organization. For the child, stages in the development of its psychosexual concepts represent an organizing focus in the development of its attitudes toward love, work, and parenthood: the main themes of adult life.

The study about to be described was designed to examine the nature of sex-typed concepts at various ages and to identify some of the dimensions on which change occurs. The basic task was to discover the qualitative changes in attitudes that occur with increasing age.

One may view statements on sex roles in two ways. First, one might ask, "How does the subject describe the male and female roles as he perceives them?" And second, "What are the subject's conceptions of what a male and female ought to be like?" The first component we refer to as the *descriptive*, for it refers only to perceptions of male and female differences, and the second is referred to as the *prescriptive*, for it pertains to the issue of how men and women ought to be, as opposed to how they are perceived. Based on this distinction, one might further ask how these components of sex typing are related to each other in the process of development. What is the relationship of the descriptive to the prescriptive factor; of what "is" to what "ought to be"?

On the basis of preliminary data, we can suggest the following changes that occur in the development of sex typing: At the earliest level, sex-role differences are based on observable physical criteria, such as size, strength, and material status. What one wants to be at this stage is limited by the physical characteristics associated with one's gender identity. A conventional level of development follows in which differences in sex roles define social duties. Males and females are seen as occupying a particular role within a larger social system. At this stage, what one wants to be in terms of roles is largely defined by conformity to existing sex roles. At the third level, sex-role characteristics are personally chosen from a conception of what one wants to be. The choice is based on a need for mutuality and equality of individuals in sexual relationships. In the remainder of this chapter, our findings with regard to these levels of cognitive development will be discussed.

Seventy boys and girls were given an extensive interview asking what they perceived as salient sex-role characteristics, why such sex-role characteristics existed, and whether one sex might have more valuable characteristics than the other. In addition, they were asked how extensively and why sex-typed characteristics ought to be expressed or conformed to by males and females. Subjects were selected at 2-year intervals between the ages of 6 and 18. The findings reported here are based on a preliminary analysis of two randomly selected interviews with male subjects in the first, fifth, and ninth grades, and with college freshmen. It was our impression that the two males in each of these four subgroups were representative of their group as a whole. Since the data on females were unavailable at the time of writing, they are not included.

Let us now turn to our first-grade subjects. With regard to the descriptive aspect of sex typing, the most important characteristic of our 6-year-old boys is the equation of sex roles with the possession of specific physical characteristics. This group of subjects showed a consistent orientation to physical, external features in differentiating between males and females. For the 6-year-old child, male and female identities are defined by such things as size, strength, depth of voice, skin characteristics, ornaments, and clothes. For example, a 6-year-old boy is asked:

WHAT ARE LADIES LIKE?

Ladies have long hair and men don't.

HOW ELSE ARE THEY DIFFERENT FROM MEN?

They wear lipstick and men don't.

In accord with this physical emphasis, mental or psychological differences between the sexes were confused with the physical attributes of men and women. A boy is asked why girls seem to get hurt more easily than boys. He responds:

Because the boys have a little tougher skin.

Later he is asked why he thinks boys are smarter than girls, and he responds:

Because they have a bigger brain, I guess.

Thus physical characteristics are also assumed either to cause or to be identical with a variety of sex-linked social and psychological attributes, such as competence, power, or nurturance. In this way, strength is equated with energy, so that males are seen as capable of more difficult physical and mental labor. A 6-year-old boy illustrates this point when he observes that

Women can't do as much as men, like I said, that is why men are smarter. . . . Men, they learn harder, because their job is harder.

WHO SHOULD HAVE A HARDER JOB?

The man. Because the woman wouldn't be that strong to do a hard job. She wouldn't be able to build.

WHAT ABOUT A SMART JOB?

The man. He is smarter because he works, he can be a fireman, a policeman, and a worker.

Similar conclusions are reached in the context of family roles. When asked who would be the boss in the family, a student answers:

The man. Because if the man wasn't and the lady was, then the lady wouldn't know what to do so very often.

WHY?

Because the man is smarter. He works harder and he plays harder.

This equation of psychological differences with physical differences and activity differences leads to a belief in male superiority because strength, energy, intelligence, and working for money are all equated.

Let us now turn to the 6-year-old's *conception of sex identity*. Here we see that deviations from any of the usual external signs of one's sex (such as clothing or hair style) are perceived as a possible change in one's real or perceived basic gender identity. As a result, others will think they are of the opposite sex and consequently will see them as funny, bizarre, or distorted:

SHOULD A BOY EVER WEAR A GIRL'S NECKLACE?

No, because it would look funny and everyone would say he was a girl.

Because social role differences between males and females are believed to be tied to their biological or physical identities, only men can play typically male roles, and only women can play typically female roles. Like 6-year-olds, we think that boys cannot become mothers because of their bodily characteristics and gender identities. Unlike 6-year-olds, we do think that boys can become nurses or secretaries, or engage in other stereotypically feminine roles. This is because we see the role of the nurse as a function, not as a set of physical characteristics and activities. In contrast, when a 6-year-old boy is asked whether a male could be a nurse, he responds:

He could still be in the hospital because the doctor is almost like a nurse. He could wear the stuff, but he would still be called a doctor.

WHY?

Because he is still a boy and doctors are supposed to be boys.

The differences between doctors and nurses is not in their function but in their gender identity and the uniforms they wear.

Turning to the prescriptive aspect of sex typing, we find that 6-year-old boys derive what males and females *should be* from what they are; that is, from their physical attributes and gender identity. All observed differences between the sexes ought to be maintained because they are necessary to the basic gender identity of each sex. Earlier we referred to the boy who thought that women are different from men because "they have long hair and wear lipstick." When asked, "Is it all right for a man to wear lipstick?" he answered, "No, they should have men not wearing lipstick and ladies wearing lipstick because they are different from each other." Clearly, any change from the customary attributes of one's sex is perceived as a violation of one's biological or physical nature and hence as "dumb," "funny," or "weird."

There are two major characteristics that distinguish the sex-role concepts of fifth-graders from those of the first-graders. First, psychological distinctions between males and females are seen as deriving from differences in wishes or intentions, rather than from physical differences. Asked who is more active, a boy replies:

Boys are more active.

WHY?

Well, they might be active because they like to play sports and that. And a lot of girls like to play sports.

Second, differences between males and females are seen in terms of the differences in the social roles they play. Fifth-graders are aware of differences in social roles and define sex differences in terms of social roles instead of relying on physical or biological characteristics. Whereas first-graders conceive of roles as classes of activities and physical characteristics, fifth-graders see roles as defined by social or shared expectations and norms. The fifth-grader sees these differences in role expectations as due to the social function of the role, its function for other people or society. How do these two characteristics—definition of sex differences in terms of psychological intention and definition of sex differences in terms of social roles—relate to one another? Primarily in that the fifth-grader's intentions and wishes are dictated by social roles they are expected to play in the future. A boy answers the following question:

HOW COME GIRLS LIKE TO STAY HOME AND DO THE HOUSEKEEPING?

I don't know, maybe they like to do what their mother does. Because they are going to be a mother.

Psychological sex differences also derive from society's definition of different roles for men and women. One boy was asked:

WHO IS SMARTER, IN GENERAL, MEN OR WOMEN?

Men, because they have to do a lot of things, like thinking. They have to work at their jobs. They have to think a lot and they have to work and they have to figure things out.

In terms of sex-role identity, we recall that first-graders saw what we now call social sex roles as fixed by one's gender identity and saw deviations from these physicalistic roles as distortions of identity. In contrast, fifth-graders are aware that some social sex roles are chosen, rather than prescribed. A fifth-grader tells us that if a boy wants to become a nurse, "it is okay because they can do what they want." While it is believed that social sex roles are chosen, the limits of individual choice are determined by an awareness of social expectation. The fifth-grader goes on to say:

But I still think a boy should become a doctor because I think a doctor's job is mostly for men, not for women.

Awareness of social roles implies awareness of social prescriptions or expectations. Role differences between the sexes are seen by the fifth-graders as expected or prescribed. In this sense, then, fifth-graders' sex-role identities are determined by what they ought to be, whereas for first-graders, what they ought to be is determined by what they are. As a subject is asked whether it would be right or wrong for a woman to ask the man to stay home with the children, he responds:

> Wrong, because I think the woman should take care of them. Because the woman is usually the one to take care of them.

Although sex roles are socially prescriptive at this age, they are not prescriptive in the moral sense. There is no standard or moral principle behind sex-role prescriptions or for justifying sex-role differences. While in the first-grade, sex-role prescription derives from the physical "is," now it derives from the social "is," from the way things usually are or are expected to be. A fifth-grade boy tells us:

> Men should act like men and ladies like ladies. They should act like they should. Take care of things, and that. You do what most women usually do.

If moral reasons for sex-role differences cannot be given beyond "that's what is supposed to be," neither can functional reasons for sex-role differences be given. Although these children are aware of social role functions divided by sex, they have no conception of the basis on which such sex-linked roles are assigned.

Let us turn now to the ninth-grader's sex-role concepts. By the ninth grade, adolescents are able to define internal psychological differences between males and females which are independent of, or prior to, the social sex roles they play:

> They (girls) have a lot of views on things, they are more—I think they have more emotions than men do and they show it more than men do.

All the usual psychological sex-role stereotypes are present: women are more sympathetic, more dependent, more emotional, less sexually driven. Insofar as there is a general rationale for differentiating male and female sex roles, it is now seen in terms of the psychological attributes distinguishing the sexes. However, these psychological sex differences are freed from fixed and prescribed social-sex roles. This allows a degree of individual variation and individual choice in expressing these sex-differentiating traits. For example, one subject said:

Some women are weaker, some are stronger, and some are the same as men. They are also brilliant, smart, just the same as men are, but some are just different as some men are different than women and some are the same.

As a result, sex-role identity or choice is no longer an all-or-nothing matter. One can choose to be feminine in some ways and not in others:

IS IT IMPORTANT FOR A GIRL TO ACT LIKE A GIRL?

Sort of. A lot of them want to be like a girl and should be. And a lot of them aren't. And maybe they don't want to be like what a girl is supposed to be pictured as.

Turning to the prescriptive aspect of sex-typed behavior, it is now recognized that sex-role stereotypes are not demanded either by society as a whole or by moral values. Sex-role stereotypes are clearly distinguished from societal or moral rights, or from a personal sense of obligation:

I don't think there is a certain set-up thing about what a girl should exactly be like. Sometimes you have a picture, but they shouldn't have to be like that.

WHY? EVEN IF THEY ACT LIKE MEN?

Right, I think they have the right to live their life the way they really want to. Because it is not right. The other people live their life the way they want to, why can't they live their life the way they want to?

IS IT IMPORTANT FOR A MAN TO BE MASCULINE AND A WOMAN TO BE FEMININE?

If they want to, go ahead. It all depends on what they think is right. If they don't think it is right, they shouldn't.

At the fifth grade, sex-role differences were justified as "what you're supposed to be." Now social expectation is merely seen as custom or tradition, which is only partially valid:

It doesn't seem right to see a woman outside cutting the grass or something. That is the way it has been for so long, I don't see why they should bother breaking that tradition.

In summary, the ninth-graders' sex-role stereotypes, identities, and prescriptions are still almost completely grounded on social expectations and conventions, as was true for the fifth-graders. But now there is a recognition that these stereotypes are not binding in either the rational-logical or the moral sense. They are chosen, rather than required by biology.

Ninth-graders are in a state of transition in their perception and prescription of sex roles. They recognize that conventional sex roles are largely arbitrary, but they have no alternative standards to offer. In contrast, college students have a set of personal values as to the way men and women should be individually and in relation to others. They have an awareness of many of the arbitrary features of conventional stereotypes; they are not simply bound by the customary definitions of sex roles.

At the ninth-grade level, adolescents defined sex differences by the usual sex-typed psychological traits. Although the college students still recognize these differences, they do not believe that they are innate to the nature of men or women. Rather, they are the product of conventional expectations and stereotypes internalized by children. For example, a college freshman points out:

> Women get put into a role; by the nature of their being born men or women, they are put into social positions and their social actions are laid out for them and they are expected to do certain things and not to do certain things. Men are expected to be aggressive and dominant, and the characteristics associated with masculinity.

Attempting to go beyond customary sex-role stereotypes, they may define images of masculinity and femininity that are ideals as opposed to what is socially expected. Masculinity and femininity are no longer defined in terms of bipolar traits like rational/emotional, aggressive/passive. An ideal male is not the opposite of an ideal female. Differences between the ideal male and the ideal female lie in a somewhat different balance or harmony of psychological traits that are common to both males and females. Asked to define the ideal woman, a student responds:

> Personally, the ideal woman to me again can be beautiful and soft, but the ideal man may also be soft in the same way, because he is soft-spoken, not domineering over anybody, but still with ambition so he could get things done.

The "principle" of this balance is that of either complementarity or mutuality between the sexes. Complementarity means that each cluster of traits makes up for the limits of the other; mutuality means that each cluster of traits is reciprocal or responsive to the other. Both complementarity and mutuality imply a conception of fundamental equality in the relation between a man and a woman. In the context of family roles a college freshman says:

> I think the husband and wife should be kind of even. And I don't think you could have a good relationship based upon the fact that one person; his role is not taken into consideration. I think the only way would be to have a dual effort.

We have noted the college student's rejection of conventional standards as the basis of sex differences. We have also noted his attempt to formulate a principle of equality to govern interpersonal relationships. In spite of these developments, the college student recognizes an inconsistency between his ideals and images, which resemble traditional notions of masculinity and femininity, and the moral requirements of equality and freedom in social relations. When a student is asked to describe an ideal woman, he replies:

> She would not necessarily be unambitious or unaggressive, but say aggressive and ambitious in a less obvious way. I feel like a moron admitting it, but it is bred into me, and so if I see a woman who is competing with men and who is being openly aggressive with men, it just sets off a mechanism.

Thus, though idealized images are personally preferred, they are simultaneously viewed as violations of the principles of equality and individual freedom. When the same student is probed further about his ideal standards, he says:

> I say (stereotypes) should be abolished, but I can't help what has been put into me over the years.

We saw that ninth-grade students rely on social custom to define appropriate sex-typed behavior. This was because they lacked alternative standards or values on which to base their judgments. Although the college student has adopted an egalitarian standard, which he views as right from both a rational and a moral perspective, he finds it difficult to reconcile these principles with his personal preferences, and thus he labels himself as "moronic," "biased," or "male chauvinist." The dilemma posed by the college student is surely one we all have faced; that is, the issue of integrating abstract moral principles of equality and individual freedom with individual values and choices in one's personal experience. It is interesting to speculate about how this conflict can be resolved, whether through continued psychological growth or through increased opportunities for exploring a variety of sex roles. It is probably a function of both. However, without data from older subjects, and in the absence of viable social alternatives, this must remain pure speculation.

The data presented here indicate the importance of examining the reasoning from which sex-typed judgments are derived. Although the content of sex-typed responses at all ages seems to conform to social stereotypes of masculinity and femininity, it is apparent that the mode of thinking about sex roles may indicate a particular developmental level. For example, subjects at each developmental level felt that women should be soft and gentle. However, when asked why they felt so, variations in reasoning became evident. The youngest group of subjects based their judgments on physical differences between men and women. Thus women should be softer than men because their skin is softer or their bones are smaller. Older subjects, on the other hand, conceptualized female gentleness in terms of the need to conform to social or familial expectations. Women should be softer because "mothers are supposed to be that way." The college student cited earlier also prescribed softness as a characteristic for women, but this standard derived from an autonomous value system with universal applicability. Thus he felt not only that women should be soft and gentle but that it was a positive attribute for members of either sex.

This content–structure distinction implies that, though the content of sex-typed responses may suggest increasing conformity to social norms, there are differing bases for these responses. The data presented here support the view that changes in thinking about sex roles do, indeed, follow age-developmental trends.

REFERENCES

1. Kohlberg, L., in Maccoby, E. E. (ed.), *Development of Sex Differences*, Stanford University Press, Stanford, Calif., 1966.
2. Piaget, J., *The Construction of Reality in the Child*, Basic Books, New York, 1954.
3. Money, J., J. G. Hampson, and J. L. Hampson, *AMA Arch Neurol Psychiatr* **77**: 333, 1957.

CHAPTER 12

The Emergence of Genital Awareness During the Second Year of Life

ELEANOR GALENSON and HERMAN ROIPHE

Department of Child Psychiatry
Albert Einstein College of Medicine
Bronx, New York

Psychoanalytic developmental psychology has posited an intimate relationship both temporally and dynamically between castration anxiety, the
oedipus complex, and the phallic phase of pyschosexual development. It
has been the purpose of the research reported here to reconsider these
interrelationships against the background of a body of clinical experience
gained through the observation of children during the second year of life
at a research nursery established within the Department of Psychiatry at
the Albert Einstein College of Medicine.

The importance of the castration complex in shaping the course and
fate of oedipal and postoedipal sexual development is a key concept in
psychoanalytic psychology. The castration complex has been understood
to arise when the child is confronted with the genital difference at the
phallic phase of development, which is usually thought to occur after the
second year of life. At this state of life then, this "momentous discovery"
of the genital difference, to use Freud's phrase, challenges the child to

cope, in the case of boys with a *threat* of loss, and in the case of girls with a *sense* of loss.

Freud (1) makes reference to the idea that oedipal-directed masturbation probably arises out of preoedipal masturbation, which is brought into relation with the oedipus complex at a later date. In subsequent writings on female sexuality (2, 3), he discussed the diverging sexual development of boys and girls as they dealt with the knowledge of genital differences. He particularly stressed the circuitous and lengthy route the girl must traverse in relinquishing her attachment to the mother, a task that, in some cases, is never completed. Although reference was made to early vaginal sensations, prephallic libidinal development in boys and girls was seen as essentially similar, with the clitoris serving a function analogous to that of the penis.

Jones (4) and Klein (5) postulated genital sensation in girls during the first 2 years of life, but their views are complicated by the theoretical formulation of an early oedipal constellation along with this early genital arousal. Although such a hypothesis is open to serious question, their inference from clinical work with children and adults of the presence of genital arousal during preoedipal development finds confirmation in later observations.

Anna Freud (6) reported intense penis envy in girls at her residential nursery occurring between 18 and 24 months of age, a finding she attributed to the extensive bodily intimacy between boys and girls in this setting. Finally, Sachs (7) discussed a case of severe castration anxiety in an 18-month-old boy. She suggested that this reaction might be indicative of early oedipal development and speculated that oedipal conflicts at a younger age might be more common than is generally assumed.

These tentative explanations of the early appearance of penis envy and castration reactions would not account for the specific age cluster of this behavior, nor would it account for the high narcissistic cathexis of the genitals implied in such reactions.

In 1968, Roiphe (8) reported a case of a moderately severe castration reaction in a 19-month-old girl, where the child's distressed reaction to the genital difference was linked with fear of object loss. In another paper, Roiphe (9) proposed that boys and girls, as part of their normal development between the ages of 15 and 24 months, experienced heightened genital sensation and awareness, as manifested by various behaviors, including increased genital handling and frank masturbation. Roiphe also related the appearance of severe castration syndromes to three preconditions:

1. Genital arousal universally experienced during this developmental stage.

2. The observation of anatomical differences between the sexes.

3. Previous trauma that produced an instability in the self and object mental representations (e.g., severe physical illness, surgical intervention, or congenital defect—or events that prevented the establishment of a stable maternal relationship, such as parental loss, maternal depression, gross neglect).

The theoretical premise that boys and girls sustain increased genital arousal during the latter half of the second year of life is further demonstrated by play expressing genital, anal, and urinary themes and by interest in certain objects, such as dolls, which are thought to have symbolic significance (10).

It is postulated that this genital arousal follows upon changes in bowel and bladder functioning that normally occur during the first half of the second year of life, independent of any attempt at toilet training. It takes place during the separation-individuation phase of development (11), when the body image is being consolidated, and is in some way concerned with the crystallization of self and object representation. We believe that this development occurs prior to the establishment of the oedipus complex and therefore is not interwoven with oedipal dynamics.

In 1967, a research nursery was established to investigate genital behavior during the second year of life. Mothers and babies attend together and spend four 2-hour morning sessions a week, in a large room with a bathroom directly accessible and a diapering table openly in view. The nursery is equipped with appropriate toys, snacks for the children, and coffee or tea for the mothers. By June 1973, after 5 years of observation, 53 children had been studied, ranging in age from about 12 to 23 months. The sample was almost evenly divided between the sexes.

Each year, two or three children were selected for particularly detailed evaluation on the basis of having sustained the type of stressful life experience that we hypothesized was necessary for subsequent development of an intense castration reaction. The majority of children in the nursery, however, were normal volunteers whose parents were members of the university community.

In order to clarify how the observed behaviors were shaped by developmental events, careful attention was paid to history. Furthermore, an attempt was made to delineate the role of genital experience in organizing the child's relationship to its human environment and in influencing its continuing development.

SUMMARY OF FINDINGS ALREADY REPORTED:
THE PREOEDIPAL CASTRATION REACTION

Several findings have been presented previously (12–15). One report concerned the development of a little girl, Ruth (12), who suffered from a congenital malformation requiring corrective apparatus and repeated medical examination during her first year. In this already vulnerable child, genital awareness and the discovery of sexual anatomical difference at 17½ months was followed by feelings of intense disappointment and anger at her mother, a loss of self-esteem, marked inhibition in both sexual and general curiosity, and the onset of an affective reaction marked by irritability and a "depressed" appearance. Both language and play development showed some loss of her capacity to symbolize, she became attached to two dolls as constant companions, and at the same time manual masturbation ceased. A year later, Ruth was still constricted in general behavior and play, and unduly anxious concerning even minor injuries and separations. Her speech still showed traces of the earlier language disturbance.

Billy (13) was a boy whose father had been absent since the early years of life and who had been separated from his mother for several weeks. At 13 months, marked separation anxiety appeared, some weeks before his genital interest began. At 15 months, he developed a ritual of sleeping with his nursing bottle pressed against his penis, and he clutched his penis whenever he became frustrated or angry. Six weeks later, his masturbation became frank and open, he would roll with his penis pressed on a toy as his facial expression became dreamy and withdrawn, and he continually straddled and rocked against his mother's crossed-over leg, finally trying to use her hand as a means of masturbation. It was felt that Billy's fear of genital loss had merged with his earlier marked separation anxiety, both of which were present to a marked degree on follow-up 18 months later.

We have proposed elsewhere (14) that inanimate objects (e.g., dolls and nursing bottles) that may be used for masturbation should be considered infantile fetishes. Early fetishistic behavior may be more common than has previously been thought and may have dynamic continuity with fetishism occurring later in life. In Ruth (12) and Billy (13) it was observed that the emergence of fetishism was preceded by a distinct castration reaction. We hypothesized that inanimate objects may serve as supports for the wavering sense of the genital body outline at the time of genital arousal and discovery of genital difference, precisely when the boy's fear of losing his phallus, and the girl's sense that she has already lost hers, undermined already unstable feelings of the body integrity and revived earlier fears of object loss.

Recently we described an early castration reaction of moderate intensity in a little girl, Sarah (15). This child had become attached to a soft doll at the unusually early age of 11 months. At 16 to 18 months, anxiety felt to be related to genital arousal and awareness of genital differences was allayed by this transitional object. Following a separation from her parents, there was a serious intensification of her castration reaction. The beloved doll was abandoned in favor of a toy bull that possessed a removable phallus and now served as a form of infantile fetish.

SEX DIFFERENCES IN THE DEVELOPMENT
OF GENITAL BEHAVIOR IN NORMALS

The children described so far manifested unusual reactions to the onset of genital arousal and the discovery of genital difference, all of which occurred prior to the oedipal period of development. Spitz (16) has found that some form of genital play appears in the *normal* infant by the end of the first year of life. He believes that this developmental sequence indicates the quality of the child's relationship with his primary object, the mother. In designating this behavior "genital play" rather than masturbation, Spitz distinguished a random, nondirected phenomenon without concomitant psychological content from masturbation, where such content can be inferred from the type of behavior accompanying genital manipulation.

We have outlined the normal patterning of early genital play more specifically. It began for most of the boys in our group at about 6 to 7 months of age; most girls began at 10 to 11 months. Boys then continued this casual play with additional visual and tactile exploration of the penis starting at about 10 to 12 months. In contrast, genital play in girls tended to disappear within a few weeks of onset.

An unusually early genital stimulation at 4 to 5 months occurred in the cases of five boys and one girl. All had experienced undue parental physical intimacy during the first 6 months of life. This early genital play, although erotic in character, never involved other people, nor did the children appear aware of genital activity in the sense of looking at or examining the genital area. In contrast, the later type of genital manipulation that begins at 15 to 16 months of age is accompanied by distinct signs of pleasure, such as giggling and smiling, along with visual and tactile attention to the genital area and definite affectionate gestures and behavioral signs of feelings directed toward other people. Although the mother is usually the first object of such feelings, masturbation is soon carried out using the crossed leg of a familiar adult or a convenient toy, particularly the rocking horse, with a withdrawal of attention from the external world.

With the onset of masturbation proper at 15 to 16 months, the patterns of genital behavior again are different in the two sexes. These differences appear to correlate with variations in the patterning of concurrent anal and urinary behavior, as well as with certain aspects of developing ego functions. In boys, the genital behavior and related development tend to follow a typical pattern, illustrated by the following report:

At 15 months, Arthur became interested in his own umbilicus as well as his parents' and also in keys. For the first time, at 15 months and 3 weeks, he tried to touch his father's phallus and urinary stream, and his mother's nipples, and at 16 months, he noticed his own urination. He looked at his penis, touched it after urination had ceased, and smiled. At 16 months and 3 weeks, he showed pleasurable affect when straining at his bowel movement and continued to be interested in his father's urination. He also became fascinated with trucks, cars, and playing ball.

At 17 months and 1 week, Arthur looked at his penis intently and touched it; in addition, he tried to put his hand between his mother's legs to touch her pubic hair. He was noted to have erections, and he pointed with glee to his father's urination. He then started handling his own penis frequently, became very interested in the toilet, tried to lift up the skirts of several mothers, and looked between the legs of some little girls.

At 18 months, he had spontaneous erections during diapering. By 19½ months his interest in inserting keys had become a passion: he manipulated every car-door handle he could find, and he loved water-faucet play (which seemed connected with his developing urinary awareness). For the first time he looked up at his mother and smiled while he was pulling at his penis in the bathtub, although he had no erection at the moment. By 19 months and 3 weeks, he was definitely aware of his urination just before it began, had started to manipulate his penis roughly and intensely with both hands, and was clearly aware of impending defecation. He was, however, unwilling to use the potty, although he showed considerable interest in flushing the toilet. At 20 months and 3 weeks, he manipulated his penis through his clothes and tried to grasp at his father's penis. He was now using the word "penis."

In the development of girls, masturbation usually continues for about 2 months after its onset at approximately 15 months. Manual masturbation is then relinquished in favor of such indirect means of stimulation as the rocking horse or thigh pressure, behaviors that are frequently still present at 3 years of age when the children are seen in follow-up. Many girls develop attachments to certain objects, such as a special doll, a wristwatch, a barrette, or a toy umbrella. Their interest in pens belonging to their fathers and their devotion to writing and drawing implements and activities is impressive.

The majority of girls do not have any particular word for the genital area (most of their mothers had not supplied one). If they had acquired a term, it was frequently lost or confused with the words for anal and urinary functions following their discovery of the genital difference. In contrast with this, those boys who had acquired a specific label for their genitals from their parents continued to use it.

In many of the girls there was extensive anal exploration after the first few months of genital masturbation, in contrast with the boys, who did not show marked anal interest. Finally, many girls showed a distinct change in mood and a decrease in general activity level and curiosity for some time after the discovery of the genital difference. This was not the case with boys.

In general, the typical genital and related patterning turned out to be far more difficult to delineate in girls than in boys. Not only were there greater individual differences during the early phase, but related developments that followed initial genital arousal were more disorganized. The following excerpt from our data illustrates the nature of the material:

At 14 months, Ruth began to finger her mons pubis and pull at her genitals in the bath; at 15 months, she occasionally fingered her clitoris directly, as well as her umbilicus. Her doll play was unremarkable. At 17 months, she regularly inserted her fingers between her labia during diapering, looking pleased and flushed as she did so. She often peered up between her widespread legs, tried to lift her mother's skirts, and examined the perineal area of dolls. She designated her own genital area "tushy" at this time, a label offered by her parents for both genital and anal zones. Her awareness of bowel functioning was evident, her interest in water-faucet play and in car-door handles had intensified, and she loved the rocking horse.

By 18 months, her masturbation had begun to decline. She refused to sit on her potty (she had not yet been trained), and she signaled the urinary and anal functions only after these were completed. She had become so insistent on accompanying her father to the bathroom, that at 19 months she was allowed to witness his urination; she seemed amazed and awed, and tried to put her hand in the urinary stream. In contrast with her prior type of doll play, she developed an intense attachment to two special dolls. She required their presence constantly, insisted they be fed when she was, took them to bed with her, and labeled one of them "boy." The rocking horse had become her favorite nursery activity, although manual masturbation had apparently ceased. At 20 months, Ruth "borrowed" her father's pen, hoarded crayons, and developed a passion for drawing and scribbling.

SUMMARY

The pattern of normal genital emergence for both sexes during the first 2 years of life has been outlined. Boys usually begin genital play at about 6 to 7 months of age, whereas girls begin at about 10 to 11 months. In boys, early genital play is continuous until the onset of masturbation proper at 15 to 16 months of age, whereas in girls, a pattern of intermittent genital play is seen.

Girls often suppress manual masturbation completely, substituting such indirect methods as thigh pressure or rocking. This substitution takes place in the wake of anxiety related to the sexual difference, with reactions which range from mild to very intense and which, in our group, appear far more frequently among girls than among boys. Symptoms related to this preoedipal form of castration anxiety include depressed mood, inhibition of sexual as well as general curiosity, interference with symbolic functioning, and the development of special attachments to certain inanimate objects. Anal zone exploration following the discovery of the sexual difference is much more pronounced in girls than in boys; so are such activities as drawing and writing.

Our data suggest that boys tend to continue using the genital zone for direct and conscious discharge of the genital drives, with additional indirect discharge through heightened general motor activity and the use of mobile toys. In contrast to this, girls tend toward the inhibition of direct and conscious genital zonal discharge with the development of indirect pathways of which they are probably less consciously aware. They also tend to turn to the anal zone as well as the substitute use of inanimate objects both for fetishistic purposes and for such early sublimatory activities as pictorial and written representation.

Although it is as yet a highly speculative hypothesis, we suggest that there may be some correlation of our data with the common finding of earlier language development in girls than in boys and with the greater vulnerability of symbolic function in boys. The different patterns of reaction between boys and girls to the awareness of genital differences may serve to organize aspects of concurrently developing ego functions and lead to the use of specific defensive measures. Distinctive male–female differences in these other areas may then emerge.

ACKNOWLEDGMENT

The research reported in this chapter was carried out in the Research Nursery, Department of Child Psychiatry, Albert Einstein College of Medicine. We wish to express our deep appreciation to all members of our staff without whose dedicated work this work would have been impossible.

REFERENCES

1. Freud, S., *Standard Edition*, Vol. 21, Hogarth Press, London, 1925, p. 243.
2. Freud, S., *Standard Edition*, Vol. 21, Hogarth Press, London, 1931, p. 225.
3. Freud, S., *Standard Edition*, Vol. 22, Hogarth Press, London, 1932, p. 7.
4. Jones, E., *Papers on Psychoanalysis*, 5th ed., Balliere, Tindall & Cox, London, 1927, p. 438.
5. Klein, M., *Contributions to Psychoanalysis*, Hogarth Press, London, 1948, p. 202.
6. Freud, A., *Psychoanal Study Child* 6: 18, 1951.
7. Sachs, L. J., *J Am Psychoanal Assoc* 10: 329, 1962.
8. Roiphe, H., Unpublished data.
9. Roiphe, H., *Psychoanal Study Child* 23: 348, 1968.
10. Galenson, E., in McDevitt, J. B. and C. F. Settlage (eds.), *A Consideration of the Nature of Thought in Childhood Play*, International Universities Press, New York, 1971, p. 41.
11. Mahler, M. S., *Psychoanal Study Child* 8: 307, 1963.
12. Galenson, E. and H. Roiphe, *Psychoanal Study Child* 16: 195, 1971.
13. Roiphe, H. and E. Galenson, *Psychoanal Quart* 42: 73, 1973.
14. Roiphe, H. and E. Galenson, unpublished data.
15. Roiphe, H. and E. Galenson, unpublished data.
16. Spitz, R. A., *Psychoanal Study Child* 17: 283, 1962.

CHAPTER 13

An Ethological Study of Children Approaching a Strange Adult: Sex Differences

DANIEL N. STERN and ESTELLE P. BENDER

Department of Developmental Processes
New York State Psychiatric Institute
New York, New York
Department of Psychiatry
College of Physicians and Surgeons
Columbia University

Young children are forced to deal with unknown, older, and larger human beings at close range. The term "fear of strangers" is used to refer to the reaction of infants to strangers during the latter half of the first year of life. At this age the fear is thought to be largely a function of the discrepancy between the appearance and perhaps the behavior of the stranger compared with that of familiar figures (1, 2). However, by the time a child is 3 years old, in nursery school, and entered into a larger world than his family, strangers have become an expected class composed of the vast majority of the human world. What remains unknown is what the stranger will do and how to react to that. In ethological terms, to the 3-year-old child, most adults and older children are now seen as larger, stronger, dominant members of the same species. The nature of an interaction with an unknown dominant conspecific is initially uncertain and potentially threatening. However, there exist in man, as in other animals, kinesic behaviors available for conspecifics to signal and, so to speak, negotiate the nature of the interaction to follow: friendly, unfriendly, and so on. In primates, these behavioral signals include flight patterns, submissive and appeasement behaviors, the observation of proxemic and territorial "rules," and aggressive behaviors (3). What may these patterns look like in young human males and females?

This chapter describes the repertoire of behaviors used by 3- to 5-year-old girls and boys in a specific human situation: approaching a strange adult. Although the experimental situation was designed to be mildly threatening and fear producing, we do not assume that the behaviors observed are the expression of fear alone or belong solely to a motivational system of fear. Our assumptions are rather that, though some specific behaviors "belong" almost exclusively to a single motivational system, most behaviors can be recruited into the service of more than one motivational system and that, when several different motivational systems are activated (fear, affiliation, curiosity, aggression), as we assume to be the case in this experimental situation, the constellation of behaviors that are performed represent an integrated result reflecting the mixture and balance of the motivational systems activated. It is the integrated performance of many separate behaviors that functions as the signal to influence the behavior of the adult and accordingly the outcome of the interaction. Bischof (4) has recently provided an elegant model to conceptualize the operations of such a system. Slight shifts in the organization of the integrated behaviors account for the often subtle but crucial nuances in the communicative value of the signal. Even in a 1-year-old child it is at times difficult to speak of fearful behaviors in isolation. Bretherton and Ainsworth (5) report that the large majority of 1-year-olds exposed to a stranger show a succession of behaviors that can be interpreted as belonging to both an attachment and affiliative system and a fear system, as well as to an exploratory system.

By the time a child is 3 years old, he has developed a richer and more articulated repertoire of facial, gestural, and postural behaviors, the precursors to many of which can be seen in the 1-year-old infant. Not only is the repertoire larger, but as development proceeds, the separate behaviors can be recombined and reorganized into a wider array of patterns. Some behaviors, which earlier in development could be performed only in succession, can now be performed simultaneously. The result is a richer and wider array of communicative signals.

The research presented here is part of a larger study on the development of the repertoire and signal functions of child behavior. We report here those results that are relevant to the study of sex differences.

METHODOLOGY

Subjects

The 204 children in the study were 3- to 5-year-old boys and girls at the Riverside Church Nursery School, a racially and economically integrated day nursery school administered by the Presbyterian Church in New York. All children in the school participated except 5% who refused.

Experimental Procedure, Setting, and Design

Children were met in the morning in their classrooms by the experimenter and asked to participate in a study of how boys and girls walked. The experimenter was neutral in expression. Children were brought individually into the testing room, which was known to them but rarely used. On entering the room with the experimenter, the child saw at the far end two other strange adult observers who looked at him or her without smiling or talking. The experimenter asked the child to stand on the end of a long rug (18×3 ft) marked with 12 different-colored, 1-in.-wide cloth tapes that repeated the color sequence every foot. The experimenter then instructed the child to "walk up to me and stop when you get there. I'll ask you to do that three times." The experimenter then went to his position at the other end of the rug, flanked by the two other observers who stood 5 ft to the side and several feet behind him. Once he was in place, the experimenter repeated "O.K., walk up to me and stop when you get there." A similar technique has been used to measure body buffer zones in adults (6). The child was asked to make three separate approaches, each time with the experimenter in a different position. The three different experimental positions or stimulus conditions were (1) the experimenter standing with feet together and hands at sides; (2) the experimenter sitting on a chair with hands on knees and knees together; and (3) the experimenter standing 6 ft behind a chair placed at the end of the rug. For this last stimulus condition the child was asked to "walk up to the chair and stop when you get there."

In a pilot study, not reported here, 60 children were tested to determine stimulus-condition order effects. None was significant, and only the two most divergent orders were used for this study: "increasing stimulus threat" (chair, sit, stand) and "decreasing stimulus threat" (stand, sit, chair).

Two experimenters were used, a male and a female who wore slacks. These two experimenters differed in many other respects besides sex. The male was 7 in. taller, 40 lb heavier, wore a mustache, and had a somewhat gruffer manner.

An analysis of variance was performed with the following independent variables: sex of child (two); age of child—3, 4, and 5 years (three); order of stimulus condition (two). Twelve groups resulted. There were 10 subjects in each of the 12 groups approaching a female experimenter, and 7 subjects in each of the 12 groups approaching a male experimenter. A separate analysis of variance was performed for each of these 12 groups.*

The experimental situation is considered threatening for several reasons. The experimenter and two observers are strange adults who initiate no friendly social contact. The child finds himself in a closed room in a situation and procedure that are novel. Especially important is the fact that the experimenter and observers are without expression and maintain a constant visual fixation on the child before, during, and after his approaches. In apes (8), chimpanzees (9), as well as human adults and children (9), in fact, among almost all primates, a maintained visual fixation without other expression is an aggressive behavior, reacted to as a threat. The child thus is placed in a conflict situation where he is asked to approach a strange staring adult (in fact, three of them) where he normally would not make such an approach. Jones (9) comments that the commonest reaction of a child to a strange adult in a nursery school setting is to stop and stare without expression from a distance, but not to approach. If the stranger stares back, the child looks away and goes away. Smith and Connolly (10), in watching nursery school children reacting to a strange adult observer, also comment on the child's staring from a distance. They also observed approaches to the strange adult, but under experimental conditions where the adult never visually fixated the child without either smiling or smiling and talking. Clearly, then, the children in this study would not have approached unless "requested" to. They are placed in a situation in which, inferring from their behavior, several different motivational systems appear to be activated: fear, affiliation,

---

* Of the children tested, 10% were black and 2.5% were Puerto Rican. Aiello and Jones (7) have reported differences in the proxemic behaviors of children of different racial and cultural backgrounds. The 21 black children in this study were distributed among the different groups and perhaps because of the resultant small N showed no difference from their white counterparts. No attempt was made to control for socioeconomic class differences.

curiosity, and in some cases, aggression. Although most of the children looked forward to the experiment as "fun" and afterward said it was "O.K.," once they got in the room and began the task, their demeanor became more sober. Only four children who entered the room cried and would not make an approach.

Child Behaviors Scored

A. *Children's Approaching Behaviors* (while the child is walking up to the adult). The behaviors chosen were those observed to occur with sufficient frequency during the pilot study and those amenable to reliable scoring at the distances involved. Where possible, we have adopted the definitions of behavioral units described by Brannigan and Humphries (11), especially for the facial behaviors.

  1. *Facial behaviors*

    a. Common smiles

      (1) simple smile (lips together)
      (2) upper smile (upper teeth showing)
      (3) broad smile (upper and lower teeth showing)

    b. "Apprehensive" mouth behaviors

      (1) bite lip
      (2) tight lips (lips pressed together)
      (3) lips in (lips pressed together and turned into the mouth)

    c. "Ambivalent" smiles (designated "ambivalent" because they combine elements of the common smile plus elements of apprehensive mouth behaviors)

      (1) compressed smile (a simple smile with lips compressed)
      (2) lip-in smile (the lower lip is drawn in between the teeth during the smile, i.e., an upper smile plus bite lip)

    d. Other (these units were scored but will not be reported on here)

      (1) open mouth
      (2) tongue between lips
      (3) eyebrow raise
      (4) eyebrow flash

  2. *Hand and arm behaviors*

    a. Hand(s) to mouth
    b. Hand(s) to face (beside mouth)

    c. Hand(s) to hair

    d. Hand(s) to head

    e. Hand to hand front (hand touching or holding other hand against or in front of chest or abdomen)

    f. Hand(s) in pocket(s)

    g. Hand(s) to side (held against outer sides of legs)

    h. Hand(s) behind back

    i. Hand(s) on hips

    j. Hand(s) up over head

    k. Arms extended to side

3. *Speed of approach* (measured by a stopwatch)

4. *Gaze behaviors* (number of gazes at experimenter before coming to a stop)

B. *End-of-Approach Behaviors*

1. *Approach distance.* After the child stops his approach, the distance from the closest part of the child's closest shoe to the experimenter's toes is measured in inches from the stripes on the rug.

2. *Angular distance* (body orientation relative to the experimenter). Angular distance is the degree to which the child avoids directly facing or fully "squaring off" with the adult (toes directed at the adult's toes and shoulder axis in parallel with the adult's). Because of the relative ease of scoring the angle of foot orientation using the lines on the rug as referents compared to judging shoulder axis orientation, we have scored only foot orientation. Foot and shoulder orientations closely match each other in this situation where there is relatively little twisting at the waist. [With only a few exceptions (7) the angular orientation of the body has been generally neglected in studies of proxemics.] The child can achieve angular distance in two possible ways. One way is to orient himself away from the experimenter. A four-point scale was used to measure this parameter: (1) the child's toes point toward the experimenter; (2) the child's toes point up to 45 degrees away from the experimenter; (3) between 45 and 90 degrees away; (4) more than 90 degrees away. The child can also achieve angular distance by placing himself other than directly in front of the adult, regardless of which direction he then faced. A four-point scale was used to measure this parameter: (1) child placed himself directly in front of the experimenter; (2) child placed himself up to 45 degrees away from the direction of the

experimenter's toes; (3) between 45 and 90 degrees away; (4) more than 90 degrees away. The two scores, which represent different ways of altering the angle of orientation or turning away, were combined to give the total angular distance between child and experimenter.

3. *Head orientation toward the experimenter*
   a. Head orientation in the horizontal plane (turning away to the side). A four-point scale was used: (1) facing the experimenter; (2) facing up to 45 degrees away from the experimenter; (3) between 45 and 90 degrees away; (4) more than 90 degrees away.
   b. Head orientation in the vertical plane (in effect this involved only head lowering). A four-point scale corresponding in units to the above-described scale was used.

4. *Gaze.* The presence or absence of gaze at the experimenter within 2 seconds after the end of approach was recorded.

One observer scored the gaze behavior and operated the stopwatch. The other scored the arm–hand behavior on approach and scored the distance and foot orientations on stopping. The third scored the facial behaviors on approach and the head orientations on stopping. The interrater agreements were as follows: distance (to the inch) .88, foot angular distance .86, head orientation horizontal .80, head orientation vertical .86, hand–arm behavior .96, facial behaviors .86, gaze at end of approach .90.

RESULTS

End-of-Approach Behaviors

For each of the end-of-approach behaviors an analysis of variance was performed against the independent variables of age, sex, order, and stimulus condition. The results of the analysis of variance are shown in Table 1.

Approach Distance. Figure 1 shows the approach distances plotted by age and by stimulus conditions for boys and girls, when approaching a male and a female adult. The F values for this are taken from Table 1. There were no differences between boys and girls, and no significant differences depending on whether a male or female adult was being approached. However, all children at all ages clearly differentiated the three stimulus conditions, coming closest to the chair and remaining

Table 1 *Analysis of Variance for End-of-Approach Behaviors* (F *Values*)

	Age	Sex	Order	Stim-ulus	Age × Sex	Age × Order	Sex × Order	Age × Stim.	Sex × Stim.	Order × Stim.
Degrees of Freedom	2	1	1	2	2	2	1	4	2	2
Approaching a Female Adult										
Approach distance	0.71	0.09	1.71	17.19***	0.13	1.15	2.72	0.25	4.99**	7.64**
Angular distance (ft)	0.75	4.04*	0.42	2.00	0.11	0.23	4.67*	0.76	1.03	0.90
Head orientation (horizontal)	0.48	4.13*	0.78	8.44**	0.61	0.55	0.78	2.00	2.55	0.35
Head orientation (vertical)	3.08*	0.51	0.69	51.63***	0.13	1.07	0.00	0.95	0.98	0.60
Approaching a Male Adult										
Approach distance	3.83*	1.14	6.65*	28.48***	0.47	0.87	0.91	1.03	0.21	0.23
Angular distance (ft)	7.27**	4.56*	0.94	1.71	0.75	0.56	0.21	1.51	0.70	0.21
Head orientation (horizontal)	0.17	4.31*	0.83	4.93**	0.91	2.37	0.56	0.84	1.54	2.51
Head orientation (vertical)	3.32*	0.35	1.54	72.92***	4.47*	0.47	0.00	0.17	0.04	0.62

$*p < .05.$
$**p < .01.$
$***p < .001.$

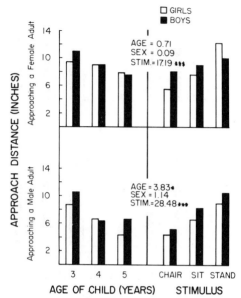

Figure 1 Approach distance (in inches) for boys and girls plotted by age and by stimulus conditions when approaching a male and a female adult. The F values from the analysis of variance are shown (*p<.05, **p<.01, ***p<.001).

farthest from the standing experimenter. This finding is of interest from the developmental point of view in that 3-year-olds utilize distance much as do 4- and 5-year-olds in the approach situation. As will be seen, use of head and body orientation in 3-year-old children also differs little from that in the older children.

Angular Distance (Body Orientation). Figure 2 shows the angular distance score plotted by age and by stimulus condition for both sexes when approaching a male and a female adult. At all ages and in all stimulus conditions, the boys avoid the full-facing position more than do girls and create a greater angular distance between themselves and the adult. Unlike approach distance, there is only a tendency for the children to turn away most from the standing adult and least from the chair.

Head Orientation. Figure 3 shows the horizontal head orientation scores plotted by age and stimulus condition for both sexes when approaching a male and a female adult. In all cases boys turn their heads away to the side more than do girls. Again the children turn their heads away most from the standing adult and least from the chair. There were no sex differences on the degree of head lowering (i.e., head orien-

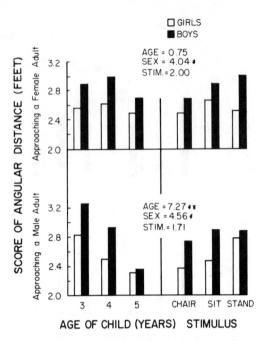

Figure 2   *Angular distance scores for boys and girls plotted by age and by stimulus conditions when approaching a male and female adult. The F values from the analysis of variance are shown (*p<.05, **p<.01, ***p<.001).*

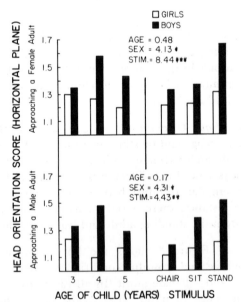

Figure 3   *Horizontal head orientation scores for boys and girls plotted by age and by stimulus conditions when approaching a male and female adult. The F values from the analysis of variance are shown (*p<.05, **p<.01, ***p<.001).*

242

tation in the vertical plane). However, all children lowered their heads more in front of the standing adult.

Gaze. There were no sex differences in the avoidance of gaze at the experimenter at the termination of the approach: 33% of all girls and 37% of all boys avoided gaze. Whereas 22% of all children avoided gaze when they stopped in front of the sitting experimenter, 59% avoided gaze in front of the standing experimenter.

Relationship between the Various End-of-Approach Behaviors. Table 2 shows the correlations between the scores of the various end-position behaviors when facing a standing adult. The relatively low degrees of correlation suggest that approach distance, angular distance, and the two head orientations are, in the main, separate kinesic subsystems that function relatively independently of each other in this situation. Angular distance and horizontal head orientation (both measures of turning away) showed the highest positive correlations, which still only accounts for a quarter of their occurrences. Also head turning away and head lowering show a positive correlation. Approach distance can show a positive, negative, or no correlation with other behaviors. The major sex difference is that for girls approach distance and angular distance correlate positively when approaching a male and negatively when approaching a female. This is one of the few evidences of discriminating the sex of the adult, and it is made by girls.

Approach Behaviors

Approach behaviors to the male and female experimenters did not differ and will be reported together. Differences between girls and boys were computed by performing chi-square tests on the percentage of each group showing the behaviors.

Facial Behaviors. Boys show more common smiling than girls (simple, upper, and broad smiles). Girls show more "ambivalent" smiles than boys (compressed and lip-in smiles). Girls show more "apprehensive" mouth behaviors than do boys (bite lip, tight lips, lips in). Figure 4 shows the percentages of girls and boys performing these behaviors plotted by age and stimulus condition.

The greater amount of common smiling by boys occurs mainly in the 3-year-old group. The girls approach the boys' level more closely by age 5. The sex difference in common smiling is most pronounced during the stimulus conditions of chair and sit (i.e., under relatively lower intensities of stress). The greater amount of "ambivalent" smiling in girls is seen

Table 2 Correlations between the End-of-Approach Behaviors: Approach Distance, Angular Distance, Horizontal and Vertical Head Orientation

Behavior	Sex of Child	Approaching a Standing Male				Approaching a Standing Female			
		N	Angular Distance	Head orient. horiz.	Head orient. vert.	N	Angular Distance	Head orient. horiz.	Head orient. vert.
Approach distance	M	42	-.04	-.15	-.12	60	-.04	-.18	-.29
	F	42	-.23	-.28*	-.38**	60	.37*	-.06	-.11
Angular distance	M	42		.53**	.17	60		.55**	.20
	F	42		.37**	-.04	60		.57**	.12
Head orientation horizontal	M	42			-.33**	60			.33*
	F	42			-.31**	60			.23

*p < .05.
**p < .01.

244

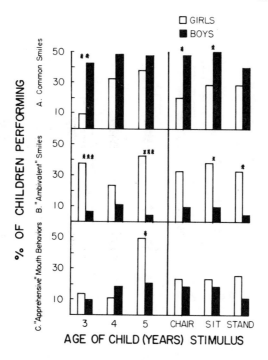

Figure 4   The percentage of girls and boys performing common smiles, "ambivalent" smiles, and apprehensive mouth behaviors, plotted by age and by stimulus condition. The sex differences were determined by a chi-square statistic (*p<.05, **p<.01, ***p<.001).

under the more intense conditions of sit and stand, and is present at ages 3 and 5. The greater amount of "apprehensive" mouth behaviors by girls is not seen until age 5.

Hand and Arm Behaviors.   Girls show many more hand-to-mouth gestures than do boys. In addition, they show more hand gestures to the head and face region (i.e., hand to face, hair, head). Figure 5 shows the percentages of girls and boys performing these behaviors, plotted by age and stimulus condition. For both of these gestures the greater performance by girls is limited to the younger age groups. No difference is seen at age 5, at which time both sexes have decreased the performance of the gestures, but girls have done so more. By the age of 5 girls perform more hand-to-hand-front gestures and boys place their hands behind their backs more. Figure 6 shows the percentages of boys and girls who perform these behaviors plotted by age and stimulus condition.

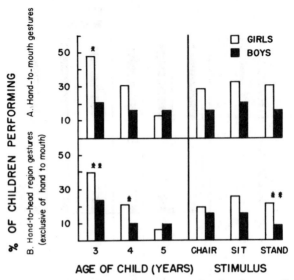

Figure 5 *The percentage of girls and boys performing hand-to-mouth and hand-to-head region (exclusive of mouth) gestures, plotted by age and by stimulus condition. The sex differences were determined by a chi-square statistic (*p<.05, **p<.01).*

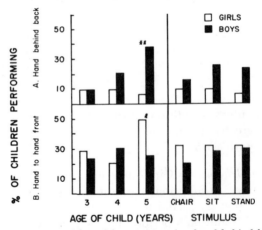

Figure 6 *The percentage of girls and boys performing hand-behind-back and hand-to-hand-front gestures, plotted by age and by stimulus condition. The sex differences were determined by a chi-square statistic (*p<.05, **p<.01).*

All Automanipulations. Automanipulations include all gestures of hand to body or clothing. Girls generally manifest more automanipulation of their body and clothing than do boys. Again this is only evident in the younger age groups. Figure 7 shows the number of automanipulations performed by both sexes, plotted by age and stimulus conditions.

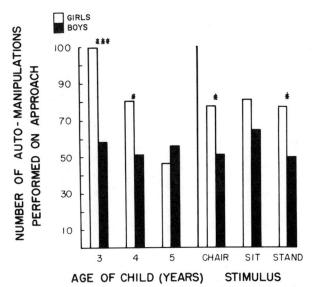

Figure 7   *The number of automanipulations performed by girls and boys, plotted by age and by stimulus condition. The sex differences were determined by a chi-square statistic (* <.05, **p<.01, ***p<.001).*

Gaze on Approach.   The number of looks at the experimenter while approaching showed no sex differences. There were far fewer looks for both sexes when approaching the standing adult.

Speed of Approach.   Specific gaits were not recorded. Speed of approach, however, showed no sex differences, but was recorded only for the group approaching the male adult.

Relationships between the Various Behaviors

To ascertain whether each separate approach behavior was associated with any other approach behaviors or with particular end-position behaviors (i.e., if larger patterns existed) we determined the observed frequency and that expected by chance of any two behaviors occurring together and calculated the chi-square values with the Yates correction for continuity (12). Table 3 shows those behaviors that were associated with each other on a greater-than-chance occurrence.

The hand-to-mouth gesture, which was more common in girls, was also associated with different other behaviors when performed by girls. In girls, hand-to-mouth gesturing was associated with gaze avoidance, with greater turning away of the head, and with not smiling. In boys, the hand-to-mouth gesture showed no association with any of these other

Table 3 The Association between Various Separate Behaviors[a]

	Sex of Child	Hand to Side	Hand to Hand Front	Hand Behind Back	Common Smile	"Ambivalent" Smile	Bite Lip, Tight Lip, or Lip in	Avoid Gaze	Angular Distance Score				Head Orientation Score (Horizontal + Vertical)				
									2	3	4	5	2	3	4	5	N
Hand to mouth	F	6	4	0	1* (5.0)	3	1	17** (11.3)	12	6	3	1	2* (6.8)	2	11	7	22
	M	3	2	0	4	0	1	5	9	1	2	1	6	2	1	4	13
Hand to face and head	F	7	5	3	3	3	1	22** (14.8)	14	8	5	2	4* (9.0)	3	14	8	29
	M	4	2	0	5	0	1	6* (10.3)	11	1	4	2	7	3	2	6	18
Hand to side	F		3* (7.4)	2	1* (5.2)	8* (4.1)	3	17* (11.8)	14	7	2	0	3	4	9	7	23
	M		3	1	4	0	0	13	11	2	2	4	4	3	6	6	19
Hand to hand front	F			1	7	6	5	14	14	8	3	2	11	4	8	4	27
	M			1	9	0	0	9	10	6	1	3	9	5	1	5	20
Hand behind back	F				6* (2.5)	2	0	6	1** (6.0)	4	5** (1.6)	1	4	1	3	3	11
	M				4	1	4* (1.2)	10	6	3	1	3	2	0	4	7	13

248

Common smile	F	5	5	7	11	3	5	0	1	5	1	19
	M	1	3	9** (16.5)	19	7	2	1	12** (5.9)	3	2	4** (10.0)	29
"Ambivalent" smile	F	6** (2.0)	9	10	4	1	0	20*** (9.7)	6	4	3	15
	M	1	2	1	1	1	0	1	0	2	3
Bite lip, tight lip, or lip in	F		7	9	1	1	0	4	0	5	2	11
	M		6	5	3	0	1	1	1	2	4	8

[a] Based on the observation of 168 children approaching a standing adult (84 approaches to a female adult plus 84 approaches to a male adult). The number of times each behavior was observed with each other behavior is shown. The number of times each behavior was expected by chance to occur with each other behavior is shown in parentheses when the difference between observed and expected occurrence is significant.

*p < .05.
**p < .01.
***p < .001.

behaviors. The larger pattern seen in girls (hand to mouth, head turned away, gaze avoidance, no smile) is commonly observed in children in situations of low-level fear—or as part of a behavioral complex interpreted as shyness. When a smile is added, the behaviors appear coy. It is interesting that boys do not show the fuller behavioral pattern in this situation, but rather perform the gesture independently of the other behaviors.

Several other sex differences exist in the constellation of behaviors performed along with different hand gestures. When placing hands behind the back, girls are more likely to turn their bodies away and smile; boys are more likely to leave their body orientation unchanged and exhibit apprehensive mouth behaviors.

Not only, then, is the frequency of separate behaviors different but so are the larger behavioral patterns into which individual behaviors may be integrated.

DISCUSSION

One major developmental finding of this study is striking, although unrelated to sex differences. Separate behaviors (approach distance, angular distance, horizontal and vertical head orientation) that reflect the internal motivational state of the child and act as signals are functioning in a predictable way by the age of 3 and change little over the next 2 years. We found that 3-year-olds showed the same differential use of approach distance and head orientation depending on the position of the stranger as did 5-year-olds. Gesture and facial expression showed more developmental change than did these postural and positional behaviors. The combination of factors involved in adjusting these behaviors to different stimulus conditions are already present at age 3, and obviously further studies must be pushed backward in time. In observing free play interactions among preschool children, Jones (9) comments on his surprise that behavioral items for 4-year-olds were present and organized in much the same way in 2-year-olds. Clearly we are dealing with some behaviors that become organized in a relatively stable form quite early.

The major sex differences and similarities are the following:

1. Girls and boys come equally close to the adult in approach distance.
2. Boys, however, consistently orient away more, both with their bodies and with their faces (i.e., they establish greater angular distance from the adult than do girls).
3. Girls at younger ages perform more automanipulations than do boys.

4. Specifically, girls perform more hand-to-mouth, hand-to-face, and hand-to-head region gestures than do boys.

5. Younger boys tend to perform more common smiling, whereas girls show more "ambivalent" smiling and more "apprehensive" mouth behaviors.

6. Several specific gestures that may be considered to be culturally sex typed emerge during the period from 3 to 5 years.

7. Larger patterns involving these behavioral units show some sex differences.

Distance

The lack of sex differences in the distance to which children approached the adult requires some comment. Several investigators have examined the personal space of children through the use of silhouettes of dyads where the nature of the relationship between the dyad is given different assignments (friendly, unfriendly, liked, feared) and the two figures are placed at various distances apart. Guardo (13) found that, among sixth-graders, girls chose closer placements to someone liked than did boys, and boys chose closer placements to someone feared than did girls. Meisels and Guardo, also using projective techniques (14), found that from the third to tenth grade girls chose greater distances than boys in negative affect situations. Generally, the explanation has been that boys are expected to show less fear and girls are allowed to experience and demonstrate more intimacy. With regard to approach distance, our findings do not support the contention that girls stay farther away from a strange or threatening person. However, this study involves younger children, the use of direct observation of actual behavior rather than semiprojective techniques, and did not measure approach distance to liked or friendly adults.

The literature is generally consistent in the finding that children over 5 years old approach a same-sex child closer than an opposite-sex child until adolescence, when a reversal occurs (14). Children in this study did not approach closer to a like-sexed strange adult. Most probably the sex of the experimenters was less important than, or overshadowed by, the fact that both were strange, threatening, and adult.

Lastly, it is usually held that males, in our culture at least, maintain a greater interpersonal distance (7, 15). Among primates dominant males "command" a larger space—if not generally, at least when assuming a threat posture. It is reported that in schoolyard play, children observed a greater distance from the more dominant boys (16). We find that by the age of 5 years, but not before, boys will not approach each other as closely as girls will approach girls (17). Nonetheless, when approaching a strange adult, the boys gave no evidence of utilizing a larger space or observing a larger space around the adult male. Under the conditions of this experiment, the instructions to "walk up to me and stop when you get there" may have prevented sex differences in approach distance from appearing, although it did not prevent the boys from maintaining a greater angular distance than did girls.

It could be argued that while our instructions limited the use of approach distance, boys "made up" for that by angling away more, and that under more natural conditions boys might remain further away, as they do with their peers, but then they might not angle away more. However, there is no evidence to suggest that approach distance and angular distance functionally substitute for each other in this situation. The correlations performed between the scores of approach distance and angular distance showed no significant negative correlations. Approach distance and angular distance operate independently of each other and appear to serve different signal functions.

Head Orientation

In apes, turning the head away to the side in response to a stare from another animal is considered to be one of the cardinal behaviors indicating appeasement, submission, or the nonintention of aggression (8). Head aversion appears to act as an appeasement gesture in other primates where visually fixating an opponent functions as a threat or sign of dominance (18). In humans, too, gaze aversion with its attendant head to the side or down is considered to be a submissive gesture in the context of mutual gaze. At an earlier point in development than 3 years, head aversion appears more purely as an avoidance or withdrawal reaction. However, head aversion in the experimental situation is not simply a withdrawal or flight behavior but partakes more of an appeasement or a "cut-off" behavior (19), since, rather than being part of a complete withdrawal or escape pattern, it allows the child to remain in very close proxemic contact with the threatening adult, during which time he may even perform smiles while face averting.

In this light it is interesting that boys of all three ages show a greater degree of this submissive or appeasing gesture common to all primates than do girls.

Body Orientation

Facing the body away, as well as the head, appears to be an important appeasement gesture in most primates where staring, facing, and "squaring off" are signs of dominance or threat. In primates, Sparks (18) considers turning the body away to be an important general feature of two specific appeasement behaviors: sexual presenting and presenting to be groomed. Although these two appeasement behaviors have no apparent analogy in human behavior, the common feature of turning the body away, may. Orienting the body away redirects the threat, or potential threat display and may also be part of a flight or preparation-for-flight pattern. In either event, this behavior is more marked in boys. This finding is consistent with the report that men maintain a greater angular distance (shoulder axis) during interactions than do women (20).

In general, then, with both head and body, boys maintained greater angular distance from the adults, and to the extent that these behaviors are appeasement gestures or signals of the nonintention of aggression, boys performed them more readily.

Facial Expression on Approach

Boys showed more common smiling, girls showed more ambivalent smiling and more lip biting, tight lips and lips in. The place of the human smile in comparative ethology is uncertain. Morphologically, the human smile with teeth showing resembles the grin face of many primates, which is clearly an appeasement sign (21). Forms of the human smile are thought to function in low-level fear situations as a sign of appeasement or the nonintention of aggression (3). However, the human smile also clearly functions in purely affiliative situations.

Some human smiles arise in conflict situations where there is a tendency to flee and a simultaneously roughly equal tendency to approach (22). This perhaps most closely approximates the situation these children experienced.

Children who smiled neither came closer to the adult nor remained further away ($t = 0.49$). Among both boys and girls common smiling (but not "ambivalent" smiling) was associated with a more direct face orientation toward the adult ($t = 4.66$). This could be interpreted as a more affiliative response on the part of these children, or the smile can be seen as an appeasement behavior which the child performs when more directly facing the staring adult, instead of turning his head away. Some smiles gave the clear impression of being affiliative behaviors. A larger number of smiles that were often fleeting or frozen gave more the impression of appeasement behaviors. The signal value of the smile (affiliative versus appeasing) appeared to be determined not only by the form in time and space of the smile itself but also by the combination of postural and gestural behaviors with which it occurred.

In general, the facial behavior of the girls in this situation appeared to be more clearly either affiliative or fearful, whereas that of the boys was more indeterminate, having more the character of appeasement behavior. These subjective judgments of the signal value of the children's facial behavior are not documented by the data and require a finer and more extensive behavioral analysis than that performed.

Hand Behaviors

McGrew (23), who studied the introduction of 3-year-old children into a nursery group, considers automanipulation to be one of the signs of social stress, fearfulness, and uncertainty. Characteristically, when the mother brought the child into the group, the child held his mother's hand with one hand while performing some automanipulation with the other, often thumb sucking. When the new children were approached by established children at the school, all showed automanipulations, and 4 of 15 sucked their fingers. Grant (24) considers automanipulations to be displacement activities. McGrew (25) has observed that they are behaviors of subordinate individuals. In squirrel monkeys, Rosenblum, Levy, and Kaufman (26) have reported that a female introduced into an established group shows an increased rate of autogrooming for several days. They attribute this in part to the general agitation associated with disruptions of dominance relations. Van Iersel and Bol (27) consider autogrooming to be a "displacement activity" elicited when two opposing social tendencies (approach and avoidance) are activated.

The girls in this experiment performed more automanipulation than the boys. This is consistent with the impressions of new nursery members reported by McGrew (23). The greater amount of hand-to-mouth and hand-to-head region gestures in girls is striking at ages 3 and 4 but is no longer present by age 5. Korner (28) has reported greater oral sensitization and more mouth-dominated hand-mouth behaviors in female newborns and suggests that this innate sex difference may relate to the more frequent and persistent thumb sucking in girls as well as their higher proclivity for other oral symptomatology. More hand-to-mouth gestures in a fearful situation may be another derivative of this early difference.

There are two sex-typed hand gestures that emerge between the ages of 3 to 5: by the fifth year boys do more hand placement behind the back, by the fifth year girls show more hand-to-hand-front gestures. These gestures that are moderately sex typed in this culture are acquired between the fourth and fifth year.

GENERAL DISCUSSION

A central issue of this conference concerns the biological and cultural factors influencing the emergence of sex differences. One biological factor that may bear on the finding that girls and boys act differently in approach behavior situations is the possibility of differential rates of maturation. The general tendency for girls to mature more rapidly has confounded the interpretation of several sex differences (29). However, the sex differences we find are not easily attributable to a more rapid maturation in girls. In fact, if any maturational pattern is evident, the girls seem to utilize many hand and facial behaviors that are more characteristic of younger children.

A second issue concerns whether the experimental situation elicits a different internal experience for boys and girls—that is, whether each of the motivational systems (fear, affiliation, curiosity, aggression) may be activated to different extents in each sex, thus resulting in different behavioral expressions. Equally likely, girls and boys may have the identical internal experience but for biological and/or cultural reasons may recruit slightly different behaviors, or even the same behaviors, but in either case, organize them differently into distinguishable behavioral constellations expressing the same internal state. The data permit no decision between these possibilities.

In addition, it is difficult to determine relative degrees of activation of any one motivational system for one sex versus the other. For example, in evaluating the degree of fearfulness, as inferred from behavior, girls would be rated more fearful by the criteria of facial expressions (more apprehensive mouth behaviors and ambivalent smiles) and hand gestures (more hand-to-mouth gestures and more automanipulation). Boys would be rated more fearful on the criteria of angular distance and head orientation away. With regard to the important parameter of approach distance, there is no sex difference. Clearly, we cannot answer the question whether girls or boys are generally more fearful within the moderate level of activation that occurs when approaching a strange adult. We are left, then, with the finding that in the same stimulus situation girls and boys perform behaviors that differ in many interesting elements. The subtle but significant differences in the behaviors of girls and boys are important to the extent that they may provide subtly but significantly different signals to the interacting partner.

Some speculations will be ventured on the possible functions of the different behavioral signals emitted by girls and boys in this situation. The more characteristic female pattern gives the impression that girls are more afraid. This impression comes mainly from the greater amount of automanipulations, particularly hand-to-mouth gestures, and from the increased presence of ambivalent smiling and apprehensive mouth behaviors. The more characteristic male pattern gives the impression less of fear and more of the boys being in an interpersonal contest of some kind. An important feature of the male behaviors of turning the head and body away and common smiling is that these same behaviors can also be used in competitive aggressive encounters to modulate the interaction without signaling fear. In an antagonistic encounter, real or playful, turning the head and body away and common smiling serve two signal functions: as appeasement behaviors to inhibit the aggression of the opponent and as signals of the nonintention of aggression on the part of the performer. A cardinal feature of the human threat display is to face, stare at, and "square off" against the opponent. Appeasement behaviors commonly consist of redirecting away the threat behavior (3). The more the boy turns away, the more his behavior functions as appeasement; the more he turns toward, the more it approaches a threat display—providing he does not manifest other behaviors that signal fear, such as hand-to-mouth gesturing, ambivalent smiles, or apprehensive mouth behaviors. The degree of turning allows him to modulate his response on a continuum between appeasement and aggression. This response to a threat permits the boy to remain in close proxemic contact with his opponent and signal from moment to moment the degree to which he accepts or refuses the threat, but without displaying overt signs of fearfulness. The male response pattern to threat, then, consists of behaviors that function as signals in an aggressive system as well as in a fear system. The female response pattern to threat consists of behaviors that do not function in an aggressive system.

The relative activation of the different motivational systems in response to threat may be no different for boys and girls. However, it may become integrated into different behavioral pathways for each. The particular response pattern in boys may have adaptive value if nature or the culture had to equip them with appropriate behaviors to deal with the fear that arises from the greater amount of competitive aggression that their biology or the culture demands of them.

Since the behaviors performed are not only patterns of reaction but at the same time signs and signals that affect the immediately subsequent behavior of the person receiving them, the existence of different patterns has implications for the nature of the interaction that each sex will contribute to creating for themselves—that is, for the ongoing course of their developmental experience. For example, rough-and-tumble play, which young males, both primate and human, engage in more than do females

(9, 30), involves the back and forth of being the "aggressor" or the chased, the threatener or threatened. Many of the frequent switches in who is the primary "aggressor" are negotiated by shifts in head and body orientation (i.e., assuming the face on, staring, "squared off" threat position or turning away from it). Children know well these signals to temporarily exchange roles. Part of the excitement and arousal of rough-and-tumble play must involve elements of fear; however, overt expressions of fear are not seen—in fact the opposite, the "play face" is seen (9). Expressions of fear would likely terminate the play. Perhaps one reason girls engage less in this activity is that their behavioral response patterns to threat, even in play, are more likely to terminate the activity rather than act as signals that contribute to maintaining the activity.

The greater availability of this response pattern to the activation of fear in boys may thus greatly facilitate the likelihood of their engaging in competitive, aggressive encounters and accordingly expand the male experience with aggression. The suggestion that a given pattern of fear response could lead to more aggression is complementary, rather than an alternative, to the possibility that males have a stronger aggressive drive.

This study demonstrates clear sex differences in the behaviors of children approaching a strange, mildly threatening adult. However, it throws no light on the origins of these differences. The existence of sex differences by the early age of 3 argues only very weakly, if at all, for a biological origin. In any event, the question of origins can only be approached once the behaviors to be explored have been identified.

ACKNOWLEDGMENTS

We thank Mary Ann Ford and Gail Wasserman for their assistance in the study, and Dr. Joseph Fleiss for statistical consultation.

The research has been supported by the Grant Foundation and the Research Foundation for Mental Hygiene, New York State.

REFERENCES

1. Schaffer, H. F., *J. Child Psychol Psychiatr* **7**: 95, 1966.
2. Bronson, G. W., *Monogr Soc Res Child Dec* **37**: No. 3, 1972.
3. Eibl-Eibesfeldt, I., *Ethology, the Biology of Behavior*, Holt, Rinehart and Winston, New York, 1970.
4. Bischof, N., in Lewis, M. and L. Rosenblum (eds.), *The Origins of Behavior*, Vol. 2, Wiley, New York, 1974.

5. Bretherton, I. and M. D. S. Ainsworth, in Lewis, M. and L. Rosenblum (eds.), *The Origins of Behavior*, Vol. 2, Wiley, New York, 1974.

6. Horowitz, M. J., D. F. Duff, and L. O. Stratton, *Arch Gen Psychiatr* **11**: 651, 1964.

7. Aiello, J. R. and S. E. Jones, *J Pers Soc Psychol* **19**: 351, 1971.

8. Schaller, G. B., *The Mountain Gorilla*, University of Chicago, Chicago, 1963.

9. Jones, N. B., in Morris, D. (ed.), *Primate Ethology*, Weidenfeld and Nicholson, London, 1967.

10. Smith, P. K. and K. Connolly, in Jones, N. B. (ed.), *Ethological Studies of Child Behaviour*, Cambridge University Press, Cambridge, 1972, p. 65.

11. Brannigan, C. R. and D. A. Humphries, in Jones, N. B. (ed.), *Ethological Studies of Child Behaviour*, Cambridge University Press, Cambridge, 1972, p. 37.

12. Fleiss, J. L., *Statistical Methods for Rates and Proportions*, Wiley, New York, 1973.

13. Guardo, C. J., *Child Dev* **40**: 143, 1969.

14. Meisels, M. and C. J. Guardo, *Child Dev* **40**: 1167, 1969.

15. Willis, F. N. *Psychonomic Sci* **5**: 221, 1966.

16. Freedman, D. G., paper presented at the Society for Research on Child Development Meeting, Philadelphia, March 1973.

17. Stern, D. N., manuscript in preparation.

18. Sparks, J., in Morris, D. (ed.), *Primate Ethology*, Weidenfeld and Nicholson, London, 1967, p. 148.

19. Chance, M., *Symp Zool Soc London,* **8**: 71, 1962.

20. Jones, S. E., *J Soc Psychol* **84**: 35, 1971.

21. Van Hooff, J. A. R. A., in Morris, D. (ed.), *Primate Ethology*, Weidenfeld and Nicholson, London, 1967, p. 7.

22. Ambrose, J. A., *J Child Psychol Psychiatr* **4**: 167, 1963.

23. McGrew, W. C., in Jones, N. B. (ed.), *Ethological Studies of Child Behaviour*, Cambridge University Press, Cambridge, 1972, p. 129.

24. Grant, E. C., in *Proceedings of the Leeds Symposium on Behavioural Disorders,* May and Baker, Dagenham, 1965.

25. McGrew, W. C., in Carpenter, C. R. (ed.), *Behaviour, Proceedings of the Second International Congress of Primatology*, Karger, Zurich, 1969.

26. Rosenblum, L. A., E. J. Levy, and I. C. Kaufman, *Anim Behav* **16**: 288, 1968.

27. Iersel, J. J. A. van, and A. Bol, *Behavior* **13**: 1, 1958.

28. Korner, A. R., *J Child Psychol Psychiatr* **14**: 19, 1973.

29. Coates, S., this volume, Chapter 14.

30. Young, W. C., R. W. Goy, and C. H. Phoenix, *Science* **143**: 212, 1964.

CHAPTER 14

Sex Differences in Field Independence Among Preschool Children

SUSAN COATES

Department of Psychiatry
Division of Child and Adolescent Psychiatry
State University of New York
Downstate Medical Center
Brooklyn, New York

Field independence is one of the most extensively and thoroughly studied constructs in all of personality research dealing with cognitive style. This particular perceptual ability, usually assessed by embedded-figures tests and the rod-and-frame test, involves the capacity to disembed items from organized perceptual contexts. These perceptual tests produce a continuum of scores, with ability to overcome an embedding context referred to as field independence, whereas being dominated by the organization of the field is referred to as field dependence. Performance on this dimension has been demonstrated to be closely interlocked with fundamental aspects of personality functioning (1).

Sex differences favoring males in field independence have been so consistently and pervasively found in older children and adults that Kagan and Kogan (2) refer to these findings as "something of a cause

259

célèbre" of personality cognition research. Indeed, field independence and its counterpart in cognition, analytic thinking, have come to be considered a basic male characteristic, whereas women are thought to be more field dependent and global in their thinking.

Sex differences favoring males appear consistently in most studies by the time of adolescence. Although they persist through most of adulthood, there is some evidence to suggest that they disappear in geriatric populations (3, 4). Sex differences favoring boys have been documented not only in most samples studied within the United States but also in most samples from other parts of the world, including France, Holland, Italy, Africa, Japan, and Hong Kong (5). Only in the Eskimos of Canada do sex differences not appear (6).

Although sex differences in field independence appear with remarkable consistency in older children and adults, the distribution of scores for the two sexes overlaps considerably, and the magnitude of difference between the sexes rarely amounts to more than half a standard deviation.

FIELD INDEPENDENCE AND PSYCHOLOGICAL DIFFERENTIATION

During the last 20 years, studies of field independence that have been carried out by Witkin's group and others have demonstrated that individuals tend to function consistently across such apparently diverse areas of psychological functioning as perception, intelligence, and personality (1).

It has been shown, for example, that field-independent persons are not only able to disembed when presented with perceptual problems but can disembed as well when presented with intellectual problems that require set breaking, restructuring, and insight. In the realm of interpersonal- and self-perception, evidence suggests that field-independent people usually have a more developed sense of separate identity as well as a more articulated body concept. As conceptualized by Witkin, a developed sense of separate identity refers to an "awareness of the needs, feelings, and attributes" that a person identifies as his own and perceives as separate and "distinct from the needs, feelings, and attributes of others" (ref. 1, p. 134). Figure drawings have been used to assess the body concept by means of a body sophistication scale that takes such things as level, degree of detail, and sex differentiation into consideration (1).

Several studies suggest that field-dependent and field-independent subjects differ in the direction of their motivational interests. Field-dependent people tend to be more socially oriented in a variety of situations, whereas field-independent people tend primarily to have nonsocial interests (7–9). Despite their greater social orientation, there is some evidence that field-dependent people are less accurate in making fine discriminations of other persons' affective states (10, 11).

In the area of defense mechanisms, it has been shown in a number of studies that field-dependent people tend to rely primarily on such defenses as denial and repression, whereas field-independent people primarily use intellectualization and isolation (1, 12).

In attempting to conceptualize these self-consistent findings, Witkin has drawn on the concept of differentiation that had been applied to psychological functioning at an earlier date by H. Werner and K. Lewin. According to this scheme, development proceeds from the global to the articulated. Witkin's unique use of this construct is to suggest that, as differentiation develops in individuals, it does so to a consistent degree across many areas. In the context of this scheme, he currently conceives of each of the separate indicators of differentiation (field independence, sense of separate identity, and articulation of the body concept) as "tracers" of the broader unitary process of differentiation (13).

One's level of differentiation, as indicated by the perceptual measures (14) as well as figure drawings (15) and defenses (12), has been shown to increase with age, whereas one's position relative to others tends to remain stable even during periods of such rapid and profound change as adolescence. These studies suggest, then, that field independence is not only an indicator of a central dimension of personality functioning but also one that has remarkable continuity over time.

EXPLANATIONS FOR SEX DIFFERENCES IN FIELD INDEPENDENCE

In attempting to understand the origins of field independence and differentiation, as well as sex differences in this dimension, Witkin has turned primarily to the mother–child relationship, although he has not ruled out the possibility that biological influences are involved. Several studies have provided evidence suggesting that field independence is related to the extent to which a child's experiences, especially with a mothering person, enable it to separate and develop as an autonomous person (1). Witkin has hypothesized that sex differences favoring boys in field independence are a consequence of cultural pressures that encourage girls to remain more dependent than boys. Empirical support for this position comes from a cross-cultural study (6) in which the sexes were compared for field independence between the Temne of Africa, a society in which females are treated as dependent, and the Eskimos of Canada, where women are in no way treated as dependent. Berry found that in several samples of Eskimos no significant sex differences emerged in embedded-figures tests, in contrast to several Temne samples in which there emerged significant sex differences favoring males.

Two other investigators have offered explanatory hypotheses for sex differences in field independence. Like Witkin, Maccoby (16) feels that girls and boys are subjected to differing cultural pressures, but she has placed specific emphasis on the motivational impact of these societal influences. She feels that tendencies toward passive dependence in females and active independence in males may act as mediating processes in the development of field independence in either of the following ways: First, the passive-dependent female may be primarily oriented to social cues and, as a result, finds it difficult to give up this orientation in order to use the internal cues that are needed for field-independent functioning. Second, sex differences in initiative and assertion may effect the capacity to solve certain cognitive tasks, including field-independence problems. Passive-dependent females, who are oriented toward having the environment act on them, rather than the reverse, may be particularly handicapped when attempting to solve cognitive problems that require analytic ability, whereas the greater assertiveness of boys may give them an advantage.

An alternative explanation of the field-independence sex differences has been offered by Sherman (17). Like Witkin and Maccoby, she feels that sex differences result from cultural stereotyping of behavior, but she believes that the mediating processes are experiential rather than motivational. She reasons that since boys are encouraged to spend their time at tasks involving block building, aiming, construction, and a variety of other types of sensory motor activities, they consequently have a greater opportunity to develop and practice spatial skills. Girls, on the other hand, who spend their time playing with dolls and in other activities that primarily involve social interaction, have less opportunity to develop these skills. Although this theory was intended to explain sex differences in spatial ability (under which Sherman subsumes field independence), it may be relevant as well to the development of disembedding ability, which is that aspect of field independence that is distinct from spatial ability.

Although there is some evidence to suggest that cultural factors are involved in the development of sex differences in field independence, there are few data yet available with which to appraise the motivational and experiential explanations: they are not, however, mutually exclusive. In all likelihood, both motivational and experiential differences are causally involved.

EMPIRICAL STUDIES OF SEX DIFFERENCES
IN FIELD INDEPENDENCE IN PRESCHOOL CHILDREN

Although sex differences favoring boys at older age levels are well established, much less is known about these differences in young children. This is partly due to the fact that valid measures of field independence have not been available. Recently, however, the Preschool Embedded-Figures Test (PEFT) was developed to assess field independence in young children (18). This test is the counterpart of the embedded-figures tests used at older age levels to assess field independence. There is considerable evidence that its validity and reliability are adequate.

With the PEFT available, studies of early sex differences in field independence have now been made possible.

Table 1 summarizes the principal studies (including some that are unpublished) on sex differences in field independence using the PEFT.

As can be seen in Table 1, overall sex differences favoring girls during the years of 3 to 5 were found in the original standardization study (18). These findings have now been replicated in several subsequent studies. Block (19) found significant sex differences favoring girls in a middle-class sample in a group of 4-year-old children, but not in a sample of 3-year-olds. Using a sample of middle- and lower-middle-class children, Costrich and Kurash (20) found similar results using a modified version of the PEFT that was developed for a special experimental procedure. Sex-difference findings favoring females have been replicated as well on lower-class samples. Derman and Meissner (21) report significant sex differences favoring females on Headstart samples in the Educational Testing Service longitudinal study. In two groups of children enrolled in a Get Set program, Beller (22) and Beller and Howell (23) found significant sex differences favoring females.

To date, only three studies using the PEFT with preschool children have failed to reveal sex differences favoring girls. Two of these samples consisted of 4-year-old lower-class children (24, 25), and the third tested 2-year-old middle-class children (26). In all, six out of nine studies using the PEFT at the preschool age level have found sex differences favoring females, and in three, no sex differences were observed.

There are, however, a few studies of sex differences in preschool children that have used another instrument for assessing field independence. This instrument, the Children's Embedded-Figures Test (CEFT), was developed to assess field independence in older children (27). It appears to be reliable in the preschool age range, but its validity has not been established at this age level (13). In two of these studies, no sex differ-

Table 1 Summary of Studies of Sex Differences in PEFT

Investigator	Sample	Age	Sex with Higher Mean	Significance
Beller (22)	Lower and middle class, $N=255$	3–4	F	$p<.05$
Beller and Howell (23)	Lower class, $N=108$	4–5	F	$p<.05$
Block (19)	Middle class, $N=110$	3	F	N.S.
	Middle-class, $N=122$	4	F	$p<.01$
Coates (18)	Middle class, $N=248$	3–5	F	$p<.05$
Costrich and Kurash (20)	Middle and lower middle class, $N=41$	3–5	F	$p<.01$
Derman and Meissner (21)	Lower class, $N=601$	4–5	F	$p<.005$
Seitz (25)	Lower class, $N=47$	4–5	M	N.S.
Shipman (24)	Lower class, $N=1288$	4–5	F	N.S.
Waldrop (26)	Middle class, $N=63$	2–3	F	N.S.

ences were found (27, 28). In the third study, however, a significant sex difference favoring boys was noted (29). The Dreyer results are difficult to interpret because they are based on averages of extremes for each sex. A survey of 12 studies shows that although sex differences are not always found, when they do occur, they seem to favor females.

This conclusion might appear to conflict with Maccoby's (30) recent review in which she cites five studies where no significant sex differences were found in disembedding ability at the preschool age level. However, in three of these studies, tests of visual perception were employed, such as matching figures, disk sorting, and a visual memory task (31–33). In none of them was disembedding required by the subject.

In one of the studies cited by Maccoby that does *not* yield a significant sex difference, the disembedding required was of a different nature from that required by the PEFT and the CEFT (34). This task involved disembedding from a distracting and disorganized context rather than from an organized context, which is an essential component of field-independence tasks. At older age levels, the processes underlying disembedding from organized and disorganized contexts have been demonstrated to differ substantially (35). Only those tasks that involved disembedding from organized contexts loaded a factor shared by other field-independence measures. Distraction tasks loaded a separate factor. Therefore lumping together those disembedding tasks that involve set breaking and those that involve resistance to distraction cannot be justified on empirical grounds. Furthermore, the failure to make such a distinction has tended to perpetuate conceptual confusion in this area of research.

The only study reported by Maccoby as finding no significant sex differences that used a valid measure of field independence is the one conducted by Shipman (24), to which we have already referred. However, when her sample was retested the following year, at age 5, with the PEFT, sex differences were significant for the combined 4- and 5-year-old group. Since means and standard deviations were reported separately for each age group, we were able to test the significance of sex differences for the 5-year-old group separately. Significant sex differences emerged favoring females at this age level ($p < .001$).

The fact that several studies did not find sex differences favoring females, combined with the fact that Shipman found no sex differences in her 4-year-old subjects but significant sex differences in the same sample when they were retested at age 5, raises the question of whether sex differences favoring females on field-independence tasks occur only within a limited period during the preschool years.

CHANGES IN FIELD INDEPENDENCE OVER THE PRESCHOOL AGE RANGE

Most of the studies reviewed so far have investigated male–female differences in field independence by lumping together data from children of all preschool ages from 3 to 6. Two exceptions to this are Block (19), who studied 3- and 4-year-olds separately, and Shipman, who studied 4-year-olds. Recently, however, the author has obtained sex differences separately at each age level between 3 and 6 years of age using the standardized measure, the PEFT. The subjects studied were 297 children from private schools for middle-class children in New York City.

In order to test the significance of the mean sex differences in PEFT performance at each age level, Kramer's (36) extension of D. Duncan's multiple-range test to groups with unequal numbers was used. As can be seen in Table 2, and at each level except age 6, the mean for girls is higher than the mean for boys. At age 3, the difference is negligible, but by age 4, it amounts to about one-quarter of a standard deviation. Only at age 5, where the mean difference is equal to half a standard deviation, does this difference reach statistical significance ($p<.05$). These results parallel the findings of Shipman on her longitudinal sample, where sex differences on PEFT were not significant at age 4 but became significant by age 5.

Unlike Dreyer, we did not find significant sex differences at the higher age ranges. However, by age 6, there was a trend in this direction. It may be that some of the previous studies have not found sex differences because lumping together several age levels has masked this difference. Finally, some of the inconsistency in sex-difference findings may have resulted from sampling fluctuations.

SEX DIFFERENCES IN COGNITIVE TESTS CORRELATED WITH PEFT

Evidence that some cognitive tests known to be highly correlated with field-independence measures follow a sex-difference pattern similar to that observed with the PEFT at the preschool age level comes from a study by Herman (37). He studied sex differences in the standardization data of the Wechsler Preschool and Primary Scale of Intelligence (WPPSI). Included in this battery is a block-design subtest that has been shown to be highly correlated with PEFT performance in preschool children (18). Its counterpart on the WISC is so highly correlated with field-independence measures at older age levels that it has often been used as an alternative measure of field independence (38). At the preschool age level, block design loads the perceptual organization factor of the WPPSI (39) as well as a larger perceptual-analytic factor that includes all

Table 2   PEFT Means and Standard Deviation by Age

Age	N	Mean Girls	SD	Age	N	Mean Boys	SD
3	30	10.73	3.74	3	26	10.58	4.93
4	70	13.99	4.39	4	48	12.87	3.43
5	34	16.29	3.90	5	39	14.21	4.00
6	25	17.00	2.34	6	26	17.85	2.58

of the perceptual organization subtests of the WPPSI and the PEFT (40). At older age levels, sex differences in the block-design subtest from the Wechsler Adult Intelligence Scale, like other measures of field independence, tend to favor males (41). However, in Herman's study of the WPPSI, sex differences in block-design performance favored females in preschool children. Thus the pattern of sex differences in block-design performance, where females excel in early childhood and males excel at older age levels, appears to be similar to the pattern in embedded-figures tests.

In order to determine whether the PEFT pattern of sex differences at the preschool age level generalizes to other cognitive measures known to be highly correlated with it, the WPPSI block-design means for each sex between the ages of 4 and 6½ from the Wechsler standardization data (37) were compared with the PEFT means.

For the PEFT, means for each sex were available at ages 3, 4, 5, and 6. For block design, means for each sex were available at ages 4, 4½, 5, 5½, 6, and 6½. As we can see in Figure 1, if PEFT and block-design mean scores are converted into a male/female ratio, so that ratios under 1.00 reflect differences favoring females and scores greater than 1.00 reflect differences favoring males, a considerable increase is seen in PEFT scores favoring females up until age 5 (at which time they become significant). By age 6, a shift has taken place so that the direction now favors males, although this difference is not statistically significant. A similar pattern emerges for block design where sex differences are initially

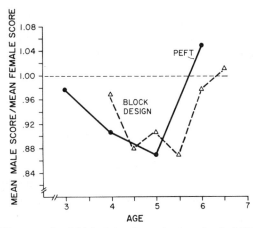

Figure 1   Sex differences in field independence in preschool children. Data for the PEFT from Coates (18); data for the block-design test from Herman (37).

small; they reach their peak at age 5 and reverse to a direction favoring males at age 6½.

These results suggest that both measures of field independence, PEFT and the WPPSI block design subtest, follow a similar descriptive course in their pattern of sex-difference development during the preschool age period.

Finally, two studies of the WPPSI geometric design subtest have found sex differences favoring females in preschool children (37, 42). This subtest, like the PEFT, requires the subject to visually analyze organized gestalts for successful performance and has been shown as well to load the same perceptual–analytic factor as PEFT and the WPPSI block-design test (40). Taken together, these findings suggest that sex differences favoring females in preschool children are not a function of the specific format of the PEFT but generalize to other measures of perceptual disembedding as well.

DIRECTIONS FOR FUTURE RESEARCH

Since the theories of the origins of sex differences in field independence that have been proposed by Witkin, Maccoby, and Sherman are all based on the assumption that sex differences favor males when they occur, these theories now need some revision. Some explanation is needed that would offer either reasons why girls may be superior at the preschool age level or why boys may have particular difficulty.

Although Maccoby has focused on the importance of assertive behavior for the development of field independence, she has also proposed a broader conception of the relationship of passive dependence and active aggression to the development of intellectual functioning in general. She has suggested that the optimal position on the passive dependent–active aggressive continuum for successful intellectual functioning is an intermediate one. Thus she views extreme passivity and extreme aggressiveness as both inhibiting successful cognitive functioning. She reasons that, since girls as a group tend to fall closer to the passive *end* of the continuum and boys as a group closer group to the aggressive *end*, optimal cognitive functioning will occur in girls when they shift to the more active *end* and in boys when they shift to the more passive *end*. In support of this explanation she cites empirical evidence suggesting that girls with high analytic ability tend to be more aggressive than other girls, whereas boys with high analytic ability tend to be more passive than other boys (16).

Recent evidence from our own laboratory suggests that Maccoby's conceptualization may also be relevant to field-independent functioning in preschool children. Girls who were rated by their teachers as primarily interested in feminine activities, such as playing house or playing with dolls, tended to be field dependent (8). Somewhat more masculine girls who were entirely uninterested in dolls and preferred to spend their time making collages, painting, and solving puzzles, tended to be more field independent. In contrast, boys who were rated by their teachers as the toughest and most aggressive in the group were almost always field dependent, whereas their relatively more passive counterparts tended to be more field independent. In the few instances, however, where boys had extreme cross-sex interests, to the point that they were primarily interested in doll and house play, they too, were field dependent. These results suggest that a degree of cross-sex typing, but not complete cross-sex typing, may be associated with the development of field independence in young children.

If one uses Maccoby's conceptualization to understand sex differences in field independence in older children and adults, one would have to assume that, since boys are more field independent, as a group they must fall closer than girls to the middle and optimal point on the passive–active continuum.

Given evidence from the present review that preschool girls appear to be more field independent than preschool boys, it seems important to ask whether there is any evidence at this age to suggest that girls as a group occupy a position on the passive–active continuum that is closer to the middle and optimal point than do boys.

There is already evidence to suggest that some of the same variables related to passivity and activity that have been correlated with the development of field independence in older children and adults are also correlated in preschool children. For example, Coates (18) found that greater autonomous achievement striving, which refers to task orientation and the capacity for sustained directed activity, was associated with the development of field independence in preschool children. Similar findings at older age levels have been reported by Crandall and Sinkeldam (43) and Wertheim and Mednick (44).

Since sex differences in autonomous achievement striving are known to favor boys at older ages and since this variable may be one that is involved in the development of sex differences in field independence at older age levels, it seemed important to determine whether there was any evidence of a sex-difference reversal or shift in this variable in preschool children. Indeed, there are at least two studies that have found greater autonomous achievement striving in preschool girls than in preschool boys. Baumrind (45, 46) found sex differences in autonomous achievement striving favoring preschool girls. More recently these results have been replicated in our own laboratory (47). It appears, then, that there is some evidence that there may be a sex-difference reversal in at least one kind of assertiveness in preschool children.

Evidence suggesting that a developmental shift may occur in the direction of increased assertion and aggression for both boys and girls comes from Kohlberg's (48) review of the development of sex typing and cross-sex interests in young children. Cross-sex interests refers to having greater interests of those of the opposite sex than others of one's own sex. The findings tended to indicate that the cross-sex interests of girls first increase during the preschool period and then decrease. For boys, same-sex interests and preferences increased during the same period.

Theoretical support for the idea that assertiveness increases during the preschool years for both sexes comes from the psychoanalytic theory of psychosexual development, which maintains that en route to establishing feminine and masculine identity, both sexes pass through a phallic period of development.

Thus both Kohlberg's work and psychoanalytic theory suggest that there may be a period during development when both sexes have shifted to a position on the passive–active continuum that is closer to the aggressive end. These findings may appear to be inconsistent with the findings of Baumrind (45, 46) and Coates and Lord (47) that girls display more autonomous achievement striving than boys. A closer look at other data suggests that this may be only an apparent contradiction.

Sex differences in aggression favoring boys are well established by the preschool years (49). Furthermore, there is evidence to suggest that aggression in boys in the preschool years interferes with autonomous achievement striving as well as field-independent functioning. Beller (50) found that aggression in boys was significantly and highly negatively correlated with field independence. These findings have recently been replicated in our own laboratory (47). The same variables were uncorrelated for girls. Since there were large sex differences in aggression, in both studies, the authors interpreted their findings as suggesting that high levels of aggression interfere with field-independent functioning.

Furthermore, Coates and Lord (47) found that in boys aggression was significantly negatively correlated with autonomous achievement striving. Again, these variables were unrelated in girls. Such data suggest that high levels of aggression interfere with the kind of organized assertiveness that the construct of autonomous achievement striving refers to. Therefore it is not inconsistent for girls to show greater autonomous achievement striving and boys greater aggression. In fact, these results suggest that boys show less autonomic achievement striving because they are too aggressive.

Taken together, several lines of evidence suggest that at some time during the preschool years girls may temporarily move sufficiently toward the active end of a passive–active continuum so that they are assertive enough for their field-independent functioning to be enhanced, whereas boys may move sufficiently to the aggressive extreme so that they are unable to carry out the internal processing necessary for field–independent functioning.

These hypotheses should be tested by further research. Furthermore, future studies need to determine whether these personality variables affect sex differences in field independence by itself or over a wider range of cognitive abilities.

Finally, one must consider the possibility that biological forces may be involved in the development of sex differences favoring females. In other areas of development, girls are known to mature more rapidly. Perhaps the development of sex differences in field independence in girls is at least partially contributed to by these forces. In all probability, a complex mixture of motivational and biological forces is involved.

What happens between the school-age years and adolescence to establish male superiority in field independence is by no means obvious. Kohlberg's work (48) suggests that in the female same-sex interest increases at this time. Psychoanalytic theory would predict that an increase in passivity occurs in girls during this period.

By age 8, consistent and significant sex differences in dependency behavior emerge favoring girls (49). Furthermore, sex differences in autonomy striving reverse from the time of preschool years, and the first evidence of greater autonomy striving in boys begins to emerge (51). Given this motivational shift to a direction of greater passivity for girls and greater achievement striving for boys, one would predict that by age 8 boys would become more field independent than girls. The fact, however, that clear and consistent sex differences favoring boys in field independence do not emerge until adolescence is puzzling.

Two explanations seem possible for the lack of emergence of significant sex differences favoring boys at this time. First, it is possible that the motivational differences that appear by school age are not sufficiently polarized to result in statistically significant sex differences but emerge, rather, in the form of trends. This possibility is suggested by the fact that, in the standardization data on the CEFT between the ages of 7 and 12, all of the means favor males, although none of these reach statistical significance (27).

It may be that not until adolescence, when sex roles become sharply polarized and motivational and experiential differences become strongly dichotomized, is there a sufficiently large difference in personality functioning for it to have a statistically significant impact on cognitive functioning.

A second possibility is that motivational and experiential differences have a decisive impact on cognitive functioning only after an extended period of time. This hypothesis would imply that motivation and experience are involved in the structuring of cognitive development in a gradual way that builds up slowly over several years.

Finally, biological influences may be involved in creating the sex differences at adolescence as well as at the younger age levels.

SUMMARY AND CONCLUSIONS

A review of the literature of preschool sex differences in field independence suggests that the traditional sex differences favoring boys that are found later do not exist in young children. In fact, a review of the majority of studies in which a valid measure of field independence was used, such as the PEFT, indicates that, in more than half the studies surveyed, girls tend to be more field independent than boys. Furthermore, in the remaining studies no sex differences were present.

In the most recent study carried out by the author on sex differences in PEFT performances between the ages of 3 and 6, the data showed a trend toward female superiority at ages 3 and 4, and a statistically significant sex difference favoring girls at age 5. A nonsignificant trend favoring boys emerged at age 6. It is possible that some of the previous studies did not find sex differences because the averaging of age groups washed out the differences, or the results may have been due to sampling fluctuations.

A pattern of sex differences favoring girls in preschool children was also found in two cognitive tests known to be highly correlated with PEFT: the WPPSI block design and geometric design subtests.

Finally, several hypotheses were explored as to the role that personality and motivational variables may play in the development of these sex differences.

ACKNOWLEDGMENTS

The author is particularly grateful to Dr. David O. Herman for making available his sex-difference data from the WPPSI standardization study and to Drs. Mae Lord, Ethel Person, Evelyn Raskin, Daniel Stern, and

Herman Witkin for their helpful suggestions on an earlier draft of this chapter.

REFERENCES

1. Witkin, H. A., R. B. Dyk, H. F. Faterson, D. R. Goodenough and S. A. Karp, *Psychological Differentiation*, Wiley, New York, 1962.
2. Kagan, J. and N. Kogan, in Mussen, P. H. (ed.), *Carmichael's Manual of Child Psychology*, Vol. 1, Wiley, New York, 1970, p. 1334.
3. Comalli, P. E., paper presented at the symposium on research on cognitive processes of elderly people. Eastern Psychological Association meetings. Atlantic City, N.J., 1965.
4. Schwartz, S. W. and S. A. Karp, *Percept Mot Skills* **24**: 495, 1967.
5. Witkin, H. A., in Goslin, D. A. (ed.), *Handbook of Socialization Theory and Research*, Rand McNally, New York, 1969.
6. Berry, J. W., *Int J Psychol* **1**: 207, 1966.
7. Eagle, M., L. Goldberger and M. Breitman, *Percept Mot Skills* **29**: 903, 1969.
8. Fitzgibbon, D., L. Goldberger and M. Eagle, *Percept Mot Skills* **21**: 743, 1965.
9. Goldberger, L. and S. Bendich, *Percept Mot Skills* **34**: 883, 1972.
10. Conklin, R. C. and H. W. Zingle, *Western Psychologist* **70**: 426, 1968.
11. Wolitzky, D. L., *Percept Mot Skills* **36**: 619, 1973.
12. Schimek, J. G., *J Abnorm Psychol* **73**: 575, 1968.
13. Witkin, H. A., P. K. Oltman, E. R. Raskin and S. A. Karp, *A Manual for the Embedded-Figures Test*, Consulting Psychologists Press, Palo Alto, Calif., 1971.
14. Witkin, H. A., D. R. Goodenough, and S. A. Karp, *J Pers Soc Psychol* **3**: 291, 1967.
15. Faterson, H. F. and H. A. Witkin, *Dev Psychol* **2**: 429, 1970.
16. Maccoby, E. E., in Maccoby, E. E. (ed.), *The Development of Sex Differences*, Stanford University Press, Stanford, Calif., 1966.
17. Sherman, J. A., *Psychol Rev* **74**: 290, 1967.
18. Coates, S., *The Preschool Embedded-Figures Test-PEFT*, Consulting Psychologists Press, Palo Alto, Calif., 1972.
19. Block, J. H., personal communication, 1972.
20. Costrich, N. E. and C. Kurash, unpublished study, 1972.
21. Derman, D. E. and J. A. Meissner, in Shipman, V. S. (ed.), *Disadvantaged Children and Their First School Experience*, Educational Testing Service, Princeton, N.J., December 1972.
22. Beller, E. K., unpublished study, Temple University, 1973.
23. Beller, E. K. and D. A. Howell, unpublished study, Temple University, 1971.
24. Shipman, V. C., *Structure and Development of Cognitive Competences and Styles Prior to School Entry*, Educational Testing Service, Princeton, N.J., 1971.
25. Seitz, E., unpublished Ph.D. thesis, New York University, 1971.

26. Waldrop, M., personal communication, January 1972.

27. Karp, S. A. and N. L. Konstadt, *Manual for the Childrens' Embedded-Figures Test*, Cognitive Tests, Brooklyn, N.Y., 1963.

28. Maccoby, E. E., E. M. Dowley, J. W. Degerman and R. Degerman, *Child Dev* 36: 761, 1965.

29. Dreyer, A. S., C. A. Dreyer and E. G. Nebelkoff, *Percept Mot Skills* 33: 775, 1971.

30. Maccoby, E. E. and C. N. Jacklin, *Proceedings of the 1972 International Conference on Testing Problems*, Educational Testing Service, Princeton, N.J.

31. Lewis, M., M. Rausch, S. Goldberg and C. Dodd, *Percept Mot Skills* 26: 563, 1968.

32. Eckert, H. M., *Percept Mot Skills* 31: 560, 1970.

33. Sitkei, E. G. and C. E. Meyers, *Dev Psychol* 1: 592, 1969.

34. Repucci, N. D., *Dev Psychol* 4: 248, 1970.

35. Karp, S. A., *J Consult Psychol* 27: 294, 1963.

36. Kramer, C. Y., *Biometrics* 12: 307, 1956.

37. Herman, D. O., *Proceedings 76th Annual Convention APA, 1968*.

38. Witkin, H. A., D. Price-Williams, M. Bertini, B. Christiansen, P. K. Oltman, M. Ramirez and J. Van Meel, *J Psychol*, in press.

39. Coates, S., and P. M. Bromberg, *J Consult Clin Psychol* 40: 365, 1973.

40. Coates, S., unpublished study, Downstate Medical Center, State University of New York, 1973.

41. Wechsler, D., *The Measurement and Appraisal of Adult Intelligence*, William and Wilkins, Baltimore, 1958.

42. Corey, M. T., paper presented at American Psychological Association meeting, Miami, Fla., September 1970.

43. Crandall, V. J. and C. Sinkeldam, *J Pers* 32: 1, 1964.

44. Wertheim, J. and S. A. Mednick, *J Consult Psychol* 22: 38, 1958.

45. Baumrind, D., *Young Children* 26: 104, 1970.

46. Baumrind, D., *Dev Psychol Monogr* 4: 1971.

47. Coates, S. and M. M. Lord, unpublished study, Downstate Medical Center, State University of New York, 1973.

48. Kohlberg, L., in Maccoby, E. E. (ed.), *The Development of Sex Differences*, Stanford University Press, Stanford, Calif., 1966.

49. Oetzel, R. M., in Maccoby, E. E., (ed.), *The Development of Sex Differences*, Stanford University Press, Stanford, Calif., 1966.

50. Beller, E. K., progress report, NIMH M-849, January 1962.

51. Crandall, V. and A. Rabson, *J Genet Psychol* 97: 161, 1960.

Discussion: Development of Sex Differences in Behavioral Functioning

MICHAEL LEWIS, Moderator

ZIRA DeFRIES, Rapporteur

The discussion began with Dr. Lewis observing that the concept of consistency has been used differently by different workers. One can describe developmental patterns in terms of their consistency, particularly with regard to sex differences. The relationship of an individual's performance to the performance of members of a group can also be described in terms of consistency over a period of time. He emphasized the need for clear understanding of the meaning of this concept as used in the present discussion.

Dr. Korner added that there is a long-range consistency in development and a day-to-day consistency—both of which are significant. She thought that Dr. Lewis placed more importance on long-range consistency.

Dr. Lewis then asked why Dr. Korner assumed that identification of early neonatal sex differences would help clarify the source of later differences, which may be either learned or biologically determined. Dr. Korner replied that some of the behavioral sex differences noted in neonates seem to persist into later life. For example, there is evidence that adult females, too, are more responsive to taste differences and to cutaneous stimulation, and that they have shorter latency in responding to photic stimulation.

Dr. Hunt inquired whether any experiments had been performed to judge the sex of the swaddled neonates. He wondered how much sex-differentiated behavior comes from parental expectations and how much is rooted in the child. Dr. Korner replied that Dr. Eleanor Maccoby is currently conducting a study at Stanford University in which great care is taken to hide the sex of the infant from the observer and which attempts to replicate and extend Bell's earlier findings to the effect that the male infant is able to lift his head higher while prone and that the female infant has greater tactile sensitivity.

Dr. Green wondered whether a longitudinal study of children at extreme ends of the curve for various behaviors known to be sex differentiated might have practical value for identifying adults who subsequently develop sexually atypical behavior, such as homosexuality.

Dr. Ehrhardt commented that the period shortly after birth is one in which hormonal differences exist in males and females, and speculated as to whether the higher level of testosterone in boys may contribute to the differences observed.

Dr. Michels then brought up the subject of genital awareness and asked Dr. Galenson whether she had studied children with physical disabilities who were unable to manually explore their genitals. He also noted that we usually regard toilet training as an experience whereby the child's drive is inhibited by social factors, but he questioned whether it might not be the reverse: a way of unswaddling the genitalia and thus giving the child free access to them.

Dr. Galenson did not have data on children with physical disabilities. She commented that she has yet to come across a boy who was not allowed into the bathroom with his mother or a girl who had not been to the bathroom with her father by the age of 16 months and observed that many interactions concerning toilet training need further clarification.

Dr. Rosenblum then turned the discussion to Dr. Stern's study of preschool children and their approach-avoidance response patterns. He described an experiment made with two species of baboons whose ranges are contiguous. In one, estrous females are followed and courted by males. In the species inhabiting the adjacent area, males are followed and courted by females. A female was removed from the male-following group and released in the territory of the female-following species. Initially, when courted by an assertive male, she fled in terror. Within 4 hours, however, he trained her to respond, so that whenever he approached, she followed rather than withdrew. By the next day, she manifested the typical female pattern of her adopted group. Dr. Rosenblum warned against assuming that a given mode of behavior is endogenous.

Dr. Michael stated that Dr. Stern's experiment demonstrated that a man may "smile and be a villain, still." He asked whether eyelid flash had been described and wondered if the primordia of an arm across the body and of the head turning away, as seen in adults in a ritualized social situation, was present. Dr. Stern replied that he had attempted to score eyebrow raise and eyelid flash, but that this was difficult to do and had not occurred very often.

Dr. Sachar inquired whether there were any hyperaggressive children in the group selected. Dr. Stern answered that deviant children had been removed from the study.

Dr. Hamburg then referred to Ms. Coates's research on field dependence–independence in children. She noted that there is some hard evidence of sex differences in the maturation rate and wondered whether different spatial abilities might not be related to the fact that male brains mature later than female brains. Ms. Coates wanted to know whether any data existed that established the time at which boys catch up with girls. Dr. Hamburg replied that this occurred when they were approximately 8 years of age.

Dr. Green observed that 6- and 16-year-old males who had been exposed to estrogen *in utero* are less aggressive and that 16 year-olds are more field dependent than controls.

Dr. Zubin then commented on Dr. Kohlberg's study concerning gender identity and related attitudes during the first 6 years of life. He questioned the validity of the interview technique used. Might not leading questions produce biased responses? Ms. Ullian responded that she never actually asked direct questions and that the questions were more open-ended than they may have appeared from the presentation.

Dr. Person inquired whether Dr. Kohlberg could use his model to explain functional psychopathology of sex and gender. Dr. Kohlberg replied that in the young child conflicts may be represented in somatic terms, frequently involving the sexual apparatus. This mechanism of thinking may persist and lead to psychopathology. For example, a male's excessive preoccupation with dominance over other males may become represented concretely in homosexual terms and then acted on.

Dr. Michels asked Dr. Kohlberg to comment on the age of irreversible gender consolidation, based on his own work and the work of J. Money and A. A. Ehrhardt. Dr. Kohlberg felt that consolidation of gender identity occurs, with some individual variability, between 2 and 6 years of age. Dr. Ehrhardt agreed.

Dr. Green commented on the social learning versus the cognitive view of development of gender identity. He noted that both differential parental expectations and dimorphism of behavior exist prior to the age of irreversible cognitive labeling suggested by Dr. Kohlberg.

5 *Gender Identity*

RICHARD C. FRIEDMAN, *Moderator*

RUTH TENDLER, *Rapporteur*

CHAPTER 15

Cryptorchidism, Development of Gender Identity, and Sex Behavior

HEINO F. L. MEYER-BAHLBURG, ELIZABETH McCAULEY
and C. SCHENCK

Departments of Pediatrics and Psychiatry
State University of New York at Buffalo
School of Medicine
Children's Hospital of Buffalo
Buffalo, New York

THOMAS ACETO, Jr.

Department of Pediatrics
State University of New York at Buffalo
School of Medicine
Children's Hospital of Buffalo
Buffalo, New York

LEWIS PINCH

Department of Surgery
State University of New York at Buffalo
School of Medicine
Children's Hospital of Buffalo
Buffalo, New York

The testes have important effects on all aspects of psychosexual differentiation. Testicular hormones in fetal life determine the somatic sexual differentiation and—possibly in man as well as in subhuman mammals—have a direct influence on the sexual differentiation of the nervous system (1). At and after puberty, testicular hormones are the basis for the virilization of the body and activation of sexual behavior. Apart from their hormonal function, the testes, together with the penis and the scrotum, are part of the genital triad that usually determines the assignment of a newborn to male sex. Consequently, lack of the testes in the scrotal sac may affect sex assignment and parental sex typing of the child, reactions of his peers toward him, and the boy's own body image, thereby influencing the development of gender identity and gender-role behavior. In addition, male fertility rests on testicular spermatogenesis, and infertility may have its own psychological concomitants (2, 3).

The condition of cryptorchidism, in which there is no spontaneous descent of the testes into the scrotum, provides an experiment of nature to clarify the role of the testes in human psychosexual development. During most of the prenatal life, the human testes while located in the abdomen are actively producing gonadal hormones. At about the seventh to ninth month of pregnancy, the testes descend into the scrotum. However, in a sizable proportion of newborns [2.7% in full-term, 21% in premature infants (4)] the testes have not assumed their scrotal position, and although in most cases the testes will have completed their descent by the end of the first year of life, there is still an incidence of undescended testes in later life of about 0.8% (4–6). There are various forms of cryptorchidism with different associated etiologies. The majority of cryptorchid males appear to have had prenatal testicular hormone production within normal limits when judged from their somatic sex characteristics. If cryptorchidism is not spontaneously or surgically corrected before puberty, fertility will usually be impaired in all forms of cryptorchidism and pubertal hormone production may also be affected.

Little psychological research has been done on cryptorchidism. The largest sample so far has been described in a pilot study by Cytryn, Cytryn, and Rieger (7). These authors present psychologic findings on 27 cryptorchid boys (age 3–17 years). They infer from human-figure drawings an increased incidence of boys with confusion of body image and gender identity. The main focus of the Cytryn study is general psychopathology, which the authors frequently find to be associated with cryptorchidism. Their study has a number of methodological shortcomings: it mixes preoperative (N 19) and postoperative (N 8) patients, bilateral (N 6) and unilateral (N 21) cryptorchidism, and includes nine boys of strikingly short stature, which by itself is a psychopathogenic factor.

A report by Blos (8) describes three cases of emotionally disturbed unilaterally cryptorchid boys (age 8–9 years) in psychoanalytic terms. Blos also found problems of sexual identity, which he ascribes to the parents', especially the mother's, reaction to the boy's genital defect.

A series of psychoanalytic publications by Bell and co-workers (9–13) is concerned with the scrotal sac, testes, and cremasteric reflex. The authors try to reconstruct the history of emotional problems, including gender-identity problems in young boys, to concerns about their retractable testes. However, the data are insufficient to establish such a relation.

Thus the available psychological literature implies that cryptorchidism may lead to gender-identity problems. However, there is a need for a systematic study focused directly on the effects of cryptorchidism on psychosexual development. Therefore we started a study of our own, which in its initial stage is designed to provide some data on the prevalence of deviancy in gender-role behavior, gender identity, and sexual orientation in a relatively homogeneous sample of cryptorchid males.

METHOD

Sample Selection

Our target population consisted of 67 patients with bilateral cryptorchidism (not including retractable testes) operated on at the Children's Hospital of Buffalo between 1963 and 1970. About one-third of these patients were excluded because of additional congenital malformations or because of mental retardation.

Procedure

The surgeon (L.P.) made the initial contacts with the patients. The patients were admitted to the Clinical Research Center of Children's Hospital for a period of about 25 hours. Medical studies involved a physical examination, with particular emphasis on somatic sexual development, collection of blood and urine samples for sex-hormone determinations, bone-age determination by X-ray, sperm count, if feasible, and medical photography. Developmental ratings, for example, of genital maturity according to Tanner (14), were done independently by two physicians. Disagreements were settled by combined reporting.

The psychological examination consisted of the Wechsler Adult Intelligence Scale (15) or the Wechsler Intelligence Scale for Children (16), the Guilford–Zimmerman Temperament Survey (17), the Benton Test (18), the Cornell Index (19), an interview with the patient's mother, and an interview with the patient. Both interviews were half-structured and covered the following topics: reaction to medical condition; developmental history, including gender-role behavior and gender identity, peer relations, school, family interactions; and, in the patient interview only, sexual development. The interview with the mother lasted about 90 minutes to 3 hours, the patient interview about 2 to 4 hours. Both interviews were tape-recorded; pertinent responses were either directly transcribed from the tape and listed under previously established categories or were rated on verbally anchored highly reliable scales as used by Ehrhardt (20). A few disagreements between the two raters employed were settled by discussion.

RESULTS

We report the findings on our first 10 patients with regard to sexual behavior, gender-role behavior, and gender identity.

Sample Characteristics

Table 1 shows that seven of our 10 patients had two operations for the repair of cryptorchidism, two had one operation, and one had three operations. Mean age at first operation was 11 years and 5 months—considerably later than the age of initial gender-identity formation (2–4 years). Our follow-up examination took place at a mean age of 18½ years, which corresponds to an average interval of 6 years and 8 months between the last operation and follow-up.

At the time of follow-up (Table 2), all patients' heights were within ±2 standard deviations from the mean of their age group; no short-stature male is included in this sample. All 10 patients had entered puberty spontaneously, and none had received sex-hormone treatment. Pubic hair development was adult, corresponding to a Tanner rating of 5 or 6 in seven patients, a rating of 4 in two patients, and a rating of 3 in one patient. The picture for genital maturity was similar. None of the patients had any penile abnormalities. Four patients showed minor abnormalities of the scrotum. Eight patients had two testicles in the scrotum, and two patients were unilaterally anorchid.

All 10 patients came from the middle or lower social classes, ranging from III to V on the Hollingshead Index (21), which corresponds well to the general patient population being seen in the Children's Hospital

Table 1 Sample Characteristics: Surgery Data

Patient Code	Number of Operations for Cryptorchidism	Age at Operation 1	Age at Operation 2	Age at Follow-up	Interval between Last Operation and Follow-up
1 LB	2	$10^6/_{12}$	$11^3/_{12}$	$18^4/_{12}$	$7^1/_{12}$
2 FB	2	$13^1/_{12}$	$13^8/_{12}$	$16^9/_{12}$	$3^1/_{12}$
3 SB	1	$10^4/_{12}$	—	$14^4/_{12}$	4
4 TH	2	$6^1/_{12}$	7	$13^9/_{12}$	$6^9/_{12}$
5 JS	2	$11^7/_{12}$	$11^8/_{12}$	$16^3/_{12}$	$4^7/_{12}$
6 JV	1	$13^1/_{12}$	—	$19^{11}/_{12}$	$6^{10}/_{12}$
7 AW	3	11	11^a	$19^3/_{12}$	$5^{11}/_{12}$
8 DN	2	$11^2/_{12}$	$11^3/_{12}$	$20^{10}/_{12}$	$9^7/_{12}$
9 RW	2	$9^9/_{12}$	$9^{11}/_{12}$	$18^6/_{12}$	$8^6/_{12}$
10 TL	2	$17^4/_{12}$	$17^5/_{12}$	$27^4/_{12}$	$9^{11}/_{12}$

[a] This patient had a third operation, a unilateral orchiectomy, at the age of 13 years and 4 months.

Table 2   Somatic Characteristics at Follow-up Examination[a]

Patient Code	Height (cm)	Tanner Stage, Pubic Hair	Tanner Stage, Genital Maturity	Scrotal Abnormalities	Number of Testes in Scrotum
1 LB	188	5	5	None	2
2 FB	183	5	Not given	None	2
3 SB	153	4	Adult penis	None	1
4 TH	161	3	4	No pigment	2
5 JS	157	5	4–5	None	2
6 JV	174	5	4	None	2
7 AW	184	4	3	Atrophic	1
8 DN	182	6	6	Thin	2
9 RW	171	5–6	5–6	Dark color, long	2
10 TL	178	6	6	None	2

[a]None of the patients had any penile abnormalities.

Table 3   Social Class, IQ, and Education

Patient Code	Social Class (Hollingshead)	Full IQ (Wechsler)	Educational Status: Current Grade
1 LB	IV	111	12
2 FB	IV	103	11
3 SB	IV	86	7
4 TH	III	109	7
5 JS	V	105	10 (vocational school)
6 JV	III	122	2nd year college
7 AW	V	105	1st year college
8 DN	III	109	12 completed, working
9 RW	IV	97	12
10 TL	IV	87	12 + course work completed, working

of Buffalo (Table 3). Mean Wechsler IQ was 103.4. Educational status ranged from vocational school to college.

Sexual Behavior

Tables 4 and 5 give an overview of the masturbation activities and sexual fantasies of our 10 patients. Nine had experience in masturbation, and the onset of masturbatory activities ranged from age 9 to 16. In the seven patients who practiced masturbation at the time of the examination, the frequency of masturbation ranged from one occurrence in 6 months to two times a week. Five of these seven patients stated that they needed about 3 to 5 minutes to reach ejaculation, whereas two needed 10 to 20 minutes. Two out of 10 patients denied having sexual fantasies; the sexual fantasies of the other eight were clearly heterosexually oriented and covered the full range of heterosexual behavior, including intercourse. Only one patient reported past sexual fantasies of vaguely homosexual character. One other patient from a rural environment reported that he had had fantasies about having intercourse with a cow.

Tables 6 and 7 show the sexual partner activities of the patients. The age of the first crush on a girl or a first girlfriend was between 10 and 15 years, as usual. Only one subject claimed that he had not yet had a crush on a girl. In the seven subjects with petting experience, the onset of petting fell between the ages of 12 and 16. Four patients were experienced in intercourse; the activity had started between 12 and 17 years of age. Only one of them had a relatively high frequency of intercourse activity, three to four times a week. The current frequency of all sexual

Table 4 Masturbation Activity (Patient's Report)

Patient Code	Age at First Masturbation	Peak Frequency	Age at Peak Frequency	Present Frequency	Present time to Ejaculation (minutes)
1 LB	13½	Twice a day	15	Once a week to once in 2 weeks	3–5
2 FB	15½	Once a week	15½	Once a month	3–4
3 SB	12	One experience only	—	—	—
4 TH	—	—	—	—	—
5 JS	13–14	Once a week	15	Once in 6 months	15–20
6 JV	16	Once in 2 days	19	Once in 10 days to 2 weeks	4–5
7 AW	16	Twice a week to almost daily	16	Twice a week	10–20
8 DN	14–15	Once a day	17	Once a week	Immediately to 5–10
9 RW	Before operation (age 9%₁₂)	Once in 2 or 3 days	17	Once in 2 weeks	5
10 TL	One experience, undated	—	—	—	—

le 5   *Sexual Fantasies in Masturbation, Wet Dreams, and Other Night and Day Dreams*

nt	Sexual Orientation	Heterosexual Content	Homosexual Content	Deviant Sex
B	Heterosexual	Intercourse	In 5th grade ("Taking a walk with a guy my own age.")	Intercourse with a cow
B	Heterosexual	Intercourse	None	None
B	No sex dreams	No sex dreams	No sex dreams	No sex dreams
H	Heterosexual	Intercourse	None	None
S	Heterosexual	Intercourse	None	None
V	Heterosexual	Intercourse	None	None
W	Heterosexual	Intercourse	None	None
N	Heterosexual	Intercourse	None	None
W	Heterosexual	Intercourse	None	None
L	No sex dreams	No sex dreams	No sex dreams	No sex dreams

outlets—combining intercourse, masturbation to orgasm, and wet dreams —ranged from five times per week to once in a couple of months, and two of our 10 patients did not have any sexual outlets at the time of our study. With regard to homosexual behavior, four of our 10 patients reported some short-term experience in late childhood or around puberty. One of the patients reported other deviant sex behavior, namely, one incidence of exhibitionism, which probably developed out of the general psychiatric disorder this patient had shown in the past.

Gender-Role Behavior and Gender Identity

Table 8 shows the rating scales used in this context. Tables 9 and 10 present the results of the mother interviews and patient interviews, respectively. In younger years, all 10 patients had played preferably or exclusively with boys' toys rather than girls' toys. No mother reported cross-gender role play, though four of the boys related instances of cross-gender dressing. According to their mothers, none of the patients showed any wedding or marriage anticipation in play and daydreams. The majority of the patients had done some babysitting, once or a few times, usually for their own siblings; none had regular babysitting activities outside the family. None of the patients had preferred girls to boys as playmates. Eight patients were judged as participating frequently in intense outdoor activities, and only one as having little or no interest in this. According to both their mothers' and their own reports (Tables 9 and 10), all 10 patients had a definite preference for the male role. Five patients had

Table 6 *Sexual Partner Experiences (Patient's Report): Heterosexual Experience*

Patient Code	Age at First Crush on a Girl or First Girlfriend	Age at First Petting	Age at First Intercourse	Current Frequency of Intercourse	Currency Frequency of All Sexual Outlets
1 LB	10	16	No experience	—	Once in 2 weeks to once a week
2 FB	12–13	16	No experience	—	Once in 3 weeks
3 SB	10	12	12	Once a month	Once a month
4 TH	No experience	No experience	No experience	None	None
5 JS	13	13	14–15	None	Once in a couple of months
6 JV	15	19	No experience	None	Once a week
7 AW	12–13	14–15	17	Ten times in several years	Once a week
8 DN	13	16	17	Three to four times a week	Five times a week
9 RW	13	No experience	No experience	None	Three times a month
10 TL	High school	No experience	No experience	None	None

Table 7   Sexual Partner Experiences: Homosexual Experience[a]

Patient Code	At Age	Homosexual Experience
1 LB	7	Prepubertal sex play with male peer
	9	Homosexual peer fantasies
2 FB		None
3 SB		None
4 TH		None
5 JS	12–13	Occasional sex play with male cousin for a 2-month period; cousin masturbated patient
6 JV	16	Cousin masturbated patient
	19	Businessman put arm around patient in elevator, patient walked away
7 AW		None
8 DN		None
9 RW	10	Genital play with male peer (no orgasm)
10 TL		None

[a] Except for one incident of exhibitionism, engaged in by TL in adulthood, no deviant sex behavior occurred in any of the patients.

been called "fem" or "sissy", but only two (1 LB, 10 TL) with possible reference to some nonmasculine appearance or behavior. In agreement with these interview data are the results of the Guilford–Zimmerman Temperament Survey (Table 11), where the masculinity/femininity scale shows a mean of 4.22 for the whole group, which is not significantly different from the male-population mean of 5.0 (C-scores).

Table 12 describes the patients' past and present concerns about their medical condition and the teasing response of their peers. Most patients stated that they either did not have any worries, did not think about it, or did not understand what the operation was all about when their condition was discussed at the time of surgery. Only one stated that right after the operation he had doubts about his potency and sterility, but the doubts were dispelled by the experience of masturbation and sexual arousal. At the time of our follow-up exams, seven patients claimed not to have concern about their medical condition; one wondered about fertility, another was a little bothered by having only one testis, and a third was worried about not having sex. In the past, only two patients had experienced peer teasing directly related to their cryptorchid condition.

Table 8   Gender-Role Behavior and Gender Identity: Rating Scales

1. Preferences in toys and games
   a. No interest in dolls, boys' toys only
   b. Boys' toys preferred, dolls occasionally
   c. Dolls preferred, boys' toys occasionally
   d. Plays with dolls only
2. Instances of cross-gender role play
   a. No
   b. Yes
3. Wedding and marriage anticipation in play and daydreams
   a. No
   b. Yes
4. Babysitting activities
   a. Never
   b. Once or a few times
   c. Regularly
5. Friends in preschool age
   a. Males only
   b. Boys preferred, girls occasionally
   c. Same interest in boys and girls
   d. Girls preferred, boys occasionally
   e. Girls only
6. Friends in elementary school age
   a. Males only
   b. Boys preferred, girls occasionally
   c. Same interest in boys and girls
   d. Girls preferred, boys occasionally
   e. Girls only
7. Friends in high school age
   a. Males only
   b. Boys preferred, girls occasionally
   c. Same interest in boys and girls
   d. Girls preferred, boys occasionally
   e. Girls only
8. Athletic interests and skills
   a. Intense outdoor activities
   b. Periodic outdoor activities
   c. Few or no outdoor activities
9. Sex-role preference
   a. Boy
   b. Girl
10. Known to self and others (peer, mother) as "fem" or "sissy"
    a. Never
    b. Passing episodes
    c. Always

Table 9 Gender-Role Behavior and Gender Identity (Mother's Report)[a]

Patient Code	Toy Preference	Role Play	Wed-ding	Baby-sitting	Friends, Pre-school	Friends, Elemen-tary School[b]	Friends, High School[b]	Athletics	Sex-Role Prefer-ence[b]	Known as Sissy
1 LB	b	a	a	b	b	NI	NI	a	a	a
2 FB	a	a	a	b	b	a–b	c	a	a	a
3 SB	a	a	a	a	c	a	a	a	a	a
4 TH	a	a	a	a	a	NI	NI	a	a	a
5 JS	b	a	a	b	b	b	b	a	a	a
6 JV	a	a	a	a	b	b	b	a	a	a
7 AW	a	a	a	a	c	NI	NI	a	NI	b[c]
8 DN	b	a	a	b	a–b	a–b	a–b	a	a	a
9 RW	a	a	a	a	b	b	b	c	a	a
10 TL	a	a	a	b	b	a	a	b	NI	a

[a]For key to ratings see Table 8.
[b]NI = no information.
[c]Patient was teased "sissy" by mother occasionally in the past.

293

Table 10   Gender Identity (Patient's Report)[a]

Patient Code	Cross-Gender Role Play	Difference from Average Peer	Called "Fem" or "Sissy"
1 LB	Once as a witch for Halloween	None	Before surgery because testes were not down and he was obese
2 FB	None	None	No
3 SB	None	"I can play more positions in football, I can always get girlfriends."	Yes, to instigate a fight
4 TH	None	"Different personality"	No
5 JS	None	None	No
6 JV	Once as a witch for Halloween	None	Yes, to start a verbal argument
7 AW	Used to dress up as female every other week when 10–11 years old for a couple of years	None	No
8 DN	None	None	Yes, just joking
9 RW	None	"I didn't have intercourse, I read the Bible and believe in Jesus."	No
10 TL	Dressed up once as a girl or a sheik while an in-patient in a psychiatric hospital	None	Yes ("When I was younger, they (the kids) said I'd be a big sissy when I grew up.")

[a] All patients had a definite preference for the male sex role.

General Psychopathology

The Cornell Index (Table 11) gives an average index score for the group of 7.80, which is well within the normal range. However, three patients are in the borderline range; two of these show one positive stop question

Table 11   Questionnaire Data

Patient Code	GZTS M–F[a] (C–Score)	Cornell Index	
		Index Score	Stop Questions
1 LB	8	2	0
2 FB	5	7	0
3 SB	Unfinished (reading problem)	7	0
4 TH	2	17	1[b]
5 JS	1	16	0
6 JV	7	2	0
7 AW	4	2	0
8 DN	4	3	0
9 RW	4	8	0
10 TL	3	14	3[c]

[a] *Guilford–Zimmerman Temperament Survey, masculinity/feminity scale.*
[b] One positive stop question (troublesome psychopathology).
[c] Two positive stop questions indicating nervousness and anxiety, one indicating troublesome psychopathology.

and one patient, three. The latter patient (TL) is the only one that impressed us as clearly psychopathologic during the interview, and he is the only one who has been under extensive psychiatric care in the past. We have no indication that his behavior disturbance is primarily linked to his cryptorchid condition.

DISCUSSION

Sexual Behavior

Sexual behavior does not seem to be grossly disturbed in our cryptorchid sample. Sexual fantasies and activities seem to be predominantly heterosexual. None of the homosexual experiences reported appear to be more than the typical transient homosexual play of childhood and adolescence, which, according to Kinsey (22), is engaged in by about half of all males. If there is anything unusual in this sample, it is that the boys tend toward later than normal onset and lower frequency of masturbation and other sexual outlets. This could be related to endocrine pathology and is presently being evaluated. However, only a study of matched control subjects will allow a definitive statement on this issue.

Table 12 *Patient's Reactions to Medical Condition (Patient's Report)*

Patient Code	Past Reactions	Present Concerns	Teasing about Condition
1 LB	Didn't think about it that much; tried to ignore remarks and questions	No doubts about masculinity; wonders about fertility	Peers wondered about surgery scars; teasing about obesity in earlier years
2 FB	Didn't think about it	None	None
3 SB	Didn't think about it	None	"Shorty"
4 TH	No worries	None	None
5 JS	Didn't understand before the operation took place	None	Yes, after he had told his friends after his initial medical workup; he told them that it was a serious operation and to stop kidding around; teasing about short stature in earlier years
6 JV	Right after operation, had doubts about potency and sterility; they were dispelled by masturbation and sex arousal	None	None
7 AW	Not bothered	Bothered by having only one testis	At age 14, he told a friend he trusted about condition: the friend spread the word and he was really teased, especially in 7th grade; teasing about obesity in earlier years
8 DN	No worries	None	None
9 RW	Didn't know what was happening	None. ("I still wonder what the operation was about. I can't seem to grow more muscles on my chest and arms [last 2 years].")	None
10 TL	No worries	Worried about not having sex	None

Gender-Role Behavior and Gender Identity

As a group, our patients showed typically male gender-role behavior. None presented the typical picture of the effeminate boy who deviates from his peers across a number of gender-dimorphic behaviors (23). Only one patient had shown a clear-cut effeminate habit: frequently repeated cross-gender dressing during early adolescence, which seems to have been transient. Thus absence of the testes from the scrotum during the time of sex assignment, early sex typing, and gender-identity formation does not usually lead to serious and permanent damage to gender role and gender identity.

General Psychopathology

Apparently, bilateral cryptorchidism is not invariably associated with gross behavioral abnormalities. Only one patient had a clear-cut psychiatric disorder, which, however, did not seem to be related to the cryptorchid condition.

Thus, overall, our results appear more favorable for the patients than what has been stated in the literature. Of course, our sample is not directly comparable to the samples of Cytryn et al. (7) or Blos (8). For instance, we do not have the inherent bias of a psychiatric sample as Blos had. On the contrary, we may have a volunteer bias toward good adjustment.

In addition, most of our patients had been operated on relatively early, at least before middle teenage, and Cytryn et al. (7) had claimed that, the later the operation takes place, the more likely it is that there will be a behavior disorder. Both Blos (8) and Cytryn (7) suggested that psychopathology in a cryptorchid patient may improve with the operation. All of our patients had successful surgery in the sense that at least one testis was permanently down in the scrotum; thus their abnormality appeared to be basically corrected and spontaneous onset of puberty could assure them of their masculinity. It is also important to note that most of our patients were unaware of any risk of infertility.

At any rate, we can tentatively conclude that bilateral cryptorchidism by itself does not lead to gender-identity and gender-role confusion even when it is not corrected by the time of initial gender-identity formation. Also, cryptorchidism in otherwise normal boys does not inevitably lead to psychopathology, at least when corrected at a reasonably early age. To corroborate these results, an expansion of the patient sample as well as a control group will be needed.

ACKNOWLEDGMENTS

We wish to thank Drs. J. E. Allen, W. L. Butsch, T. C. Jewett, I. V. Magoss, and R. Spier for their collaboration, Dr. Earl Hodin for participation in the physical examination of the patients, and the nursing staff of the Clinical Research Center of the Children's Hospital of Buffalo for excellent assistance.

This investigation was supported by a grant (RR-05493) from the General Research Support Branch, Division of Research Resources, National Institutes of Health; by a short-term fellowship grant from the United Health Foundation of Western New York; by the Erickson Educational Foundation; and by the Human Growth Foundation.

REFERENCES

1. Money, J. and A. A. Ehrhardt, *Man & Woman, Boy & Girl*, Johns Hopkins University Press, Baltimore, 1972.
2. Noyes, R. W. and E. M. Chapnick, *Fertil Steril* **15**: 543, 1964.
3. Mai, F. M. M., *Aust NZ J Psychiatry* **3**: 31, 1969.
4. Scorer, C. G., *Arch Dis Child* **39**: 605, 1964.
5. Baumrucker, G. O., *Bull US Army Med Dept* **5**: 312, 1946.
6. Cour-Palais, I. J., *Lancet* **1**: 1403, 1966.
7. Cytryn, L., E. Cytryn, and R. E. Rieger, *J Am Acad Child Psychiatry* **6**: 131, 1967.
8. Blos, P., *Psychoanal Study Child* **15**: 395, 1960.
9. Bell, A. I., C. F. Stroebel, and D. Prior, *Psychoanal Quart* **40**: 415, 1971.
10. Bell, A. I., *Int J Psychoanal* **49**: 640, 1968.
11. Bell, A. I., *Psychoanal Quart* **34**: 182, 1965.
12. Bell, A. I., *J Am Acad Child Psychiatry* **3**: 577, 1964.
13. Bell, A. I., *J Am Psychoanal Assoc* **9**: 261, 1961.
14. Tanner, J. M., in Gardner, L. I. (ed.), *Endocrine and Genetic Diseases of Childhood*, Saunders, London, 1969, p. 19.
15. Wechsler, D., *Manual for the Wechsler Adult Intelligence Scale*, The Psychological Corporation, New York, 1955.
16. Wechsler, D., *Wechsler Intelligence Scale for Children, Manual*, The Psychological Corporation, New York, 1949.
17. Guilford, J. P. and W. S. Zimmerman, *The Guilford–Zimmerman Temperament Survey, Manual of Instruction and Interpretation*, Sheridan Supply Co., Beverly Hills, Calif., 1949.
18. Benton, A. L., *The Revised Visual Retention Test*, 3rd ed., The Psychological Corporation, New York, 1963.

19. Weider, A., H. G. Wolff, K. Brodman, B. Mittelmann, and D. Wechsler, *Cornell Index, Manual* (revised), The Psychological Corporation, New York, 1949.

20. Ehrhardt, A. A., in Duhm, E. (ed.), *Praxis der Klinischen Psychologie II*, Verlag für Psychologie, Dr. C. J. Hogrefe, Göttingen, 1971, p. 94.

21. Hollingshead, A. B., *Two Factor Index of Social Position*, privately printed, New Haven, Conn., 1957.

22. Kinsey, A. C., W. B. Pomeroy, and C. I. Martin, *Sexual Behavior in the Human Male*, Saunders, Philadelphia, 1948.

23. Zuger, B., and P. Taylor, *Pediatrics* **44**: 375, 1969.

CHAPTER 16

The Behaviorally Feminine Male Child: Pretranssexual? Pretransvestic? Prehomosexual? Preheterosexual?

RICHARD GREEN

Department of Psychiatry and Behavioral Science
State University of New York at Stony Brook
Stony Brook, New York

Study of the feminine male child is my research strategy in attempting to understand the origins of sexual identity. As used here, sexual (or gender) identity consists of three components: (1) earliest, a person's self concept of being male or female; (2) later, nongenital behavior that is typical of most males or females in that culture; (3) still later, genital sexual orientation. The feminine male child may have a basic female identity, manifests feminine gender-role behavior, and has a greater than average probability for later preferring same-sex sexual partners.

BACKGROUND MATERIAL

During the year 1968–1969, the UCLA Gender Identity Program interviewed 25 adult male transsexuals requesting sex-change surgery to live as women. Their reported childhood histories included culturally atypical preferences for toys, clothing, and playmates as well as ambiguity concerning whether they felt like boys or girls: 57% preferred girls as playmates, only 3% preferred boys; 67% preferred girls' toys, 48% preferred girls' clothes; and only 57% clearly saw themselves as being boys. These reports are similar to those of other clinicians (1). Although such retrospective reports are frequently difficult to validate, they do suggest that a population of young boys behaving similarly to the recalled childhood of these transsexuals may constitute a high probability group for those who will later request sex change.

Retrospective reports of some adult male homosexuals also suggest that certain behaviors, culturally labeled feminine or nonmasculine, more frequently constitute their childhood. Bieber and colleagues (2) interviewed about 100 homosexuals and 100 heterosexuals in psychoanalytic treatment. They found that one-third of the homosexuals recalled preferring girls as playmates compared with only 10% of the heterosexual sample. Additionally, less than one-fifth of the homosexuals participated in competitive group games versus two-thirds of the heterosexuals. Saghir and Robins (3) found that 2/3 of their sample of about 90 homosexuals recalled "girl-like" behavior during childhood.

Three follow-up studies of previously evaluated feminine boys lend the strongest support to the heightened probability of feminine boys later manifesting atypical sexuality. J. Money and I (unpublished data) have reinterviewed five young adult men first seen 12 to 15 years previously when they had been referred for boyhood femininity. Femininity had included overt statements of wanting to be a girl, dressing in girls' clothes, considerable doll play, and gestures and mannerisms more typical of girls. Four currently appear to be primarily homosexually oriented, and the fifth is bisexual. A second follow-up evaluation of six late-adolescent and young-adult males, previously seen for boyhood femininity, found three to be homosexually oriented and one possibly transsexual (4). A third report, reevaluating 16 males, found three to be transsexual, two to be homosexual, and one to be a transvestite (5).

The effects of treatment intervention during the boyhood of feminine boys are unclear. The boys that Money and I saw were not systematically treated; rather the parents were advised not to continue encouraging feminine behavior (where this had been the case), and the fathers (when available) were encouraged to involve themselves more in their sons' lives. The boys were told of the impossibility of becoming girls, and the clinic facility was made available to the boy and his parents for periodic reassessment and advice. The extent and type of treatment in the other two published studies are not reported.

RESEARCH STRATEGY

Based on the above findings, a composite picture has been drawn of a preadolescent male at "high risk" for subsequent atypical sexuality. These are boys who prefer the dress, toys, activities, and companionship of girls, role-play as females, display feminine mannerisms, and perhaps overtly state their wish to be girls. During the last 6 years, a population of 50 such boys and their families has been evaluated. Referrals have come from family physicians, clinical psychologists, psychiatrists, and school counselors; some cases were self-referred after newspaper or television reportings of the project. The age range for the boys has been 4 to 10 years, with about half between 4 and 7 years old. The boys have all been anatomically normal (not intersexed) and, with two exceptions, otherwise unremarkable medically (one boy has Marfan's syndrome; another was earlier an autistic child). Their socioeconomic level is varied, with a somewhat disproportionately high representation from the upper middle and working classes. Three families are black, and five are Mexican-American.

Procedure

On referral, the family is sent a screening questionnaire, which is a simple behavioral item checklist (the cross-gender index). On this sheet each parent indicates on a "never," "occasionally," or "frequently" trichotomy the occurrence of cross-gender dressing, playing with dolls, use of cosmetics, female-role playing, feminine gestures, assertions of wanting to be a girl, and whether the boy is labeled "sissy" by peers. If cross-gender behavior is present frequently across all or most parameters, an evaluation interview is scheduled. Parents are interviewed together and singly, with all interviews tape-recorded and transcribed. The interview format is structured and covers the following areas: the boy's feminine and masculine behavior and parental attitudes toward each; the boy's appearance and behavior as an infant and during the first years of life; availability of mother and father to the child during these years, with comparative data on siblings; the parents' own childhood, relationship with their parents, parental psychosexual development, and the current marital relationship. Meanwhile the child is administered a variety of testing procedures. These include the Draw-A-Person Test, the It Scale for Children, the Family Doll Preference Test, the Parent and Activity Preference Test, the Playroom Toy Preference Test, and the Quick Test.

The Draw-A-Person Test requires the child to draw a person (6). No clue is given the child whether a male or female should be drawn. The

It Scale presents the child with a card depicting a neuter stick figure (It). "It" then selects from a series of cards masculine or feminine toys, activities, clothes, playmates, and household articles (7). The Family Doll Preference Test has the child construct a 10-minute story in which dolls representing a set of grandparents, parents, a boy, a girl, and an infant may be utilized. Time spent utilizing each figure is recorded (8). The Parent and Activity Preference Test presents the child with 28 sets of two-card picture sequences that constitute the first two pictures in a three-card sequence. One card depicts an adult male engaged in either a masculine, a feminine, or a gender-neutral activity. The third card is selected by the child from two options. One shows a child of the same sex as the subject having joined the male in his activity; the other shows the child having joined the female (9). The Playroom Toy Preference Test permits the child free access to a variety of culturally masculine and feminine toys in a room equipped with a one-way mirror. The time spent with each toy is recorded by the observer in the adjacent room (10). The Quick Test is a brief measure of intelligence (11). The child is also interviewed regarding his understanding of the reason for coming to the clinic, his ideas about being a boy or a girl, his activity and role preferences, the reasons for them, and his understanding of the possibilities of becoming a girl.

Families with feminine boys are matched with contrast families in which the same-age boy displays culturally typical masculine behavior. The families are matched for marital intactness, ethnic background, father's educational and occupational level, and the child's sibling order. Contrast families are obtained from classified newspaper advertisements offering payment for participation in a "pleasant psychological study."

BEHAVIORAL FEATURES OF THE BOYS

All the boys commenced their compelling interest in cross-gender dressing prior to their sixth birthday and in two-thirds of the cases by the fourth birthday. When genuine articles of feminine attire have been unavailable, a variety of materials have been utilized to improvise costumes. Beach or bath towels have been used to simulate dresses, as have adult-sized T-shirts. Small towels have been used to simulate long hair. Felt-tipped marking pens have simulated nailpolish and cosmetics. The typical reply of a mother to the question, "How often does your son cross-dress?" is "As often as you let him."

Playmate preference is decidedly in favor of girls. Boys are avoided with the typical comment, "They play too rough." When playing house or mother–father games, the boys are usually mother. Since their playmates are girls (who also want to be mother), the boys may settle for being sister or school teacher. "I don't know what a daddy does" summed up one boy's reason for refusing to play daddy. "Barbie" doll is the favorite toy of the feminine boy. Hours may be spent costuming and recostuming Barbie to the exclusion of all other play. Should parents attempt to divert the boy's attention to a male-type doll ("Ken," Barbie's counterpart), they are unsuccessful. Feminine gestures and mannerisms are prominent with some of the boys. This latter behavior contributes further to their being labeled "sissy" by their male peer group. The boys may state they wish to be girls. "Girls get to do better things," "Girls wear nicer clothes," "Mommies get to go to nice places, daddies just go to work," "Girls don't have a penis" (or a childhood equivalent of penis) are some reasons given. Extensive verbatim statements by these boys are reported elsewhere (9).

PSYCHOLOGICAL TESTING RESULTS

On several tests the feminine boys score similarly to same-age girls and differently from same-age boys. On the Draw-a-Person Test, they are more likely to draw a female when requested to draw a person. Typical boys draw a male first, whereas girls draw a female (12). On the It Scale their toy and activity preferences are decidedly feminine, and their score is in the normal range for girls (13). On the Family Doll Preference Test their fantasy play utilizes female family members more than male family members and additionally includes considerable attention to the infant doll. Girls respond similarly. The contrast boys utilize the male figures more and spend relatively little time with the infant. In the Parent and Activity Preference Test, feminine boys (and girls) more often complete the picture sequence with the child having joined the adult female in a feminine activity. The contrast boys more often select the card with the child and the adult male engaged in a masculine activity. In the experimental playroom the feminine boys and girls spend more time engaged in doll play and less time engaged in truck play. This differs significantly from the contrast boys (9). Thus, in a variety of testing situations, the boys in the experimental study group behave similarly to same-age girls and differently from typical same-age boys. Their identity, role, and activity preference appears to be culturally feminine.

TREATMENT

General Principles

The primary goal of intervention for those boys who are unhappy about their current behavior is to increase the boy's comfort in being anatomically male, enable him to perform behaviors typical of boys his age, and promote a positive anticipation of an adult male role.

Toward these goals we have initiated several strategies. First, we have utilized an adult male as the agent of intervention. By the nature of his authority, prestige, and comfort in being male, it is hoped that the boy's identification with this person will be effected. The boy is told (if he does not already know) the anatomic and physiologic differences between boys and girls, men and women. The irreversibility of these differences is stressed, with the philosophy that it makes more sense to learn to be satisfied with what you are than strive for something that is impossible.

An attempt is made to modify gestures and mannerisms that are decidedly feminine and label the child "sissy" with its consequent stigmatization. The boy is alerted to those mannerisms in his gait, use of the hands, or speech that result in teasing.

An attempt is made to find a male peer group that will not reject the feminine boy, thus permitting him to develop a wider range of socialization than previously experienced. To effect this it may be necessary for the parents to scout for other boys in the school or neighborhood who are themselves not overly aggressive or rough-and-tumble. These boys, if they live at a nonwalking distance, may need to be "bussed" to provide a new milieu for their son. Boys who reject the "traditional" roles of the young male, with sports and aggressiveness as priority features, may rebound to the "only" alternative—girls' activities. However, a third choice is available—one that will cause them less social discomfort.

Activities may be found that are agreeable to both father and son, will enhance the quality of their relationship, and will promote a more positive male identification in the boy. The fathers need to know that their sons are innately not aggressive, rough-and-tumble boys and do not enjoy athletics. These boys should not be pushed into Little League or some other highly competitive experience that will further alienate them from the male peer group. We have found Indian Guides to be a compatible father–son group experience. Here boys and fathers may share experiences that are within the competence of the boy and can be fun for the father. The boys' aesthetic interests are met by handicrafts and outdoor camping and cooking, as a group experience. The latter is not threatening to the boy and permits the father a relaxing break from his work schedule.

Parental positive reinforcement of the boy's femininity can be stopped. Prior to referral, the typical parental response to the femininity has been positive or neutral. No consistent pattern of discouragement has been practiced. The boys may have been shown off to other adults while dressed in women's clothes, posed for pictures for the family album, and laughed at in a positive way. More subtle forces may also have been operative. Parental attitudes may be such that male-peer-group contact has been discouraged because boisterous play is less tolerable than quieter doll play with girls. Furthermore, a boy manifesting behavior he knows to be more typical of girls and receiving a neutral reaction may conclude (accurately) that his parents do not object to his atypical behavior. Whatever the source of encouragement, overt or covert, the parents need to be sensitized to the manner by which they are promoting behavior causing their son conflict.

The image of the father and his life role may provide additional negative input to the boy's anticipation of an adult male role. A father denigrated by his wife and lamenting his job may not provide a compellingly positive image for current identification or future behavior. Many children lack a clear idea of what their father does while away from home during the workday, a vacuum that can be filled by pleasant imagery from a trip to the place of employment and positive input from the father's co-workers. In families in which marital role division is decidedly skewed, with mother the sole decision-maker and provider of sustenance to the child, some equalization of authority and prestige can be encouraged.

Father–son interaction can be augmented where it has been weak. Typically fathers of feminine boys have an alienated relationship with their son. In some families this is the result of the boy's having rejected the activities and role of the father, with the father withdrawing and directing affection toward another sibling. Fathers, in consequence of their son's evolving toward a feminine orientation, may see themselves as having failed in their role as the prime source of male-role modeling. Other fathers are overly demanding of masculinity in their sons, resulting in withdrawal of the boy and subsequent anger and rejection by the father. In conversation with the fathers, the special nature of their son's interests can be stressed as well as the special effort needed by these fathers for promoting comfortable interaction. Strategies toward this goal have been detailed elsewhere (9).

Theoretical Considerations

Ethical and research issues are engaged by intervention in the lives of children with atypical gender-role behavior. What is the basis for expecting or desiring a child to manifest gender-role behavior that is conventional within his culture? If a boy wants to wear a dress instead of pants and play with dolls rather than trucks, so what? Regrettably such idealism is challenged by the social milieu in which the child lives coupled with the milieu that will accompany future adulthood. The very feminine boy is teased, bullied, and ostracized. In spite of all that is written, read, and said about a unigendered movement taking hold in this society, that ethic has barely (if at all) filtered down to the pediatric age group under study. The atypical male child of today is being subjected to a comparable degree of alienation experienced by the "sissy" of a generation ago. The children who come to us are unhappy in consequence of peer-group stigmatization. Although privately one might wish to immediately eradicate the sexism that exists within our culture, such a goal remains out of reach, and there is more basis for optimism for promoting change in the individual child.

What of the change to be promoted? Are these feminine boys to be forged into rough, aggressive, athletically driven males with all elements of aesthetics and sensitivity erased? Hardly. An alternative is available. These boys' gender-role orientation is so skewed as to preclude any options for what the culture defines as typical boyish behavior. They cannot effectively integrate into a male peer group because they lack the required confidence and social skills. They may, with assistance, be able to experience comfort in playing with boys *and* girls, not just girls. They may find that some "boyish" things are fun after all. Initially, they see no positive feature in being a boy and maturing into a man. Are they to be reassured that, with modern hormonal and surgical technology, they should just be patient and in a decade's time will receive sex-change surgery? What of the years of social pain prior to that time? What of the fact that males who "change sex" do not become normal females, but are biologically nonreproductive and have a flaw in their female sexual identity—the inescapable fact that they are chromosomally male and were born with male genitalia.

What if the very feminine boy is pretransvestic, not pretranssexual? Are there social consequences during adolescence and adulthood that derive from the compulsion to wear articles of women's clothing or their requirement for penile erection? Clearly, social limitations confront such behavior. Aside from the illegality of cross-gender dressing in some parts of the United States (which may fall before civil suits), will not such a male experience greater difficulty in finding a compatible dating or marital partner? Will not intrafamilial conflict result from the issue of cross-gender dressing in view of the couple's children?

What if the very feminine boy is prehomosexual, without subsequent desire to change sex or be a transvestite? Will the results of current reform efforts by the American homophile movement (Gay Liberation Front, etc.) be successful in changing laws and public opinion so as to render the adult homosexual's life comparable with that of the hetero-sexual? Can we expect a style of behavior that is illegal in 80% of the United States, labeled until 1974 a mental illness by American psychiatry, considered a sin by most organized religions, and a social threat by so many Americans be comfortably embraced in time for today's prehomosexual boy? Although laws may become equitable and psychiatry may limit pejo-rative labeling, if extrapolation from other societal biases is appropriate (such as religious and racial prejudice), how much basis is there for optimism with respect to homosexuality? The idea of two males kissing or engaging in fellatio or anal intercourse will probably remain an anathema at worst, and offensive at best, for at least a generation.

What will be the effects of treatment intervention during the preadoles-cent years? If the very feminine boy is pretranssexual, pretransvestic, or prehomosexual, at what ages will intervention produce an effect and on which components of sexual identity?

Most of the adult transsexuals I have interviewed were not psychi-atrically treated during childhood. Their parents had considered their behavior to be a "passing phase," and not until adolescence or adulthood was professional consultation sought. Their basic identity (female) and their gender-role behavior (feminine) remained atypical, and their genital orientation became directed toward same-sex partners. Most transvestites who have responded to research questionnaires were not treated during childhood or adulthood, and their atypical gender-role behavior and its fetishistic aspect remained unmodified (14). Most male homosexuals were not treated (nor recognized as atypical) during childhood. The few femi-nine boys J. Money and I have seen were treated only with respect to inculcating the idea that they could not become girls, and their parents were advised to discourage feminine behavior. The basic identity of these subjects during adulthood was male, their gender-role behavior was masculine, and their sexual orientation was homosexual.

In considering which aspect(s) of sexual identity are engaged by inter-vention during childhood, age at referral is a first consideration. Basic sexual identity is crystallized during the first 3 years of life. While it continues to be heavily overlaid during the next 2 to 3 years (and to a lesser degree beyond), much has been effected by the time the atypical male is first seen (usually 7 to 8). With a younger child, relatively more may be done with respect to sex categorization and satisfaction with that designation. However, clues revealing an enduring atypical identity are less clear at these earlier ages, and most parents do not recognize them even when present.

It may be that enough comfort with typical gender-role behavior may still be imparted when these children are first seen to preclude the relentless quest for genital-altering surgery of the transsexual. Grossly feminine children, through identification with a male therapist and training in certain physical behaviors, may appear more masculine. Social feedback in the face of these new behaviors may alter the boy's self-concept. Thus basic identity may undergo change with greater comfort in anatomic maleness. The long-term effect may be that the person will not need to resort to years of hormonal and surgical intervention to make (as best as is technically feasible) the body fit the mind. If so, anyone who has interviewed a large number of transsexual adults should agree that major distress and many unnecessary difficulties in life will have been avoided.

What will be the effect of better male-peer-group integration (promoted in treatment) on current life and future sexuality? First, it should reduce boyhood social distress. Second, there is the suggestion that peer-group alienation may influence adult sexuality. Many adult homosexuals report alienation from their male peer group during preadolescence and early adolescence. Whether this alienation led to wanting love from that group during later years and/or was a reflection of an early identification with a peer group that also later seeks males (the female peer group) is speculative. Furthermore, gross femininity in a male during early adolescence poses extraordinary difficulties to developing heterosexual relationships and perhaps augments opportunities for homosexual ones. Within the teenage social hierarchy, the grossly feminine male will probably hold a lower ranking. Furthermore, his obvious femininity may render him a more attractive partner for a homosexual male interested in feminine males and more vulnerable to homosexual assaults by sadistic males. It may also render him a more likely object of a sexual invitation by homosexual males seeking a partner deemed less likely to reject them.

Thus modification of atypical gender-role behavior in preadolescent males may reduce social alienation during childhood and increase the opportunity for heterosexual experiences during adolescence and later. It may be that the results of intervention will permit bisexuality or exclusive heterosexuality, should the person so elect.

DISCUSSION

Treatment questions bring into focus the complex and incompletely understood relationship between basic sexual identity, gender-role behavior, and genital sexuality. At what age(s) are the determinants of sexual orientation meshed? What are the relative weightings to be given prenatal influences, neonatal labeling of the child as male or female, preadolescent gender-role behavior, and adolescent socialization experiences?

Prenatal influences are the object of a vigorously renewed spirit of investigation. In the wake of decades of negative studies, a cluster of reports has appeared suggesting neuroendocrine influences on patterns of human sexuality. Case reports document chromosomally intersexed males with deficiently functioning testes (Klinefelter's syndrome) whose gender identity is female and whose sexual orientation is toward males (15). Whether these patients represent a coincidental association between the physiological anomaly and the atypical behavioral pattern is unknown. Other studies report differences between adult male homosexuals and heterosexuals with regard to plasma testosterone levels, sperm count, and urinary levels of testosterone metabolites (16, 17). The former finding has not been confirmed with other subjects (18), but the latter has been replicated (19). Whether these hormonal differences are primarily responsible for homosexuality or are a nonspecific by-product of it (such as increased stress) is yet to be determined.

Other reports suggest that prenatal gonadal hormone levels have an effect on specific aspects of gender-role behavior, notably rough-and-tumble play, aggressiveness, doll play, and maternalism. Females exposed to elevated levels of androgen (those with the adrenogenital syndrome or those whose mothers received synthetic progesterone agents during gestation) (20, 21) appear more tomboyish and less maternal. Males whose mothers received estrogens during pregnancy (along with lesser amounts of progesterone) are reported to be less aggressive and athletic (22). Whether these preadolescent tomboys will have a higher incidence of adult homosexuality or transsexualism remains to be determined, but one study of adult females with the adrenogenital syndrome does not indicate such an increased likelihood. Regarding the female-hormone-exposed males, it is difficult to distinguish the influence on these boys' behavior of their mothers' chronic illness (diabetes, for which they received the hormones) from specific effects of the hormones.

What role might gonadal hormones play on the subjects in this study? We need to view that role in a social-biological context, rather than as a simple brain–chemical interaction yielding heterosexual or homosexual behavior.

Neuroendocrine influences do not appear to relate directly to basic sexual identity. Earliest establishment of sexual identity appears to be essentially influenced by parental labeling of the child as a boy or girl. This is supported by studies of patients, comparably intersexed at birth, one designated male and one female (23). The bulk of the evidence indicates that the child unambiguously raised as a female will consider itself female, and the child unambiguously raised as a male will consider itself male—this in spite of the fact that they may be chromosomally and gonadally identical.

By contrast, the evidence from primate research, human and non-human, points to the influence of androgen on gender-role behavior, specifically aggressiveness and rough-and-tumble play. In the Western cultural context, children who do not exhibit these two characteristics are "feminine." Opposites are "masculine." The innately passive child will elicit different responses from mother and father. Earliest peer-socialization experiences are also influenced. The male who innately resonates with non-rough-and-tumble play will accommodate more to the social activities of young females. Maternalism (and its play-equivalent doll play) has also recently come under the scrutiny of neuroendocrinologists. Previously thought to be a purely sex-typed social-learning phenomenon, recent data suggest that it is, in part, neurally programmed. Nonhuman male and female primates show a clear difference in the extent and type of attention they pay to the newborns of their species. Female rhesus monkeys do not even require exposure to adult maternal models for their greater interest in infants to emerge. Human female preadolescents exposed *in utero* to masculinizing hormones show a significantly diminished interest in both doll play and the wish to bear children. Doll play is a sex-typed childhood behavior with salient social implications.

What of later socialization experiences? Study of the period of adolescence and its effect on adult sexuality remains an essentially unharvested research field. This is the life period in which one person enters the sexual waters a toe at a time while another plunges in with the whole body. These initial experiences may leave an enduring imprint. Self-image, in terms of desirability–undesirability, rapidly consolidates. Sexual conditioning, the temporal association of fantasy, external experience, and orgasm provides new and varied linkages. The occurrence of transient psychic phenomena during early adolescence is widely acknowledged. An aphorism of psychiatry is that behavior that at any other age might well be considered schizophrenic must be much more carefully evaluated here.

The same holds for certain sexual behaviors. I have seen several early-adolescent males who discovered (for them) the erotic properties of wearing women's garments and commenced cross-gender dressing with masturbation. For these boys, it *was* a passing phase that was later replaced by heterosexual, interpersonal relationships. We do not know the incidence of fetishistic cross-gender dressing during adolescence that permanently disappears. By contrast, we do know that most early adolescent same-sex genital experience does not endure as exclusive homosexuality. However, some adult homosexuals assert they were conditioned into a homosexual life style by adolescent genital experiences. Whether this sexual pattern emerged primarily as a result of conditioning on a neutral substrate or reinforced an already receptive recipient is not yet thoroughly understood. The picture for transsexualism is no more clear. Significantly, the only transsexual-appearing male patient to be reoriented in therapy to a male identity and heterosexual orientation was an adolescent (24). However, other adolescent transsexuals have persisted in their cross-sex identity, and at least one has undergone sex-reassignment surgery (25).

How, then, may these influences, varied appearing as they are, interact? Perhaps the model is one of coupling a male child's temperamental suitability to activities culturally labeled feminine with the visual appeal of certain articles that are feminine (cosmetics, bright clothes) and parental indifference to those preferences (or encouragement) during the child's first years. Typically, parents do not consider atypical gender role behavior during preschool years to be significant for adult behavior. Others consider it funny or cute and provide positive reinforcement. In our experience, no parents, actively discouraged these atypical preferences. The male child then begins school with greater facility for culturally feminine play and is labeled "sissy." This further contributes to male-group ostracism and drives the child further toward feminine socialization and father–son alienation.

In summary, we have presented a model in which innate factors, environmental support of atypical behaviors, and early peer-group experiences interact in a manner that is only partially understood. Our research must continue to delineate in greater detail the complex intermediate steps that result in the formation of an enduring atypical sexual identity.

ACKNOWLEDGMENTS

The work reported here was supported by a grant (G69-471) from the Foundations' Fund for Research in Psychiatry as well as a grant (MH 24305) and a Research Scientist Development Award (MH 31-739) from the National Institute of Mental Health, U.S. Public Health Service.

REFERENCES

1. Benjamin, H., *The Transsexual Phenomenon*, Julian Press, New York, 1966.
2. Bieber, I. and Colleagues, *Homosexuality. A Psychoanalytic Study of Male Homosexuals*, Basic Books, New York, 1962.
3. Saghir, M. and E. Robins, *Male and Female Homosexuality*, Williams and Wilkins, Baltimore, 1973.
4. Zuger, B., *J. Pediat* 69: 1098, 1966.
5. Lebovitz, P., *Am J Psychiatry* 128: 1283, 1972.
6. Machover, K., *Personality Projection in the Drawing of the Human Figure*, Charles C Thomas, Springfield, Ill., 1949.
7. Brown, D. *Psychol Monogr* 70: 14, 1956.
8. Green, R. and M. Fuller, *Am. J. Orthopsychiatry* 43: 123, 1973.
9. Green, R., *Sexual Identity Conflict in Children and Adults*, Basic Books, New York, 1974, Gerald Duckworth, London.
10. Green, R. M. Fuller, and B. Rutley, *Person Assess* 36: 349, 1972.
11. Ammons, R. and C. Ammons, *Psychol Rep Monogr Supp* 1-VII, 1962.
12. Jolles, I., *J Clin Psychol* 8: 13, 1952.
13. Green, R., M. Fuller, B. Rutley and J. Henler, *Behav Ther* 3: 425, 1962.
14. Prince, C. and P. Bentler, *Psychol Rep* 31: 903, 1972.
15. Baker, J. and R. Stoller, *Arch. Gen. Psychiatry* 18: 361, 1968.
16. Kolodny, R. W. Masters, J. Hendryx and G. Toro, *New Eng J Med* 285: 1170, 1971.
17. Margolese, S., *Horm Behav* 1: 151, 1970.
18. Tourney, G. and L. Hatfield, *Biol Psychiatry* 6: 23, 1973.
19. Evans, R., *J Cons Clin Psychol* 39: 140, 1972.
20. Ehrhardt, A., K. Evers and J. Money, *Johns Hopkins Med J* 123: 115, 1968.
21. Ehrhardt, A., in Zubin, J. and J. Money (eds.), *Contemporary Sexual Behavior*, The Johns Hopkins University Press, Baltimore, 1973.
22. Yalom, I., R. Green, and N. Fisk, *Arch Gen Psychiatry* 28: 554, 1973.
23. Money, J. and A. Ehrhardt, *Man & Woman, Boy & Girl*, The Johns Hopkins University Press, Baltimore, 1973.
24. Barlow, D., E. Reynolds and S. Agras, *Arch Gen Psychiatry* 28: 569, 1973.
25. Newman, L., *Arch Gen Psychiatry* 23: 112, 1970.

CHAPTER 17

The Psychodynamics of
Male Transsexualism

ETHEL S. PERSON and **LIONEL OVESEY**

Psychoanalytic Clinic for Training and Research
Department of Psychiatry
College of Physicians and Surgeons
Columbia University
New York, New York

For the last 3 years we have been engaged in a psychiatric study of transvestites, cross-dressing male homosexuals, and male and female transsexuals. In this chapter, we summarize some of our findings on male transsexualism—findings that are presented in detail elsewhere (1–3).

We have defined transsexualism operationally as the wish in biologically normal persons for hormonal and surgical sex reassignment. The wish may present as a symptom, in which case it is transient, or it may present as a syndrome, in which case it is insistent and progressive. In the latter instance, the wish grows to obsessive proportions and invades all other aspects of the patient's life.

The transsexual syndrome in males is not a unitary disorder, but a final common pathway for patients who otherwise differ markedly in family history, developmental history, clinical course, and personality. Clinically,

315

there are three prototypic histories in patients who seek sex reassignment, and we have classified transsexuals in accordance with these prototypes (2). Primary transsexuals progress toward a transsexual resolution of their gender and sexual problems without a significant history of either heterosexuality or homosexuality. Secondary transsexuals reach a transsexual resolution only after some period of time in which they are behaviorally homosexual or transvestitic. We have designated these two subgroups of secondary transsexuals as homosexual transsexuals and transvestitic transsexuals.

Our original work (1–3) was based on psychiatric interviews with 20 transsexual patients in various stages of sex-conversion therapy. Ten were primary transsexuals, five were homosexual transsexuals, and five were transvestitic transsexuals. All of the patients were volunteers referred from several clearing houses for patients seeking sex reassignment. Five patients were seen in single interviews only; 15 patients were seen approximately once a week for several weeks, then irregularly for periods ranging from a few months to as long as 2 years. In addition to the subjects in our original study, we have subsequently seen at least 30 other transsexuals in different settings, such as group meetings and consultations. We have drawn our observations from these patients as well as from the original ones.

We shall describe the primary transsexual syndrome and briefly contrast the findings in homosexual transsexualism and transvestitic transsexualism with the primary group. We shall present a psychodynamic hypothesis of transsexualism and discuss etiology. In conclusion, we shall make some remarks on the relationship of gender identity to gender behavior—remarks that derive from the comparison of the three groups of transsexuals.

PRIMARY TRANSSEXUALISM

Developmental History and Clinical Course

In the literature, transsexuals are described as effeminate from childhood onward, with a lifelong aversion for masculine pursuits (4, 5). We believe this finding is a result of the failure to distinguish among the three types of transsexual histories. In our series of 10 primary transsexuals, nine showed no evidence of effeminacy in childhood and were never referred to as "sissies". At school, all participated in rough-and-tumble play when required, but with an inner sense of abhorrence. They did not engage in girls' activities or play with girls any more than did normal boys. As children, our patients were envious of girls and fantasized being girls, but none actually believed that he was a girl. The wish to be female may fluctuate, but it usually becomes progressively intense as psychological adaptation in the masculine role deteriorates.

All 10 of our primary transsexuals were socially withdrawn and spent most of their time after school by themselves at home. In effect, they were childhood loners with few agemate companions of either sex. This isolate behavior was accompanied by feelings of anxiety, depression, and loneliness.

As he advances through childhood, the primary transsexual becomes increasingly aware of the difference between himself and other boys. This difference is sharply accentuated in adolescence, when most boys become sexually aware. The primary transsexual shows little sexual interest in either sex and remains relatively asexual. Most often, he has no sexual experience other than masturbation, and even the masturbation is infrequent. Seven of our 10 patients masturbed less frequently than once a month. Masturbation was usually performed in a mechanistic, dissociated way, either with no fantasy at all or with a vague heterosexual fantasy in which the patient saw himself as a woman. The pleasure yield was minimal, at times almost to the point of anhedonia.

A major component of this asexuality in all of our primary transsexuals was a specific self-loathing of male physical characteristics. The loathing typically began in late adolescence and was a progressive phenomenon. It encompassed not only the genitalia but also the secondary sexual characteristics.

In postadolescence, the primary transsexual often makes "one last effort" to be a man in order to resolve the confusion about the difference he feels from other males and to overcome his sense of isolation. This effort is usually an intense involvement in some activity commonly regarded as distinctly masculine. For example, the patient may join the army or go out for football. This attempt rarely fails behaviorally, since primary transsexuals are usually adept in manifest mastery. Nonetheless, the symptoms of isolation and the sexual withdrawal continue unabated. At this point, the patient becomes even more isolated, anxious, and depressed than he originally was.

Ashamed, confused, without outlet for intimate conversation, or even confession, he begins a quest for some explanation of his distress. He avidly reads the psychological and sexual literature, searching for clues to explain his problems and to define his real nature to himself. Eventually, he stumbles on an account of transsexualism, usually an account of Christine Jorgensen. The discovery of transsexualism, with its attendant explanation, offers relief, first of all, by giving the patient an identity.

Second, the literature on transsexualism offers a medical vehicle for a fantasy—the wish to be a woman—to be converted into a reality. It is at this point that the wish to be female hardens into the conviction that the patient is indeed a woman trapped in a man's body.

There is a uniform history of cross-dressing in our sample, in all cases beginning sometime between the ages of 3 and 10, usually in the mother's clothes. The cross-dressing appears to be the dramatization of the wish to be female. In all 10 patients, the cross-dressing was surreptitious. Typically, in early adolescence, the practice evoked shame and was voluntarily abandoned as unmasculine, but was resumed openly on a full-time basis after the transsexual resolution. The memory attached to the first experience of cross-dressing was invariably the same: "I felt very warm, very comfortable." . . . "I had company." . . . "I felt relieved." "I felt wanted." . . . "I felt my mother's arms around me."

Personality

We found little variation in personality among the primary transsexuals. Psychological aptitude was minimal, although all patients were extremely cooperative. Depression, most often experienced as loneliness, was characteristic. The depression was not of the guilty, self-accusatory, or angry type—it was essentially an empty depression. The patients described their lives, as men, historically and in the present as sad, lonely, empty, and colorless. Suicidal ideation and suicide attempts were frequent. The depression could perhaps be attributed mainly to failure in the masculine role with subsequent anxiety and loss of self-esteem. Our clinical impression, however, is that these patients are describing an ongoing depressive core, intensified by current stress, but not caused by it. In their histories, there are frequent occurrences of prolonged thumb sucking, enuresis, and eating disorders, either anorexia or gluttony.

A schizoid quality is pervasive in the primary transsexual's personality. As already described, childhood is characterized by isolate behavior. Nonetheless, by adolescence or adulthood, some of these patients acquire the skill of establishing cordial, but not intimate, asexual relationships.

As a group, we found the primary transsexuals to be extremely gentle and self-effacing people. Assertiveness was seriously crippled, though it survived enough in the work area to allow adequate and, on occasion, even outstanding performance. These patients were always pliant and agreeable in their relationships with others unless thwarted in their demands for sex reassignment. Under such circumstances, they became stubborn, strong-willed, and intractable. Otherwise, they were generally incapable of manifest anger.

Mental life, before and after surgery, is characterized by obsessive preoccupation with gender-related items. The obsessive form remains throughout; only the content changes. Thus, in childhood, the primary transsexual is obsessed about being a girl. In adolescence, he is obsessed about "one last effort" to be a man. In adulthood, before surgery, he is obsessed about sex conversion. After surgery, he is first obsessed about the anatomical results and then centers on how to be more and more feminine both in appearance and in behavior.

In summary, primary transsexuals are schizoid-obsessive, asexual, unassertive, and out of touch with anger. The question arises as to whether the life-long suffering and personality malfunction are manifestations of the thwarted desire to be female or of some other underlying problem. We believe that the estrangement, loneliness, and emptiness uniformly reported by these patients constitute evidence of severe separation anxiety engendered early in life. Diagnostically these patients fall in the range of the borderline syndrome, characterized by separation anxiety, empty depression, sense of void, oral dependency, defective self-identity, and impaired object relations (6, 7).

SECONDARY TRANSSEXUALISM

Homosexual Transsexuals

The homosexual transsexual is effeminate at all times, from early childhood into adulthood. The typical personality of homosexual transsexuals falls on a spectrum with passive, hysterical features at one end and hyper-aggressive narcissistic features on the other end; in no instance can a homosexual transsexual be described as withdrawn and isolated. All are emotionally labile, expressive, and theatrical. Those on the narcissistic end of the spectrum may be paranoid, grandiose, and even violent. Cross-dressing begins in childhood; it is nonfetishistic and intermittent. The clothes are used for narcissistic aggrandizement and, later, to attract male sexual partners. Unlike the primary transsexual, the homosexual cross-dresser wants to be noticed, and in general, puts on a theatrical performance. To this end, he wears colorful, flamboyant clothing, often to the point of caricature, especially at parties and drag balls. Sexuality may be attenuated, as in the primary transsexual, and may even range to hyperactivity, but the sexual object is always male and prior to the transsexual resolution, his self-identification is always homosexual. Sexual preference is usually the passive role in anal intercourse, but at the narcissistic paranoid end of the spectrum, it may be the active role in anal intercourse. The transsexual wish and, in some, the transsexual resolution arise at times of intense stress, usually rejection by a lover or some failure in the homosexual adaptation.

Transvestitic Transsexuals

Transvestitic transsexuals are masculine in childhood; in adulthood, their personalities are distinguished by extreme assertiveness and competitiveness. Even in feminine attire, these individuals have difficulty effectively mimicking female behavior. Cross-dressing is most often fetishistic, but is also used nonsexually to relieve gender tension. It is at first intermittent, but in most transvestitic transsexuals (as compared with transvestites), it is escalatory, progressive, and eventually becomes continuous. The clothing is often dated and out of style, more like the clothes "mother" used to wear. Sexual object choice is almost invariably female; sometimes the individual may prefer the subordinate role in intercourse. Sexuality is attenuated, though not to the degree we see in primary transsexualism. The transsexual wish or resolution occurs at times of stress. In this group, the stress consists of threats to both masculinity and dependent security; for example, vocational failing, competitive defeat, broken marriage, death of the mother, or birth of a child.

PSYCHODYNAMIC RECONSTRUCTION

Primary Transsexualism

Most investigators claim that male transsexuals have a female core gender identity. Stoller (8), for example, believes that the child acquires a female core gender identity by virtue of an "imprinting" or learning mechanism, the origin of which is not the result of conflict. On the basis of our experience, we cannot concur that transsexuals have a female core gender identity. Although the presenting complaint may be the stereotyped one, "I am a female soul trapped in a male body," this statement is not a life-long conviction, but the evolutionary end point in a search for gender certainty. It is true that there is a history of gender discomfort, an inner abhorrence of certain masculine activities, and early cross-dressing accompanied by emotional relief. Nonetheless, the fantasies of childhood and adolescence are cast in the form of a wish, not in the form of a conviction; for example, "I would like to be a girl," not "I am a girl". The conviction of femaleness crystallizes out rather abruptly when the patient learns of the existence of transsexualism. These patients commonly speak of their great confusion as to what they were—heterosexual, homosexual, transvestite—until they learned of transsexualism, usually through reading an account of Christine Jorgensen.

We believe it is more accurate to describe core gender identity in the transsexual as flawed or *ambiguous* by virtue of the *wish* to be female, rather than as female. This is a distinction that allows us to conceptualize transsexualism in psychodynamic terms. To do so we must attempt to account for the origin of the wish to be female and ultimately trace the metamorphosis of the wish to be female into the transsexual syndrome.

All our transsexual subjects suffer from the manifestations of extreme separation anxiety engendered early in life. In order to alleviate separation anxiety, the child resorts to a fantasy of symbiotic fusion with the mother. Through this fantasy, mother and child become one and the danger of separation is reduced. We infer that this fantasy is laid down before the child is 3 years old; otherwise, core gender identity would be firmly established by that age. The wish to be female usually emerges later in childhood and is the conscious component of the unconscious fantasy of symbiotic fusion with the mother.

The fusion fantasy is dramatized in childhood through cross-dressing. To date we have never seen a primary transsexual without a history of this. Adult memories of the first experience of dressing in the mother's clothes, as already quoted, represent clinical evidence of the fusion fantasy. In addition, the recurrent fantasy of mothering a girl infant, which appears in many histories, represents an attempt to establish a symbiotic bond.

The separation anxiety is not completely allayed through utilization of the fusion fantasy but continues into adulthood. The final transsexual resolution is an attempt to get rid of this anxiety through sex reassignment; that is, the transsexual acts out his unconscious fantasy surgically and "literally" becomes his own mother. Through the self-identification as a transsexual he "solves" the problem of confused core gender, offers justification for his failure in the masculine gender role, and establishes hope for the future.

In essence, we see the fantasy of symbiotic fusion with the mother as the anlage of the transsexual resolution. Both the fusion fantasy and ultimately the transsexual resolution are reparative or adaptive maneuvers to counter early separation anxiety. As such, transsexualism is a "self-cure." Indeed, in certain patients, sex reassignment reverses some of the personality defects characteristic of the preoperative transsexual.

Secondary Transsexualism

We suggested in an earlier paper (1) that the symptomatic distortions of sex and gender in transsexualism, transvestism, and effeminate homosexuality reflected different ways of handling unresolved separation anxiety engendered during progressive steps of the separation–individuation phase of infantile development. We suggested that the three disorders originated along a developmental gradient: transsexualism first, transvestism and effeminate homosexuality later. The separation anxiety is nonspecific and can derive from any situation, real or imagined, that threatens the child with separation.

In contrast to transsexualism, separation anxiety in transvestism and homosexuality is allayed not by the fantasy of symbiotic fusion with the mother, but by resort to transitional and part-objects. These mechanisms are not as primitive as symbiosis and do not become available to the infant until he has moved further along on the separation–individuation gradient. These mechanisms may become operative before the age of 3 years, but their major effects come later, since there is no ambiguity about core gender identity either in the transvestite or in the homosexual; on the contrary, core gender identity in both is very definitely male. Their gender-role identity, however, is markedly disturbed.

The stages of maturation along a developmental gradient are not neatly compartmentalized, but overlap each other, so that preceding stages merge with those that follow. In consequence, under conditions of stress, the fantasy of symbiotic fusion with the mother may arise defensively as a regressive phenomenon in some effeminate homosexuals and transvestites, and present as a transsexual symptom or evolve into the transsexual syndrome.

Etiology

Despite a plethora of explanations, the etiology of transsexualism remains unknown. Benjamin (9) has postulated an endocrine etiology. Stoller (8) has suggested an "imprinting" mechanism. Many investigators (10–15) have suggested a psychological etiology, with the origin antedating the phallic-oedipal stage. Our observations are in agreement with these latter investigators; more specifically, we postulate an early separation anxiety in transsexualism. In our group of primary transsexuals, symptoms generally considered referable to separation anxiety are well documented; for example, the empty depression and the frequent eating disorders. In addition, 50% of our sample, 5 patients out of 10, had had an actual separation from the mother, necessitated by the child's hospitalization for illness before the age of 4 (2). However, we do not believe that the presence of separation anxiety in transsexual patients can be viewed as the etiologic agent. Separation anxiety is nonspecific; it may be caused by a variety of traumas, and different infants may be differently affected by the same trauma. In addition, separation anxiety is not limited to transsexuals. It is a widespread finding in many disorders, particularly in the borderline ranges of psychopathology.

What is specific to transsexualism are the methods of counteracting early separation anxiety: (1) the fantasy of symbiotic fusion with the mother and (2) the evolution of the fusion fantasy into the insistent wish for surgical and hormonal sex reassignment. At this time, we have little understanding as to why some children with early separation anxiety utilize such a fantasy, whereas others do not. Some few clues emerge from the family psychodynamics. We have found a predominant, though not exclusive, type of mother–son interaction in each transsexual group (2, 3). However, these findings are not precise enough to "explain" transsexualism. The problem of etiology is further complicated by the fact that not all children who utilize a fantasy of symbiotic fusion grow up to be transsexual.

It is possible that the history of transsexualism as a clinical entity may shed some small light on its essential nature. In 1952, when the transformation of George to Christine Jorgensen was reported in the press and became a matter of wide general interest, the word "transsexual" had not yet been coined, though a few cases of sex conversion had been reported earlier (16). In the intervening 20 years, an estimated 10,000 transsexuals surfaced. The question naturally arises as to whether this increase represents a real increase in incidence or whether transsexuals have always existed in comparable numbers. This is a difficult question and one that can be answered only speculatively.

It is only recently (since the 1930s and 1940s) that the "impulse" to transsexualism has been able to find release in medical and surgical intervention. This is the first historical time in which the potential transsexual can modify his physical body to match the psychological predilection. We believe that this fact alone modifies the clinical course. Prior to this time, the potential transsexual had to modify the psychological predilection, live with the dichotomy in gender identity, or seek temporary relief by cross-dressing.

In our experience, all patients with confused sexual identity are avid readers of the scientific sexual literature. Transsexuals are a dramatic case in point. We have never met a transsexual who has not read at least one book on the subject; many transsexuals can give a complete bibliography on transsexualism. This fact has certain concrete ramifications. On the one hand, it leads many patients to retroactive distortion (both conscious and unconscious) in order to fit the criteria for the syndrome. This may be done for practical reasons, for example, to qualify for surgery. On the other hand, and more important, familiarity with the literature offers a concrete identity, albeit a bizarre one, to people who are terrified of being isolated freaks. Each of our patients described a sense of relief on discovering that he fit into some category. Even Jorgensen did not come to the transsexual resolution unaided. He sought some medical explanation for his gender confusion and resolved the confusion by a pseudohermaphroditic identification culled from the medical literature.

It is certainly true that persons with confused gender identity have always existed. In this sense, transsexuals have always existed potentially. By this we mean that there have always been individuals with early separation anxiety who counter this anxiety with a fantasy of symbiotic fusion with the mother and enact the fantasy through cross-dressing. Nonetheless, the transsexual resolution *per se* is a relatively recent historical phenomenon dependent on borrowing an "identity" from the medical literature.

CONCLUSION

We have proposed a psychodynamic formulation of transsexualism. The etiology, in our opinion, remains unknown. The breakdown of the transsexual syndrome into the primary group and into the secondary group (homosexual and transvestitic) has prognostic significance for sex-conversion therapy (2, 3), but it also suggests further areas for inquiry.

We are struck with the finding that only one of the three groups of transsexuals, the homosexual, presents signs of effeminacy in childhood. Despite the wish to be female and despite the unconscious fantasy of symbiotic fusion with the mother, the primary group essentially presents as neuter throughout life, at least until sex conversion. The transvestitic transsexual, on the other hand, appears masculine or even hypermasculine in both childhood and adulthood.

How are we to account for this finding? Overt signs of masculinity and femininity (gender-role behavior) in transsexuals appear to be related to sexual preference rather than to self-identification. The transvestitic transsexuals who are heterosexual (some of whom continue to prefer female sexual partners even after sex conversion) appear masculine. The asexual primary group does not emit either feminine or masculine cues, but is behaviorally neuter. Only the homosexual group, whose sexual preference is male, appear effeminate.

The origin of masculine or feminine characteristics in transsexuals does not automatically derive from core gender identity, which is ambiguous. It seems to be related to the choice of sexual object, but precedes emerging sexuality. For example, effeminacy in childhood has been reported to occur as early as 2 years of age (4) and consequently must antedate sexual preference. Gender-role behavior (masculinity and femininity) may well organize the direction of emerging sexuality and then come to serve as a signaling device for sexual preference. Nonetheless, its own derivation—that is, the ultimate source of masculine and feminine behavioral manifestations—remains obscure.

REFERENCES

1. Ovesey, L. and E. Person, *J Am Acad Psychoanal* **1**: 53, 1973.

2. Person, E. and L. Ovesey, *Am J Psychother,* **28**(1): 4, January, 1974.

3. Person, E. and L. Ovesey, *Am J Psychother,* **28**(2): 174, April, 1974.

4. Green, R., in Green R. and J. Money (eds), *Transsexualism and Sex Reassignment,* Johns Hopkins University Press, Baltimore, 1968, p. 23.

5. Money, J., in Green, R. and J. Money (eds.), *Transsexualism and Sex Reassignment,* Johns Hopkins University Press, Baltimore, 1968, p. 115.

6. Grinker, R., B. Werble and R. C. Drye, *The Borderline Syndrome,* Basic Books, New York, 1968.

7. Kernberg, O., *Am J Psychoanal* **15**: 641, 1967.

8. Stoller, R. J., *Sex and Gender,* Science House, New York, 1968.

9. Benjamin, H., *The Transsexual Phenomena,* Julian Press, New York, 1966.

10. Segal, M. M., *Int J. Psychoanal* **46**: 209, 1965.

11. Socarides, C. W., *The Overt Homosexual,* Grune & Stratten, New York, 1968.

12. Socarides, C. W., *Int J Psychoanal* **51**: 341, 1970.

13. Golosow, N. and E. L. Weitzman, *J Nerv Ment Dis* **49**: 328, 1969.

14. Gershman, H., *Am J Psychoanal* **30**: 58, 1970.

15. Weitzman, E. L., C. A. Shamoian and N. Golosow, *J Nerv Ment Dis* **151**: 295, 1970.

16. Money, J. and R. J. Gaskin, *Int J Psychiatry* **9**: 249, 1970–1971.

Discussion: Gender Identity

RICHARD C. FRIEDMAN, Moderator

RUTH TENDLER, Rapporteur

Dr. Kohlberg opened the discussion by saying that, in speaking of gender identity, Dr. Green actually seemed to be making observations on sex-role preference, and he asked whether Dr. Green had evaluated children who believe they are of the opposite sex. Dr. Green replied that by the time the children are seen (modal age 6 years), they do not say "I am a girl" except when they are dressed in women's clothes and role playing, although they had said this when they were younger. Primarily they say "I wish I were," "I want to be," or "I will become." Similar statements are made by adult male transsexuals, who, unless they are psychotic and delusional, do not say "I am," but rather "I feel like" or "I want to live as" (a female).

Commenting on the childrens' reasons for their sexual preference, Dr. Green stated that some boys explain they would rather not have a penis. He also noted that there is a problem in defining what instruments most accurately assess gender identity. It is not yet clear whether the most sensitive indicator is the Draw-a-Person Test, doll-play fantasies, peer-group preference, toy choice, or some other measure.

Dr. Kohlberg thought that cognitive measures were called for in view of parental reports that the children had made "I am" statements at early ages. He also asked Dr. Green to elaborate on the therapeutic interventions made by his group. Dr. Green described a group experience with six or seven boys and a male therapist with whom they can identify.

Group sessions are also held with the boys' families, with mothers alone, and with fathers alone, in an effort to teach family members how to avoid reinforcing very feminine behavior.

In addition, boys may be placed in one-to-one play therapy with a male therapist, with the family also being seen. Systemic reinforcement schedules are suggested for use at home, but this measure is usually ineffective because of psychological needs within the family to preserve the child's atypical behavior. Another group of parents who do not wish to involve themselves or their children in a formal therapeutic program have become a control group, since periodic contact with them is maintained.

Dr. Green did not think that this type of study lent itself to the matching of cells for different varieties of intervention because there is never an absolute "no-intervention" group. He pointed out that the act of seeking an evaluation of the behavior demonstrates that the family has begun to perceive it as undesirable. Dr. Green asked Dr. Kohlberg for suggestions regarding the cognitive measures that might be appropriate, but none were described.

Dr. Sackett reported on a recently completed study to determine sex-role effects in rats. Litters were arranged to provide for three control groups: one of four females, one of four males, and the third of two females and two males; and for two experimental groups: one litter of a male and three females, the other of one female and three males. In the two experimental groups, therefore, one of the sexes acquired experience only with pups of the opposite sex.

Two measures, distributed almost independently for male and female rats, were used. One was motor activity in an open field, where females are known to be more lively than males. The second was the hole-in-the-wall test, in which females regularly leave through the hole faster than males. The rats remained in the litters until they were 3 weeks old, after which the mother was taken out for 1 week. Then they were adapted to an open field, once a day, for 1 week, and the amount of activity was measured. After they were 37 days old, the hole in the wall was opened.

Females were more active than males in an open field. Males raised with another male and two females were indistinguishable from all males, and females raised with another female in the litter were indistinguishable from all females. The male raised with females was, proportionately, about intermediate, whereas the female raised with males showed a greater change from female norms. Results of the hole-in-the-wall test showed the same pattern. Although the male raised with females was different from other males, he was much more like normal males than a female raised with males, who was much closer to the male norm.

Dr. Sackett's conclusions were that, though both sexes were considerably influenced, the female was more affected than the male, and that the sex of the pups with whom a given rat pup lives during the first 3 weeks of life has a major effect on sex-typical behavior.

Dr. Green commented that this kind of experience may be an important variable for the boys he studied. Many families reported that only girls were accessible as early playmates for their sons, so that toy availability and socialization during preschool years were exclusively feminine. When these boys entered kindergarten or first grade, they had not developed social skills in relating to male peers. As a result, alienation from the group and social stigmatization occurred, further estranging the boys.

Dr. Michels was interested in Dr. Green's findings on sibling order, intervals and composition. Dr. Green stated there were no significant trends as regards sex, ordinal position, or sibling intervals. When selecting control families, matching is routinely made for sibling sequence.

Also in terms of these variables, Dr. Michels asked what data were available on homosexuals and transsexuals. Dr. Green responded that there was considerable diversity among published reports in the area of sibling order as well as on measures of masculinity and femininity.

Dr. Moss elicited the fact that the photographs Dr. Green had shown of effeminate boys had all been taken by their parents. He asked Dr. Green why the families had saved these pictures. Dr. Green felt that the pictures reflected a positive parental attitude toward the feminine behavior. The behavior is typically identified and either rationalized or subtly encouraged, but not labeled negatively. The atypical gender preferences expressed by children between the ages of 2 and 4 are usually not interdicted by their parents.

Dr. O'Connor inquired whether Dr. Green had taken a detailed psychosexual history on the parents in his study and whether families were seen jointly or separately. Dr. Green said that 2 to 3 hours were spent with each parent. In addition to a complete history, there were observations of familial interactions involving both parents, or a parent and child, or a parent and sibling. He added that they had a control group in which children were matched for age, ethnic background, marital intactness, socioeconomic level of parents, and sibling order; these control families went through the same procedures.

The discussion was then directed to Dr. Person's presentation on the psychodynamics of transsexualism. Dr. Ehrhardt wanted to know how subjects were selected and what type of people came for psychotherapy after surgery. Dr. Person replied that her group was not random; subjects came from clearing houses for sexual reassignment in New York and from referrals from other subjects. Although there were a few who subsequently desired treatment, they participated in the study as subjects, not as patients.

Dr. Friedman inquired whether the external environment of any of Dr. Person's subjects was normal during their developmental years. She thought this depended on the weight given to family dynamics as they are presented by the transsexual. Since all describe defects in their mothers' maternal capabilities, presumably none of them had normal childhood experiences. She is currently trying to obtain direct information from their mothers.

Ms. Ullian commented that Drs. Green and Person seemed to be saying that female gender preference is largely based on externals, such as clothes and makeup, and asked for data on what other aspects of the female role transsexual males prefer or how they conceptualize the female role and what they dislike about the male role. Dr. Person thought that the attachment to clothes is for security reasons and not primarily related to appearance; it is linked to the necessity for cross-gender dressing, which is symptomatic of severe separation anxiety. She also noted that there are reports of people who are dissatisfied with either gender and exhibit a fluctuating gender identity, although they are not in the majority. Illustratively, she told of a man who was married, then became a transvestite, later a homosexual, and finally a transsexual—and is now a radical lesbian.

Ms. Ullian asked whether transsexuals expressed a desire to have or to take care of babies. Dr. Person said that the fantasies and behavior of the three groups of transsexuals are different in this respect. Primary transsexuals have many fantasies about mothering girl children. Homosexual transsexuals focus instead on the narcissistic aspects of femininity, such as furs and jewels. Transvestitic transsexuals are more difficult to describe in terms of what attributes of femininity they are attuned to. Their fantasy life and behavior at parties suggest that they see themselves more as daughters than as mothers.

Dr. Rosenblum asked Dr. Person to comment further on separation trauma in the histories of these patients. Dr. Person referred to the earlier paper of Dr. Galenson, who made the point that separation anxiety and castration anxiety among young children were expressed in attachment to inanimate objects. She related her material to this, citing the fusion fantasy in the transsexual and the transvestite's affinity, from very early years, for part-objects, transitional objects, and fetishes. Involvement with these objects is understood as a substitute for perceived lack of relationship with the mother. It is not clear whether this reflects a realistic mothering deficit or whether these people have a greater need to be mothered and are more sensitive to maternal deprivation than normal. It is clear, however, that this involvement is compensatory.

Dr. Rosenblum wanted to know whether this kind of separation trauma is equally prevalent in female and male transsexuals. Dr. Person responded affirmatively and noted that a study of women who have breast-augmentation procedures concluded that the primary motivation for surgery is reunion with the mother, rather than physical attractiveness to men. Female transsexuals are rare, and Dr. Person has never evaluated a *primary* female transsexual. Transvestism is so unusual in women that Dr. Person stated she would expect most female-to-male transsexuals to have first identified themselves as homosexual.

Dr. Green highlighted some differences between male and female transsexuals as noted by his group. Female-to-male transsexuals have less of a social network before surgery; afterward they are more likely to drop their former contacts and blend into conventional marriages, often with women who have been divorced. Male-to-female transsexuals may remain publicly identified as transsexuals postsurgically by becoming stage professionals, and they less frequently form stable marital relationships. After sex change, female-to-male transsexuals usually adopt a traditional male middle-class value system: they are punctual, responsible, pay their bills, and hold steady jobs. Male-to-female transsexuals, on the other hand, are more likely to develop a dramatic syndrome characterized by financial undependability, lack of vocational goal directedness, transitory relationships with others, and frequent moves between rented rooms.

6   *Aggression, Adaptation, and Evolution*

HEINO F. L. MEYER-BAHLBURG, *Moderator*

DANIEL N. STERN, *Rapporteur*

CHAPTER 18

Sex Differences in Aggression

KENNETH E. MOYER

Department of Psychology
Carnegie-Mellon University
Pittsburgh, Pennsylvania

In all mammalian species, from mouse to man, the male is the more aggressive sex. In man, the male is the primary perpetrator of violent crimes. According to the National Commission on Violence (1), violent crime in the city is overwhelmingly committed by males. In 1968, the homicide rate was five times higher for males; for robbery it was 20 times higher. It has been suggested that the trait that has the greatest statistical significance in differentiating criminals from noncriminals is that of sex status (2). Broom and Selznick (3) summarize the particular propensity of the male for all types of criminal behavior with the observation that, since history has been recorded, males have committed more crimes of violence than have females in all nations and all communities within those nations. Furthermore, with the exception of those types of crime related specifically to the female sex, such as abortion, men have committed more of all types of crime.

This chapter is based on material from the author's forthcoming book *The Psychobiology of Aggression*, to be published by Harper and Row, New York.

However, the fact that, in this particular area, the statistics are over-whelmingly higher for the male should not lead us to conclude that the female is incapable of aggression. She is not. She does, however, tend to engage only in certain kinds of aggressive behavior.

Our understanding of the differences between the sexes in regard to aggressiveness necessitates that we discriminate among various kinds of aggression and not lump all varieties of hostile behavior into a single category. This argument has been presented in some detail elsewhere and need not be covered again here (4). Suffice it to say that different kinds of aggression can generally be discriminated on the basis of the stimuli that elicit them, the topography of the aggressive response, and the physiological basis. The following classification of aggressive behavior may be useful: predatory, intermale, fear induced, irritable, maternal, sex related, and instrumental. In this chapter I deal with the differences between the sexes on intermale, maternal, and sex-related aggression as well as with one form of irritable aggression that is the exclusive province of the female—premenstrual irritability. The sexes also differ in instrumental aggressive behavior because they are differently reinforced for hostile behaviors; the role models they learn to emulate differ in the amount of aggression that they manifest. There does not appear to be a physiological basis for the sex differences in instrumental aggression, and those differences will not be covered here.

Although care must obviously be used in applying data obtained from animal research to humans, we can learn much about ourselves by understanding the behaviors and the physiological bases of the behaviors of those lower on the phylogenetic scale. This chapter therefore includes much of what is known about sex differences in aggression in animals as well as man.

INTERMALE AGGRESSION

The most frequent target of male hostility is a male conspecific to which the attacker has not become habituated. Intermale aggression is unique and can be differentiated from other types of hostile behavior on the basis of the kinds of stimuli that elicit it, the stimuli that inhibit it, the species-specific topography, and its particular physiological basis.

Although there are particular situations in which the female can display intense and effective aggression (e.g., in the defense of the young), in the day-to-day encounters among animals, it is the male that shows the highest and most consistent level of spontaneous aggression.* Calhoun (7), in his extensive study of a rat colony under seminatural conditions, came to the conclusion that males actively "seek" competitive situations. He based this conclusion on the observation that the number of intermale conflicts was far beyond that to be expected on the basis of chance encounters. The number of conflicts between two females, however, was within the range of chance interactions, and the agonistic contacts between pairs of males and females was so low that Calhoun concluded that the sexes tend to avoid conflict with one another. A number of other investigators have arrived at similar conclusions (8, 9).

It has been repeatedly shown that pairs of male mice placed together in a neutral environment will promptly engage in fighting; if the animals are relatively well matched, the fight may be intense and result in wounding. Fredericson (10) found that spontaneous fighting in 30 pairs of male mice occurred in 100% of the time over 13 trials. However, when females were tested in the same apparatus under the same conditions, only one pair of mice manifested spontaneous aggression (11). In an attempt to develop an aggressive strain of mouse, Lagerspetz (12) found so little spontaneous fighting among females that she was obliged to base selective breeding entirely on the behavior of the males. The tendency for pairs of male mice to fight is so strong and so consistent that it has frequently been used as a dependent variable in the testing of drug effects on aggression (13).

In most of the species that have been studied, it has been found that the male is the more aggressive sex. Among the Pacific pilot whales (*Globicephala scammoni*), the young males are described as tattered with scars both new and healing, and there appears to be good evidence that the wounds result from attacks by older males. Bull sperm whales fight by grappling with their jaws; these fights reach sufficient intensity to result in broken, dislocated, or twisted jaws (14).

Under certain conditions, such as the crowding that results during high tide on a narrow beach, aggression among male elephant seals may reach such dramatic proportions that the whole social structure is disrupted, with resulting chaos (15). Matthews (16) describes the aggressive social interactions of the hippopotamus, deer, musk ox, seals, walruses, wolves,

* Exceptions to this general rule include hamsters and gibbons. When hamsters are tested in pairs in a neutral area, considerable agonistic behavior occurs, with overt fighting in about half the cases. However, no sex differences are discernible (5). After extensive field observations, Carpenter (6) has concluded that male and female gibbons are generally equally dominant and aggressive.

and a variety of Australian marsupials and in each case attributes the bulk of the aggressive behavior to the males.

Among nonhuman primates, most of the aggressive behavior that does occur is manifested by males. For example, Thompson (17) studied irus macaques and observed dyadic encounters within and between sexes in a laboratory situation. He reports that the principal interaction between pairs of males consisted of biting or rough handling of one male by the other. Pairs of females manifested almost no aggressive behavior, but spent their time in grooming and inspecting one another. In male–female pairs, the males initiated most of the social interactions, which involved mounting, grooming, and anogenital inspection with relatively little hostile behavior.

Although there are some species differences, the naturalistic observations of a variety of nonhuman primates tend to support the laboratory findings indicating that intraspecific aggression is displayed more by the males than by the females (18–20). A number of additional studies are cited by Gray (21).

Although actual fighting does not generally occur until endocrine maturation takes place, the males in some species seem to have an early predisposition to rough-and-tumble play, which simulates adult aggressive behavior. Among chimpanzees and baboons, males spend considerably more time engaging in aggressive play than do females (22). Infant male rhesus monkeys wrestle and roll and engage in sham biting significantly more than do females, and from approximately 10 weeks of age males show more threat responses than do females. These results were obtained during the study of infant monkeys raised with inanimate surrogate mothers, who could hardly transmit cultural differences to the young (23). Sexual dimorphism in regard to the frequency of threat, rough-and-tumble play, and chasing play in the infant rhesus monkey has also been confirmed by Goy (24), and it seems unlikely that this difference between the sexes is due to blood levels of testosterone since that hormone is undetectable in the blood at that age (25). Furthermore, these sex differences are maintained even though the males are castrated at 3 to 4 months of age (26). Field studies have also confirmed the tendency for the young male monkey (Old World) to engage in rough-and-tumble play (27).

Human children also show sex differences in aggressive tendencies at a very early age. Large amounts of data have been collected in various parts of the United States on the amount and kinds of aggression displayed in relatively standardized doll-play situations, and there is a clear distinction between the sexes on these variables as early as age 3. Boys spend more time in aggressive play than do girls, and the type of aggression shown by boys tends to be more vigorous, destructive, and hurtful than that shown by girls (28). Careful observation of nursery school children reveals that boys more frequently engage in mock hostile play than do girls. This activity involves rough contact with considerable running, chasing, jumping up and down, and laughing (29). It has also been reported that boys up to the age of 6 or 7 in a Melanesian society show much more rough-and-tumble play than do girls (30).

Response Topography in Intermale Aggression

A number of authors have emphasized the stereotyped ritualized nature of fights between male conspecifics (31–35). The behaviors displayed by fighting males are characteristic of the species and differ considerably from aggressive behavior involved in the capture of prey or defense against predators.

The response sequences characteristic of intermale aggression have been referred to as fixed action patterns, and although there is some increase in the precision of the movements and an increase in coordination with practice, there is little evidence that these response sequences are learned. Eibl-Eibesfeldt (36) raised male wild Norway rats in isolation so that they would not have an opportunity to learn fighting responses through social interactions. After reaching adulthood, the isolates were matched with strange, socially reared males, and fighting ensued almost immediately. Eibl-Eibesfeldt reported that the general display of aggressive behavior was essentially the same for both groups. They showed apparently innate and fixed behavior patterns. Other investigators have also shown that learning is not essential to the manifestation of aggressive responses (37–39).

The species-specific topography of intermale fights has been described in detail for a number of different animals [see Fox (34) for canids, Barnett (8, 40) for the rat, Kummer (18) for baboons, and Banks (41) for the mouse; also see general summaries by Eibl-Eibesfeldt (32, 33, 36)].

Minor Damage from Intermale Contests

One of the most remarkable characteristics of intermale aggression is the relatively small amount of injury that occurs during fighting. In other kinds of aggression, the animal uses its available weapons as effectively as possible to dispatch the antagonist. In contests between males, however, the fighting behaviors have evolved in such a way that the encounters result in a demonstrable superiority of one animal over the other with little physical damage. At a given stage in the conflict, one of the animals may flee and his opponent is unlikely to pursue for any distance; alternatively, the defeated animal may assume a posture that results in the inhibition of aggression on the part of the victor. In other instances, the attack is aimed at portions of the opponent's anatomy that have evolved in such a way as to minimize injury. For example, fighting among male elephant seals is vigorous and intense. It is conducted with the large upper canine teeth, which have considerable potential for damage. The bulls are frequently wounded, and the older, more dominant veterans of many encounters display a large number of wrinkled scars in the neck region, where the attacks are directed. However, the elephant seal is well equipped with tough skin and fat pads to take a great deal of punishment in that part of the body (16).

The agonistic behavior between males of the same species is highly ritualized and stereotyped. Again, the nature of the response is such that the possibility of serious wounding is minimized. Among fallow deer (*Dama dama*), rival stags engage in vigorous fighting. Their encounters consist of headlong charges against one another. However, they charge only when facing, with the result that the contact is antler to antler. An attack is never directed against the more vulnerable parts of the body. Fighting among male giraffes is common. They engage in neck-to-neck pushing matches, or they swing their heads against the opponent's body or legs. They do not, however, attack with their sharp and dangerous hooves, which are reserved for defense against predators. The oryx and other antelopes may have extremely sharp horns for use in interspecific defense. In intraspecific interactions they are used only to lock the heads of the animals together during intermale pushing contests (42).

Another aspect of the hostile interactions among male conspecifics that tends to minimize serious injury is the role of learning. After a limited number of agonistic contacts between a given pair of animals, a dominance–submission relationship is set up between them. When this is accomplished, the probability of actual fighting is diminished because the more submissive animal has learned to respond to anticipatory aggressive responses (threat behavior) with submission or escape, which terminates the encounter. Thus the threat gestures functionally replace actual fighting.

Stimulus Situation Eliciting Intermale Aggression

Although males are more aggressive in many situations, a strange male conspecific constitutes a unique aggression-eliciting stimulus complex in a large number of animal species. Aggression will be manifested toward another male even though the animal will either ignore or interact peaceably with other animals or humans. Gibbons will feed in the same general area with macaques and langurs without conflict, but will not tolerate the approach of other male gibbons (6). The Mongolian gerbil makes an excellent pet because its reaction to humans is gentle and without hostility (43). However, if two strange males are placed together in a cage, blood will be drawn in a few minutes, and when there is no escape, one of them may be killed. According to Matthews (16), barred bandicoots (*Perameles,* a South Australian marsupial) become very tame and gentle toward humans during captivity, but they are desperately pugnacious among themselves.

It is relatively rare that females of any species elicit aggression from the male. Barnett (8) reports that even when strange rats intrude on an established colony, it is the mature males, and not the females or juveniles, that are attacked by the residents. Under conditions of high population density, the amount of fighting among mice increases significantly. Some of the more dominant mice roam about the area attacking other colony members without provocation. Once again, however, females and immature mice are ignored (44). In a fighting situation, male mice attack males more frequently and longer than they do females (45).

The Role of Olfaction in Intermale Aggression

There is now a great deal of experimental evidence in animals to show that odors are of considerable importance in the control of aggressive behavior. An experiment by Mugford and Nowell (46) was particularly well conceived and can serve as an example of a large number of studies in the area. On the basis of a series of earlier experiments, Mugford and Nowell postulated that the transport mechanism for the aggression-eliciting cues in mice was through the urine. Their hypothesis was confirmed by an experiment in which they applied the urine of mice of different sex, endocrine, and dominance status to the coat of castrated male mice. Castrated male mice treated with water elicit only a modest amount of attack behavior from an intact isolated male mouse. However, if the castrated male is wet with the urine of a mouse that has previously been shown to be an aggressive and dominant animal, the amount of elicited aggression is significantly increased. Wetting the castrate victim mouse with the urine of an intact but submissive mouse results in an attack by the aggressor mouse that is intermediate in intensity between the experimental conditions cited above. It is further interesting to note that a castrate mouse wet with the urine of a female mouse is essentially protected from attack. The amount of aggression is significantly less than under all other experimental conditions.

It can be concluded from these studies that the urine of an intact male mouse contains an endocrine-dependent pheromone that elicits attack from another male. Dominant males evidently produce larger amounts of this pheromone than do submissive animals, and the urine of females contains a pheromone that has an inhibitory effect on male aggression.

Stimulus Situation Inhibiting Intermale Aggression

Intermale aggression is unique in that it can be blocked or inhibited by a specific, generally species-specific, stimulus input. The defeated animal successfully avoids serious injury by engaging in particular ritualized behaviors that function to prevent further attack by the superior contestant. These behaviors have been referred to as submissive (16) or appeasing (47) responses. Schenkel (48) has characterized "active submission" in the wolf and dog as "impulses and effort of the inferior toward friendly harmonic social integration" or as a request for "love" from the superior animal. It is important to recognize that one need not project such complex cognitive affective mental states on to animals in order to recognize that a particular behavior in one animal has a high probability of eliciting a particular behavior on the part of a responding animal. The terms "submission," "appeasement" "love," and the like are descriptive of mental states recognizable by humans. They may, of course, have nothing at all to do with the mental states (if any) that are concurrent in animals behaving in the manner described as "submissive" etc.

Although the intent and the derivation of these ritualized aggression-inhibiting responses have been variously interpreted, there can be little doubt that active, ongoing, intermale aggression can be immediately blocked by the assumption of a particular stance or posture by the defeated animal. The ethological literature is replete with examples (33, 36, 42, 47, 49). Lorenz (47) devotes an entire chapter ("Behavioral Analogies to Morality") to descriptions of various aggression-inhibiting signals. The wolf, it is said, turns its head away from his opponent and offers the jugular vein; this immediately inhibits further aggression from its rival. [Similar reports have been made on the hamadryas baboon (18).] Alternatively, when the fight is clearly lost, the weaker wolf throws itself on its back exposing all of the vulnerable parts of the body to the victor, who "cannot" then follow up his advantage (16).

Submissive postures have also been described in some detail for a variety of laboratory animals (8, 50–52).

The submissive postures, in general, tend to be quite different from those displayed during threat or actual fighting, and it may be that there are few components in the submissive posture that elicit aggression. Darwin (49), in developing his principle of antithesis in emotional expression, has emphasized that gestures of greeting and gestures of affection present a stimulus pattern that is quite the opposite of the pattern presented during threat.

An analysis of many of the submissive postures observed in mammals seems to indicate that, at least in a general way, Darwin's principle of antithesis appears to hold (53). The animal that appears large in threat appears small in submission. The erect stance of threat is replaced by the supine posture of submission. The canines, which in many species are prominently displayed during threat, are hidden, covered, or turned away during gestures of appeasement.

However, it seems likely that more is involved in the act of submission than merely the absence of aggression-eliciting stimuli. Lorenz (47) makes the salient point that in the aroused and "angry" animal there is considerable emotional momentum and that the shift from one motivational state to another tends to be gradual rather than abrupt. Thus it seems that the appeasement postures provoke direct response inhibition on the part of the attacking animal.

As yet nothing is known about the neurological mechanisms underlying the aggression-inhibiting capacity of submissive postures. However, the available descriptive literature suggests the possibility that elements of the submissive pose function to activate neural systems that are incompatible with the neural system for intermale aggression.

Reinforcing Properties of Intermale Aggression

There are several lines of evidence to indicate that the opportunity to engage in intermale aggression may be positively reinforcing to the participants. The opportunity for one male to attack another will suffice to support the learning of new response patterns. Male mice trained as fighters learned a position response in a T-maze when the only reinforcer used was the opportunity to attack a "victim" mouse. When the reinforcer was withdrawn, the response was extinguished, and the position response was reversed when the victim mouse was moved to the opposite side of the T (54). If a fight between mice is interrupted, the victorious mouse will push open a door and run from one compartment to another to get at its opponent, as will one of a pair of evenly matched mice. The only reward for this behavior is the opportunity to continue the fight. If a fight immediately precedes a trial, aggressive mice will also cross an electrified grid to get at a defeated opponent. Again, there is no reward available except the opportunity to fight (55).

Sexual Maturity and Intermale Aggression

There is now abundant evidence that the male sex hormones play a critical role in the development and maintenance of the intermale aggressive response. As already indicated, there are distinct differences in the play activities of young males and females of many species, including man. The play of the males involves much more vigorous physical activity, and there is more mock combat and sham biting. However, until sexual maturity occurs, the interactions among these juveniles are well tempered in intensity, with the result that there is seldom any pain inflicted by either participant. Fighting in earnest only occurs after the male gonads become functional. In the rat, there is a heightened increase in hostile behavior after the descent of the testes (at 86 to 115 days of age) overt antagonism being rarely observed before that time. Furthermore, prepubescent males do not elicit unrestrained aggressive behavior from adults. The juveniles may be driven from the home burrow or from a food source by a mature animal, but they are seldom bitten. Instead, they are attacked and may be knocked over and trounced with all four feet. It is rare, however, for the younger rat to be wounded in this type of encounter (7). The physiological basis for this restraint by the adults is not yet understood. After puberty, however, fighting among rats becomes serious and frequently includes a considerable emotional component (9). Similar findings have also been reported for mice (38, 56) and for mink (57). The direct measurement of plasma androgens and onset of fighting in mice reveals that the initiation of intermale aggression occurs at a time when the secretion of androgens is increasing (58).

If the androgen level in immature male mice is raised by testosterone injections, there is a significant increase in the amount of aggression (59) or the aggression reaction appears earlier (38). A similar finding has been reported in primates. Two of six juvenile male macaques, after testosterone injections, showed more than double the amount of aggressive behavior observed during control periods (60). The administration of exogenous androgens to immature female mice, however, does not result in a facilitation of aggressive behavior (61).

Several species of nonhuman primates show an increase of various agnostic behaviors with the onset of sexual maturity, and although there are wide individual differences, there appear to be dramatic increases in testosterone and androstenedione (a biologically active form of testosterone) levels in adolescent human males. There are differences between the sexes prior to puberty, but after the age of 9, boys show a gradual increase in testosterone levels. However, at ages 10 to 15 the increases are on the order of tenfold. Adolescent boys do, of course, show an increase in aggressive behavior, but the increases in testosterone levels have not yet been related to any measures of aggression in adolescents (62).

Effects of Castration and Androgen Replacement on Intermale Aggression

When the level of androgens in the bloodstream is reduced by castration, there is a decrease in the manifest aggression between males in many species. [Although this chapter is concerned primarily with mammals, there is considerable evidence of the role of the gonads in intermale aggression in lower vertebrates (63–65).]

The classic experiment on this problem was done by Beeman in 1947 (66). She demonstrated that male mice showed considerable aggression when they were placed together after a period of isolation. However, if the mice were castrated in prepuberty, they did not develop intermale aggression. When testosterone pellets were implanted in the same mice, the aggressiveness appeared, only to disappear again when the pellets were removed.

A large number of studies have now essentially confirmed these basic findings. The spontaneous aggressive behavior between males is reduced by castration and can be restored by appropriate doses of male hormones. It has been confirmed for mice (67–79), and it has also been demonstrated in the rat (9, 80, 81), in the gerbil (82) and in the hamster (83). Of course, persons involved in the practical problems of animal husbandry have known for centuries that the castration of males produces docility in a wide variety of species from the camel to the bull.

It is interesting, however, that castration does not appear to inhibit the development of aggression in the dog as measured by the frequency of social fighting or the dominance position arising from competition for females or bones (84). The administration of testosterone to castrated macaques did not change the hierarchical status of subordinate animals. However, the hierarchies had been well established before the testosterone administration (85). Castration has been shown to affect the behavior of rhesus macaques, but there is considerable individual variability, which evidently depends in part on the types of social experiences the animal has. After 10 young males from the free-ranging colony of Cayo Santiago Island off Puerto Rico were castrated, it was observed that the castrates tended to associate with one another, responded more to immature monkeys, and in general had a lower dominance status. However, some who formed coalitions did engage in fighting and were successful, even against larger animals (62, 86).

Relationship between Endogenous Androgen Levels and Aggressive Behavior

The plasma testosterone levels of male rhesus monkeys have been shown to correlate with a number of agonistic behaviors. Threatening and chasing behavior and being submitted to by another member of the colony all correlate significantly with plasma testosterone levels. Submissive behavior is negatively correlated with testosterone levels, but not significantly so. This is interpreted as indicating that an animal with a high frequency of aggressive contacts with his subordinates will generally show a higher testosterone level regardless of how frequently he responds submissively to those above him in the dominance hierarchy. Dominance rank within the colony is also correlated with plasma testosterone concentration. The animals in the highest quartile had significantly higher testosterone levels than those lower in the hierarchy (87).

The Role of Other Hormones in Intermale Aggression

Although the experimental results are not completely consistent, it is possible to sketch a tentative picture of the role that other endocrine glands play in intermale aggression. Space precludes a complete discussion of this material, but some representative studies can be covered.

Briefly, intermale aggression is essentially dependent on circulating androgens in the bloodstream, and any endocrine manipulation that limits the quantity of circulating androgens tends to decrease aggressive responding. Also, any process that blocks the effectiveness of androgens reduces the tendency to intermale aggression. An increase in the adrenocorticotrophic hormone (ACTH) also tends to decrease the aggressive tendencies, and any manipulation that increases circulating ACTH also inhibits the fighting tendency.

Hypophysectomy completely prevents the development of fighting behavior in isolated mice. This effect is evidently due to the lack of gonadatrophic hormone, because aggressiveness does develop in hypophysectomized mice given subcutaneous implants of testosterone (17.5 mg/mouse) (71).

It has now been reported several times that estrogenic compounds tend to inhibit intermale aggression in intact male mice (68, 69, 76, 88). Progesterone and progesterone-like compounds also block aggression in intact male mice (68).

Isolated adult male mice injected with ACTH are significantly less aggressive in a standard fighting situation than are sham-injected controls (89). One of the effects of adrenalectomy is an increase in ACTH levels in the blood because ACTH production by the pituitary is released from inhibition by the adrenal hormones (90). It would follow, then, that fighting should be reduced by adrenalectomy. Some investigators have failed to find this relationship (91, 92). However, the more common finding has been that, though adrenalectomy does not eliminate inter-male fighting in the mouse, it does significantly reduce it (89, 93–96).

Dexamethasone, which is a powerful blocker of ACTH, causes an increase in fighting behavior in male mice (89). Hydrocortisone, another adrenal glucocorticoid that suppresses ACTH output, has also been shown to increase fighting behavior in isolated male mice (88, 97).

Permanent Effects of Early Endocrine Manipulations on Intermale Aggression

The changes induced by the endocrine manipulations discussed so far are essentially reversible. The deficits produced by adult castration can be restored by testosterone injections, and the changes induced by hormone injections disappear when the material is fully metabolized.

However, there are certain critical periods in the development of the nervous system during which some biochemical influences can perma-nently alter the direction of its development. The result is an adult animal whose nervous system is either more or less sensitive to the influ-ence of various blood chemistry components and to particular types of complex sensory input. It is important to recognize that most of the experimental work on this phenomenon has been done on a single species, the mouse, and that the specific paradigm has generally involved some measure of isolation-induced aggression. Considerable caution must therefore be exercised in generalizing to other species. The limited amount of work done on other animals seems to indicate that the general construct of permanent nervous system alterability by endocrine manipu-lations in early life is valid, but it is also clear that there are significant differences in the specific details.

Most of the experimental manipulations that have an effect on aggres-sive behavior also have an influence on some aspects of sexual behavior. However, this discussion will be limited to aggression.

MASCULINIZING THE FEMININE NERVOUS SYSTEM

Nature appears to have a general rule that the nervous system, if left alone, will develop into one that is characteristically feminine (98). In order for a male type of system to be formed, some exposure to androgens at particular developmental periods is necessary. In the normal course of development in the genetic male, the nervous system comes under the influence of the available testicular androgens. In the genetic female, no androgens are available and consequently the female nervous system develops. Thus any manipulation that subjects the nervous system to adequate androgen influence at the proper time will result in what is essentially a masculine nervous system in a genetically feminine soma.

It has now been repeatedly demonstrated that the perinatal administration of androgens, usually in the form of testosterone propionate (TP), to females results in permanent changes in the responsiveness of the nervous system to androgens administered in adulthood. A large number of these studies have been reviewed by Bronson and Desjardins (99). As indicated earlier in this chapter, female mice seldom display spontaneous fighting. However, if they are given a single early androgen treatment (10–100 μg of TP) and are again treated as adults (50–100 μg), they display fighting that is quite comparable to that displayed by normal male mice (72, 100–102). It is important to note that the mice do not display spontaneous aggression in adulthood unless they are given an androgen treatment as adults. In this respect, the treated females are also like normal males. As already indicated, males do not begin to fight seriously until sexual maturity, when the levels of circulating testosterone increase.

The developing system is not indefinitely malleable. The effectiveness of androgen stimulation declines rapidly from birth through the first 12 days of life. A single androgen injection on the day of birth is more effective in producing fighting among females in adulthood than is a single dose at day 10. However, the day 10 androgen treatment is more effective than a control injection of oil (103). In an extensive parametric study, Bronson and Desjardins (102) showed that a single injection of TP is more effective on the day of birth than it is on days 3, 6, or 12 and that single doses become ineffective sometimes between day 12 and day 24. Prolonged treatment with TP can alter the sensitivity of the female nervous system to later androgen treatment. Female mice gonadectomized at 30 days of age and administered 100 μg of TP daily for 20 days did show more aggression than oil-injected controls when tested under androgen influence 45 days later (104). Thus very small amounts of androgens are effective during certain critical periods, but relatively massive amounts are necessary later.

FEMINIZATION OF THE GENETIC MALE

The nervous system of the genetic male is presumably masculinized by the action of minute amounts of androgens circulating in the bloodstream during early life. Thus any manipulation that reduces the level of those androgens will block that process. There are now a number of studies to indicate that neonatal castration is an effective procedure for preventing normal masculinization in male mice (101, 103, 105–107). Once again, there is evidently a critical period after which this treatment is no longer effective. In mice, it appears that the masculinization of the nervous system is completed sometime between the second and the sixth day after birth. Castration 12 hours after birth is more effective than castration at 2 days after birth in preventing fighting in male mice given androgens in adulthood. Castration after 6 days, however, is no more effective than a sham operation (106).

The mouse is different in this respect from the rhesus monkey. Genetic male rhesus monkeys castrated on the day of birth and tested at 3½ to 9 months of age are clearly different from female counterparts on such measures as threat behavior, play initiation, and rough-and-tumble and chasing play (26). There is some indication that there is no circulating testosterone in the neonatal monkey as there is in rodents (24).

PRENATAL MASCULINIZATION IN MONKEYS

Relatively little work has been done on the masculinizing effects of endocrine manipulations in primates, and no direct measures of overt injurious aggression have been taken in the studies that have been done. However, there is some indication that the aggressiveness of primates can be altered by prenatal, rather than postnatal, manipulations. This work has been well summarized by Goy (24). If 600 to 700 mg of TP is administered to pregnant rhesus monkeys over a 25- to 50-day period after day 39 of gestation, the genetically female offspring will be pseudohermaphroditic, with a well-developed scrotum and a small but complete penis. The behavior of these animals is also altered in a masculine direction. They display frequencies of rough-and-tumble and chasing play that are either intermediate or overlap extensively with the normal male standards. During the entire 150 days of observation the masculinized females always scored higher on these variables than did normal control females.

NEUROLOGY OF INTERMALE AGGRESSION

Almost nothing is known of the neurology of intermale aggression. However, one study using electrical stimulation of the hypothalamus in the rhesus monkey appears to have been concerned with pure intermale aggression to the exclusion of any other type. A remote telestimulator was used, and the points stimulated were in the anterior portion of the lateral hypothalamus and in the preoptic region. The experimental subjects were two male rhesus monkeys that had been shown to be submissive to the test males during control periods. During the test periods the experimental animal was caged with the dominant test animal and its female consort. Initially, the test male displayed clearly dominant responses. It paced the cage with tail erect and actively aggressed against the experimental monkey. It also monopolized all the sexual and grooming responses of the female. The experimental animal reacted with the typically submissive pattern, including grimacing and crouching, when approached by the dominant monkey. Direct hypothalamic stimulation of the experimental animal in both groups resulted in a vicious directed attack on the dominant male. It is important to note that the stimulated animal showed no tendency to attack the female and no tendency to attack inanimate objects. Furthermore, it showed no fear reactions and no escape tendencies. Thus this aggression could not be considered to be generalized irritable aggression or fear-induced aggression. The test animal reacted to these attacks as though they were normal monkey behavior and counterattacked vigorously. After 10 stimulations in one group and 43 stimulations in the second, the dominance roles between the two animals were reversed. The formerly dominant test animal began to give shrill screams each time it was attacked. The now dominant experimental male paced freely about the cage and mounted the female and was groomed by her (108).

Another point of considerable interest is that one of the three points that produced attack behavior also supported self-stimulation; that is, the monkey pressed a bar at a rate of at least 50 presses per minute on a lever that produced stimulation at that point. The other two points yielded reliable escape behavior.

To date, this is the only study on the electrical elicitation of intermale aggression in the monkey. However, the results are so clear-cut and the specificity of the stimulus object so high that it appears to be excellent evidence of a relatively specific neural system for intermale aggression. Experimental animals similar to the ones used in this study would be excellent preparations for the study of the actions of hormones on neural systems, an area in which almost no information is currently available.

MATERNAL AGGRESSION

A mother animal with young will behave aggressively toward a large number of intruders. It has been suggested that this strong tendency to aggression is characteristic of all vertebrate mothers (63). Although maternal aggressive behavior may not be universal, there is abundant evidence that it is a characteristic of many species. In general, the stimulus situation eliciting this type of aggression involves the proximity of some threatening agent to the young of that particular female. Thus both the young and the threatening agent are part of the necessary stimulus complex and differentiate this class of aggression from all others. It is generally true that, as the mother gets further from her young, the tendency to aggression decreases. The probability of attack is also frequently a function of particular stimulus characteristics of the young and the hormonal status of the mother. The attack tendency waxes and wanes as the levels of hormones associated with the birth process fluctuate.

Although there have been relatively few detailed experimental studies of maternal aggressivity, there is considerable qualitative documentation of the phenomenon. Grizzly bear sows with cubs account for 82% of all bear attacks on hikers and campers in the national parks of Canada and the United States (109).

A few days before giving birth, the female mouse may be so aggressive that it will kill any males unable to escape from her ferocious and unrelenting attack (110). After the birth of litters in the laboratory situation, mouse mothers will savagely attack a forceps placed close to the nest. The most aggressive animals will cling to the rubber tips so firmly with their teeth that they can be lifted from the nest (111). Lactating female rats will chase any intruder away from their nests or burrows when unweaned young are present, but that behavior is rare in other circumstances (40, 112).

A moose cow with her calf will attack any intruder, including a large bull moose, and it will pursue the offender for a considerable distance. Altman (113) describes a moose cow that chased a horse into the water, beat it intensively, and did not give up the chase until the horse was driven to another island. In another case, a moose cow attacked and badly wounded a bear that was attempting to carry off her calf.

Chimpanzees will attack a model leopard. However, the model will be attacked much more vigorously if it has a model baby chimpanzee as its victim. Mother chimpanzees with young are more aggressive toward the model whether it has a victim or not (19).

Attacks by mother with young are also common in squirrels (114), langurs (115), baboons (116), snowshoe hares (117), rabbits (118), sheep (119), weasels (120), cats (121), and many other animals.

Not All Animals Show Maternal Aggression

There are some significant exceptions to the general rule that mother animals show increased attack tendencies. Only one of four different breeding groups of rats (Wistar-SPF, Long–Evans, Wistar conventional, and Sprague–Dawley), the Wistar-SPF, showed any increased aggression toward a black mouse during lactation, and only 60% of those animals exhibited attack behavior (122, 123). Calhoun (7) concludes that there has been a general reduction in aggressiveness, including that associated with lactation, as a result of domestication. Some species of mice manifest no maternal aggressiveness (111, 124), and some strains of rabbits show that behavior whereas some other strains are not aggressive at all (118).

Under certain circumstances animals will not only fail to show aggression toward an intruder, but will actually attempt to mother it and retrieve it to the nest. Karli (125) has reported that some lactating female rats exhibit marked maternal behavior toward a mouse, attempting to retrieve it. These animals do not become aggressive toward the mouse even though it disrupts the nest and scatters the pups. Similar findings have been reported by Revlis and Moyer (126) and Baenninger (127). Although many mice with pups will behave like an "unrelenting tigress" toward a male (111), it has been reported that some actually attempt to grasp the male and bring it back to the nesting area (124).

For reasons that are not at all clear, the mother's aggression is sometimes directed toward her own young. In mice, the mother not infrequently kills and cannibalizes her young, usually shortly after giving birth, but sometimes as long as a week later (11). In one laboratory, 93 of 278 litters were killed and eaten. There is some evidence that this cannibalistic characteristic is under genetic control, and it does not seem to be correlated with the tendency of the mother to attack intruders approaching the nest area (118). Pup killing by female rats can be induced by injections of testosterone propionate, and it has been suggested that the female attack on the young may be due to abnormally high levels of endogenous androgens of adrenal origin (128).

Relationship of Maternal Aggression to Pregnancy, Parturition, and Lactation

In most animals, increased aggressiveness of the female toward intruders is directly related to pregnancy, parturition, and lactation. There is, however, a good bit of variability both within and among species. Mice become highly aggressive during the last few days of pregnancy (110) and remain so during the first 14 days postpartum. In one of the few experimental studies on this problem, it was shown that 86% of the lactating females tested between day 1 and day 14 of lactation exhibited immediate and intense aggression toward either a male or a female intruder. After day 14 of lactation, only 13% of the animals attacked, and none attacked when tested 21 days after lactation (129). Scudder, Karczmar, and Lockett (124) report that three of the four genera of mice that they studied showed aggression toward humans during the first 7 or 8 days postpartum.

In natural or seminatural conditions, female rats drive other animals from their nests only during lactation (7, 40, 112). Endroczi, Lissak, and Telegdy (130) report that only lactating female rats will attack a frog placed in the home cage. This finding is evidently strain specific because other investigators have been unable to replicate it (126). The attack behavior of non-mouse-killing female rats on mice increased from parturition and reached its maximum on day 5 of lactation (60% occurrence). Thereafter the incidence of aggression decreased and disappeared entirely by day 15 of lactation. This behavior was also strain specific and occurred in only one of the four strains studied (123).

The female weasel, normally submissive toward the male, assumes a position of dominance from about midpregnancy until the young are about 12 weeks of age, whereupon she again becomes submissive to the male (120). Similarly, the female langur may be dominant to the male during the last few weeks of pregnancy (115).

In sheep, there is a very sensitive period immediately after birth during which the mother will show strong approach tendencies toward any lamb. However, this strong maternal drive toward all young fades within a few hours after parturition, after which the dam attempts to butt any young other than her own, as well as any other sheep, male or female (119).

The relationship between maternal aggressiveness and pregnancy, parturition, and lactation in the animals discussed here implies a hormonal influence on this behavior. In some higher animals—baboons, chimpanzees, and Japanese macaques—hormonal influences seem to be less important than the external stimulus control in the elicitation of this type of aggression. Among the baboons, for example, a baby baboon is the center of attraction for the whole troop. Females other than the mother attempt to groom the baby and respond to its distress. The older males also show great interest in the infant and are highly sensitive to any hint of distress from it. They will viciously attack any human that comes between it and the troop (116). If, because of injury, the infant baboon manifests considerable distress, the amount of threatening by the males rises considerably. They threaten each other, the females, and human observers. If the infant dies, the males may threaten the mother if she moves even a short way from her baby (131).

The type of behavior described here might well be classified as *paternal aggression*, since it appears to be elicited by a particular and relatively specific stimulus situation. However, except for a few naturalistic descriptions, relatively little is known about it.

Types of Stimulus Situations Eliciting Maternal Aggression

There have been no experimental attempts to systematically manipulate the stimuli most relevant to the elicitation of maternal aggression in mammals. It is therefore necessary to make inferences about the relevant stimuli from naturalistic studies and experimental work designed to study other questions.

In the turkey, a very wide range of stimuli elicit attack during the time that the poults are of a given age. The turkey may be described as being in a general state of irritability, attacking almost anything that moves except turkey chicks. In the case of the turkey, the problem is not to find what stimuli elicit aggression, but to find those factors that prevent the bird from attacking its own chicks. The relevant aggression-inhibiting stimulus is the distinctive call of the turkey poult. A dumb poult will be attacked and killed, but the turkey will foster a model of a polecat (a natural predator of turkey chicks) if it has a built-in speaker that emits recorded calls of a turkey poult. It is not known whether the turkey's general aggressivity is enhanced by the presence of vocal turkey chicks (132).

Although there are definite species differences, it is generally true that nursing mother mice are less aggressive when their young are not present; thus the presence of the young is an important variable in eliciting of maternal aggression. Furthermore, some stimulus complexes are more prepotent in the elicitation of aggression than others. Male mice will elicit ferocious attacks from a female in day 8 of lactation. However, if she is tested 5 hours after her pups are removed from the nest, she shows no aggression at all (129). Before the birth of their young, pregnant females can be easily chased from the nest with a 10-in. forceps. After the birth of the litters, however, some species will savagely attack the forceps (111). The mouse *Peromyscus maniculatus gracilis* will show a relatively mild attack on the forceps, but is intensely aggressive toward a male mouse placed in the cage. She continues her attack even when the male shows the species-typical submissive posture. Thus the male mouse is a more potent stimulus complex for the elicitation of maternal aggression than is the inanimate forceps. The mouse *P. m. bairdii* will also attack the male, but will not continue the attack with the intensity of the *gracilis* (111). Eisenberg (133) also reports species differences in maternal aggression. The *californucus* are "defensive" of the nest even when not with the young, whereas the *maniculatus* does not react aggressively in the nest area unless she is parturient.

A lactating female rat seems to show increased irritability, but her attack tendencies are limited to particular stimulus situations. As already indicated, she is aggressive toward all alien rats in the vicinity of her burrow. However, she also reacts aggressively, though less so, in the food pen, which may be some distance from her nest. These aggressive tendencies in the food area are elicited only by male rats, there being remarkably little aggressive interaction among lactating females in the food pen, even though their nests are widely separated (7).

Sheep recognize their young on the basis of visual cues, and aggression toward them is inhibited. An ewe will butt away any other animal that approaches her regardless of age or sex. However, she exhibits the same behavior even in the absence of her young. Thus, in sheep, the young are not a critical variable in the elicitation of aggression, and the state produced by the physiological changes accompanying parturition appears to be one of generalized irritability.

A similar generalized irritability apparently occurs in various cat species shortly before and after the birth of the young. Schneirla, Rosenblatt, and Tobach (121) suggest that the increase in irritability may be due to the general "stressor" effects of parturition.

The cues that elicit both cherishing behavior and maternal (paternal) aggression in primates are, as might be expected, complex. The mother recognizes her own young and is more responsive to them than she is to young in general. Among baboons, adult females show considerable interest in young baboons. They tend to pay less attention to them when the young reach the age of about 8 months and may threaten and mildly attack these juveniles. If the young baboon is attacked, it screeches in terror; the mother runs to its side and threatens or attacks the aggressor if it is a female of lower status (116). One factor that appears to elicit attention and the tendency to aggression during infant distress is the coat color of the infant. In langurs, the infant's coat is brown; when it changes to gray, the adults tend to lose interest (115). The young of baboons, vervet monkeys, and chimpanzees also have distinctive coat colorations serving a similar purpose.

Response Topography in Maternal Aggression

There have been few studies dealing with the response topography of maternal aggression. What little is known about it, however, seems to indicate that the response patterns are somewhat different from other kinds of aggressive responding. In mice, the maternal attack on an intruder is immediate. The female lunges at and bites the strange animal. There is no prelude of behaviors, such as genital sniffing and tail rattling, which are usually observed when two male mice are paired. The attack is continuous, consisting primarily of bites to the flanks and the neck region (129).

Generally, mother animals with mobile young will move away from a possible source of conflict. For example, no person in our national parks has been molested by a sow bear with cubs if the individual was making noise, talking loudly, or singing. The bear mother maintains an individual distance of up to several hundred yards. However, if the bear is unable to avoid an intruder (e.g., in the case of surprise), she may actively attack and pursue an escaping individual. The bear need not be cornered for the attack response to occur (109).

A female moose with a calf also attempts to maintain a distance from other animals. If approached too closely, however, she will attack the intruder and pursue it for a considerable distance. The attack is carried out with the hooves and follows the mother's signal to the calf to heel. The signal consists of a warning posture of freezing and a "bristling" with the head lifted (113).

SEX-RELATED AGGRESSION

There can be no doubt that there is a relationship between sexual and aggressive behavior. The dubious and unsupported hypothesis that "sex is the cause of nearly all crime, the dominant force that drives nearly all criminals" has been proposed by no less an authority than the former warden of San Quentin (134). Freud (135) has suggested that aggression is an essential and integral part of sexual feelings in the male. When sexually aroused, he actively subdues the female in the mating process. The woman, in turn, submits to the aggressive behavior and prefers to be subdued. This is presumed to be of value to the species because it enables the stronger males to make a greater proportional contribution to the gene pool.

Under optimal conditions the aggression involved in sex relations should be under sufficient control to prevent serious injury to either participant. However, because of normal biological variability, sex-related aggression sometimes exceeds optimal bounds and becomes sexual violence with severe injury and, frequently, death as a result. Evidence of sex-related aggression abounds in the daily newspaper. Case studies are presented *ad nauseam* in a number of different sources (136–140) and need not be elaborated here.

It is proposed in this section that sex-related aggression should be considered as a separate class of aggressive behavior in that the stimulus situation eliciting it is relatively specific and because it most probably differs in physiological basis from other types of aggression. In spite of the prevalence of sex-related aggression and the constant and morbid interest in it (many tabloids would go out of business if a sudden universal cure were found), there is remarkably little experimental evidence on the topic.

Sex-related aggression can be defined as aggressive behavior that is elicited by the same stimuli that elicit sexual behavior. It is found primarily, but not exclusively, in the male, and the stimulus variables are those related to the opposite sex. Although this type of aggressive behavior assumes its most variable and bizarre forms in the human, it is also found in other species.

Sex-Related Aggression in Animals

Mating behavior in many species involves motor components that are very similar to those found in intermale aggression or in prey catching. Fighting—including a great deal of scratching, biting, and vocalization—is an important part of the courtship process in the cat and weasel family. In some cases, it is difficult to distinguish mating behavior from an intense aggressive encounter. Among ferrets and mink, mating has the characteristics of a prolonged fight, which may endure for an hour or more (141). During copulation, the male mink grabs the female by the scruff of the neck in a manner that is very similar to that observed in intermale encounters (57). Similar responses can be found in the gray fox (34) and a number of carnivores and marsupials. Eisenberg and Leyhausen (142) relate this neck grip during mating to the killing bite of predation and suggest that the potential for the lethal bite is always present but is controlled or partially inhibited during mating.

In general, aggressive courtship displays can be distinguished from true fighting by their consequences: only minor injuries are inflicted in the former. However, sex-related aggression in animals sometimes exceeds adaptive bounds, as it does in humans. Carpenter (143) has made extensive field observations of the rhesus monkey and reports that males frequently attack estrous females. Observations of 45 estrous periods revealed that 22 females were attacked, and 6 of them were severely wounded. One of them lost parts of both ears, received severe cuts on the arm, and a number of wounds on the face and muzzle. Another had a leg wound severe enough to make her limp for several days. Others had deep thigh cuts, bruised noses, deep gashes, and one received such a deep wound in the hip that the motor nerve was damaged and she became a permanent cripple. Carpenter's interpretation of these findings is worth quoting (143):

A final, partial explanation of the increase in fighting is that aggression may constitute a sadistic component of the normal mating behavior of Rhesus monkeys. A necessary condition to serial copulation and the consort relation seemingly is that the female be driven to a state of submission, of "awe" and of complete "rapport" in relation to the male.

Experimental work on the aggressive behavior of the male rhesus monkey indicates that the male is responding to some stimulus characteristic of phases of estrus in the female, because that behavior can be manipulated by the administration of hormones to the female. Threat behavior on the part of the male is directed away from the female at one stage. When the male's sexual interest is high, the "threatening away" is more frequent and intense, and is not elicited by any particular external stimulation. The threat may be directed at a distant animal or at nothing. Females, when they are most receptive, also display threatening-away behavior. However, if their receptivity is reduced by the administration of progesterone, the threat behavior is also reduced (144). There are also hormonal states during which the aggressive behavior of the female toward the male increases (administration of estrogen and during pregnancy) but during which the male is remarkably tolerant of the female. It is speculated that aggression by the male at this time is inhibited by a female pheromone (145).

SEX DIFFERENCES IN AGGRESSION IN HUMANS AND THEIR PHYSIOLOGICAL BASES

There seems to be little doubt that there are different kinds of aggression in humans in that hostile and destructive behaviors have more than one physiological substrate. However, because of man's exceptional ability to manipulate symbols and substitute one stimulus for another, it is not possible to differentiate the kinds of aggression on the basis of the eliciting stimuli. The topography of human aggressive responding is also highly variable and, of course, is not different for different types of aggressive behavior. However, there are physiological differences between the sexes that do appear to account for some of the sex differences in aggression. Some of those physiological factors are considered in this section.

Premenstrual Syndrome

Although in humans violent and aggressive behavior is overwhelmingly committed by the male, any husband can testify that women are not immune to hostile feelings and aggressive tendencies. Feminine hostility has, of course, many causes, but there is now good evidence that there is a periodicity to the irascibility of women and that it is related to the hormonal changes occurring over the course of the menstrual cycle. There is some evidence that during the period of ovulation anxiety and feelings of hostility are at a relatively low level (146). Just prior to menstruation, however, a significant number of women manifest a variety of symptoms that have been collectively called the premenstrual syndrome. This syndrome includes physical changes, such as headache, edema (particularly of the face, hands, and feet), and significant weight gain. Changes in appetite, a craving for sweets, and unusual bursts of energy may also be a part of the syndrome (147, 148). Emotional instability is characteristic of a number of women during the premenstrual period. There is an increased tendency for women to seek psychiatric help during the premenstrual period (149), and there is a general increase in psychiatric symptoms at that time (150, 151). There is also an increase in suicide attempts (150, 152–154).

Of particular interest here is the general increase in various manifestations of irritability and hostility. Shainess (155) describes it as defensive hostility. Ivey and Bardwick (156), who used Gottschalk's technique of analysis of verbal reports, found consistent themes of hostility during the premenstruum. In a recent study of 1100 women who were the wives of graduate students in a large American university, 52% reported that they were sometimes markedly irritable in the premenstrual phase; 30% reported marked irritability during their most recent cycle. The feeling of irritability was more marked than that of depression or tension (22). Similar findings have been reported by other investigators (157–159). Women in a prison population are more irritable during the premenstrual and menstrual phases of the cycle (160).

Irritable feelings are frequently acted out. In the Ellis and Austin study (160), significantly more aggressive acts occurred during the menstrual and premenstrual period. According to Dalton (161), women prisoners themselves frequently recognize that their behavior during this critical period is likely to get them into trouble and as a result request to be isolated. School girls show more infractions of the rules and receive more punishment during the critical period in the cycle, and older girls with legitimate disciplinary power tend to mete out more punishment during their own menstruation (162). The majority of women prisoners who are sufficiently violent to require removal to maximum security quarters menstruate during the first few days of confinement (163). Women prisoners are more frequently reported for "bad behavior" during the critical period (164).

There is also evidence that more crimes are actually committed during the irritable period in the menstrual cycle. Cooke (165) indicated that 84% of all of the violent crimes committed by women in Paris during a given year were committed during the period of menstruation (160), although that estimate certainly seems to be excessively high. A study of prison records revealed that 62% of the crimes of violence were committed during the premenstrual week and only 2% at the end of the period (166). A similar finding is reported by Dalton (164), who found that 49% of all crimes committed by women occurred during menstruation or in the premenstruum. Thus the association between menstruation and crime is highly significant. One would expect only 29% of all crimes to be committed during the 8-day period if they were normally distributed. The probability of the obtained distribution's occurring by chance is less than 1 in 1000. The possibility of impulsive aggression and law breaking during the menstrual and premenstrual period is of sufficient magnitude for the criminal law in some countries to recognize menstruation as an extenuating circumstance (167). Severe premenstrual tension is placed in the category of temporary insanity in France (168).

Feelings of irritability, hostility, and other manifestations of the premenstrual syndrome are not confined to a few asocial individuals who get into difficulties with the law. Moderate or severe degrees of the syndrome occur in about 25% of all women (157, 169). Some authors estimate that as many as 90% of women are subject to some irritability, hopelessness, depression, or other symptoms prior to or during menstruation (170, 171).

The underlying physiology of the tendencies to hostility associated with the menstrual–premenstrual syndrome is obscure. There seems to be rather general agreement that the symptoms are associated with a fall in the progesterone level and a relatively greater amount of estrogen in the estrogen-progesterone ratio (169, 172, 173). Bardwick (174) maintains that the symptoms are due to the absolute fall in estrogen. Several studies have shown that the symptoms can be alleviated by the administration of progesterone (161, 175, 176). Women who take oral contraceptives that contain progestational agents show significantly less irritability than do women who are not taking the pill (169, 177, 178). It may be that the irritability-reducing effects of progesterone are a function of their direct effect on the hostility-related neural systems in the brain. However, the explanation may be much less direct. Janowsky, Gorney, and Mandell (170) hypothesize that the irritability results from the cyclic increase in aldosterone inasmuch as weight, behavioral, and aldosterone changes seem to parallel each other. The increase in sodium and water retention caused by aldosterone results in a secondary neuronal irritability and consequent psychic symptoms. The therapeutic effects of lithium (160) and diuretics

(172, 179, 180) in treating premenstrual tension may then be due to their tendency to reverse the aldosterone effect on sodium metabolism.

Another physiological characteristic of the premenstrual syndrome is hypoglycemia. Billig and Spaulding (181) found evidence of hypoglycemia during the period immediately prior to the onset of the menses, and Harris (182) noted an increase in the symptoms of hyperinsulinism in women at the same time in the cycle. Morton (172) suggests that the increased sugar tolerance is due to the action of the unopposed estrogen on carbohydrate metabolism and indicates that many of the psychic symptoms as well as weakness and fatigue can be largely ascribed to the hypoglycemia. He recommends diet changes, including supplementary protein, as an adjunct therapy.

Endocrinology of Aggression in Human Males

As already indicated, there is good evidence that various agonistic behaviors appear in a number of animals with the onset of sexual maturity. Although postpubic adolescent boys show increased aggressive behavior and increases in testosterone level, correlation between these two parameters has not been definitely established (62).

Until recently there has been essentially no information available relating the endocrine function and affective response tendencies in man. However, with the improvement in assay techniques (183), such studies are beginning to appear. A suggestive relationship was found between the activity of the pituitary (luteinizing hormone) testicular axis and feelings of hostility, anger, and aggression (184). A further study was undertaken on the basis of those findings using more refined techniques involving the measurement of plasma testosterone level and the testosterone production rate (185). Two groups of men were studied. The 18 individuals in the younger group ranged from 17 to 28 years of age; the 15 older men were between the ages of 30 and 66 years. The average testosterone production rate of the older men was about half that of the younger men, and when all of the subjects were considered as a group, it was shown that there was a significant negative correlation ($r = -.62$) between age and testosterone production rate. This is an interesting finding in itself inasmuch as it has been shown that violent crime in the United States is most prevalent among males between the ages of 15 and 24.

This study also showed that, in the younger men, the testosterone production rate was highly correlated with an aggression measure that was derived from the Buss–Durkee Hostility Inventory, and a multivariate regression equation was obtained between the testosterone production rate and four different measures of aggression and hostility. This equation accounted for 82% of the variance in the testosterone production rate for the younger men. In the older age group, the only variable that correlated highly with testosterone production was age, and the regression equation that was highly predictive for the young men was not valid for the older age group.

In another study, aggressive behavior and plasma testosterone levels were assessed in a young criminal population (186). The subjects were selected to provide a high- and a low-aggression group, using the number of times that an individual had been placed in solitary confinement as the index for assignment to the two groups. That index was associated with fighting behavior and resulted in highly differentiated groups. Fighters were defined as those individuals who had been in more than one fight during their imprisonment. Plasma testosterone levels were measured in six plasma samples taken within 1 hour of awakening. Although there was a significant difference between the two groups in terms of actual fighting behavior and in verbal aggression, the differences between the groups on plasma testosterone level were not significant. Pearson product–moment correlations between (1) the number of fights and plasma testosterone level and (2) the number of incidents of verbal aggression and plasma testosterone level were also not significant. Paper-and-pencil tests were also given to the subjects. Hostility was measured by the Buss–Durkee Hostility Inventory, but there was no significant correlation between the hostility test scores and fighting in prison, and the hostility scores did not correlate with plasma testosterone levels. However, an investigation of the type of crime for which the subjects were incarcerated revealed that those individuals who had committed violent and aggressive offenses during adolescence had a significantly higher testosterone level when compared with men without that type of offense. There was also a significant correlation between the age of the first conviction of a violent crime and the plasma testosterone level. However, the past history of assaultive behavior was not correlated with either fighting in prison or hostility as measured by the paper-and-pencil test.

The results of the Kreuz and Rose study (186) are somewhat surprising in light of the Persky, Smith, and Basu study (185), which used the same hostility inventory. It may well be that a variety of potent pressures in the prison setting influence the instrumental aggression of the subjects. Reinforcement in the prison tends to be swift and severe, and may be a more important determinant of actual testosterone level. The behavior that did correlate with plasma testosterone level occurred outside the prison. The reason for the lack of relationship between the scores on the Buss–Durkee inventory and testosterone level is not clear at the moment.

These studies on blood testosterone levels and aggressive tendencies used males as subjects, but it is not possible from the data to determine whether the hostility measured is a form of intermale or irritable aggression, or some combination of both.

Although uncontrolled clinical studies must be interpreted with caution, several reports on humans offer support for the idea that exogenous androgens enhance aggressive tendencies. One series of schizophrenic patients showed a decrease in fearfulness and apprehension and increased self-confidence when treated with dehydroisoandosterone (Diandrone) (187). A decrease in feelings of inferiority, timidity, and apathy with an increase in self-confidence occurred in young males with "inadequate personality" after 4 days to 4 weeks of therapy with the same preparation (188). Dehydroisoandosterone is also reported to exert an androgenic effect in the social and psychological rather than in the physical or sexual field. Masculine activity, aggression, and self-confidence are enhanced. The timid "shrinking violet" becomes more adequate, and the aggressive tendencies of individuals with manifest hostility are made much worse (189).

Effects of Castration on Aggression

A further understanding of the role of androgens in the aggressive behavior of humans can be gained from a study of the effects of castration. This operation is an available form of therapy for certain sex criminals in a number of countries. Bremer (190) did a follow-up study on 224 Norwegian cases and concluded that the sex drive was drastically reduced by castration: "It can be stated at the beginning that in all cases without exception the amount of sexual activity has been altered. It has been reduced or abolished irrespective of the direction or the form of sexual urge—heterosexuality, homosexuality, fetishism, zoophilic actions, masturbation, exhibitionism, or fetishistic actions—which are those represented in the material." In two-thirds of the cases, sexual interest and activity essentially disappeared within the first year after the operation, and in most cases the asexualization occurred immediately or shortly after the operation.

About half of the cases considered by Bremer were dangerous. The others were considered to be merely asocial or troublesome, manifesting such offenses as exhibitionism, fetishism, and zoophilia. Castration was most effective in all respects when the sexual factor was the dominating cause of the criminal or disturbed behavior. Seventy-seven of the subjects were castrated in the hope of achieving a general pacifying effect to make them more tractable and easier to control. Many of these individuals were low-grade oligophrenics and schizophrenics. Bremer reports that the operation was ineffective in controlling the disturbed mental cases and has no definite pacifying effect. This is an interesting and somewhat paradoxical finding in the light of the animal literature, which seems to indicate that there is a reduction of intermale and irritable aggression with a reduction in the blood androgen level.

Other investigators have found that castration (and androgen blocking by other means) does reduce hostility that is not directly associated with the individual's sexual behavior. Hawks (191) describes several cases in which a generally aggressive individual has had his sexual aggression curbed and has been made less aggressive in other ways by castration. He also reports on a series of observations in which relatively large doses of testosterone were given to large groups of castrates over a period of several weeks. In a number of cases, it was necessary to terminate the injections because the patients became generally destructive. They "had reverted to all of their antisocial tendencies, were attacking small children, starting fights, breaking windows and destroying furniture" (ref. 191, p. 222). When the administration of the hormone was stopped, the individuals became tractable once again within a period of a few days and no longer created disturbances in the ward. Many of the 330 individuals in the Kansas sample who were treated by castration were brutal homosexuals who were generally unstable and constantly created disturbances. After the operation, they became stabilized and could be paroled or became useful citizens within the institution (191).

Sex criminals treated by castration seldom repeat their crimes. Danish statistics indicate that the recidivist rate for individuals treated without castration and released is about 10 times that of the ones who have been castrated (192). The figures are almost the same for Norway (190). Hawke (191) reports that a sex crime has never been committed by a parolee or a castrate who escaped from the Kansas institution.

Estrogens as Antihostility Agents

A number of clinical studies have shown that female hormones may be used in the control of aggressive tendencies in man. Golla and Hodge (193) indicate that estrogens could be used as a form of chemical castration and would be more efficient than the operation itself because they would block the effects of the adrenal androgens, which would not be controlled by castration. A number of authors have reported series of cases in which the aggressive tendencies of adolescents and young adults were controlled by the use of stilbestrol (189, 194, 195). Stilbestrol is a synthetic drug that has been demonstrated to have the estrogenic qualities of natural estrogens. It depresses anterior pituitary gonadotrophic function. A case is reported in some detail by Dunn (196) in which stilbestrol was used to control hyperirritable aggression and excessive libido. This patient was a 27-year-old male under maximum sentence for sexual offenses against female minors. He was a persistent troublemaker in prison and was frequently placed in solitary confinement for insubordination. The prisoner had abnormal amounts of male hormone and gonadotrophic hormone in the urine before therapy and was preoccupied with his sex life. After 4 weeks of daily treatment with stilbestrol, he reported that his sexual responses, both physical and mental, were reduced. He had also adapted much better to prison discipline and was no longer considered a troublemaker. He continued relatively symptomfree for more than 3 months after discontinuance of the therapy. Subsequently, however, he had a return of his symptoms and requested a resumption of therapy.

Two investigators have used subcutaneous or intramuscular injections of long-acting estrogens (estradiol B.P.C. and estradiol valerianate) in order to avoid the necessity of daily oral therapy (197, 198). This approach permits the release of otherwise highly dangerous individuals and does not depend on their cooperation in taking the medication. Both reports indicate that the aggressive behavior and the sexual offenses were essentially eliminated while the patients were under estrogenic therapy.

Antiandrogens and Aggression Control

There are now several available substances that have demonstrated antiandrogenic activity (199). A-Norprogesterone (200), Chlormadinone acetate (201), cyproterone acetate (202), and medroxyprogesterone (203) have been shown to be potent antagonists of androgens. These synthetic hormones are steroids, as are the natural sex hormones. When administered to intact animals, they produce, in some measure, chemical castration. Cyproterone acetate appears to block the use of naturally produced testosterone by competing with it at the receptor sites (204), and medroxyprogesterone lowers the plasma level of testosterone from the testes (205).

It is interesting that cyproterone acetate does not block intermale aggression in either the gerbil (82) or in the mouse (73), but it does appear to have some effect in the control of excessive libido and apparently sex-related aggression in man (206, 207). There is not, as yet, sufficient evidence to evaluate the effectiveness of cyproterone on aggression, particularly in man. However, further work is certainly indicated.

Medroxyprogesterone (Provera, Upjohn) also needs further evaluation, but there is some evidence that it may also be effective in the control of excessive and impulsive sexual behavior and aggression in man. Lloyd

(208) indicates that sexually hyperactive and aggressive adolescent boys are made more tractable by Provera therapy. Although he did not investigate aggressiveness as such, Money (205) reports that Provera significantly and rapidly reduces a variety of illegal sexual behaviors in male offenders.

REFERENCES

1. *Report of the National Commission on Violence*, U.S. Government Printing Office, 1969.
2. Cressey, D. R., in Merton, R. K. and R. A. Nisbet (eds.), *Contemporary Social Problems*, Harcourt, Brace & World, New York, 1961.
3. Broom, L. and P. Selznick, *Sociology: A Test with Adapted Readings*, Harper & Row, New York, 1957.
4. Moyer, K. E., *Commun Behav Biol* **2**: 65, 1968.
5. Payne, A. P. and H. H. Swanson, *Behaviour* **36**: 259, 1970.
6. Carpenter, C. R., *Comp Psychol Monogr* **16**: 1, 1940.
7. Calhoun, J. B., Public Health Service Publication No. 1008, U.S. Department of Health, Education and Welfare, Washington, D.C., 1962.
8. Barnett, S. A., *A Study in Behavior*, Methuen, London, 1963.
9. Seward, J. P., *J Comp Physiol Psychol* **38**: 175, 1945.
10. Fredericson, E., *Anat Rec* **105**: 29, 1949.
11. Fredericson, E., *J. Comp Physiol Psychol* **45**: 254, 1952.
12. Lagerspetz, K., *Ann Acad Sci Fenn* **131**: 1, 1964.
13. Valzelli, L., *Adv Pharmacol* **5**: 79, 1967.
14. Norris, K. S., in Clemente, C. D. and D. B. Lindsley (eds.), *Aggression and Defense: Neural Mechanisms and Social Patterns*, University of California Press, Los Angeles, 1967.
15. Bartholomew, G. A., in Clemente, C. D. and D. B. Lindsley (eds.), *Aggression and Defense: Neural Mechanisms and Social Patterns*, University of California Press, Los Angeles, 1967.
16. Matthews, L. H., in Carthy, J. D. and F. J. Ebling (eds.), *The Natural History of Aggression*, Academic Press, London, 1964.
17. Thompson, N. S., *Anim Behav* **15**: 307, 1967.
18. Kummer, H., *Social Organization of Hamadryas Baboons: A Field Study*, University of Chicago Press, Chicago, 1968.
19. Chance, N. and C. Jolly, *Social Groups of Monkeys, Apes and Men*, Dutton New York, 1970.
20. Carpenter, C. R., *Naturalistic Behavior of Nonhuman Primates*, Pennsylvania State University Press, University Park, Pa., 1964.
21. Gray, J. A., *Acta Psychol* **35**: 29, 1971.
22. Hamburg, D. A., *Nature* **230**: 19, 1971.
23. Harlow, H. F., in Beach, F. A. (ed.) *Sex and Behavior*, Wiley, New York, 1965.

24. Goy, R. W., in Michael, R. P. (ed.), *Endocrinology and Human Behaviour*, Oxford University Press, London, 1968, p. 12.

25. Resko, J. A., *Endocrinology* **81**: 1203, 1967.

26. Goy, R. W., *J Anim Sci* **25**: 21, 1966.

27. DeVore, I. (ed.), *Primate Behavior: Field Studies of Monkeys and Apes*, Holt, Rinehart & Winston, New York, 1965.

28. Sears, R. R., in Beach, F. A. (ed.), *Sex and Behavior*, Wiley, New York, 1965.

29. Blurton-Jones, N. G., in Morris, D. (ed.), *Primate Ethology*, Doubleday, London, 1969, p. 437.

30. Davenport, W., in Beach, F. A. (ed.), *Sex and Behavior*, Wiley, New York, 1965, p. 164.

31. Lorenz, K., in Carthy, J. D. and F. J. Ebling (eds.), *The Natural History of Aggression*, Academic Press, New York, 1964.

32. Eibl-Eibesfeldt, I., in Clemente, C. D. and D. B. Lindsley (eds.), *Aggression and Defense: Neural Mechanisms and Social Patterns*, University of California Press, Los Angeles, 1967, p. 57.

33. Eibl-Eibesfeldt, I., *Ethology: The Biology of Behavior*, Holt, Rinehart and Winston, New York, 1970.

34. Fox, M. W., *Behaviour* **35**: 242, 1969.

35. Ardrey, R., *The Territorial Imperative*, Atheneum, New York, 1966.

36. Eibl-Eibesfeldt, I., *Scientific American* **205**: 112, 1961.

37. Scott, J. P., *J Hered* **33**: 11, 1942.

38. Lagerspetz, K. and S. Talo, *Rept Inst Psychol Univ Turku* **28**: 1, 1967.

39. Poole, T. B., in Jewell, P. A. and C. Loizos (eds.), *Play, Exploration and Territory in Mammals*, Academic Press, New York, 1966, p. 23.

40. Barnett, S. A., in Garattini, S. and E. B. Sigg (eds.), *Aggressive Behaviour*, Wiley, New York, 1969, p. 3.

41. Banks, E. M., *J Genet Psychol* **101**: 165, 1962.

42. Cloudsley-Thompson, J. L., *Animal Conflict and Adaptation*, Dufour, Chester Springs, Pa. 1965.

43. Ginsburg, H. J. and W. G. Braud, *Psychon Sci* **22**: 54, 1971.

44. Llody, J. A. and J. J. Christian, *J Mammal* **48**: 262, 1967.

45. Lee, C. T., *Am Zool* **10**: 56, 1970.

46. Mugford, R. A. and Nowell, N. W., *Nature* **226**: 967, 1970.

47. Lorenz, K., *On Aggression*, Harcourt, Brace & World, New York, 1966.

48. Schenkel, R., *Am Zool* **7**: 319, 1967.

49. Darwin, C., *The Expression of Emotions in Man and Animals*, Appleton, New York, 1896.

50. Brain, P. F. and N. W. Nowell, *Commun Behav Biol* **5**: 7, 1970.

51. Grant, E. C. and J. H. Mackintosh, *Behaviour* **21**: 246, 1963.

52. Grant, E. C., *Behaviour* **21**: 260, 1963.

53. Eisenberg, J., *Univ Calif Publ Zool* **69**: 1, 1963.

54. Tellegen, A., J. M. Horn, and R. G. Legrand, *Psychon Sci* **14**: 104, 1969.

55. Lagerspetz, K. and R. Nurmi, *Rept Inst Psychol Univ Turku* **10**: 1, 1964.

56. Fredericson, E., *J Psychol* **29**: 89, 1950.

57. MacLennan, R. R. and E. D. Bailey, *Can J. Zool* **47**: 1395, 1969.

58. McKinney, T. D. and C. Desjardin, *Biol Reprod* **7**: 112, 1972.

59. Levy, J. V. and J. A. King, *Anat Rec* **117**: 562, 1953.

60. Kling, A., *J Comp Physiol Psychol* **65**: 466, 1968.

61. Levy, J. V., *Proc W Va Acad Sci* **26**: 14, 1954.

62. Hamburg, D. A., *Int Soc Sci J* **23**: 36, 1971.

63. Beach, F. A., *Hormones and Behavior*, Hoeber, New York, 1948.

64. Collias, N. E., *Physiol Zool* **17**: 83, 1944.

65. Guhle, A. M., in Young, W. C. and G. W. Corner (eds.), *Sex and Internal Secretions*, Williams and Wilkins, Baltimore, 1961, p. 1240.

66. Beeman, E. A., *Physiol Zool* **20**: 373, 1947.

67. Urich, J., *J Comp Psychol* **25**: 373, 1938.

68. Suchowsky, G. K., L. Pegrassi, and Bonsignori, in Garattini, S. and E. B. Sigg (eds.), *Aggressive Behaviour*, Wiley, New York, 1969, p. 164.

69. Suchowsky, G. K., L. Pegrassi, and A. Bonsignori, *Psychopharmacology* **21**: 32, 1971.

70. Sigg, E. B., C. Day, and C. Colombo, *Endocrinology* **78**: 679, 1966.

71. Sigg, E. B., in Garattini, S. and E. B. Sigg (eds.), *Aggressive Behaviour*, Wiley, New York, 1969, p. 143.

72. Edwards, D. A., *Science* **161**: 1027, 1968.

73. Edwards, D. A., *J Endocrinol* **46**: 477, 1970.

74. Bevan, J. M., W. Bevan, and B. F. Williams, *Physiol Zool* **31**: 284, 1958.

75. Kochakian, C. D., *Endocrinology* **28**: 478, 1941.

76. Anton, A. H., R. P. Schwartz, and S. Kramer, *J Psychiatr Res* **6**: 211, 1968.

77. Bevan, W., G. W. Levy, J. M. Whitehouse, and J. M. Bevan, *Physiol Zool* **30**: 341, 1958.

78. Yen, H. C. Y., C. A. Day, and E. B. Sigg, *Pharmacologist* **173**: 1962.

79. Erpino, M. J. and T. C. Chappelle, *Horm Behav* **2**: 265, 1971.

80. Beach, F. A., *Physiol Zool* **18**: 195, 1945.

81. Barfield, R. J., D. E. Bush, and K. Wallen, *Horm Behav* **3**: 247, 1972.

82. Sayler, A., *Physiol Behav* **5**: 667, 1970.

83. Vandenberg, J. G., *Anim Behav* **19**: 589, 1971.

84. Le Boeuf, B. J., *Horm Behav* **1**: 127, 1970.

85. Mirsky, A. F., *J Comp Physiol Psychol* **48**: 327, 1955.

86. Wilson, A., unpublished dissertation, University of California, Berkeley, Calif., 1968.

87. Rose, R. M., J. W. Holaday, and I. S. Bernstein, *Nature* **231**: 366, 1971.

88. Banerjee, U., *Commun Behav Biol* **6**: 163, 1971.

89. Brain, P. F., N. W. Nowell, and A. Wouters, *Physiol Behav* **6**: 27, 1971.

90. Cox, G. S., J. R. Hodges, and J. Vernikos, *J Endocrinol* **17**: 177, 1958.

91. Burge, K. G. and D. A. Edwards, *Physiol Behav* **7**: 885, 1971.

92. Welch, B. L., *BioScience* **18**: 1061, 1968.

93. Harding, C. F. and A. I. Leshner, *Physiol Behav* **8**: 437, 1972.

94. Walker, W. A. and A. I. Leshner, *Am Zool* **12**: 652, 1972.

95. Svare, B. B. and A. I. Leshner, paper presented at the 43rd Annual Meeting EPA, 1972.

96. Leshner, A. I. and W. A. Walker, paper presented at the Psychonomic Society Meeting, November 1972.

97. Kostowski, W., W. Rewerski, and T. Piechocki, *Neuroendocrinology* **6**: 311, 1970.

98. Money, J. and A. A. Ehrhardt, *Man & Woman, Boy & Girl,* Johns Hopkins University Press, Baltimore, 1972.

99. Bronson, F. and C. Desjardins, in Eleftheriou, B. and J. Scott (eds.), *The Physiology of Aggression and Defeat,* Plenum Press, London, 1971, p. 43.

100. Edwards, D. A. and J. Herndon, *Physiol Behav* **5**: 993, 1970.

101. Bronson, F. H. and C. Desjardins, *Endocrinology* **85**: 971, 1969.

102. Bronson, F. H. and C. Desjardins, *Gen Comp Endocrinol* **15**: 320, 1970.

103. Edwards, D. A., *Physiol Behav* **4**: 333, 1969.

104. Edwards, D. A., *Physiol Behav* **5**: 465, 1970.

105. Peters, P. J. and F. H. Bronson, *Am Zool* **11**: 621, 1971.

106. Peters, P. J., F. H. Bronson, and J. M. Whitsett, *Physiol Behav* **8**: 265, 1972.

107. Miley, W. M., unpublished dissertation, Temple University, 1973.

108. Robinson, B. W., M. Alexander, and F. Bowne, *Physiol Behav* **4**: 747, 1969.

109. Herrero, S., *Science* **170**: 593, 1970.

110. Brown, R. Z., *Ecol Monogr* **23**: 217, 1953.

111. King, J. A., in Rheingold, H. L. (ed.), *Maternal Behavior in Animals,* Wiley, New York, 1963, p. 58.

112. Barnett, S. A., in Carthy, J. D. and C. L. Duddington (eds.), *Viewpoints in Biology* **3**: 170, 1964.

113. Altman, M., in Rheingold, H. L. (ed.), *Maternal Behavior in Mammals,* Wiley, New York, 1963, p. 233.

114. Taylor, J. C., in Jewell, P. A. and C. Loizos (eds.), *Play, Exploration and Territory in Mammals,* Academic Press, New York, 1966.

115. Jay, P., in Rheingold, H. L. (ed.), *Maternal Behavior in Mammals,* Wiley, New York, 1963, p. 282.

116. DeVore, I., in Rheingold, H. L. (ed.), *Maternal Behavior in Mammals,* Wiley, New York, 1963, p. 305.

117. Burt, W. H., *J Mammal* **24**: 346, 1943.

118. Ross, S., P. B. Sawin, M. X. Zarrow, and V. H. Denenberg, in Rheingold, H. L. (ed.), *Maternal Behavior in Mammals,* Wiley, New York, 1963, p. 94.

119. Hersher, L., J. B. Richmond, and A. U. Moore, in Rheingold, H. L. (ed.), *Maternal Behavior in Mammals,* Wiley, New York, 1963, p. 203.

120. Lockie, J. D., in Jewell, P. A. and C. Loizos (eds.), *Play, Exploration and Territory in Mammals,* Academic Press, New York, 1966.

121. Schneirla, T. C., J. S. Rosenblatt, and E. Tobach, in Rheingold, H. L. (ed.), *Maternal Behavior in Mammals,* Wiley, New York, 1963, p. 122.

122. Flandera, V. and V. Novakova, *Physiol Bohemoslov* **20**: 61, 1971.

123. Flandera, V. and V. Novakova, *Physiol Behav* **6**: 161, 1971.

124. Scudder, C. L., A. G. Karczmar, and L. Lockett, *Anim Behav* **15**: 353, 1967.

125. Karli, P., *Behaviour* **10**: 81, 1956.

126. Revlis, R. and K. E. Moyer, *Psychon Sci* **16**: 135, 1969.

127. Baenninger, R., *Psychon Sci* **15**: 144, 1969.

128. Davis, P. G. and R. D. Gandelman, *Horm Behav* **3**: 169, 1972.

129. Gandelman, R., *Horm Behav* **3**: 23, 1972.

130. Endroczi, E., K. Lissak, and G. Telegdy, *Acta Physiol Acad Sci Hung* **14**: 353, 1958.

131. Hamburg, D. A., *J Psychiatr Res* **8**: 385, 1971.

132. Schleidt, W., M. Schleidt, and M. Magg, *Behaviour* **16**: 254, 1960.

133. Eisenberg, J. F., *Behaviour* **19**: 177, 1962.

134. Duffy, C. T. and A. Hirshberg, *Sex and Crime*, Doubleday, New York, 1965.

135. Freud, S., *The Complete Psychological Works of*, Hogarth Press, London, 1955.

136. Reinhardt, J. M., *Sex Perversions and Sex Crimes*, Thomas, Springfield, Ill., 1957.

137. Stekel, W., *Sadism and Masochism: The Psychology of Hatred and Cruelty*, Liveright, New York, 1929, Vols. I and II.

138. Ellis, H., *Psychology of Sex*, Brooke, New York, 1937.

139. Kraft-Ebing, R., *Psychopathia Sexualis*, Davis, Philadelphia, 1892.

140. Rothman, G., *The Riddle of Cruelty*, Philosophical Library, New York, 1971.

141. Etkin, W., in Etkin, W. (ed.), *Social Behavior and Organization Among Vertebrates*, University of Chicago Press, 1964, p. 75.

142. Eisenberg, J. F. and P. Leyhausen, *Z Tierpsychol* **30**: 59, 1972.

143. Carpenter, C. R., *J Comp Psychol* **33**: 113, 1942.

144. Zumpe, D. and R. P. Michael, *Anim Behav* **18**: 11, 1970.

145. Michael, R. P. and D. Zumpe, *Anim Behav* **18**: 1, 1970.

146. Gottschalk, L. A., in Mandell, A. J. and M. P. Mandell (eds.), *Psychochemical Research in Man*, Academic Press, New York, 1969.

147. Sletten, I. W. and S. Gershon, *Comp Psychiatry* **7**: 197, 1966.

148. Altman, M., E. Knowles, and H. D. Bull, *Psychosom Med* **3**: 199, 1941.

149. Jacobs, T. J. and E. Charles, *Am J Psychiatry* **126**: 148, 1970.

150. Glass, G. S., G. R. Heninger, M. Lansky, and K. Talan, *Am J Psychiatry* **128**: 705, 1971.

151. Torghele, J. R., *Lancet* **77**: 163, 1957.

152. Dalton, K., *Med J* **1**: 148, 1959.

153. Ribero, S. L., *Br Med J* **1**: 640, 1962.

154. Mandell, A. J. and M. P. Mandell, *J Am Med Assoc* **200**: 792, 1967.

155. Shainess, N., *Comp Psychiatry* **2**: 20, 1961.

156. Ivey, M. E. and J. M. Bardwick, *Psychosom Med* **30**: 336, 1968.

157. Coppen, A. and N. Kessel, *Br J Psychiatry* **109**: 711, 1963.

158. Sutherland, H. and I. Stewart, *Lancet* **1**: 1180, 1965.

159. Moos, R., *Psychosom Med* **30**: 853, 1968.
160. Ellis, D. P. and P. Austin, *J Crim Law Criminol Police Sci* **62**: 388, 1971.
161. Dalton, K., *The Premenstrual Syndrome*, Thomas, Springfield, Ill., 1964.
162. Dalton, K., *Br Med J* **2**: 1647, 1960.
163. Shah, S. A. and L. H. Roth, in Glaser, D. (ed.), *Handbook of Criminology*, Rand McNally, Chicago, in press.
164. Dalton, K., *Br Med J* **2**: 1752, 1961.
165. Cooke, W. R., *Am J Obstet Gynecol* **49**: 457, 1945.
166. Morton, J. H,. H. Addison, R. G. Addison, L. Hunt, and J. J. Sullivan, *Am J Obstet Gynecol* **65**: 1182, 1953.
167. Deutsch, H., *The Psychology of Women*, Grune & Stratton, New York, 1944.
168. Podolsky, E., *Pakistan Med J* **15**: 9, 1964.
169. Hamburg, D. A., R. H. Moos, and I. D. Yalom, in Michael, R. P. (ed.), *Endocrinology and Human Behaviour*, Oxford University Press, London, 1968.
170. Janowsky, E. S., R. Gorney, and A. J. Mandell, *Arch Gen Psychiatry* **17**: 459, 1967.
171. Penington, V. M., *J Am Med Assoc* **164**: 638, 1957.
172. Morton, J. H., *Am J Obstet Gynecol* **60**: 343, 1950.
173. Lloyd, C. W. and J. Weisz, paper presented at the Houston Neurological Symposium on Neural Bases of Violence and Aggression, Houston, Texas, March 1972.
174. Bardwick, J. M., *Psychology of Women*, Harper & Row, New York, 1971.
175. Greene, R. and K. Dalton, *Br Med J* **1**: 1007, 1953.
176. Lloyd, C. W., in Lloyd, C. W. (ed.), *Human Reproduction and Sexual Behavior*, Lee & Febiger, Philadelphia, 1964.
177. Wiseman, W., in *Recent Advances in Ovarian and Synthetic Steroids and the Control of Ovarian Function: Proceedings of a Symposium, Sydney, Australia*, Globe Commercial Party Ltd., 1965.
178. Paige, K. E., unpublished dissertation, University of Michigan, 1969.
179. Winshel, A. W., *Int Rec Med* **172**: 539, 1959.
180. Greenhill, J. P. and S. C. Freed, *Endocrinology* **26**: 529, 1940.
181. Billig, H. E., Jr. and C. A. Spaulding, *Ind Med* **16**: 336, 1947.
182. Harris, S., Jr., *South Med J* **37**: 714, 1944.
183. Hamburg, D. A. and D. T. Lunde, in Maccoby, E. (ed.), *The Development of Sex Differences in Human Behavior*, Stanford University Press, Palo Alto, Calif., 1966, p. 1.
184. Persky, H., M. Zuckerman, and G. C. Curtis, *J Nerv Ment Dis* **146**: 488, 1968.
185. Persky, H., K. D. Smith, and G. K. Basu, *Psychosom Med* **33**: 265, 1971.
186. Kreuz, L. E. and R. M. Rose, *Psychosom Med* **34**: 321, 1972.
187. Strauss, E. B., D. E. Sands, A. M. Robinson, W. J. Tindall, and W. A. Stevenson, *Br Med J* **2**: 64, 1952.
188. Sands, D. E. and G. H. A. Chamberlain, *Br Med J* **2**: 66, 1952.
189. Sands, D. E., *J Ment Sci* **100**: 211, 1954.
190. Bremer, J., *Asexualization*, Macmillan, New York, 1959.

191. Hawke, C. C., *Am J Ment Defic* **55**: 220, 1950.

192. Sturup, G. K., *Can J Correc* **3**: 250, 1961.

193. Golla, F. L. and R. S. Hodge, *Lancet*, **1**: 1006, 1949.

194. Foote, R. M., *J Nerv Ment Dis* **99**: 928, 1944.

195. Whitaker, L. H., *Med J Aust* **2**: 547, 1959.

196. Dunn, G. W., *J Clin Endocrinol* **1**: 643, 1941.

197. Field, L. H. and M. Williams, *Med Sci Law*, 27, 1970.

198. Chatz, T. L., *Int J Offend Ther* **2**: 1972.

199. Lerner, L. J., *Rec Prog Horm Res* **20**: 435, 1964.

200. Lerner, L. J., A Bianchi, and A. Borman, *Proc Soc Exp Biol Med* **103**: 172, 1960.

201. Rocky, S. and R. O. Neri, *Fed Proc* **27**: 624, 1968.

202. Neumann, F., R. VonBerswordt-Wallrabe, W. Elger, and H. Steinbeck, in Tamm, J. (ed.), *Testosterone. Proceedings of the Workshop Conference, Tremsbuettel,* Georg Thieme, Stuttgart, 1968.

203. Servais, J., *Acta Neurol Belg* **68**: 407, 1968.

204. Neuman, F., H. Steinbeck, and J. D. Hahan, in Martini, L., M Motta, and F. Fraschini (eds.), *The Hypothalamus,* Academic Press, New York, 1970, p. 569.

205. Money, J., *J Sex Res* **6**: 165, 1970.

206. Laschet, U., *Klin Wochenschr* **45**: 324, 1967.

207. Laschet, U., L. Laschet, H. R. Fetzner, H. U. Glaesel, G. Mall, and M. Naab, *Acta Endocrinol* **119**: 54, 1967.

208. Lloyd, C. W., in Lloyd, C. W. (ed.), *Human Reproduction and Sexual Behavior,* Lea & Febiger, Philadelphia, 1964, p. 497.

CHAPTER 19

The Psychobiology of Sex Differences: An Evolutionary Perspective

BEATRIX A. HAMBURG

Child Psychiatry Clinic
Stanford University School of Medicine
Stanford, California

In recent years there has been an enormous increase in the interest in, and knowledge about, sex differences. This field of work has reflected many of the remarkable advances of modern biology. Significant data are now available in such diverse areas as molecular genetics, neuro–endocrine relations, and primate field studies. Sex differences have also been a topic of research interest to a range of social scientists who are concerned with issues of socialization across the life cycle and social organization within and between cultures.

The modern theory of evolution is a powerful instrument for organizing our thinking about biological issues. It seems profitable to see whether this tool can help to integrate some of the data being amassed in the current explosion of knowledge about the molecular, organismic, and cultural aspects of sex difference. In this discussion, three aspects of behavior that are characterized by well-documented sexual dimorphism will be used to illustrate the utility of an evolutionary perspective in understand-

373

ing the epigenesis and the significance of the behavior. Sexual behavior, language, and spatial behaviors will be used as specific examples. Ultimately, it would seem profitable to apply the same kind of analysis to all of the behavioral categories that have been critical for human survival. This chapter only touches on such important areas as aggression, maternal behaviors, socialization, and sex status as a basis for the organization of social institutions.

The terms "sex role" or "gender role" have come to encompass the significant sexual dimorphisms in behavior. "Sex role" is a modal term that describes the clusters of behaviors that are performed characteristically or more frequently by one sex rather than another. There are virtually no behaviors that are performed exclusively by one sex, with the exception of those linked very directly with childbearing, nursing, or inseminating behavior.

Sex role is ascribed at birth based on observed characteristics of the external genitalia. In sociological terms, it is a "master role" that determines socially patterned attitudes as well as actions from birth onward. The sex role acts as an organizer of prescriptions and prohibitions regarding types of activities, personality styles, and erotic behaviors for the individual. In contemporary Western culture, the activities prescribed for adult women relate to maternal roles. For adult males, occupational and protector roles are prescribed. Personality styles of dominance and aggression are a part of the male stereotype. Passivity, dependence, and nurturance are often ascribed to the female. Erotic preferences and actions are also defined. The male is associated with low threshold and high frequency of sexual arousal, sexual initiations, and an active, thrusting role in copulatory behavior.

Not only is the behavior of the individual defined by the sex role, but the reciprocal behaviors of others toward the person are also defined. For example, girls and women are not to be hurt by counterpunitive action even when they are aggressively provocative in their behavior toward a male (1).

A multiplicity of specific sex-role definitions can be observed across cultures. Obviously, the widest possible variety of sex-role patterns can be learned and incorporated in a stable way into social institutions. At times, this plasticity of gender behavior has been used to argue for an environmental determinism of the development of sex-role behaviors. However, can sex roles be said to be nonbiological even though they show the greatest possible impact of learning?

One might use the analogy of language. There is clearly a biological basis for language. No other animal has the adaptation of brain and vocal apparatus to make meaningful speech possible. The neurological basis of speech is well described (2, 3). Despite this, language is clearly learned behavior. Langer (4) has pointed out that man does not say even the first word by instinct. All cultures learn and share a particular language. She reminds us that even in the most primitive human groups where clothing, skills, and tools are absent or rudimentary, language is always present, well developed, and culturally transmitted.

Because of the prominence of nature versus nurture in the discussions of sex difference, the current meaning and usage of the term "biological" needs careful definition. Over the years, and unfortunately still in some sectors at present, there has been a tendency to see "biological" and "social" as polarized terms. Biological or innate behaviors have been perceived as unlearned and independent of the environment. The term "innate" has often taken on connotations of considerable rigidity. This perceived rigidity takes two forms. One is the *fixed-action-pattern con-cept*. In this construct, a biological behavior is believed to represent a rigid stereotyped pattern that either inexorably appears at a specific timing, such as puberty, or is mechanically and uniformly released by a specific stimulus in the environment that acts as an automatic trigger. This is only partially true for lower animals and is certainly not a valid concept to apply to higher primates, especially to humans. In the human species, the extraordinary capacity for, and dependence on, learning has been a major adaptation. As in the example of language, the important issue is not the biological behavior *per se* but rather the biological contribution to the shaping of what is learned. For our purposes we are interested in what may be sex differences in the attentional preferences of males and females. Do males and females have sex differences in the ease of learning of certain kinds of behavior? (5) The evidence tends to confirm that there is greater naturalness in performing certain behaviors or a greater sense of congeniality in pursuing particular interests.

TYPOLOGICAL VERSUS POPULATION CONCEPTS

Another rigidity sometimes arises when characteristics defined as biological are seen as absolute. Most biological attributes occur in a normal distribution curve. The distribution curves show great overlap between the sexes. For example, it can be said that males are taller than females. This signifies that, for the total population of males, the averaged height is greater than the averaged height of the total population of females. There is a range of heights for both groups. Obviously, a specific tall female may be notably taller than a specific short male. The generalization of height difference remains valid, nonetheless. In the same vein, it is undoubtedly true that such sex differences in behavior as may be found to exist on a biological basis will represent generalizations for total populations and cannot tell us anything specific for a given individual. In these instances, as in the case of height, individual exceptions at the outer ends of the distribution curves do not disprove the generalization.

It should also be borne in mind that, although genes control the potential for expression of a trait such as height (genotype), environmental factors (e.g., health and diet) weigh very heavily in the actual height attained (phenotype). This principle applies even more strongly for the expression of behaviors, even those with a clear biological base.

In summary, the new biology recognizes that no dichotomy exists between nature and nurture. Growth and development are the resultant of the influence of environmental factors, which are superimposed on, and interact with, a biological background. Biological systems, whether at a molecular or total organismic level, are *open* systems. This means that the innate and environmental inputs are mutual influences on each other.

Modern evolutionary theory is based on two key concepts. First, there is a genetic code that determines the structural and functional characteristics of living organisms. Changes in this genetic code are continuously and randomly occurring as a result of the processes of mutation and recombinations of the genes. Second, natural selection operates on these random changes to preserve those mutations and combinations in the gene pool that have been "favorable" in adapting to the environment. "Favorable," in this context, refers to success in reproduction—that is, the enhancement of the likelihood that increased numbers of progeny will selectively survive and lead to continuation of those mutations in the gene pool of the population. This theory accounts at one and the same time for both novelty and stability in organisms since it deals with changes that occur very slowly, perhaps over a period of millions of years in some cases.

The term "population" is important. In an evolutionary context, the fate of a particular individual is not important. Reproductive success is measured in terms of the ability of the total population to have progeny at a stable or increasing rate. Also, the ultimate selective unit in the individual is not the single gene but his entire coadapted gene complex. Mutations that are greatly dissonant or incompatible with preexisting gene complexes generally prove to be lethal and are not transmitted.

In order to achieve reproductive success in more complex species, a number of processes must occur. Male and female members of the species must have the opportunity to engage in copulatory behavior. The partners must be sexually acceptable to each other and be motivated to mate. Fertilization must occur, and their gametes must be genetically compatible. The intrauterine growth and development must be normal. Offspring must be cared for and learn skills to survive to maturity and, in turn, successfully repeat the cycle. There are selective pressures operating at all of the stages of the life cycle. The net reproductive success reflects the total outcome. The behavioral contribution to reproductive success is prominent in the stages of the cycle that have to do with mating, care and training of the young, and meeting the challenges of adaptation to the ecological niche. Hamburg (5) has pointed out that natural selection has operated on the variability in behavior patterns and motivations and has preserved those behavioral and emotional patterns that have been effective in getting the tasks of survival accomplished. The social organization is also an important adaptive mechanism for most primates and especially *Homo sapiens*. For this reason, the genes that determine species-specific predispositions for patterns of group interactions (social behavior) have contributed in a major way to the evolution of man. It is appropriate to consider the development of sex difference from this evolutionary perspective.

It is clear that sexual reproduction was enormously important in increasing the diversity of a gene pool. The advantages of diversity in the gene pool have been amply demonstrated. On the one hand, heterozygosity offers the possibility of offsetting the probable negative effect of a particular mutant through the presence of a normal allele. If unpaired, a particular mutant could potentially do great harm. When counteracted by a homolog acting at the same chromosomal site, the effect of the mutant is nullified and the harmful trait cannot be expressed. There is also the advantage of diversity in enabling a population to show greater flexibility in responding to environmental change or opportunity. When the environmental change is stable and a particular genetic variant is notably more advantageous, the trait will be passed on selectively and, over time, become incorporated as a stable element of the genetic makeup of the population. In times of rapid change, a population with a large and diverse gene pool has "preadapted" individuals who are genetically prepared for a range of circumstances. Structural and behavioral mutations that have facilitated sexual reproduction have, therefore, had an adaptive advantage and have been favored in the natural selection process.

It would seem desirable for the sexes to recognize each other readily. If one takes a comparative approach and considers the placental species of animals and also studies the anthropological data from cultures around the world, it is clear that there has been a universal emphasis on maintaining nongenital, visible differences between the sexes. This suggests that there has been some adaptive advantage in maintaining this visible difference. This visible difference is usually structural. There is often a notable dimorphism in size. Characteristically, the males are significantly larger. However, depending on the species, adaptations in every aspect of external appearance have been involved, from the mane of the lion to prominent antlers in the elk. Selection pressures have shaped dimorphisms in behavioral as well as structural differences. Some of these behavioral dimorphisms may be important in signaling sex differences, which facilitate mating behavior.

It would also seem desirable for each of the sexes to emit and receive clear signals about readiness for fertile matings. In nonhuman mammals, the time of ovulation is associated with such cues as changes in the coloring of genital skin, olfactory stimuli, and hormonally mediated increase in sexual receptiveness of the female. These stimuli induce distinctive courtship and mating behaviors in the male. In humans, there are no obvious external cues as to the timing of ovulation. The implications of this will be discussed later.

The evolution of human behavior and its relation to social organization are best understood in the context of early man in the period of hunting-and-gathering societies. The best available information indicates that out of the roughly 2 million years that hominids have existed, over 99% of this time has been spent in hunting-and-gathering societies. Agriculture as a major way of life was instituted only 5,000 to 6,000 years ago. The Industrial Revolution is a recent development of the last 100 years, and only the most minute fraction of humans have lived in an industrial or technological society. Our biological heritage chiefly derives from the era of man the hunter. The long period of man's existence in the challenge of a hunting-and-gathering way of life has afforded the opportunity for those adaptations to become firmly established in the gene pool. It has been postulated (6) that our intelligence, interests, emotions, and species-specific patterns of social interaction are all the evolutionary residue of the success of *Homo sapiens* in the hunting-and-gathering adaptation. In effect, modern man carries essentially the same genetic heritage as early man.

Several important changes should be noted and will be discussed further: the descent from the trees and shift to a wide territorial range, upright posture with bipedal locomotion, development of "handedness" and use of tools, development of language. Both of the latter developments are closely related to the increase in size and complexity of the brain. This brain development has been more generally related to vast increase in learning potential.

It is significant that as "Man the Hunter" evolved, there were selection pressures for the physiological and behavioral adaptations that enhance sexual dimorphism and sexual division of labor. Some of these dimorphisms were already present in early man as part of his primate heritage, and these preexisting sex differences continue to be observed in contemporary nonhuman primates. These are the clusters of traits that pertain to male dominance and include the larger size, greater endurance and strength, and higher aggressiveness. The primate male is also characteristically less fearful and more exploratory in his behavior. These traits were highly compatible with the male hunting role.

In going from life in the trees to ground-dwelling to terrestrial and hunting life, there was much in the heritage from arboreal primate ancestry that was highly useful. The "grasping" adaptations of the hand for climbing were helpful in tool use and toolmaking. The binocular vision and excellent spatial intelligence were both readily transferable and highly adaptive for the hunters. The main changes from other primates came in brain size and function. The most notable advance was undoubtedly the acquisition of language. Communal hunting would have been made much more effective by a highly developed communication system. There was also a premium on slow maturation and learning over a period of many years. This, of course, depended on adaptations for prolonged child care. There would have been a powerful selective advantage for maternal and child behaviors that fostered strong and prolonged attachment. Both hunting and gathering involved migrations over long distances, seasonally. This implies detailed knowledge of the flora and fauna of diverse areas, knowledge of annual cycles, and recall of unusual circumstances or rare events. None of this would be possible without language and a long-learning childhood. Big-game hunting was largely a male occupation (7–9). Small-game hunting, food gathering, and child care was done by females. These female occupations were not trivial and are believed to have contributed in a major way to the total food supply.

Although in nonhuman primates a hierarchical social structure has proved useful in monitoring the use of available resources, it is also true that among nonhuman primates there is virtually no cooperation among group members in the collection of food and sharing of food among mature members (10). Even food sharing between mother and child is rare after weaning. Although man has inherited hierarchical tendencies, the social organization of human hunting and gathering stands in marked contrast to the social adaptations of other primates. It involves group cooperation and sharing, both male–male and male–female, in a coordinated way that is unknown in other primate species and depends on the existence of strong interindividual social bonds. It also depends on the existence of an agreed upon home base to which both males and females return with their kills or food collections.

There is a strong primate heritage, continued in *Homo sapiens*, for the development of intense and enduring affectional bonds between a mother and her offspring (11). The adult–adult bond affectional system in nonhuman primates seems less well developed. Grooming is used prominently among adult primates as transient social relating behavior. It seems likely that sexual behavior in humans has evolved to afford an important basis for intense and enduring adult male–female pair bonds. In typical nonhuman primates, adult male–female consort pairs are usually temporary and limited to cyclic periods of sexual receptiveness. Much more needs to be known about mechanisms for establishing and maintaining the adult–adult social bonds in humans that support close group membership in a family structure. Language also may be important in this regard.

As already mentioned, there has been remarkable similarity in fundamental cultural pattern across human societies. Cross-cultural differences reflect not basic divergence but rather the influence of learning and environment on the expression of basic biologic heritage.

To date, the most comprehensive review and analysis of cross-cultural data on sex-role behavior is that done by D'Andrade (12). He reported on data from many anthropologists and covered over 600 societies in terms of male–female division of labor, ascription of social status, patterns of interpersonal behavior, and definitions of gender identity. On the basis of the available data, he concludes that, although the behavioristic details are not universal, there are modal patterns of sex-role typing and behaviors that are strikingly widespread. The prevalent finding is that males are more sexually active, more dominant, more deferred to, less responsible, less nurturant, and less emotionally expressive than females. Women almost universally were given child-rearing roles. Division of labor by sexes was also almost universal. In general, male occupations tended to involve behavior that was strenuous, cooperative, and tended to require long periods of travel. The making of tools and weapons, although not involving more strength or skill than the manufacture or repair of clothing, was also a male occupation. The making of tools and weapons appears to be an activity that is assumed by men because of their direct relationship with activities defined as masculine. Women have major responsibility for gathering fuel, water, and foods. They manufacture and repair clothing. In agricultural societies, often men and women work together in the fields.

Maleness and femaleness are institutionalized as statuses in all cultures In addition to gender being used as a basis for assigning occupational tasks, it also serves as a basis for organizing social institutions. In general, cultures are organized around males rather than females. In fact, D'Andrade points out that the institutional subordination of women is more pervasive and complete than can be explained solely on overt differences in dominance or aggression. He discusses the sex bias that can lead to a devaluation of female activities—that is, activities performed by women are evaluated less highly because they are performed by women.

Finally, he describes the almost universal learning of appropriate sex-role identity, and individuals seem to learn to want to occupy their assigned sex status. There is some discussion of the circumstances under which one sex envies the status of the other.

It is interesting to look at the current appraisal of sex-role stereotypes in the United States (13) in a study that cut across lines of age, sex, marital status, and education. Broverman and co-workers conclude that there is strong consensus across all groups as to the sex roles of men and women. The characteristics ascribed to men reflect a "competency" cluster. Men are described as independent, objective, active, competitive, logical skilled in business, adventurous, decisive, self-confident, ambitious, and taking leadership roles. The stereotypic perception of women is as dependent, noncompetitive, passive, gentle, warm and expressive, sensitive to the feelings of others, able to express tender feelings. The characteristics ascribed to males are more positively valued than the traits ascribed to women. In general, the sex-role definitions are implicitly and uncritically accepted and incorporated into the self-concepts of both men and women. These stereotypes are considered desirable by all groups, even college students, who are often critical of traditional social norms. The studies of college students reported in this symposium replicate this finding. This research confirms contemporary existence in America of the sex-role behaviors and typings similar to those that have been postulated for early hominid societies and those that appear to have characterized the majority of contemporary societies studied in cross-cultural surveys. It seems reasonable to assume that this acceptance, pervasiveness, and consistency of sex roles reflects selection pressures that have operated to preserve and enhance dimorphisms in behavior. It would seem profitable to examine for sex difference in all of the behavioral areas that have been critical for human survival. The categories that would seem to merit special attention are reproductive behaviors (copulatory and maternal behaviors); language; socialization of the young; defense against dangers, relationship to the territory; and social organization. We shall look at three of these areas: copulatory behavior, language, and spatial abilities.

COPULATORY BEHAVIOR

Sex hormones have long been known to influence both the physiological events that control the production of ova and sperm, and also to control the sexual behaviors ensuring a high probability of fertile mating. There is evidence that, in humans, these processes are influenced by neuro-humoral events that occur prior to birth through organizational effects on the developing brain and are regulated, postnatally, by the circulating levels of sex-appropriate hormones. A brief summary will be given here.

The elucidation of sexual dimorphism in the programming of the brain under hormonal influence is an exciting and important contribution. Harris (14) hypothesized that the brain of a mammal is essentially "female" unless exposed to testosterone at a critical period in early development. Subsequently, in work with rodents, Harris and Levine (15) determined that a single injection of testosterone at the critical period could produce the same masculinizing effect that had previously been shown with implantation of the testis. The work was replicated in rhesus monkeys by Young, Goy, and Phoenix (16). In all cases, the effects were found to be mediated through the sexual differentiation of the hypothalamus. Once this sexual differentiation of the brain occurs at the critical period, a pattern of physiological and behavioral responses is set—a pattern that is permanent and cannot be later reversed either by gonadectomy or administration of the cross-sex hormone. The pituitary gland itself does not become sexually differentiated. This was demonstrated by transplanting mature male pituitary glands into operated females, who continued to maintain normal female functions (17). Furthermore, sex differences in the ultramicroscopic structure of the hypothalamus have been found (18).

There are several major functional differences between male and female brains. In female brains, the secretion of pituitary gonadotrophic hormones is regulated in a *cyclic* fashion that effects the rhythm of ovulation and the formation of the corpus luteum in the ovary and results in an estrous or a menstrual cycle. In males, on the other hand, the secretion of pituitary gonadotrophins is maintained at a more nearly constant level, the cyclicity typical of the female not being apparent.

A second functional sex difference is the programming of the brain for differences in characteristic mature sexual copulatory patterns. Not only is the characteristic behavioral response determined, but the threshold point is set for later sensitivity of the brain to circulating gonadal hormone levels. For example, it is normally almost impossible to elicit female patterns of sexual behavior in a mature male rodent by injecting him with female sex hormones, even in large amounts. However, if newborn male rats are castrated at the critical period and the brain is permitted to proceed to a female differentiation (in the absence of testosterone), as adults these operated males will show typical female sexual patterns when even small doses of female sex hormones are administered. This differential response to stimulation as a result of early sex typing of the brain may have its analogues in threshold responses to other stimuli as well and may be a paradigm for differential response sets and learning patterns of the sexes under similar environmental stimulation.

Over the course of evolutionary development in mammals there has been increasing complexity of the neuro–endocrine–environmental mechanisms that control sexual behavior. Mature human sexual behavior represents a culmination of this trend, and social learning appears to play a superordinate role. Comparative studies of guinea pigs, rats, cats, and monkeys (19–22) show a decreasing dependence on levels of sex hormones and an increasing dependence on sensory stimulation and cortical brain function with ascent of the mammalian scale. The variability of outcomes in man, after castration, highlights the impact of expectation and motivation as key factors in subsequent sexual interest and performance. Indeed, at times, due to secondary effects of fear and negative suggestion, there is loss of sexuality after vasectomy, even though this procedure does not affect hormone levels. It is worth noting that across species the male sexual patterns are more vulnerable than the female. For example, both male and female monkeys reared in isolation showed profound loss of sexual function in adulthood (23). The males were never able to recover from this, but the females did adapt sufficiently, in many cases, to achieve fertile matings.

It was suggested earlier that the abolition of cyclic sexual receptiveness in the human female may play a role in facilitating attachment bonds between adult male–female consort pairs. The potential for continuous sexual receptiveness in the human female represents an uncoupling of copulatory behavior from the gonadally controlled monthly cycle of ovulation, the menstrual cycle. In this respect, there would be a loss of immediate reproductive efficiency. The human male is not as efficiently signaled as other mammals as to the most ideal timing for fertile matings. Despite the fact that the neuroendocrine factors controlling the cyclic occurrence of ovulation do not also seem to mediate well-defined cyclic copulatory behavior patterns in humans, it cannot be said that sexual and copulatory behaviors are independent of these neurohumoral influences. Furthermore, it seems well established that some nonsexual behaviors are strikingly influenced by the hormonal events of the menstrual cycle. Considerable research effort is now being devoted to fuller understanding in both of these areas.

Other chapters in this volume cover the menstrual cycle in detail, particularly with respect to the cyclic emotional responses. It may be worthwhile, however, to report an interesting line of research that relates ovarian hormones to patterns of sexual behavior during the menstrual cycle.

Rhesus monkeys are a useful laboratory model for the experimental study of sex hormones and sexual behavior. They are uniquely comparable to man in that they are the only other primate species in which continual sexual receptiveness occurs. This continuous receptiveness is characteristic of laboratory animals. They also have a 28-day menstrual cycle. Also, as in humans, there is a striking factor of individual variation in consistent partner preference as a significant determinant of absolute level of sexual activity. In the experimental procedures, animals were selected for good levels of sexual interaction. The experimental work in this area has been well reviewed by Michael (24) and can be summarized as follows. These animals show heightened sexual receptivity near midcycle. They also show a direct relationship between agonistic and sexual behavior. The female rhesus monkey is more aggressive to the male when sexually receptive. She is less aggressive and more liable to be attacked by the male just prior to menstruation. Mounting attempts on the part of the male increase in number toward midcycle and ejaculation time becomes shorter. There is a decline of this behavior during the luteal phase. Males spend more time grooming females near midcycle than near menstruation. Female invitations to encourage male mounting behavior seem to remain at a fairly constant level throughout the menstrual cycle, but the "female success ratio," or proportion of such invitations accepted by the male, markedly declines during the luteal phase. There is also a female refusal of male mounting efforts during the luteal phase.

Using ovariectomized animals and controlled injections of estrogen and progesterone, some mechanisms have been elucidated. After ovariectomy, the cyclic sexual behavior of both males and females described above was abolished. When estradiol was administered, male interest was restored to normal levels as evidenced by attempted mounts and grooming activity. Administration of progesterone showed that the female refusal of male mounts is due to a progesterone effect. Concomitantly, males lose interest in females receiving high doses of progesterone. Their mounting attempts sharply decline. These data are interesting when related to reports of loss of libido in couples where the woman has been on progestational oral contraceptives for long periods of time (25–27). Michael (24) administered progestational oral contraceptives to his normal, intact rhesus females in a pattern comparable to the human regimen. The results are still being analyzed, but marked changes in sexual interaction occurred. The most conclusive finding so far has been a progressive decrease in the number of ejaculations per test with successive cycles of treatment.

Much remains to be learned about the mechanisms controlling the effects of gonadal hormones in sexual behavior. It is currently believed that hormone-dependent (activation) effects within the brain mediated by progesterone are responsible for the female refusal responses. Michael and colleagues have shown that olfactory cues mediate sexual initiating behaviors in the male. His work strongly suggests the existence of an estrogen-dependent vaginal pheromone mechanism. Male monkeys rendered anosmic failed to press a bar to gain access to estrogen-treated females after it had been demonstrated that with normal olfaction they consistently did so.

This indication of an estrogen-dependent pheromone mechanism influencing behavior is interesting in the light of recent work on menstrual synchrony in human females (28). It was found that groups of women living together, particularly close friends, tended to have entrainment of menstrual cycles to the same timing. A pheromone mechanism was postulated. Social factors were also recognized because emotional reactions to the other women in the group appeared to affect the synchrony. Also, exposure to males seems to affect cycle length. Whether or not this, too, represents a pheromonal effect is not clear. It is also not clear whether there is anything in the human that is analogous to the effect in mice (29), where the pheromones of stranger males serve to precipitate abortions in pregnant mice. In the same species, the females show regular estrus cycles when the excrements of familiar males are present. Although cortical factors do seem superordinate in human sexual behavior, some of these other factors may play a significant role.

How does all of this relate to the previous discussion of the universal hominid tendency across time and space for adult males and females to mate in stable pairs, show a powerful tendency to stay together, and rear their young jointly? What has been briefly outlined here deals with the chromosomal, structural, and neuroendocrine apparatus that is important in the development and mediation of male and female sexual behavior. Natural selection favors those members of the population who, in addition to having this apparatus, also possess the motivation to enact the adaptive behavior. It is not enough for the organism to have the equipment to accomplish a given task. There must be a dependable basis for ensuring the appropriate emotional set. For example, even an animal of large size with powerful jaws and teeth will be unsuccessful in defending himself against predators unless he is also temperamentally endowed with the courage, tenacity, and aggressiveness to put up a good fight. From the evolutionary perspective, what do we know that may help in understanding the motivational and emotional patterns that have been critical in human sexual behavior? It is clear that sexual behavior has the aspect of high intrinsic reward value, which gives individuals the motivation to want to perform the behavior that is critical to survival. Sexual activity is emotionally arousing, preemptively involving, and frequently culminates in the highly pleasurable experience of orgasm. In general, the experience of orgasm in the male is a stable and dependable phenomenon that shows a long mammalian-primate heritage. The orgasm of the human female is very important and seems to be a fairly recent evolutionary acquisition. It has been sporadically reported in a few other species, but it clearly is not entrenched in the primate gene pool. Chimpanzees, for example, do not show this characteristic. Even among human females there appears to be a wide range of variability in orgiastic potency. This variability may also point to the relative recency of this trait's entry into the gene pool.

Very early in this chapter, the upright posture was mentioned as a salient and new attribute of hominids. This upright posture has been associated with extreme tilting of the pelvic axis as a part of functional adaptations for the altered muscular requirements of bipedal locomotion. An effect of these changes has been an anterior placement of associated pubic structures, including the vagina. The most obvious consequence of this altered anatomy has been a shift in the preferred mating position The ventral–ventral position is the modal pattern for most human societies (30). This is quite distinctive inasmuch as other mammals uniformly prefer the posterior position. This anterior displacement and ventral positioning enormously facilitate clitoral stimulation. It has been shown that female orgasm is chiefly dependent on rhythmic mechanical stimulation of the clitoris (31). The human female's ability to experience orgasm comparable to the male's enhances the reward value for both and gives sexual behavior an important role in interpersonal bonding. With the advent of the upright posture and altered anatomical relations, new functions were added to the old structures. Copulatory behavior came to have functions in the social organization of hominids that were as important as the reproductive role. This dissociation of sex behavior and child producing is of increasing importance in modern man. Sexual behavior may come to have importance chiefly in the functions of interpersonal bonding. This is an area for continued research.

LANGUAGE

Language is a uniquely human property and is clearly involved in social organization. There is a well-documented superiority of girls in verbal skills (32–34). Available evidence strongly suggests that this difference may be partly due to the way in which the brain is organized. There is evidence that lateralization of the hemispheres and functional activity of the language centers occur earlier in girls than in boys. At the same time, males have been shown to be more proficient in spatial tasks than females. Buffery and Gray (35) have given an excellent, detailed review of the present state of evidence of sex differences in linguistic and spatial abilities, and the research on the asymmetries of cerebral function. The following description covers the main lines of evidence and also offers some interpretations from an evolutionary perspective.

The functional division of the human brain into a dominant and nondominant hemisphere appears to be an evolutionary change that is related to the development of language and also to the adaptive advantage of "handedness" in toolmaking and other skills of manual dexterity. Because of the crossing over of nerve pathways, the dominant hemisphere is contralateral to the dominant hand. Since most people are "right-handed," the left hemisphere is usually dominant. The speech and language centers are located in the dominant hemisphere. Spatial ability has been shown to be localized in the minor (nondominant) hemisphere.

Our information concerning lateral specialization of the brain comes chiefly from patients who have asymmetric lesions of the hemispheres. We have also learned a great deal through surgical interventions necessary for tumors and epilepsy. Of late, new approaches have been possible through the technique of commissurotomy (36), that is, operations on patients whose intractable epilepsy has been found to be greatly improved by surgical disconnection of the cerebral hemispheres by cutting the corpus callosum. We also have a great fund of information about the microscopic and ultramicroscopic structures of the cerebral hemispheres.

The lateralization of cerebral language function has also been studied in normal subjects through the techniques of dichotic listening (37, 38). Dichotic presentation refers to the simultaneous presentation of different stimuli to the receptor organs (eyes or ears). Normally, in such simultaneous presentation, the stimuli are not processed by the two ears or eyes with equal proficiency. These perceptual asymmetries seem to reflect the normal functional asymmetry of the brain.

Using dichotic auditory methods, a clear superiority of the right ear (and therefore the left hemisphere) for the perception of words and speech sounds (verbal stimuli) has been demonstrated for mature individuals. With dichotic presentation, environmental (nonverbal) sounds are more accurately identified by the left ear (right hemisphere). This work demonstrates a specialization and functional differentiation of the hemispheres along the verbal–nonverbal dimension. When children were studied at 5 years of age, young males were distinctly more proficient in the procession of nonverbal stimuli (38). The authors concluded that in their sample of right-handed children "the right and left hemispheres had begun to show a functional differentiation along the verbal-non-verbal dimension by age five." The superiority of girls on the verbal identification is attributed by the authors to differential maturation, with the girls maturing faster.

There is some supportive evidence for a faster rate of maturation of the lateralization of the hemispheres in girls from a totally different line of inquiry. Taylor (39) studied 158 cases of temporal lobe epilepsy in terms of the sex distribution of the age of onset of the first seizure. There is a well-established hypothesis that a potential seizure-producing insult usually affects the less functionally active hemisphere. Taylor found that operation of this effect ceases after the fifth year. He also found that there was a consistently greater proportion of boys who were continuing to be affected by left-sided seizures up until 5 years of age. In girls, the decline in seizure rate was precipitate for left-sided seizures after 2 years of age. Right-sided lesions were equally prevalent for both sexes. This would seem to point to earlier maturation of lateralization (and functional activity of language centers) in girls. These data suggest that the left hemispheres are typically functionally active by 2 years of age in girls versus 5 years in boys.

The possible added contribution to the high verbal facility in girls might derive from differential verbal stimulation of girls and boys by the mothers in infancy (40). It can be said, in summary, that there is persuasive evidence of a biological basis for sex differences in verbal ability (due in part to maturational effects on the language centers of the brain). It is possible that girl infants may also receive more verbal stimulation than boys in an environmental interaction that would then potentiate the biological predisposition and further enhance the verbal skills of girls.

SPATIAL ABILITY

Males have been shown to be more proficient in spatial tasks than females. Spatial ability has been shown to be localized in the minor (nondominant) hemisphere. For right-handed persons, this is the right hemisphere of the brain. Much valuable information about the specialized functions of the minor hemisphere has been gained through the commissurotomy technique. Sperry and Levy (36) have found that knowledge about minor-hemisphere function can only be gained through special tests utilizing nonverbal forms of motor expression. Inasmuch as langauge is located in the dominant (left) hemisphere, information can be elicited about the function of that hemisphere through verbal report of the commissurotomy patient. This verbal report is not possible with the right or *mute*, minor-hemisphere patient. Through their studies, Sperry and Levy have concluded that the minor hemisphere is a conscious system that perceives, feels, thinks, and remembers at a characteristically human level. They confirm that the minor hemisphere is distinctly superior to the major hemisphere in the performance of certain types of tasks involving spatial ability, such as copying geometric figures, drawing spatial representations, and assembling Kohs blocks in the block-design test.

Spatial localization in the brain has also been studied through dichotic techniques. Kimura (41) demonstrated that a point can be more accurately located when presented to the left visual field than when presented to a corresponding position in the right visual field. It was also demonstrated that "on the localization task employing location within squares, the left field (spatial) superiority was absent or less marked for females compared with males." Other investigators have found the same male superiority in spatial ability on other perceptual tasks. Witkin et al. (42, 43) found differences in three tests of spatial discrimination: the embedded-figure test, the rod-and-frame test, and the tilting-room test. After age 8 years, males did consistently better on all of these tests. Prior to that age, results were variable. Porteus (44) has found that his maze test of spatial ability has yielded consistent results of male spatial superiority across a large number and wide range of cultures (from Australian aborigines to European and American school children). Finally, there is strong support for the presumption that the sex chromosomes play a role in determining spatial ability because in girls with Turner's syndrome, an XO condition, there is a profound defect in spatial perception (45).

It is interesting to speculate about the genesis of these sex differences in language and spatial abilities. It is fairly obvious that there was an adaptive advantage from an evolutionary standpoint in the lateralization of the brain into two functionally different hemispheres. Present evidence (46) indicates that where there is mixed dominance and some language competency in both hemispheres, there are perceptual deficits particularly in visualization and spatial abilities.

Gray and Buffery (47) have argued that the superiority of the female in verbal skills may be related to the possibility that mothers who were verbal and encouraged linguistic skills in their infants were selectively favored because of the enormous adaptive importance of language in the social organization. This formulation is an attractive one. The same authors postulate that male superiority in spatial skills "is in part connected with the man's role in dominance interactions and in part with his role in the protection of the group from other conspecific groups and from predators." This formulation is not spelled out and, as presented, is not as persuasive as the verbal skill and mother–infant interaction hypothesis. I should like to suggest another hypothesis. Washburn (48) has pointed out that most monkeys spend their lives in an area of 2 or 3 square miles. The gorilla and chimpanzee have a range of roughly 15 square miles. These are primates who have at least as adequate locomotor systems and special senses. Yet, according to Washburn, "one of the really remarkable characteristics of man is that even the most primitive of men operate over hundreds of square miles rather than these small areas." Man's unique spatial abilities may very well play a role in having made it possible to both vastly increase the human territorial range and give an adaptive advantage in hunting and warfare.

There may also have been additional selection pressure for male superiority in those spatial skills that are related to the aimed throwing of objects. This activity has been reported by van Lawick-Goodall (49) in contemporary free-living chimpanzees as a male behavior. In her observations, the aimed throwing occurred exclusively in agonistic encounters. In hominids, this agonistic primate throwing pattern was extended and used additionally for the aimed hurling of objects at prey animals as a hunting skill. It would appear that male superiority in spatial ability has probably conferred selective advantage in three major areas critical to human survival: expansion of territorial range, enhancement of hunting skills, and heightening of aggressive potential in agonistic encounters.

CONCLUSION

Sex difference in behavior is a relatively new field of study that has undergone rapid expansion in recent years. There has been accumulation of data from diverse disciplines of the biological and social sciences. In this chapter, an attempt has been made to utilize an evolutionary perspective to integrate some of the thinking about the ontogeny of the differences and the significance of the findings. There has been an effort to review the existing knowledge in terms of demonstrating continuities between human and animal findings, analyzing the differences, and trying, when possible, to point to some important gender differences that have been ignored. Also, an effort has been made to use the logic of evolutionary thinking to identify promising lines of research.

The essentials of the modern, synthetic theory of evolution are briefly described. Particular attention has been paid to understanding the evolution of the structural–behavioral genetic inheritance derived from the long period of hominid existence in hunting-and-gathering societies.

Three significant areas that show documented sexual dimorphism— sexual behavior, language, and spatial abilities—have been discussed to illustrate the possible utility of an evolutionary perspective.

ACKNOWLEDGMENTS

I should like to express my deep appreciation to those whose stimulation and encouragement has facilitated this work: David Hamburg, Betty Pickett, Lorraine Torres, Sherwood Washburn, and Frank Beach.

REFERENCES

1. Taylor, S. P. and S. Epstein, *J Pers* **35**: 474, 1967.
2. Geschwind, N. in Washburn, S. L. and P. Dolhinow (eds.), *Perspectives on Human Evolution*, Holt, Rinehart and Winston, New York, 1972.
3. Masland, R. L., in Washburn, S. L. and P. Dohlinow (eds.), *Perspectives on Human Evolution*, Holt, Rinehart and Winston, New York, 1972, p. 421.
4. Langer, S., *Philosophy in a New Key*, Harvard University Press, Cambridge, 1951.
5. Hamburg, D. A., in Knapp, P. H. (ed.), *Expression of Emotions in Man*, International University Press, New York, 1963, p. 300.
6. Washburn, S. L. and C. S. Lancaster, in Lee, R. B. and I. DeVore (eds.), *Man the Hunter*, Aldine, Chicago, 1968.
7. Steward, J. H., in Lowies, R. H. (ed.), *Essays in Anthropology Presented to A. L. Kroeber*, University of California Press, Berkeley, 1936.
8. Berndt, R. M. and C. H. Berndt, *The World of the First Australians*, University of Chicago Press, Chicago, 1964.
9. Spencer, B. and F. J. Gillin, *The Arunta: A Study of a Stone-Age People*, Macmillan, London, 1927.
10. DeVore, I. and S. Washburn, in Washburn, S. L. (ed.), *Classifications and Human Evolution*, Aldine, Chicago, 1963.
11. Bowlby, J., *Attachment and Loss*, Vol. I, Hogarth, London (Basic Books, New York), 1969.
12. D'Andrade, R. G., in Maccoby, E. (ed.), *The Development of Sex Differences*, Stanford University Press, Stanford, Calif., 1966.
13. Boverman, I. K., S. R. Vogel, D. M. Broverman, F. E. Clarkson, and P. S. Rosenkrantz, *J Soc Issues* **28**: 59, 1972.
14. Harris, G. W., *Endocrinology* **75**: 627, 1964.
15. Harris, G. W. and S. Levine, *J Physiol* **181**: 379, 1965.
16. Young, W. C., R. W. Goy, and C. H. Phoenix, *Science* **143**: 212, 1964.
17. Harris, G. W. and D. Jacobsohn, *Proc Roy Soc London* **139**: 263, 1951/1952.
18. Raisman, G., paper presented to the Association for Research in Nervous and Mental Disease, 52nd Annual Meeting, New York, December 1972.
19. Valenstein, E. S. and W. C. Young, *Endocrinology* **56**: 173, 1955.
20. Beach, F. A., *Physiol Rev* **27**: 240, 1947.
21. Rosenblatt, J., in Beach, F. (ed.), *Sex and Behavior*, Wiley, New York, 1965.
22. Luttge, W. F., *Arch Sex Behav* **1**: 61, 1971.

23. Harolw, H., in Beach, F. (ed.), *Sex and Behavior*, Wiley, New York, 1965.

24. Michael, R. P., in Michael, R. P. (ed.), *Endocrinology and Human Behavior*, Oxford University Press, London and New York, 1968, p. 69.

25. Grounds, A. D., in Shearman, R. P. (ed.), *Recent Advances in Ovarian and Synthetic Steroids 1965*, G. D. Searle and Co., Chicago, 1965, p. 185.

26. Kane, F., R. Daly, J. Ewing, and M. Kieler, *Br J Psychiatry* 113: 265, 1967.

27. Grant, E. C. G. and E. Mears, *Lancet* 2: 945, 1967.

28. McClintock, M. K., *Nature* 229: 244, 1971.

29. Bruce, H. M., *J Reprod Fert* 2: 138, 1961.

30. Ford, C. S. and F. A. Beach, *Patterns of Sexual Behavior*, Harper and Row, and Paul B. Hoebler, Inc., New York, 1952.

31. Masters, W. H. and V. E. Johnson, *Human Sexual Response*, Little, Brown, Boston, 1966.

32. Jacklin, C. and E. Maccoby, paper presented at AERA meeting, April 1972.

33. McCarthy, D., in Carmichael, L. (ed.), *Manual of Child Psychology*, 2nd ed., Wiley, New York, 1954, p. 492.

34. Tyler, L., *Tests and Measurements*, Prentice-Hall, Englewood Cliffs, N.J., 1963, p. 96.

35. Buffery, A. W. H. and J. A. Gray, in Ounsted, C. and D. Taylor (eds.), *Gender Differences: Their Ontogeny and Significance*, Williams and Wilkins, Baltimore, 1972, p. 123.

36. Sperry, R. W. and J. Levy, paper presented at APA Symposium, "Asymmetrical Function of the Human Brain," Miami, 1970.

37. Kimura, D., *Cortex* 3: 163, 1967.

38. Knox, C. and Kimura, *Neuropsychiatry* 8: 227, 1970.

39. Taylor, D. C., *Lancet*, July 1969, p. 140.

40. Lewis, M. and S. Goldberg, *Merrill-Palmer Quart.* 15: 81, 1969.

41. Kimura, D., *Can. J. Psych* 23: 445, 1969.

42. Witkin, H. A., H. B. Lewis, M. Herzman, K. Machover, P. B. Meissner, and S. Wapner, *Personality through Perception*, Harper and Row, New York, 1954.

43. Witkin, H. A., R. B. Dyk, H. F. Faterson, D. R. Goodenough, and S. A. Karp, *Psychological Differentiation*, Wiley, New York, 1962.

44. Porteus, S. D., *Porteus Maze Test: Fifty Years Application*, Pacific Books, Palo Alto, Calif., 1965.

45. Alexander, D. A., A. Ehrhardt, and J. Money, *J Nerv Dis* 142: 161, 1966.

46. James, W. E., R. B. Mefferd, and B. Wieland, *Percept Mot Skills* 25: 209, 1967.

47. Gray, J. A. and A. W. H. Buffery, *Acta Psychol* 35: 89, 1971.

48. Washburn, S. L., in Roslansky, J. (ed.), *The Uniqueness of Man*, North-Holland, Amsterdam and London, 1969, p. 165.

49. van Lawick-Goodall, J., *Anim Behav Monogr* 1: 161, 1968.

Discussion: Aggression, Adaptation, and Evolution

HEINO F. L. MEYER-BAHLBURG, Moderator

DANIEL N. STERN, Rapporteur

Dr. Phoenix began by commenting that, in his experience with monkeys, castration may not change the levels of aggression nor the position of the castrate in the dominance hierarchy.

Dr. Moyer noted that aggression also may not change in man after castration, which is less surprising since much of the aggression in man is instrumental and based on learned responses. Castration need not affect learned patterns of behavior.

Dr. Phoenix added that animals frequently show sexual behavior for years after castration.

Dr. Rosenblum pointed out that the data given by Dr. Michael illustrated that sexual activity in rats can also diminish rapidly after castration. Dr. Michael answered that there is enormous individual variation as to whether copulatory activity will cease in weeks after castration or will continue for several years.

Dr. Rosenblum asked whether there were any clues in the behavior of individual animals prior to castration that might predict whether or not there would be a rapid decline in sexual activity. Dr. Michael knew of no predictive signs. Dr. Moyer added that, among humans as well, case studies showed that there is great individual variability in the response to castration and that many castrates continue a normal sexual life with an adequate adjustment.

Dr. Green asked whether the adrenal androgen levels in those men who continued their sexual functioning after castration were different from those who did not. He also raised the issue of individual differences in sensitivity to androgens. Dr. Michael then introduced the role of estrogens into the discussion by pointing out that it is an error to equate androgens with aggression and, reciprocally, estrogens with docility. Much evidence in mammals suggests that females, when coming into heat and under the influence of more estrogen, become increasingly aggressive.

Dr. Rosenblum added that in nonhuman primates there is an upsurge of sexual activity in the perimenstrual period. He wondered whether increased aggressive behavior in women at this time might reflect intensified erotic feelings that are not acted on because of cultural taboos against sexual activity during menstruation. Dr. O'Connor said that women do indeed show a small but definite peak in sexual activity just prior to menstruation.

Dr. Rosenblum observed that in free-ranging rhesus monkeys there is an upsurge of copulatory behavior during the perimenstrual period, but this increase is not as great as that seen at the peak of ovulation.

Dr. Michael noted that the taboo on sex during menstruation is also shared by male rhesus monkeys, who show a marked decrease in sexual activity with menstruating females.

Dr. Rosenblum then opened the discussion on adaptation and evolutionary perspective. He commented that the data from DeVore and others on bushmen and hunter–gatherer people reveal that animal protein is a relatively minor part of the diet and therefore the selective advantage of hunting skills and associated behavior patterns is not readily apparent. In light of this, he wondered why there was not as much selective pressure to evolve better gathering skills and related behaviors. Dr. Hamburg answered that the current hunter–gatherers have been pushed by civilization into a terrain different from their original environment in which animals for hunting were probably more available as a source of nutrition. Dr. Rosenblum remarked that nonhuman primates were exposed to the same adaptive pressures in the same terrain, but remained vegetarians whereas man evolved hunting skills. Dr. Hamburg commented that only man had the requisite hand and brain adaptive capability to allow the evolutionary route leading to hunting with tools. Dr. Rosenblum rejoined that, though this was true, it still remained unclear as to what the adaptive pressure or selective advantage was to become a hunter.

Dr. Michels pointed out that an immense selective advantage in favor of hunting is not necessary for its evolvement. If there is only a minimal survival advantage for a slight increment in size, strength, aggressiveness, or ability to hunt, these factors will be selected.

Dr. Stern took up Dr. Rosenblum's point, commenting that the selective pressures for dimorphism must have involved psychological or social factors equal to, and perhaps greater than, nutritional factors. For example, behaviors that permit and maintain a stable dominance hierarchy, with all of its survival value, would be selected. Accordingly, the major adaptive pressure may have been social, and the increased hunting ability, with its greater nutritional advantages, may have been a secondary phenomenon.

7 Perspectives on Psychoendocrine Differences

ANKE A. EHRHARDT, *Moderator*

RICHARD C. FRIEDMAN, *Rapporteur*

CHAPTER 20

The Bisexual Behavior of Female Rhesus Monkeys

RICHARD P. MICHAEL, MARGO I. WILSON, and D. ZUMPE
Department of Psychiatry
Emory University School of Medicine
Atlanta, Georgia and The Georgia Mental Health Institute

There are many reports that the females of various mammalian species show bisexual patterns of behavior (1). In contrast to this, the spontaneous occurrence of female patterns of sexual behavior in male mammals has been reported less frequently. Many factors must enter into the determination of this difference between the sexes, but the frequency and ease with which malelike mounting behavior occurs in females compared with the infrequency with which the lordosis response occurs spontaneously in males could be regarded as yet another example of a biologically determined gender difference. It may perhaps be emphasized that the foregoing generalization applies to spontaneously occurring behavior (i.e., to the normal behavioral repertoire), and not to experimental situations in which, for instance, hormones are administered to neonates or pharmacological doses of heterologous hormones are applied to castrates.

The majority of early observations on the bisexual behavior of females were made on lower vertebrates and on infraprimate mammals, and our present aim is to consider the implications of some of the more recent findings in primates. Sexually excited captive female tree shrews (Tupaii-dae) mount and rub against each other: the female-on-female mounts were usually of short duration, whereas the female-on-male mounts were longer and involved more conspicuous pelvic thrusting by the female (2). Mounting with pelvic thrusting by females on either males or females occurs frequently during play in squirrel monkeys (*Saimiri sciureus*) both under free-ranging conditions (3) and in captivity (4). On Lolui Island in Lake Victoria, Gartlan (5) observed five instances in which adult female vervet monkeys (*Cercopithecus aethiops*) mounted other females, and there were other occasions when adult females also mounted adult males. These latter mounts were associated with pelvic thrusting by the females, which immediately previously had been sexually presenting to the unresponsive males. Similar data were reported for vervets by Struh-saker (6). Captive female talapoin monkeys (*Miopithecus talapoin*) also mount males and executive vigorous pelvic thrusts (7). Free-ranging female rhesus monkeys (*Macaca mulatta*) mount each other (8), and the four incidents described in detail all occurred during, or about 1 month after, a period of behavioral estrus in both females of the homosexual pair. Carpenter also described an old, sexually excited female that mounted an unresponsive adult male. Another estrous female was observed to force a juvenile male into a posture that facilitated her mounting him. Captive female pigtail monkeys (*Macaca nemestrina*) mount other females and males (9). Females mounted other females throughout the cycle, but only mounted males when swollen at the height of sexual receptivity. Sexually swollen chacma baboons (*Papio ursinus*) occasionally show malelike mounting with other females (10), and captive female yellow baboons (*Papio cynocephalus*) seem frequently to be mounted by higher ranking females (11). Swollen captive female hamadryas baboons (*Papio hamadryas*) also mount each other (12), and captive female olive baboons (*Papio anubis*) mount other females throughout their cycle and occasionally clasp males (R. G. Evans and R. P. Michael, unpublished observations). In the wild, a mature female chimpanzee (*Pan troglodytes*) was observed to mount a young swollen female that had made the invitational crouching posture to her after having been rejected by a male (13). According to Hess (14), male and female sexual behavior in captive gorillas (*Gorilla gorilla*) may be shown by and toward both sexes, but homosexual interactions appear to be restricted mainly to immature individuals. Nevertheless, older females have been observed to assume the male role in "pseudocopulations" developing out of a play context.

We have given some well-authenticated examples of bisexual behavior in female primates that have been culled from the extensive literature now available. However, they indicate that mounting activity in females occurs most frequently at the time in the cycle when females are also sexually receptive to male conspecifics: in this respect, primates resemble such infraprimate mammals as rat, guinea pig, dog, and also the larger farm animals.

MOUNTING BEHAVIOR BY FEMALE RHESUS MONKEYS

Our own observations on the mounting behavior of female rhesus monkeys were made on a total of 40 jungle-bred, fully adult animals (weighing 4.5–8.0 kg) studied systematically during different periods between June 1963 and May 1971. Observations commenced at the conclusion of the quarantine period 3 to 4 months after arrival from India and were made during 1-hour tests in which each female was paired with a fully adult male partner; details of the testing procedure have been given previously (15). Many behavioral data were obtained during these tests, but of interest here is the finding that 15 females (37.5%) either made repeated mounting attempts on or actually mounted their male partners during some of the tests. Whether or not a female's mounting attempts resulted in a mount depended on both the persistence of her efforts and the tolerance of the male partner. In some cases, the male's response was immediately aggressive, and, after being attacked, the female never attempted to mount that male again. However, in five females (12.5% of 40) the activity of the female and the tolerance of the male were such that mounting behavior occurred with sufficient frequency and regularity to warrant numerical treatment.

The mounting posture assumed by a female depended a great deal on the behavior of the partner. During a mounting attempt, the female usually approached the male from behind and clasped his hips or waist with both hands, and if the male remained in a sitting position, the female would make vigorous pelvic thrusts against his back (Fig. 1). If, however, the male was standing on all fours at the time of the female's approach or adopted this posture in response to her clasp, the female would mount the male in a typically malelike fashion, grasping the backs of his legs with her feet while making vigorous pelvic thrusts against the male's anogenital region (Fig. 2, top left). The most experienced observer could mistake this behavior for the mounting and thrusting of a normal male. Mounting by the female often occurred in response to a male's grooming invitation, and when this was made by a male lying on the floor of the cage, it resulted in the female's moving completely onto his back, grasping his fur with hands and feet, while rubbing her genital region against his back in a series of pelvic thrusts (Fig. 2, top right).

Figure 1   A female clasp with pelvic thrusting. The female stands behind the seated male, and clasps his hips with both hands. In this position, the female makes pelvic thrusts against the male's back, smacking her lips as she does so.

Females also mounted seated and standing males, as illustrated in Figure 2 (bottom left and right). These patterns of female mounting were recorded on moving film, and the drawings in Figure 2 are traces of individual film frames. That mounting by the female sexually stimulated the male (as well as being merely tolerated) was indicated by the occasional simultaneous occurrence of male masturbation. Figure 2 (bottom right) shows a male rubbing his penis during the female mount, and the rhythm of his masturbation was synchronized with that of the female's pelvic thrusting. Furthermore, another male was seen actually to ejaculate while being mounted by the female and without any masturbation. Frame-by-frame analysis of female thrusting showed that either the

Figure 2   Female mounting behavior. Traces from moving film frames illustrating four different mounting positions by normal, jungle-reared adult female rhesus monkeys.

backward or the forward movement might be the stimulatory phase while the opposite movement was a recovery phase. In three females for which we have detailed numerical data, pelvic thrusting occurred during 87% of the mounts by female 55, 68% of the mounts by female 51, and 53% of the mounts by female 93. However, the mean number of pelvic thrusts per mount was lower for females than for males; females made approximately three to five thrusts, whereas males made over six thrusts per mount.

Although the male's behavior clearly plays an important part in determining the form of the female's mount, more detailed examination of the data showed that individual females had distinct preferences for certain postures. During 2444 tests, these five females showed 3837 mounting episodes. During 223 mounting episodes, female 13 almost invariably clasped the seated male from behind and made pelvic thrusts against his back (Fig. 1), and during 216 mounting episodes, female 16 almost always climbed on the back of the seated or standing male and then made pelvic thrusts. The distribution of different mounting postures adopted by the other three females is given in Table 1. Two females (13 and 51), then, most frequently used either the full malelike mount or an incomplete form of it (the hand clasp and the half-mount), whereas three females (16, 55, and 93) generally mounted the male's back or shoulders. On six occasions female 55 appeared to reach a sexual climax while mounted, showing small but obvious rhythmic contractions of the thigh muscles and around the base of the tail. This reaction occurred after a mean of 16.3 mounts and 102.3 thrusts, 27.5 minutes from the start of the female's mounting series.

We were impressed by the completeness with which these malelike patterns of behavior were expressed by jungle-raised females, especially because the opportunity for cognitive rehearsals of mounting is so low in genetic females during the first year of life—less than 1% that of similarly aged genetic males (16). In the male rhesus monkey, a prolonged period of sexual maturation after the time of puberty is needed for the full acquisition of adult levels of performance (17). Nevertheless, without these experiential factors operating to anything like the same degree, malelike patterns of mounting readily expressed themselves in

Table 1   *Distribution of Different Mounting Positions Adopted by Three Female Rhesus Monkeys*

Mounting Position	Frequency (%)		
	Female 55	Female 51	Female 93
Hand clasp from the rear	7	40	37
Half-mount	2	1	14
Malelike mount	0	51	2
Mount on male's back	91	8	27
Mount on male's shoulders	0	0	20
Total number of female mounting episodes	1666	1015	717

these jungle-bred adult females. The neural and muscular substrates for malelike behavior clearly existed in these females, they underwent appropriate maturation during the developmental period, and could express themselves when circumstances permitted. Since these behaviors occur in the wild, they are unlikely to be a captivity artifact; however, the frequency with which they occur may well be changed under captive conditions.

INFLUENCE OF THE MENSTRUAL CYCLE
AND THE EFFECTS OF OVARIECTOMY

The mounting behavior of two females (13 and 16) was studied in relation to their menstrual cycles. Female 13 was tested with two males throughout two consecutive cycles, and female 16 was tested with one male throughout three consecutive cycles, but during the last of these she was tested with a second male also. Figure 3 shows changes in the frequency of the mounting behavior by the females in all eight cases. Female 13 showed

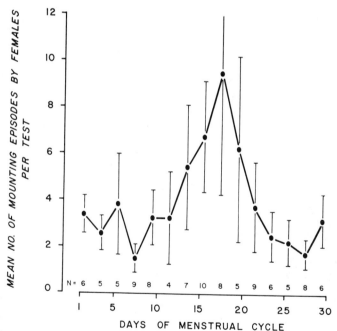

Figure 3   Changes in the frequency of mounting behavior by female rhesus monkeys in relation to the menstrual cycle. Each point gives the mean and standard error for 2 consecutive days; N=number of tests (four pairs, eight cases, 101 tests).

a marked increase in mounting near midcycle, with peak activity occurring on days 18, 15, 18, and 18 in the four cases, respectively. These peaks were near the expected times of ovulation (18), when female receptivity was high and male mounting activity was also at its height (19, 20). Female 16, on the other hand, showed a midcycle peak with only one male partner; with the other there were quite high levels of female mounting (four to seven mounts per test) throughout all three cycles.

Both females were studied during a total of 51 tests after bilateral ovariectomy (Table 2). There was a significant decrease in female mounting activity ($t = 3.95$, $p < .005$), and this was associated with a marked decrease in female receptivity: the number of sexual invitations made by females to male partners declined significantly ($t = 8.40$, $p < .001$), and there was a significant increase in the number of female refusals of male mounting attempts ($t = 2.63$, $p < .005$). The subsequent subcutaneous administration of estradiol benzoate, 25 μg/day for 22 days, to female 13 resulted in increased female mounting activity and restored her invitational behavior.

These data taken together demonstrate that the bisexual behavior of female rhesus monkeys depended on the secretory activity of the ovaries and was expressed most frequently at those times in the cycle, and under those hormonal conditions, when the female was also most receptive to the male. The results are in agreement with data from infraprimate mammals and confirm the incidental observations made in other primate species both in captivity and in the wild. However, the relative importance of the different hormones secreted by the ovaries in the control of female bisexuality has yet to be determined.

Table 2   *Effect of Ovariectomy on the Mounting Behavior of Two Intact Female Rhesus Monkeys[a]*

Behavior	Female Intact[b] Mean ± SE	Female Ovariectomized[c] Mean ± SE	t-Test
Mounts by female on male	4.06 ± 0.62	0.57 ± 0.20	$p < .005$
Invitations to mount by female to male	5.59 ± 0.46	0.72 ± 0.12	$p < .001$
Refusals by female of male mounting attempts	0.11 ± 0.04	0.61 ± 0.15	$p < .005$

[a] Four pairs, 152 tests.
[b] Total of 101 tests.
[c] Total of 51 tests.

OTHER SOURCES OF VARIABILITY–IDENTITY OF MALE PARTNER

It soon became apparent that the temperament and identity of the male partner determined to a considerable degree not only the type of female mounting posture, as already mentioned, but also its frequency. The effect of the male is clearly demonstrated in Figure 4, which shows the mounting frequency of female 13 when paired with each of two male partners during two consecutive menstrual cycles. Male 4 (upper graphs) was mounted throughout most of both cycles, and there were midcycle peaks, but male 12 (lower graphs) was mounted only on a few occasions near midcycle in each case, when her mounting on the other male was at its maximum. Similar findings were obtained with female 16 during the cycle in which she was also tested with two males: one male was tolerant of her behavior, and all mounts were complete and associated with pelvic thrusting; the other male was intolerant and permitted the female to

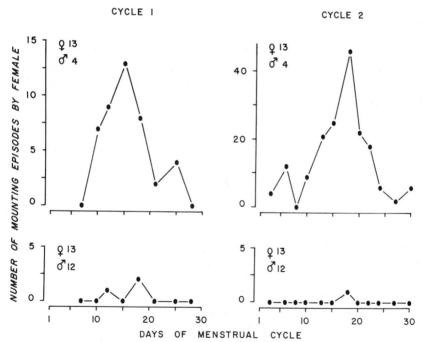

Figure 4 The influence of the male partner on the expression of mounting behavior by a female rhesus monkey throughout two successive menstrual cycles. With one male (upper graphs), mounting was at a much higher level than with the other male (lower graphs).

mount fully only once on day 14 and twice on day 16. There were indications in three of these four pairs that male tolerance of female mounting behavior declined in the early luteal phase, perhaps a pheromone-mediated change, and that male tolerance played an important part in determining the overall frequency of this bisexual behavior. The role of other factors, such as individual partner preferences, relative dominance relations within the pair, and hormone-dependent changes in female aggressivity and male tolerance (21), has still to be determined.

INFLUENCE OF THE MALE'S HORMONAL STATUS ON THE MOUNTING BEHAVIOR OF THE FEMALE PARTNER

Since the behavioral responses of the male appeared to influence the expression of bisexual behavior by the female, it seemed worthwhile to consider in more detail the factors operating within the male that might influence his tolerance of the female's behavior.

There was no very clear indication that younger, less dominant males were more tolerant of female mounting than were larger, more dominant males; in fact, although clearly dominant over the females, the four younger males for which we have data seemed quite apprehensive of mounting attempts by the females, and the mean numbers of female mounts per test were not higher for the younger than for the older group. In contrast, it was clear that older, more confident females were more likely to show this behavior, and we never saw bisexual patterns with any regularity in younger females with more timid dispositions. Unfortunately, we have no data on what the actual dominance hierarchy of these females was in relation to each other.

The influence of castrating the males, and of testosterone replacement treatment, on the bisexual behavior of the female partners was studied during 2280 tests. During these, three ovariectomized females subcutaneously injected with 5 to 10 μg/day of estradiol benzoate were partnered by eight males in a total of 12 paired combinations over a period of 36 months. The results were very striking. It can be seen in Figure 5 that castrating the males resulted in a progressive decline in their ejaculatory performance and that this was associated with a corresponding increase in female mounting activity: an effect that was reversed by administering testosterone (testosterone propionate, 1–2 mg/day, intramuscularly) to the males. Within 5 weeks of starting androgen treatment, mounting behavior by females declined to precastration levels. We concluded from these results that castrating these eight males had in some way released the bisexual behavior of their female partners from an

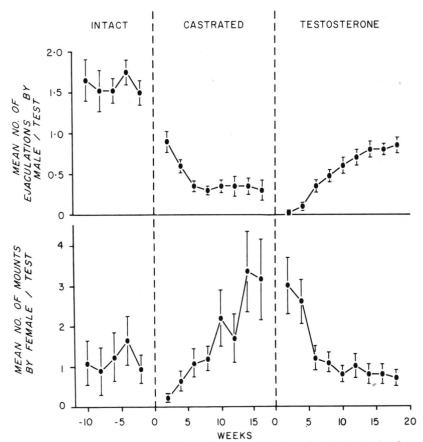

Figure 5 Castrating the males resulted in a progressive decline in their ejaculatory performance and in a corresponding increase in the mounting behavior of their female partners. Administering testosterone to the eight male castrates inhibited the bisexual behavior of the females. Each point gives the mean and standard error for consecutive 2-week periods (12 pairs, 1854 tests).

inhibition, but it is certainly difficult to understand the mechanisms that were involved. Although castrating male rhesus monkeys does not im-mediately reduce their mounting behavior (so that females continued to be mounted by males), it rapidly reduced their ejaculatory performance (22). Taking all tests (males intact, castrated, and testosterone-treated) with female mounting (783 tests), females mounted in 30% of tests in which ejaculation occurred and in 70% of tests in which ejaculation failed to occur. Thus mounting was more likely to be seen in tests with-out ejaculation. However, a more detailed examination of behavior during individual tests is needed, particularly of the relation of female mounting to the timing of ejaculation, before deriving conclusions about causation from this type of data. Nevertheless, it has been our impression that, when males failed to ejaculate despite increased female mounting invitations, the behavioral initiative swung away from the male toward the female.

It was noteworthy that female 51 never attempted to mount any male until 29 days after one of her partners had been castrated. She then made mounting attempts on her other three castrated partners within the next 48 hours. Similarly, female 93 attempted to mount one male 40 days after he had been castrated and then made mounting attempts on her three other partners, all of which were intact at the time, within the next few weeks. This seemed to indicate an extension of bisexual behavior toward other male partners when conditions had become appropriate for its first appearance.

These three ovariectomized, estrogen-treated females, two of which (51 and 55) were tested with the same four males (40, 53, 103, and 104), showed marked differences in the frequency with which they mounted different males: 82% of the mounting episodes of female 51 were with male 104, 67% of the mounting episodes of female 55 were with male 53 and 64% of the mounting episodes of female 93 were with male 102. Thus, when different females have a choice between male partners, all of which will tolerate being mounted, the females show individual partner preferences for the expression of their bisexual behavior.

SUMMARY

There was previously a lack of quantitative data on the expression of bisexual patterns of behavior in females of a primate species against which to evaluate the effects of experimental interventions. It now seems clear that malelike mounting behavior occurs as a part of the normal behavioral repertoire in about one-third of mature female rhesus monkeys that have been born and reared in the wild. However, bisexual behavior was observed with regularity only in about 12% of the females in our group. The occurrence of this behavior was influenced by the secretory activity of the ovaries: its incidence increased in intact animals near the expected time of ovulation and was greatly reduced by bilateral ovariectomy. Thus bisexual behavior was increased at those times and under those conditions when the heterosexual activity of the pair was maximal. These findings bring this primate species into line with several infraprimate mammals. Whether or not a given rhesus female would express any bisexual behavior was much influenced by the reactions of her male partner and by his tolerance of her behavior. It was noteworthy that, as ejaculatory performance declined after castration, there was also a progressive increase in the expression of bisexual behavior by the female partners. Thus the hormonal status of both male and female influenced the expression and frequency of her mounting behavior.

ACKNOWLEDGMENTS

This work was supported by grants from the Foundations' Fund for Research in Psychiatry, the Population Council, and the National Institute of Mental Health (5-R01-MH19506-01). Dr. Margo Wilson was supported by a Commonwealth Scholarship awarded by the Association of Commonwealth Universities. We thank Dr. J. Herbert for conducting some of the tests during the earlier years of this study.

REFERENCES

1. Beach, F. A., *Hormones and Behavior*, Hoeber, New York, 1948.
2. Conaway, C. H. and M. W. Sorenson, *Symp Zool Soc London* **15**: 471, 1966.
3. Baldwin, J. D., *Folia Primat* **11**: 35, 1969.
4. Ploog, D., S. Hopf, and P. Winter, *Psychol Forschung* **31**: 1, 1967.
5. Gartlan, J. S., *J Reprod Fertil Suppl* **6**: 137, 1969.
6. Struhsaker, T. T., *Univ Calif Publ Zool* **82**: 1, 1967.
7. Wolfheim, J. H. and T. E. Rowell, *Folia Primat* **18**: 224, 1972.
8. Carpenter, C. R., *J Comp Psychol* **33**: 143, 1942.
9. Tokuda, K., R. C. Simons, and G. D. Jensen, *Primates* **9**: 283, 1968.
10. Bolwig, N., *Behaviour* **14**: 136, 1959.
11. Anthoney, T. R., *Behaviour* **31**: 358, 1968.
12. Kummer, H., *Social Organization of Hamadryas Baboons*, University of Chicago Press, Chicago, 1968.
13. Goodall, J., in DeVore, I. (ed.), *Primate Behavior*, Holt, Rinehart and Winston, New York, 1965, p. 452.
14. Hess, J. P., in Michael, R. P. and J. H. Crook (eds.), *Comparative Ecology and Behaviour of Primates*, Academic Press, New York, 1973, p. 507.
15. Michael, R. P., G. S. Saayman, and D. Zumpe, *J Endocrinol* **41**: 421, 1968.
16. Goy, R. W., in Michael, R. P. (ed.), *Endocrinology and Human Behaviour*, Oxford University Press, London, 1968, p. 12.
17. Michael, R. P. and M. I. Wilson, *Endocrinology*, in press.
18. Hartman, C. G., *Contr Embryol* **23**: 1, 1932.
19. Michael, R. P. in Diczfalusy, E. and C. C. Standley (eds.), *The Use of Non-*

human Primates in Research on Human Reproduction, WHO Research and Training Centre on Human Reproduction, Stockholm, 1972, p. 322.

20. Michael, R. P. and J. Welegalla, *J Endocrinol* 41: 407, 1968.
21. Michael, R. P. and D. Zumpe, *Anim Behav* 18: 1, 1970.
22. Michael, R. P., M. I. Wilson, and T. M. Plant, in Michael, R. P. and J. H. Crook (eds.), *Comparative Ecology and Behaviour of Primates*, Academic Press, New York, 1973, p. 235.

CHAPTER 21

Plasma Testosterone Levels and Psychologic Measures in Men Over a 2-Month Period

CHARLES H. DOERING, H. K. H. BRODIE, H. KRAEMER,
H. BECKER, and D. A. HAMBURG

Department of Psychiatry
Stanford University School of Medicine
Stanford, California

The endocrinology of sex differences in behavior is a fascinating part of the more general problems of how hormones affect behavior. The study of the process of sexual differentiation from fetal development to adolescence provides a number of entrances into this complex problem area. In fetal development, numerous experimental approaches have been pursued with animals. Through the utilization of various "natural experiments," hormonal action on sexual differentiation has also been studied in humans. This approach is best exemplified by the work of Money and Ehrhardt (1). Less attention has been given to the process of differentiation in pubescence and adolescence. The advantages of a psychoendocrine study correlating behavioral and hormonal changes at puberty would be (1) the occurrence of fairly large changes and (2) the

413

use of the individual as his own control. Presently, most data are correlations of average values of the two parameters: pooled measures of behavior *versus* pooled hormone levels.

The link between hormones and behavior has, of course, been studied extensively outside the context of differentiation, as reviewed recently by Davidson and Levine (2). Classical methods involve the surgical removal and subsequent replacement of such endocrine glands as the testes, ovaries, adrenals, and pituitary. The observation is made that the removal of a gland, and consequently a hormone, can profoundly alter behavior patterns. Variations of this method involve the removal of glands at various early stages of development and the transplantation of glands.

The surgical research strategy is often coupled with experiments in which steroid hormones—generally in greater than physiological dosages—are infused and the effects on behavior are recorded. Methods of administering hormones have been refined enormously with the technique of stereotaxic implantation of micropellets into specific brain regions and, more recently, by the use of Silastic capsules and double cannulae.

The approaches just described frequently do not permit the establishment of a quantitative relationship between the hormone administered and the observed effect. An important question remains unanswered: Do the findings obtained with these fairly drastic interventions offer an explanation for natural behavior in intact animals? Do quantitative correlations observed in the experimental situation adequately describe the relationship between hormone levels occurring normally and variations in behavior in a natural setting?

One would think that answers to such basic questions would be established before issues regarding causality or mechanisms of action are addressed. However, very little information has been reported on the correlation of endogenous levels of steroid hormones and behaviors in normal individuals. The technical difficulty of making accurate and appropriate measurements on large numbers of samples was a major obstacle in this work. Only in the last 6 years have the relatively convenient protein saturation and displacement methods been developed for the analysis of androgens and estrogens in plasma, and these methods are still being improved. Earlier methods involving gas chromatography were quite flexible, specific, and accurate, but were time consuming and required relatively large plasma samples. Now it is possible to perform an assay speedily and on less than 1.0 ml of plasma. In fact, 1 ml of plasma would actually suffice to assay for four or five different hormones.

There are only a few reports in the literature concerning the correlations between individual behavior scores and endogenous hormone levels. Rose, Holaday, and Bernstein (3) brought together a colony of 34 male rhesus monkeys, who in 7 months established a stable, linear dominance hierarchy, during which time a variety of behavior was recorded for each male. Blood samples were obtained from each male and analyzed for total testosterone content. Rose et al. found that aggressive behavior correlated positively and significantly with testosterone concentration ($r = .47$; $p < .01$). Dominance rank was also positively correlated with testosterone concentration ($r = .35$; $p < .05$). Although related, aggressive behavior was not merely a reflection of dominance status. Several of the most aggressive individuals were considerably below the top-ranking male (tenth to twelfth). The human analogy to this is the report by Kreuz and Rose (4) on aggressive behavior and plasma testosterone in 21 young male criminals at a penal institution in Maryland. In contrast to the findings with the monkey colony, Kreuz and Rose report that testosterone levels neither correlated with the amount of fighting behavior nor with various psychologic test scales in this prison population. The authors noted, however, that the age of initial conviction of a more serious and violent crime in adolescence was negatively correlated with the plasma testosterone level at this later age ($r = -.65$; $p < .01$). Kreuz and Rose hypothesized that their prison inmates with higher testosterone levels "may have experienced earlier onset of testosterone rise and more rapid increase in levels and were therefore placed at increased risk to commit more violent and aggressive acts during adolescence" (4).

Another human study was conducted by Persky, Smith, and Basu (5), who determined plasma levels as well as production rates of testosterone in 18 normal young males and at the same time administered a battery of psychologic self-rating tests. Contrary to the findings of Kreuz and Rose, these authors reported a positive correlation between plasma testosterone and ratings of hostile and aggressive feelings among individuals. The best correlation was found between the production rate of testosterone and the Buss–Durkee Hostility Inventory. Moreover, a multivariate regression equation between the testosterone production rate and four psychologic measures of aggression and hostility accounted for 82% of the variance in the production rate of testosterone.

The investigation to be described was designed to answer several questions that have not been previously studied: What are the individual differences in androgen levels and in their stability over time? Are there any regular, periodic changes in androgen levels in the male? The major question, however, is whether changes in androgen level are associated with changes in self-perception of mood over a period of time. Finally, is there an association between the average levels of androgen and average mood states of each person when studied in relation to a group of individuals?

METHODS

Our subjects were 20 healthy male paid volunteers with a mean age of 23.4 years (range 20–28). They were screened by the Minnesota Multiphasic Personality Inventory and all scored within the normal range on all scales. The subjects were noninstitutionalized and carried out their normal daily activities throughout the study. For 2 months, every other morning at about 8 o'clock the subjects had a 10-ml blood sample withdrawn into heparinized Vacutainer tubes and completed the Multiple Affect Adjective Check List (MAACL) in our laboratory. The subjects also kept a daily diary recording the amount of sleep, sex, and drugs taken, as well as any outbursts of anger and other stressful events. Two other psychologic tests, the Personality Research Inventory and the Buss–Durkee Hostility Inventory, were administered to each subject once during the study.

The blood samples were refrigerated on collection. Within 2 hours plasma was separated and stored in a deepfreezer at $-25°C$ until assay. Plasma concentrations of total testosterone were determined by assaying each sample in duplicate by the modified technique of August, Tkachuk, and Grumbach (6). The method involved the extraction of 0.3 ml of plasma, purification of the extract by two thin-layer chromatograms in series, and quantitation by competitive protein binding (saturation analysis) with late-pregnancy plasma. Bound testosterone and free testosterone were separated by precipitation with ammonium sulfate. The samples in each assay were coded and analyzed in random sequence. The recovery generally ranged between 70 and 80% (determined for each sample by radiotracer.) The accuracy was determined by use of processed standards of testosterone (7) over the range of 0.5 to 2.0 ng; the average value found was 114% without blank correction. Blank values were 0.2 to 0.3 ng. The precision on the basis of duplicate determinations ranged between 8 and 14% (expressed as coefficient of variation) for the individual subjects.

Each adjective checklist was computer scored, the resulting ratings of hostility, anxiety, and depression being recorded for each subject-day. The diaries that the subjects were required to keep provided other quantifiable information, particularly on stress, anger, sleep, and sexual activity. Stress and anger were quantitated on an arbitrary four-point scale; the amount of sleep was calculated from the reported hours of retiring and awakening; and sexual activity was defined as the total number of reported orgasms per 48 hours. Sexual activity in the 24-hour period preceding and following the taking of blood samples also was extracted from the diaries and accumulated separately. Correlation coefficients were computed for each subject between each of the negative-affect scores, as well as the scores from the diaries and the corresponding plasma testosterone levels by the Pearson Product Moment procedure.

RESULTS

The mean hormone levels, mean affect scores, and several other measures of the 20 subjects are shown in Table 1. All these means are within the normal range expected for this population. For example, the mean testosterone level for all subjects of 618 ng/dl is very close to the means reported by a number of other laboratories for similar populations using a variety of methods, and the mean hostility score of 8.7 is quite close to the value of 8.5 reported by Zuckerman and Lubin (8) for their sample of college-age males on whom the MAACL was standardized.

The measures of testosterone, affect, and other categories derived from the diaries differed among the subjects not only in the overall levels of the measures but also in the labilities of the measures over time and in the degrees of correlation of these measures. We can illustrate testosterone and hostility variation over the 2-month period by showing the results for five of our 20 subjects.

Subject PR (Fig. 1) showed little variation in his testosterone and hostility ratings, and had low mean values with respect to the means for

Table 1   Mean Values for 20 Young Male Subjects Over 2 Months

	Mean	SD	Range
Plasma testosterone (ng/dl)	618	194	371 –1113
Hostility (MAACL scale)	8.7	1.6	6.0 –10.9
Anxiety (MAACL scale)	7.0	1.6	3.6 – 9.0
Depression (MAACL scale)	13.9	3.1	7.5 –18.6
Anger	0.42	0.54	0.0 – 2.1
Stress	1.2	1.1	0.0 – 4.1
Sleep in 48 hours (hours)	15.7	1.9	10.8 –19.4
Sex in 48 hours (orgasms)	1.02	0.57	0.11 – 2.08
Pretestosterone sex[a]	0.54	0.32	0.07 – 1.12
Posttestosterone sex[b]	0.48	0.28	0.00 – 0.95

[a] Number of orgasms on the day before blood sampling.
[b] Number of orgasms on the day after blood sampling.

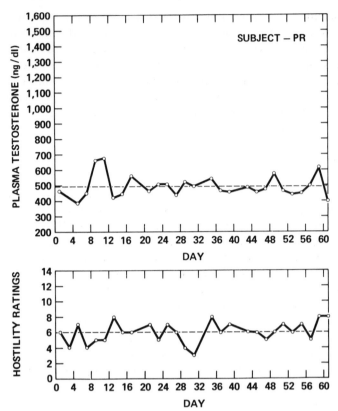

Figure 1   Concentrations of plasma testosterone and ratings of hostility obtained for PR, one of five adult males tested at the same time, over the course of 60 days. The values for testosterone are means of duplicate determinations by competitive protein binding method. The hostility ratings are derived from the Multiple Affect Adjective Check List. The broken line indicates the mean over the 60 days for the particular subject.

all 20 subjects. His testosterone and hostility ratings were inversely related: $r = -.55$, which is highly significant at $p < .005$ with 23 degrees of freedom (df).

Subject BE (Fig. 2) also showed little variation over time and had low mean values, but his testosterone and hostility ratings were significantly positively correlated: $r = .32$ ($p < .05$, 27 df).

Subject GO (Fig. 3) showed greater variability, but had an average level of hostility along with very low levels of testosterone. The two measures were significantly positively correlated: $r = .46$ ($p < .01$, 24 df).

Subject FA (Fig. 4) showed still greater variability, but had an average

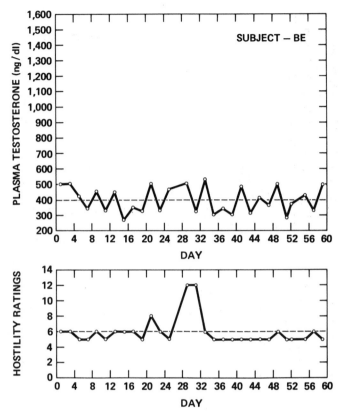

Figure 2   Concentrations of plasma testosterone and ratings of hostility for BE, an adult male subject (see caption of Fig. 1).

level of hostility along with very high levels of testosterone. The two measures, however, were not significantly correlated: $r=.17$ (N.S., 26 df).

The last of these examples is subject PH (Fig. 5), who showed enormous fluctuations in his testosterone levels. There was no significant relationship between his testosterone levels and hostility ratings: $r=.13$ (N.S., 21 df).

Intrasubject Correlations

The correlation coefficients for each subject between plasma testosterone levels and hostility, anxiety, and depression ratings ranged from significant positive values to significant negative values, with the majority being positive. Figure 6 shows the correlation coefficients for each of the 20 subjects; the majority of values cluster around zero, suggesting little con-

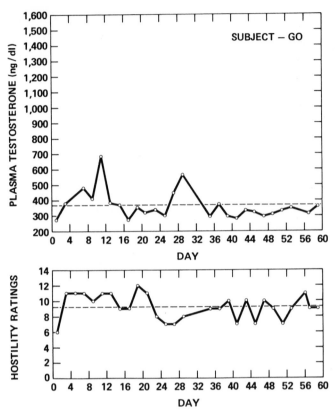

Figure 3   Concentrations of plasma testosterone and ratings of hostility for subject GO (see caption of Fig. 1).

sistent relationship between hormone levels and affect scores for an individual. As revealed by the chi-square test, we found significant individual differences among subjects in the degree of correlation between testosterone and anxiety ($\chi^2 = 33.0$, $p < .05$) and between testosterone and depression ($\chi^2 = 33.8$, $p < .05$). Testosterone and hostility correlations, on the other hand, were homogeneous ($\chi^2 = 22.5$, N.S.), and the pooled value was .09 (20).

The correlation coefficients within each subject between plasma testosterone levels and psychologic measures of anger and stress as well as amount of sleep and sexual activity also ranged from significant positive to significant negative values with a fairly homogeneous distribution. As was the case with the affect measures, there was no consistent relationship between hormone levels and anger, stress, sleep, and sexual activity for an

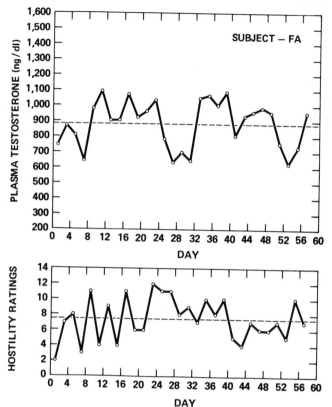

Figure 4 Concentrations of plasma testosterone and ratings of hostility for subject FA *(see caption of Fig. 1).*

individual. The pooled correlation coefficients were all close to zero (Figs. 7 and 8).

Intersubject Correlations

Calculating the mean of the approximately 30 values in each measurement of each subject we could compare such means across all 20 subjects. The resultant among-subject correlation coefficients between mean testosterone levels and mean affect scores were all positive and stronger than the pooled within-subject correlations. They are listed in Table 2. Although the correlation between testosterone and hostility and anxiety ratings failed to reach customary levels of significance, the correlation between testosterone and depression ratings was significant ($r = .45$; $p < .05$; 18 df). In the same among-subject comparison, the average levels

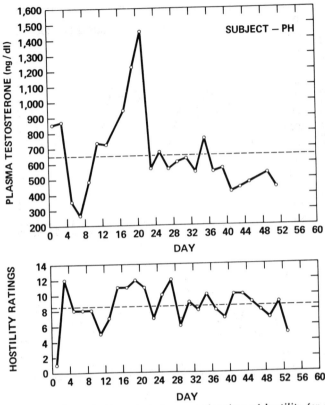

Figure 5　Concentrations of plasma testosterone and ratings of hostility for subject PH (see caption of Fig. 1).

of anger and average amounts of sleep were not associated with average testosterone levels. The correlation coefficient between stress levels and testosterone was positive and somewhat stronger, but still well below significance (Table 2).

The analysis of sexual activity data across all subjects yielded surprisingly strong negative correlation coefficients with testosterone levels. This was found in spite of the majority of within-subject correlation coefficients having been positive (see Fig. 8). For example, in the category of total sexual activity per 48-hour interval, there were 15 positive and 5 negative within-subject correlation coefficients with a pooled value of .07. The intersubject correlation coefficient, however, was computed to be a highly significant −.52 (two-tailed test; $p<.02$, 18 df).

In addition to the repeated administration of the MAACL, three other psychologic tests were administered to each subject once only. These were

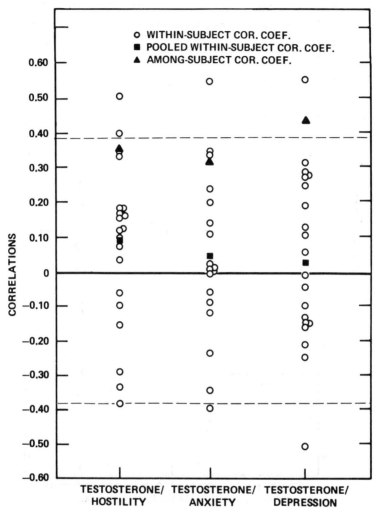

Figure 6   Correlation coefficients within each of the 20 subjects (○), the pooled value for 20 coefficients (■), and the among-subject correlation coefficient (▲) between plasma testosterone levels and the three affect ratings of hostility, anxiety, and depression. Any within-subject correlation coefficients (○) lying outside the limits indicated by broken lines are significant by two-tailed test (p<.05). The level of significance of among-subject correlation coefficients (▲) is found in Table 2.

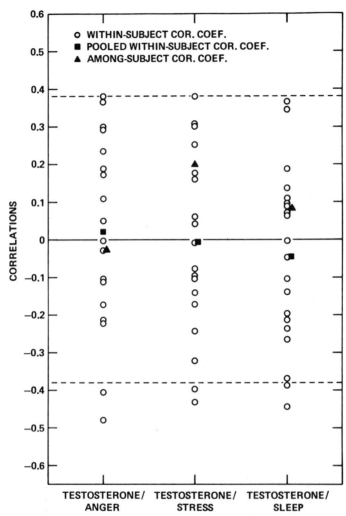

Figure 7   Correlation coefficients within each of the 20 subjects (○), the pooled value for the 20 coefficients (■), and the among-subject correlation coefficient (▲) between plasma testosterone levels and anger, stress and sleep (see also caption of Fig. 6).

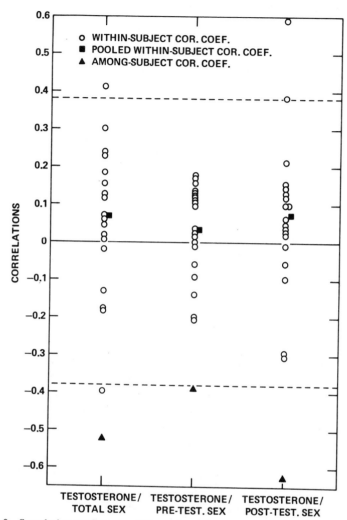

Figure 8 Correlation coefficients within each of the 20 subjects (○), the pooled value for the 20 coefficients (■), and the among-subject correlation coefficient (▲), between plasma testosterone levels and sexual activity. The total sexual activity during the usual 2-day interval is also broken down as sexual activity within the day before and within the day after the taking of a blood sample. (See also caption of Fig. 6.)

Table 2   Among-Subject Correlation Coefficients between Mean Concentrations of Plasma Testosterone and Mean Affect and Various Other Scores for 20 Young Adult Male Subjects

Testosterone versus	Correlation Coefficient	Level of Significance[a]
Hostility	.36	$p<.10$
Anxiety	.32	N.S.
Depression	.45	$p<.05$[b]
Anger	−.03	N.S.
Stress	.20	N.S.
Sleep	.08	N.S.
Sex, total	−.52	$p<.01$
Pretestosterone sex[c]	−.39	$p<.05$
Posttestosterone sex[d]	−.62	$p<.005$
Buss–Durkee, indirect subscale	.42	$p<.05$

[a]One-tailed test, 18 degrees of freedom.
[b]Also significant in a two-tailed test.
[c]Number of orgasms on the day before blood sampling.
[d] Number of orgasms on the day after blood sampling.

the Buss–Durkee Hostility Inventory (B–D), the Minnesota Multiphasic Personality Inventory (MMPI), and the Personality Research Inventory (PRI). A correlation matrix was computed for all the subscales of these tests as well as the B–D summation, B–D factors I and II, and the mean values of all the measures described above (testosterone, affect, etc.). Although this matrix included a number of strong and highly significant correlation coefficients between various psychologic test scores, the correlations between testosterone and psychologic scores were uniformly insignificant, except for those few already discussed, and the B–D indirect subscale (Table 2). It is particularly noteworthy that in our 20 subjects no significant relationship was found between mean plasma testosterone levels and the B–D summation of hostility nor between testosterone and B–D factor II (aggressive feelings).

DISCUSSION

To our knowledge, this is the first attempt to relate plasma testosterone levels and affective states over an extended period of time. The most striking observation is the lack of consistency among individuals in the hormone–affect associations. It has not been possible with our limited sample of 20 subjects to identify subsets of subjects on the basis of some other parameters.

The fluctuations of testosterone over the 2-month period were substantial for most individuals. The coefficients of variation ranged from 16 to 43%. The most probable source of this seemingly random pattern of peaks would be transient pulsatile changes of plasma testosterone concentration. The appearance of such peaks, on a time scale of hours, has been reported previously (9–12). The observed fluctuations may also reflect, in part, an unstable diurnal rhythm, as suggested by Fox et al. (13). A number of authors have described daily cycles of testosterone levels (14–19), but little is known about the stability of such cycles. Variations in amplitude and wavelength would appear as peaks and valleys of testosterone levels in samples taken at rigidly regular intervals, as we have done. Lastly, the presence of cycles with periods of several days or weeks would also contribute to the fluctuations described here and in other studies (4, 13). Regular cycles of one or two weeks' duration were not readily apparent in our subjects. The data are presently being analyzed by computer.

It is most striking that there are such large individual differences among the subjects in their labilities of plasma testosterone and affect ratings. However, a closer analysis of the labilities of all measures of all 20 subjects did not reveal any consistency of labilities; that is, subjects who are highly labile in testosterone levels may or may not be highly labile in other measures. Nor was lability related either to level of response or degree of correlation between testosterone and other measures.

Fox et al. (13) have described the relationship between sexual activity and plasma testosterone levels in one human male subject. Testosterone levels in samples taken immediately before and after orgasm were significantly higher than those found under resting conditions. These results do not contradict our finding, because in our study, orgasms may have occurred as much as 24 hours before or after blood samples were collected. In fact, a closer analysis of the report by Fox et al. (13) reveals important parallels to our study. First, two separate series of regular daily blood sampling, each for 43 days and at the same hour each day, are characterized by fairly large day-to-day fluctuations in plasma testosterone levels without a recognizable pattern. The majority of our subjects have very similar fluctuations. Second, Fox et al. have noted a relatively frequent coincidence of low control levels of testosterone on the days on which intercourse took place. The major testosterone peaks were never associated with sexual activity during their entire study of the combined length of about 86 days. Fox et al. conclude that rising levels of circulating testosterone probably are not involved in precipitating the desire for or initiating sexual activity. The literature contains several other anecdotal reports on related studies that cannot be reviewed here. More work needs to be done to clarify the underlying mechanisms operating in these relationships.

The lack of correlation between plasma testosterone and Buss–Durkee test scores, other than "indirect," is consistent with the findings of Kreuz and Rose (4) with a prison population. It is, however, in contrast to the findings of Persky et al. (5) with a normal male population. The latter reported correlation coefficients between plasma testosterone levels and the B–D summation of hostility of .49 and between testosterone levels and B–D factor II of .52 (both $p < .05$, 16 df). On the other hand, our finding of a positive relationship between plasma testosterone levels and the MAACL hostility ratings is consistent with that reported by Persky et al. (5), although their study differs from ours in that their results were based on only a single measurement of testosterone and hostility in each subject. The use of a single measurement in evaluating the degree of correlation produces an attenuation in the correlation coefficient (21) due to two factors: (1) intrinsic unreliability of the measurement and (2) lability of the subject's response over time. We have found that both sources of attenuation are substantial and believe, for this reason, that the use of single determinations of testosterone levels and single psychologic assessments leads to a poor indication of the relationship between the two. These statistical considerations make a strong case for replicate measurements on each subject. Repeated sampling is also indicated for biological reasons (i.e., the diurnal variations and the likelihood of episodic pulses of hormones in blood referred to earlier).

In connection with our strong positive correlation between mean plasma testosterone levels and mean depression ratings, we noted that the three affect ratings of hostility (H), anxiety (A), and depression (D) themselves were all highly interrelated, the correlation coefficients H/A, H/D, and A/D having been .83, .75, and .77, respectively. Zuckerman and Lubin (8), who devised the MAACL, reported similar high positive correlations. Thus our finding of similar correlation coefficients between testosterone levels and these three variables is not surprising. We had no reasons, however, to expect the testosterone and depression correlation to be the strongest, since there was no precedent in the literature. Persky et al. (5), for example, reported a correlation of .22 between plasma testosterone level and the MAACL depression ratings. Sachar et al. (22), in a study of 15 severely depressed older men who were psychiatrically hospitalized, found that plasma testosterone levels were normal and that there was no relationship among individual patients between testosterone levels and either severity of depression or recovery from it.

Assuming that correlations exist, the utilization of improved techniques should demonstrate hormone–behavior relationships less ambiguously. The influence of stress on affect and hormones may be stronger than expected and needs to be measured more carefully. It is of particular significance that the strongest correlation in our study was between testosterone and depression, and that the scale used to measure depression is probably the most accurate of the self-rating affect scales.

The biochemical measurement of circulating hormone can also be refined. A blood sample collected over about 30 seconds, as it is normally done, may contain the hormone at a concentration not at all representative of the average concentration for that individual. We are concerned that the changing blood levels heavily contribute to the methodological "noise," which can blot out the more subtle differences between individuals. This concern stems from the realization that the diurnal changes of testosterone levels have an amplitude of about 20% of the mean level and that the episodic, random peaks of testosterone levels, on the time scale of hours, may have an amplitude of up to 50% of the mean levels. The sampling technique evidently needs to be improved in future studies in order to obtain more representative samples. The pooling of multiple blood samples or the use of effusion pumps for blood withdrawal has already been advocated (11).

It is pertinent here to bear in mind that only a small percentage of circulating testosterone is not bound to protein, because it is this free testosterone that is generally considered to be physiologically active (23). In addition, the concentration of total testosterone in plasma may not be the best parameter of androgenicity nor be the best correlate for aggressivity or hostility (24). Metabolites of testosterone, the sum of certain metabolites, or the ratio of certain metabolites may be more appropriate parameters for our purposes.

SUMMARY

In a population of 20 young men, we have assessed the degree of correlation between a number of psychologic measures and the biochemical measure of plasma testosterone levels. Correlations were tested in two ways:

1. Within each individual over an extended period of time (28–30 observations per subject over 2 months). The major finding was that in each category the correlations ranged fairly evenly from significant positive to significant negative values. There was no consistent relationship between the psychologic measures, amount of sleep, or sexual activity and plasma testosterone levels over time.

2. A comparison among the subjects revealed a significant positive correlation between the average levels of self-perceived depression and the average concentration of plasma testosterone ($r = .45$).

The correlation between other psychologic measures and testosterone level was not significant, although self-perceived hostility versus plasma testosterone level closely approached significance. In addition, we found a strong inverse relationship among subjects between sexual activity and the mean level of plasma testosterone ($r = -.52$).

Even though about 600 samples were analyzed, the majority of correlations fell short of statistical significance. Furthermore, the relatively strong correlations between depression and testosterone level ($r = .45$) and between sexual activity and testosterone ($r = -.52$) account for only 19.8 and 27.2% (i.e., r^2), respectively, of the total variances. These findings, nevertheless, provide sufficient encouragement for further work.

ACKNOWLEDGMENTS

We thank Dr. Rudolf Moos for his valuable advice in the selection of psychologic test instruments. We thank Miss Anita Leung, Mrs. Kathleen Pelzmann, and Messrs. Jeffrey Shindelman and Michael Gage for expert technical assistance. We are also grateful to Misses Marianne Petersen, Judith Simms, Angela Williams, and Victoria Williams for help in evaluating the behavioral data; to Messrs. Charles Petty and Paul Sommers for computer scoring the MAACLS; and to Miss Irene Case for preparing the manuscript. We are particularly grateful to the Commonwealth Fund for their generous financial support of this work.

REFERENCES

1. Money, J. and A. A. Ehrhardt, *Man & Woman, Boy & Girl*, Johns Hopkins University Press, Baltimore, 1972.
2. Davidson, J. M. and S. Levine, *Ann Rev Physiol* **34:** 375, 1972.
3. Rose, R. M., J. W. Holaday, and I. S. Bernstein, *Nature* **231:** 366, 1971.
4. Kreuz, L. E. and R. M. Rose, *Psychosom Med* **34:** 321, 1972.
5. Persky, H., K. D. Smith, and G. K. Basu, *Psychosom Med* **33:** 265, 1971.
6. August, G. P., M. Tkachuk, and M. M. Grumbach, *J Clin Endocrinol* **29:** 891, 1969.
7. Nugent, C. A. and D. Mayes, in Diczfalusy, E. (ed.), *Steroid Assay by Protein Binding*, Second Symposium, Karolinska Symposia on Research Methods in Reproductive Endocrinology, Stockholm, 1970, pp. 257–274.

8. Zuckerman, M. and B. Lubin, *Manual for the Multiple Affect Adjective Checklist*, Educational and Industrial Testing Service, San Diego, Calif., 1965.

9. Evans, J. I., A. M. MacLean, A. A. A. Ismail, and D. Love, *Proc Roy Soc Med* **64**: 841, 1971.

10. Evans, J. I., A. W. MacLean, A. A. A. Ismail, and D. Love, *Nature* **229**: 261, 1971.

11. West, C. D., D. K. Mahajan, V. J. Chaure, C. J. Nabors, and F. H. Tyler, *J Clin Endocrinol* **36**: 1230, 1973.

12. Brodie, H. K. H. and K. Pelzmann, unpublished observations.

13. Fox, C. A., A. A. A. Ismail, D. N. Love, K. E. Kirkham, and J. A. Loraine, *J Endocrinol* **52**: 51, 1972.

14. Curtis, G. C., *Psychosom Med* **34**: 235, 1972; see references cited therein.

15. Nieschlag, E. and A. A. A. Ismail, *Klin Wochenschr* **48**: 53, 1970.

16. Okamoto, M., C. Setaishi, K. Nakagawa, Y. Horiuchi, K. Moriya, and S. Itoh, *J. Clin Endocrinol* **32**: 846, 1971.

17. Faiman, C. and J. S. D. Winter, *J Clin Endocrinol* **33**: 186, 1971.

18. Rose, R. M., L. E. Kreuz, J. W. Holaday, K. J. Sulak, and C. E. Johnson, *J Endocrinol* **54**: 177, 1972.

19. Alford, F. P., H. W. G. Baker, Y. C. Patel, R. C. Rennie, G. Youatt, H. G. Burger, and B. Hudson, *J Clin Endocrinol* **36**: 108, 1973.

20. Kraemer, H. C., submitted for publication to *Encyclometrica*.

21. Walker, H. and J. Lev, *Statistical Significance*, Holton, New York, 1953, pp. 299–301.

22. Sachar, E. J., F. Halper, R. S. Rosenfeld, T. F. Gallagher, and L. Hellman, *Arch Gen Psychiat* **28**: 15, 1973.

23. Vermeulen, A. and L. Verdonck, *J Steroid Biochem* **3**: 421, 1972.

24. Grant, J. K., in Baird, D. T. and J. A. Strong (eds.), *Control of Gonadal Secretion*, Edinburgh University Press, Edinburgh, 1971, pp. 193–202.

CHAPTER 22

Aggression, Androgens, and the XYY Syndrome

HEINQ F. L. MEYER-BAHLBURG

Departments of Pediatrics and Psychiatry
State University of New York at Buffalo School of Medicine
Children's Hospital of Buffalo
Buffalo, New York

The etiology of sex differences in aggression is still a matter of debate. Environmentalists hold parental rearing and sex typing responsible. Ethologists, by contrast, point out that sex differences in aggression are found throughout all mammalian species, from rats to monkeys, and that the same biological factors that determine sex differences in subhuman mammals probably play a role in human behavioral sex differences as well.

In this context, the XYY syndrome is of special interest: it is generally believed to be associated with aggressive behavior and is a sex-chromosome disorder, which may tell us something about how sex chromosomes affect sex dimorphic behavior. There is quite a body of physiological and behavioral data available on this syndrome which warrants close scrutiny regarding possible biological, especially hormonal, determinants of aggressive behavior in man. The discussion to follow will focus on the 47, XYY condition and disregard mosaic and other forms of the YY genotype.

433

Since the mid 1960s, the XYY male has become a kind of evil hero. Many people visualize him as the aggressive criminal, the tall supermale—a sinister hyperbole of masculinity. Such was not the case when the first XYY male was described in 1961 by Sandberg and co-workers (1). This man had been karyotyped because there was a child with Down's syndrome in his family. He was neither a criminal nor an excessively violent person, but a hard-working man living within a stable marriage. Subsequently more patients were discovered. Karyotyping concentrated first on persons with physical abnormalities—in particular, abnormalities of the genitalia. Thus it is not surprising that, among the limited number of cases known by 1965, the condition of the genitalia was described in 10 patients; eight of them had genital abnormalities.

Public interest in the XYY syndrome developed with a spectacular headline in *Nature*: "Aggressive Behavior, Mental Subnormality and the XYY Male," by Jacobs and co-workers (2) in 1965. They had karyotyped inmates of the maximum security state hospital at Carstairs in Scotland and found seven, and later, two more XYY men among 315 males, a prevalence rate of nearly 3%. This was an extraordinarily high percentage for a rare chromosomal disorder and led to speculation about cytogenetic determinants of criminality and aggression. Many surveys have since been reported on inmates of prisons, mental institutions, maximum security hospitals, and the like, and hundreds of XYY males have been found, many of whom manifest severe behavior disorders.

The main questions to be examined here are the following:

1. Is the XYY syndrome really associated with an aggressive behavior disorder?

2. If so, what are the predominant factors involved in the development of this aggressive behavior?

3. Do sex hormones play an etiologic role?

ILLUSTRATIVE CASES

In order to demonstrate the range of behavior patterns one may find in XYY subjects, nine cases that have been studied in our Buffalo unit will be described. Three of these (cases 1, 2, and 3) had been discovered in systematic genetic prevalence studies of delinquent subjects (3), the other six in routine clinical examinations for either physical disability or known chromosomal abnormalities in family members.*

* With the exception of case 4, all of these cases have been already reported (4).

XYY Subjects Found in Prevalence Studies

Case 1: Age 14 Years and 11 Months, Height 178 cm.   Severe learning "disability." Repeated kindergarten. Several years of special school for learning disorders. Severe aggressive behavior disorder since age 5. At age 11 years and 8 months, strangled a 5½-year-old neighborhood boy (almost fatally). After this, was in two institutions for juvenile delinquents. On parole since age 14 years and 9 months.

Case 2: Age 18 Years and 11 Months, Height 184 cm.   Severe learning "disability." Severe aggressive behavior disorder. Since age 9, in several institutions for same. Since age 13 years and 10 months, has been in mental institutions. Free since age 15 years and 10 months. Occasional jobs, thefts, probably robbery; at present on trial because of forcible intercourse.

Case 3: Age 27 Years and 10 Months, Height 190 cm.   Behavior problems and school failure at least since age 7. Long history of antisocial behavior, including physical attacks, thefts, armed robbery, desertion, and the like. Spent 1 year in a psychiatric hospital at age 17 for behavior problems. Later in prisons and treatment program for drug abuse. Presently on parole. Married 4 years; wife considering divorce.

XYY Subjects Found in Clinical Routine Examinations

Case 4: Age 3½ Years, Height 90 cm.   Several physical symptoms, including webbed neck and malfunction of one kidney. Due to genitourinary pathology has had 10 surgical experiences; presently wears appliance for urination. No aggressive behavior disorder known. Intelligence normal.

Case 5: Age 8 Years and 3 Months, Normal Height.   Two members of family have Down's syndrome. Severe learning "disability," repeated first grade, now attending special school. Since age 3, moderately aggressive behavior problems with children and adults.

Case 6: Age 11 Years and 9 Months, Height 147 cm.   Severe learning "disability." Repeated kindergarten, currently attends special school. Since age 6, moderately aggressive behavior problems with children and adults.

Case 7: Age 17 Years and 3 Months, Height 201 cm.   Very severe learning "disability," does not read or write. Severe aggressive behavior disorder; first problems reported at age 2 years and 4 months. Born out of wedlock, lived in three different foster families from age 1 year, 10 months to 8 years, 8 months. In mental institution since age 10.

Case 8: Age 21 Years and 11 Months, Height 202 cm. Mild learning difficulties, but clearly less talented than brothers who attend college. High school graduate. No aggressive behavior problems. Working as crane-man.

Case 9: Age 54 Years, Height 188 cm. Average student. Frequent physical fighting during his twenties; still fights occasionally when provoked. Hard working. In stable second marriage for 19 years. [This is the XYY man first described by Sandberg et al. (1).]

These nine cases are characteristic of subjects reported in the literature. Most XYY males have a normal masculine physique, frequently combined with a tall stature. They demonstrate wide variations in abilities and behavior, covering the entire spectrum from superior intelligence to mental retardation and from normal to extremely disordered behavior. Unfortunately, a severe sampling bias exists in studies of the XYY syndrome because reported cases come chiefly from prisons and mental hospitals where chromosomal surveys have been conducted (following the model of the original Carstairs project). In our sample, the three males who were discovered in genetic surveys of delinquents are much more deviant in behavior than the six diagnosed during routine clinical examination.

INCIDENCE AND PREVALENCE OF XYY MALES

Since the publication of the original Carstairs survey (2), there have been numerous incidence and prevalence studies of newborn populations as well as of various selected inmate and other samples. In 1970, the Center for Studies of Crime and Delinquency of the National Institute for Mental Health (NIMH), which had created a task force on the XYY syndrome, compiled the data available and published the following figures as best estimates (5):

1. Incidence rate of XYY syndrome in unselected newborns: 1.8 in 1000 (12 XYY babies were found among about 6700 newborns).

2. Prevalence of XYY syndrome among inmates of various penal and mental institutions, unselected for height: 7.1 in 1000 (17 XYY males were found among 2391 inmates; eight studies).

3. Prevalence of XYY among inmates selected for tall stature (approximately 6 ft upward): 29.1 in 1000 (86 XYY males were found among 2951 inmates; 37 studies).

Thus, according to NIMH, it appeared that the prevalence of the XYY genotype in criminal and mental institutions, and especially among tall inmates, was definitely higher than the incidence rate in newborn. Obviously, XYY individuals run a higher risk of being institutionalized (mentally or criminally) than do XY males. It would also seem that they are more likely to be very tall.

A second, thorough review of XYY data that incorporates more recent surveys has been presented by Hook (6), who obtained a pooled frequency of about 1 in 1000 for the incidence rate in newborns, which is somewhat below the NIMH estimate. Rates in individual studies range from 0 to about 4 in 1000. The data on inmate populations were divided by Hook into those obtained from mental institutions, from penal institutions, and from mental–penal settings, such as hospitals for the criminally insane or security wings in hospitals for the retarded. Excluding the first Carstairs report, which had described an extraordinarily high prevalence rate of XYY in mental–penal situations, Hook found 35 subsequent studies of mental–penal settings to date. In 20 of these studies which were not restricted by height and for which exact data were provided, the pooled frequency of XYY males was 72 out of 3813, or 1.89%. The median rate of the 20 studies was 2.05% and the mean, 2.05%. Thus Hook arrived at a point estimate of 20 in 1000 for the prevalence rate of XYY males in mental–penal settings of the type represented. This figure is about 20 times the pooled newborn rate of 1 in 1000. All of these investigations took place in Europe, Australia, and North America and include predominantly white samples. With regard to exclusively penal or exclusively mental settings, Hook did not find a consistent trend; if there was any increased incidence of XYY males it appeared smaller than that in combined mental–penal settings.

AGGRESSION IN THE XYY SYNDROME

Why are XYY males overrepresented in mental–penal and possibly other institutions, when compared with their newborn rate? Obviously, they must have a behavior disorder of some type. Is this behavior disorder an aggressive one? Are XYY males perhaps even more aggressive than their fellow inmates? The first relatively well-controlled study to address this question was done on the Carstairs sample in Scotland. Price and Whatmore (7) compared the nine XYY subjects with 18 randomly selected controls from the same institution and found that (1) XYY inmates displayed less violence against persons in their criminal behavior than did control inmates; (2) XYY patients initiated criminal activity approximately 5 years earlier than other inmates; (3) they had no significant family history of crime or mental illness; (4) they had severe personality disorders; and (5) in the past, their criminal behavior had proved to be resistant to conventional forms of corrective training and treatment.

A more recent comparison study (8) used pair-matched controls. Again, XYY males did not demonstrate more violent crime than did control inmates, but they did have records of more theft and breaking-in offenses and a greater number of convictions. It was not confirmed that XYY males have first convictions earlier than their fellow prisoners.

There is a third, very comprehensive, study by Casey and co-workers (9), in which XYY males are compared to fellow inmates. Here, XYY subjects had committed more sex offenses and more property offenses than the controls, but committed slightly fewer crimes against the person. There was no difference in the total number of convictions. In one of the two institutions studied by Casey's group, XYY subjects were first convicted at a significantly earlier age than the controls, but in the other institution, there was only a negligible difference.

From the foregoing three studies, one has to conclude that XYY males in mental–penal institutions are basically admitted for the same reasons as their fellow inmates and that they do not commit a greater number of violent crimes. The problem remains that the population of XYY males in these institutions is greater than would be expected from the incidence of XYY newborns in the general population.

Crimes, of course, need not necessarily involve aggressive behavior. Individuals are frequently admitted to a mental–penal institution because of social deviance rather than conviction of a criminal offense. Thus we can ask if the XYY male—irrespective of the particular crime he was convicted of—exhibits unusually aggressive behavior or certain forms of such behavior that ultimately lead to his being institutionalized. The problem one encounters in this context is the question of how to classify human aggressive behavior. Standard assessment methods like the Buss aggression machine or hostility questionnaires are often not appropriate for these clinical samples and hardly permit inferences to overt behavior. A classification system is needed for the specific nature of the behavior of these individuals that results in conflict with others.

To illustrate, the behavior of two patients mentioned earlier will be described. One is the teenage boy (case 1) who had nearly strangled a little neighbor in earlier years. During test sessions in my office, this patient poked holes into papercups, pushed wires into a test apparatus, or hammered continuously with a stylus on metal. At home, he repeatedly burned carpets with cigarettes or smashed doorframes with hammers. Although cowardly with same-size peers, he frequently harassed smaller children and animals. By contrast, the very tall boy (case 7) from a psychiatric institution was usually very quiet in the Clinical Research Center. At the state hospital, however, he had temper tantrums, attacked hospital attendants, threatened personnel with knives, and vandalized offices. Several times he thrust his arms through glass windows and produced severe lacerations. Do these two patients manifest different expressions of the same behavior disorder? Or do they display two different assortments from a variety of independent forms of aggressive behavior?

Since a satisfactory classification system does not exist, ad hoc categories will be used to characterize the aggressive behaviors exhibited by our Buffalo patients. Six of the nine patients tended to have sudden, frequent dysphoric mood changes which were often expressed explosively. In addition, the patient originally described by Sandberg et al. (1) appears to have been moderately quiet in childhood, but participated in physical fighting almost continually during his midtwenties and still becomes involved in occasional active fighting. Four of the six patients with temper tantrums have a history of violent attacks on males. Typical releasers of temper behavior in our patients were demands by authority figures such as parents, teachers, supervisors or by peers and non-specific frustrations. A tendency to destructive behavior was present in three patients, and one additional patient exhibited destructive fantasies.

Of the remaining patients, only one with cryptorchidism appeared uninclined toward aggressive behavior, although a few years previously he had broken another high school student's jaw after repeated provocation.

The impression obtained from the literature is similar. Owen, in his 1970 review on the XYY syndrome (10), listed behavioral characteristics as they were reported, again not using any systematic classification. The category that included the largest number of patients was "temper outbursts, tantrums, head banging tantrums, sudden fits of violent rage and anger, aggressive," all of which corresponds to our own findings. Many more of the reported patients fall into this category than into categories of undisturbed behavior, such as "not aggressive, not aggressive to patients, not overtly aggressive," or "not a behavior problem, no signs of an antisocial attitude," or "outgoing, friendly, extroverted, good humor," and so on. These findings, however, do not justify the conclusion that XYY males are really more frequently aggressive than XY males, because most XYY patients so far described in case reports or group studies have come from institutionalized populations.

As we lack a systematic classification system for human aggressive behavior as well as base rates for the different forms of aggression in the general population, no data can be presented that would directly answer the question whether there actually is an increase of aggression in the

XYY syndrome. Such an increase is quite likely, however, for two reasons: (1) the modal behavior category for cases reported is aggression of some type (usually temper), but not other forms of psychopathology; (2) the special character of mental–penal institutions, which are predominantly designed to hold potentially dangerous subjects (i.e., aggressive disorders). Thus let us assume for the discussion to follow that there *is* a higher incidence of severely aggressive XYY males than expected from the XYY newborn rate. A number of possible contributing factors must be considered in order to explain this phenomenon.

SEX CHROMOSOMES AND AGGRESSION

There appears to be something magic about sex chromosomes that fosters hasty conclusions. We do not know exactly why the concept of the aggressive XYY supermale "predestined to crime" became so popular but the reasoning behind it must have been as follows: Klinefelter's disease (the double X syndrome, 47, XXY), in which there are two female chromosomes and one male chromosome, typically produces a somewhat demasculinized man: hypogonadal, often with breast development at puberty, and infertile. Thus, by analogy, the double Y genotype should lead to hypermasculinity. This premature conclusion draws support from the fact that XYY males tend to have tall stature, which is expected, as XY males are taller than XX women. By the same reasoning, XYY males should be more aggressive than XY males.

The major problem with this naive approach is that we do not know to what degree sex chromosomes affect psychosexual differentiation. Sex chromosomes are certainly directly involved in the differentiation of the gonads in the early embryo. But according to present understanding, subsequent differentiation is determined by gonadal hormones. At least for the euploid genotype, sex steroids may overrule the genetic sex completely (11). So far, no one has been able to demonstrate that sex chromosomes are directly involved in the differentiation of sex dimorphic behavior.

Direct chromosomal effects appear to show up more in aneuploid conditions when there are too many or too few chromosomes. A very good example is Klinefelter's disease. If there was a simple additive mechanism, such as the Y chromosome providing for male behavior and supernumerary X chromosomes demasculinizing the male, then we should expect the XXY syndrome to be less frequently represented in mental–penal and related institutions than would be expected from the XXY newborn rate. Quite the contrary is true. The newborn rate of XXY males is about 1.1 to 1.2 per 1000 (6, 12). The prevalence figures of XXY males in mental–penal institutions pooled over available samples is 10 per 1000. Thus it appears that the XXY male also has an increased risk of showing up in a mental–penal setting, but possibly, not as great a risk as an XYY male. In addition, the XXY male is more likely to be a high-grade retarded than the XY, and probably the XYY, male (6).

In several studies, XXY and XYY patients found in the same or comparable institutions were compared with regard to deviant behavior. Only Nielsen (13) found that violent crime was significantly higher in XYY males than in patients with Klinefelter's syndrome. These results could not be confirmed by three other research efforts (11, 14, 15).

The most comprehensive study comparing XYY, XXY, and controls from the same institutions was carried out by Casey and co-workers (9). Both XYY and XXY males had a higher number of sex offenses and property offenses than did controls, but fewer offenses against the person. In one of the two institutions studied, both XYY and XXY males were younger at first conviction than controls. While there was no significant difference between XYY and XXY males in sex offenses, offenses against the person, or "other offenses," XXY males had significantly more property and absconding offenses than did XYY males. Apparently, the differences in deviant behavior between XYY and XXY males, if any, are not very dramatic. Thus it would seem more likely that an unusual chromosome count, the aneuploidy, makes for a higher risk of deviant behavior rather than any specific difference between the Y and the X chromosomes. Definite conclusions cannot be drawn yet, however, for recent findings that deviant behavior may correlate with the size of the Y chromosome (62), if confirmed, would make additional explanations necessary.

HORMONES AND AGGRESSION

The next question is whether gonadal hormones are related to aggressive behavior in XYY males. It is well known that, in many subhuman mammalian species, from the rat to the rhesus monkey, males demonstrate much more threat and fighting behavior than do females and that these sex differences are determined by androgen levels (16). In male rats, spontaneous fighting does not start before puberty (17); furthermore, castration of postpubertal males diminishes spontaneous fighting, and testosterone therapy restores their readiness to fight, at least partially (18). Testosterone therapy of adult male rats, however, does not bring about the normal male frequency of fighting behavior if the castration was performed at neonatal age—that is, during the critical phase of central nervous system differentiation. Testosterone-replacement therapy is successful if castration takes place at weaning age (21 days) or later (19). In mice, the effect of neonatal castration can be prevented by one subsequent dose of testosterone (20). Neonatal testosterone treatment of female mice followed by testosterone treatment in adulthood brings about the same fighting behavior as that shown by normal males, while neonatally untreated female mice do not respond to testosterone treatment in adulthood (21, 22). In several rodent strains where males normally show relatively low levels of aggression, aggressive behavior cannot be enhanced by exogenous testosterone injections in adulthood. However, recent studies with hamsters (23) show that, at least in this species, exogenous testosterone given to intact animals shortly after birth can increase aggression above normal adulthood levels. There are certainly strain differences as to the degree of hormonal effects. However, it appears to be generally valid for rats and mice that, in the presence of androgens during the critical time of neonatal differentiation, certain central nervous system structures are organized in such a way that they respond to androgen treatment in adulthood; thereby, the readiness for aggression or the probability of aggressive behavior with adequate environmental stimulation is increased.

To date, there have been no studies of the relationship between endogenous testosterone production and aggression in lower mammals. However, in primates, one such study has been reported: Rose, Holaday, and Bernstein (24) found that, in a group of 34 adult male rhesus monkeys, plasma testosterone levels correlated positively with behavioral dominance and other aggression measures. In a second study, Rose, Gordon, and Bernstein (25) demonstrated that the plasma testosterone level can be strongly influenced by aggression. Single male rhesus monkeys were placed with an established group of males and thereby exposed to the group's aggressive responses. The newcomers soon became submissive to all monkeys of the group. They were then isolated and blood samples were taken. Their plasma testosterone levels fell 80% from the initial values, and the decrease was demonstrable for several weeks after this event. Consequently, the blood level of testosterone is not a fixed quantity that affects behavior. Rather, endogenous hormone production can be drastically influenced by behavioral variables. Thus the cause-and-effect relations of testosterone levels and dominance status remain to be clarified.

What data are available for man with regard to the relationship of androgens to aggression? As in most subhuman mammals, man also demonstrates a pervasive sex difference in aggressive behavior (26). We do not yet know to what extent prenatal androgens contribute to this difference

(11). Evidence of the role of postnatal androgens in human aggression is still scarce. Castration is being performed in several countries as a treatment for sexual offenders (27–32). If androgens had a role in adult human aggression, castration in adulthood might effectuate a decrease. Indeed, castration of adult males *has* been of value in the treatment of aggressive sexual offenses (31). However, Bremer (29), who followed 167 castrated males of different psychiatric diagnostic groups for 1 to 10 years after surgery, came to the conclusion that castration did not inhibit aggression unless it depended directly on the sex drive. Other authors (30) have noted a clear-cut loss of energy in some castrates, but the effects are apparently less dramatic than those in lower mammals.

Testosterone levels can be lowered not only by means of surgical castration but also by the exogenous application of hormones that depress pituitary gonadotrophin production and consequently testosterone levels. Blumer and Migeon (33) tried this approach with medroxyprogesterone acetate (MPA) in a variety of aggressive patients, apparently with success. It is doubtful, however, that their success was due to the effect on androgen production, since the MPA treatment decreased aggressive behavior at a relatively low dose level—a level that was not fully effective in suppressing sexual behavior, which is known to depend on androgens. Aside from its gonadotrophin-depressing effect, progesterone can also have a direct inhibitory effect on brain activity (34), and it may well be that the latter was responsible for the effect on aggression.

Thus the castration studies do not provide satisfactory evidence of a role of androgens in human aggression. Another source of such evidence is a number of clinical reports (35–38) that testosterone treatment of juvenile patients may stimulate increased aggressiveness in both aggressive and passive children, producing deleterious effects in those who were already aggressive and beneficial effects in those who were not aggressive enough. Unfortunately, the documentation of these differential effects is unsatisfactory.

In the last 3 years, studies have been published which deal directly with the question of whether androgen production and aggression are correlated in humans. Persky, Smith, and Basu (39) studied a group of 18 young college males and obtained remarkably high correlations between questionnaire measures of aggression and plasma testosterone levels. They could not find any relationship between androgens and aggression in an older group of men (age 31–66 years), whose hormone production was considerably lower than that of the college group. An independent replication of the Persky study by this author and co-workers (40) using an extreme-groups design with another group of young college males failed.

Kreuz and Rose (41), who investigated a sample of young male prisoners, also failed to obtain a correlation between plasma testosterone levels and questionnaire aggression. They divided their sample into two groups, high versus low aggression in everyday prison life, but did not find a corresponding difference in plasma testosterone levels. However, there were correlations between biographical data and androgens: plasma testosterone levels were higher in those prisoners who had committed juvenile violent crimes against the person. Correspondingly, age at first criminal conviction correlated significantly in the negative direction with plasma testosterone levels. This result, if replicable, could be of great theoretical importance.

From the studies mentioned, it appears that judgment must be reserved regarding the degree to which androgens might influence aggressive behavior in human males. Even if a correlation could be confirmed, the cause-and-effect interactions would not be readily apparent. Also in humans, behavioral variables can affect androgen levels: emotional stress (42, 43) and surgical stress (44–46) depress plasma and urinary testosterone levels; physical exercise increases serum androgens (47). However, it is not very likely that the results obtained with monkeys by Rose and co-workers will be replicated in human males. In rhesus monkeys, both dominance status and testosterone production seem to depend on the structure of the one group the monkey belongs to. Human males, by contrast, are members of multiple groups with variable status. Moreover, dominance in human groups is less related to physical power than it is in animals.

Perhaps a different model of interaction between androgen levels and behavior is more appropriate for human aggression: the one suggested by Raboch and Stárka (48) for sexual behavior. From their findings of negligible correlations between marital coital activity and plasma testosterone levels, they conclude that a certain minimum testosterone level is necessary for sexual functioning, but that an increase beyond that minimum does not lead to a further increase in sexual activity. If this holds true for aggression, too, then a correlation between testosterone levels and aggressive behavior in endocrinologically normal males should not be expected.

In an attempt to determine whether the increased frequency of behavior disorders and, possibly, of aggression in XYY males might be related to unusually high androgen production, the literature in this area was reviewed. The results are shown in Table 1 (49–83). Plasma testosterone levels were within the normal range (as given by the authors) or comparable to those of selected controls in almost all cases reported. Urinary testosterone levels were decreased in about one-third of the subjects for which such levels were reported. This could indicate that at least a sub-

		Number of Subjects with Hormone Values				
Hormone	Total Number of Subjects[a]	Within Normal Range or Comparable to Controls	Elevated	Low	Number of Subjects with Inconsistent Results	References[b]
Testosterone:						
Plasma	56	52	2	2	0	49[2], 50[5], 51[17], 52[7], 53[9],54[7], 55[4], 56[1], 57[2], 58[1], 59[1]
Serum	3	2	0	1	0	60[1], 61[1], 62[1]
Urinary	48	13	3	14	18	54[11], 55[3], 63[9], 64[9], 65[11], 66[4], 67[1]
Androgen fraction of urinary 17-ketosteroids	24	21	0	3	0	55[4], 65[11], 68[6], 69[2], 70[1]
LH:						
Plasma	14	13	1	0	0	50[5], 71[3], 72[6]
Serum	27	13	12	1	1	52[7], 54[11], 60[1], 73[7], 74[1]
Urinary	5	2	3	0	0	59[1], 75[3], 76[1]
FSH:						
Plasma	9	8	1	0	0	71[3], 72[6]
Serum	7	6	1	0	0	52[7]
Urinary	7	6	1	0	0	55[4], 75[3]
Total Urinary Gonadotrophins	31	24	4	3	0	54[11], 61[1], 69[2], 70[1], 77[1], 78[2], 79[9], 80[1], 81[1], 82[1], 83[1]

[a]Only true 47, XYY subjects are included; mosaics and other YY forms were disregarded if identifiable. Patients whose hormone values were reported in more than one paper were counted only once per hormone category if identifiable.

[b]The reference number is followed by the bracketed number of the subjects taken from the study quoted. The total of the bracketed numbers per hormone category is identical with the number given in the column "Total Number of Subjects."

445

group of XYY subjects showed an unusual metabolism of testosterone; however, most of the subjects with relatively low excretion rates come from one study (65), which needs replication. Another third of this group was listed under the category "inconsistent results": these subjects showed an elevation of urinary testosterone excretion versus normal noninstitutionalized controls, but did not show an elevation above controls selected from the same institution (63, 64). In both studies, the non-XYY prisoners had higher urinary testosterone excretion than did normal ambulant controls. A recent study by Wakeling et al. (54) confirms these findings. We do not know if this is an example of behavioral or environmental effects on androgen production and metabolism or a constitutional factor. To date, no comparable difference between prisoners and nonprisoner controls has been found with regard to plasma testosterone levels. Price and Van der Molen (51) pair-matched a sample of XYY prisoners with non-XYY prisoners and could not detect any difference in plasma testosterone levels or in urinary testosterone excretion.

Table 1 also shows that the androgen fraction of urinary 17-ketosteroids is essentially within normal limits. There is a tendency toward an elevation in the levels of luteinizing hormone, whereas the levels of follicle-stimulating hormone are basically normal. Furthermore, measures of total urinary gonadotrophin output do not show consistent deviation from the norm. Thus the overall result reveals no gross abnormalities of androgen or gonadotrophin production in the XYY syndrome. This is in distinct contrast to the XXY genotype, where the majority of cases exhibit gross abnormalities of the pituitary–gonadal system, with very high gonadotrophin values and rather low testosterone levels. However, one has to realize that most of the measurements presented in Table 1 were executed in a clinical framework lacking rigorous experimental methodology. A major shortcoming of most of these data is that they do not represent repeated measurements and that they are compared with whatever controls the specific laboratory happens to have available, although there are some important exceptions. Although gross hormonal abnormalities like those found in Klinefelter's syndrome can be ruled out for the majority of XYY males, it is still possible that subtle, though significant, endocrine pathology will be found when appropriate methods are used.

Even if pubertal or postpubertal hormone production did contribute to the behavior abnormalities of some XYY males, endocrine factors could not be the sole behavioral determinants. If one overviews the biographical histories of our six XYY males with aggressive disorders, one finds that the earliest reports of tantrum behavior date back to ages 2½, 3, 5, 7, 7, and 9; that is, they predate puberty by several years in all cases.

Similarly, XXY patients show an increased incidence of severe behavior disorders in spite of deficient pubertal androgen production. Of course, a second possibility for hormonal effects has to be considered: irregularities in prenatal hormone production and possibly prenatal over-production of testosterone may influence subsequent unusually aggressive behavior, as in the hamster model mentioned earlier. So far, there is neither a rationale nor any evidence that there is a prenatal overproduction of androgens in the XYY syndrome.

To summarize, it is quite possible that the aggressive behavior disorder encountered in many XYY males is totally unrelated to androgens.

ABNORMAL BRAIN FUNCTION AND AGGRESSION

It is well known that many patients with severe behavior disorders suffer from brain dysfunction (84, 85). Can this factor account for the increased prevalence of abnormal behavior in the XYY syndrome? In our Buffalo sample, none of our six patients on whom a sleep-and-wake EEG could be done showed any abnormality. Two subjects had experienced petit mal symptoms in childhood. Another manifested definite finger tremor during the examination.

In a recent paper, Owen (10) reviewed the records of 79 XYY subjects containing information relevant to neurological status. Of the 57 cases referred for EEG, 24 evinced some degree of abnormality. A number of the patients had histories of epilepsy, seizures, or minor neurologic abnormalities (e.g., finger tremor). However, neurologic and EEG methods and criteria for what is normal and what is abnormal have been far from uniform. Furthermore, there is a strong selection bias: many cases have been referred because a neurologic abnormality was expected, and most cases are from institutional populations where there is increased incidence of EEG abnormalities. So far, we do not even know if the XYY syndrome shows the same frequency of neurologic abnormalities as do other institutionalized males. Moreover, the anomalies that have been found are rarely severe enough to unequivocally explain aggressive behavior in these subjects. What is needed are studies employing representative sampling, well-defined control subjects, and a uniform methodology for a large sample.

A more indirect indicator of brain dysfunction would be intelligence, especially profound mental retardation. A recent summary of 75 XYY subjects with IQ data (10) showed a range from severe mental retardation (IQ 34) to superior IQ levels (IQ 125). Thus the XYY condition is not incompatible with a high average or above average intelligence, which is quite different from what is usually found in autosomal trisomies like Down's syndrome. Still, the majority of the values are somewhat below the norm. Our own nine cases show a corresponding distribution.

Does this justify the conclusion that XYY males in general have an increased frequency of lower IQs? The answer is that it is possible, but not proved by these data. The majority of subjects have been karyotyped either as inmates of an institution or because of physical or behavioral disorders. Under such sampling conditions a group of genetically normal XY males would also show a somewhat subaverage group mean. For instance, in our prison system, the lower socioeconomic groups are over-represented. Socioeconomic class is also highly correlated with IQ. Thus one expects a greater frequency of low-IQ males in such institutions than in the general population. To answer the question of intelligence in XYY males, we again need well-designed control groups and bias-free sampling. Although a few prison studies employed matched controls, the results were conflicting, and the small samples do not allow for reliable conclusions.

An example of a basically ideal design is the longitudinal study by Valentine, McClelland, and Sergovich (86). They found four XYY males among 1066 unselected male newborns and have followed them for several years. A review of the development of these boys showed that at the age of 2 years all four had normal motor development but were somewhat below average in mental development. However, we do not know how this finding compares either with the newborn population they were selected from or with their normal XY relatives. In our Buffalo sample, the only patient with a middle-class background was clearly inferior to the other members of his family in mental ability.

Other indirect evidence indicating that the XYY condition may well have some negative effects on intelligence comes from surveys of data on all sex-chromosome anomalies as presented by Barlow (87). Barlow demonstrated a remarkable negative correlation between the number of supernumerary chromosomes (particularly X chromosomes) and intelligence. As a preliminary hypothesis, he suggested that heterochromatic sex chromosomes have a retarding effect on cell division in some phase of brain development. The degree of developmental retardation depends on the number of sex chromosomes, and the retardation is responsible for lowered intelligence. At any rate, in this model, too, the XYY condition is borderline as far as influence of the chromosomal condition on IQ is concerned.

To summarize, there may be some increased frequency of subaverage IQ in XYY males, but the evidence is not secured beyond criticism, and at present the indirect evidence from intelligence studies is not enough to formulate a hypothesis of general brain dysfunction.

SOCIAL FACTORS

Finally, some nonbiologic factors should be briefly mentioned. Several researchers have speculated that the increased height of the XYY male may render him more prone to arrest than would be the case with a shorter man. This factor has been ruled out in a careful study by Hook and Kim (88).

The role of social class must also be considered in the high risk of incarceration for XYY males: a genetic survey by Robinson and Puck (89) indicated that sex-chromosome abnormalities came almost exclusively from low social classes, whereas autosomal disorders were distributed evenly across social classes. Interestingly enough, eight of our nine patients come from social class IV or V on the Hollingshead Index (90); one comes from class II. Thus there is clearly an overrepresentation of the lower class in our sample, too. This finding is contradicted by one study in England (7), and the data available so far do not allow a definite conclusion.

Family dynamics are a most important factor in the ontogenesis of antisocial and aggressive behavior. In our Buffalo sample, three of nine subjects came from homes with severely disturbed and/or broken marriages, and one was born out of wedlock and given to a foster home before he was 2 years old. Family psychopathology has been described in many XYY cases reported in the literature. It appears to be much more frequent than abnormalities of hormone production, although a thorough review is needed to document this point.

CONCLUSION

In summary, there appears to be a distinct increase above the newborn rate of the XYY syndrome in mental-penal and, possibly, other institutions. The possibility of a higher risk for aggressive behavior has not been settled satisfactorily, although it appears to be likely. A major obstacle in obtaining definitive results is that there are no well-designed tools to assess aggression under clinical conditions.

With regard to factors that may contribute to an increased risk of behavior disorders, including aggression, in the XYY syndrome, we have considered the effects of sex chromosomes, of hormonal abnormalities, of brain dysfunction, and of social factors. Many XYY subjects with disorders in one or another of these areas have been reported. As compared with other elements, hormonal abnormalities appear to be of lesser importance. However, much more systematic and sophisticated research has to be accomplished before definite conclusions are arrived at.

ACKNOWLEDGMENTS

This investigation was supported by a research grant (HD-05023) from the National Institute of Child Health and Human Development and a grant (RR-628) from the General Clinical Research Center Program of the Division of Research Resources, National Institutes of Health, U.S. Public Health Service.

REFERENCES

1. Sandberg, A. A., G. F. Koepf, T. Ishihara, and T. S. Hauschka, *Lancet* **2**: 488, 1961.

2. Jacobs, P. A., M. Brunton, M. M. Melville, R. P. Brittain, and W. F. McClemont, *Nature* **208**: 1351, 1965.

3. Marinello, M. J., R. A. Berkson, J. A. Edwards, and R. M. Bannerman, *J Am Med Assoc* **208**: 321, 1969.

4. Meyer-Bahlburg, H. F. L., D. A. Boon, M. Sharma, and J. A. Edwards, in Eckensberger, L. H. (ed.), *Bericht über den 28. Kongress der Deutschen Gesellschaft für Psychologie in Saarbrücken, 1.–5. Oktober 1972*, Hogrefe, Göttingen, in press.

5. National Institute of Mental Health Center for Studies of Crime and Delinquency, *Report on the XYY Chromosomal Abnormality* (U.S. Public Health Service Publication No. 2103), National Institute of Mental Health, Chevy Chase, Md., 1970.

6. Hook, E. B., *Science* **179**: 139, 1973.

7. Price, W. H. and P. B. Whatmore, *Br Med J* **1**: 533, 1967.

8. Griffiths, A. W., B. W. Richards, J. Zaremba, T. Abramowicz, and A. Stewart, *Nature* **227**: 290, 1970.

9. Casey, M. D., C. E. Blank, T. M. McLean, P. Kohn, D. R. K. Street, J. M. McDougall, J. Gooder, and J. Platts, *J Ment Defic Res* **16**: 215, 1973.

10. Owen, D. R., *Psychol Bull* **78**: 209, 1972.

11. Money, J. and A. A. Ehrhardt, *Man & Woman, Boy & Girl*, Johns Hopkins University Press, Baltimore, 1972.

12. Kessler, S. and R. H. Moos, *Ann Rev Med* **24**: 89, 1973.

13. Nielsen, J., *Br J Psychiatry* **117**: 365, 1970.

14. Baker, D., M. A. Telfer, C. E. Richardson, and G. R. Clark, *J Am Med Assoc* **214**: 869, 1970.

15. Tsuboi, T., *Humangenetik* **10**: 68, 1970.

16. Bronson, F. H. and C. Desjardins, in Eleftheriou, B. E. and J. P. Scott (eds.), *The Physiology of Aggression and Defeat*, Plenum Press, New York, 1971.

17. Seward, J. P., *J Comp Physiol Psychol* **38**: 175, 1945.

18. Beach, F. A., *Physiol Zool* **18**: 195, 1945.

19. Conner, R. L. and S. Levine, in Garattini, S. and E. B. Sigg (eds.), *Aggressive Behavior*, Excerpta Medica, Amsterdam, 1969, p. 150.

20. Bronson, F. H. and C. Desjardins, *Endocrinology* **85**: 971, 1969.

21. Bronson, F. H. and C. Desjardins, *Gen Comp Endocrinol* **15**: 320, 1970.

22. Edwards, D. A., *Science* **161**: 1027, 1968.

23. Swanson, H. H., A. P. Payne, and J. S. Brayshaw, paper presented at the Symposium on Differentiation and Neuroendocrine Regulations in the Hypothalamus–Hypophysial–Gonadal System, Berlin, September 20–23, 1972.

24. Rose, R. M., J. W. Holaday, and I. S. Bernstein, *Nature* **231:** 366, 1971.

25. Rose, R. M., T. P. Gordon, and I. S. Bernstein, *Psychosom Med* **34:** 473, 1972.

26. Feshbach, S., in Mussen, P. H. (ed.), *Carmichael's Manual of Child Psychology*, 3rd ed., Vol. 2, Wiley, New York, 1970, p. 159.

27. Hawke, C. C., *Am J Ment Defic* **55:** 220, 1950.

28. LeMaire, L., *J Criminal Law Criminol* **47:** 294, 1956.

29. Bremer, J., *Asexualisation. A Follow-up Study of 244 Cases*, Oslo University Press, Oslo, 1958.

30. Langelüddeke, A., *Die Entmannung von Sittlichkeitsverbrechern*, Walter de Gruyter, Berlin, 1963.

31. Stürup, G. K., *Acta Psychiatr Scand (Suppl)* **204:** 1, 1968.

32. Cornu, F., *Katamnesen bei kastrierten Sittlichkeitsdelinquenten aus forensisch-psychiatrischer Sicht*, Karger, Basel, 1973.

33. Blumer, D. and C. Migeon, paper presented at the annual American Psychiatric Association meeting, May 1973.

34. Kopell, B. S., in Salhanick, H. A., D. M. Kipnis, and R. L. Vande Wiele (eds.), *Metabolic Effects of Gonadal Hormones and Contraceptive Steroids*, Plenum, New York, 1969, p. 649.

35. Strauss, E. B., D. E. Sands, A. M. Robinson, W. J. Tindall, and W. A. H. Stevenson, *Br Med J* **3:** 64, 1952.

36. Sands, D. E. and G. H. A. Chamberlain, *Br Med J* **2:** 66, 1952.

37. Sands, D. E., *J Ment Sci* **100:** 211, 1954.

38. Johnson, H. R., S. A. Myhre, R. H. A. Ruvalcaba, H. C. Thuline, and V. C. Kelley, *Dev Med Child Neurol* **12:** 454, 1970.

39. Persky, H., K. D. Smith, and G. K. Basu, *Psychosom Med* **33:** 265, 1971.

40. Meyer-Bahlburg, H. F. L., D. A. Boon, M. Sharma, and J. A. Edwards, *Psychosom Med* **36,** 1974, in press.

41. Kreuz, L. E. and R. M. Rose, *Psychosom Med* **34:** 321, 1972.

42. Rose, R. M., P. G. Bourne, R. O. Poe, E. H. Mougey, D. R. Collins, and J. W. Mason, *Psychosom Med* **31:** 418, 1969.

43. Kreuz, L. E., R. M. Rose, and J. R. Jennings, *Arch Gen Psychiatry* **26:** 479, 1972.

44. Matsumoto, K., K. Takeyasu, S. Mizutani, Y. Hamanaka, and T. Uozumi, *Acta Endocrinol* **65:** 11, 1970.

45. Aono, T., K. Kurachi, S. Mizutani, Y. Hamanaka, T. Uozumi, A. Nakasima, K. Koshiyama, and K. Matsumoto, *J Clin Endocrinol Metab* **35:** 535, 1972.

46. Carstensen, H., B. Amér, I. Amér, and L. Wide, *J Steroid Biochem* **4:** 45, 1973.

47. Sutton, J. R., M. J. Coleman, J. Casey, and L. Lazarus, *Br Med J* **163:** 520, 1973.

48. Raboch, J. and L. Stárka, *J Sex Res* **8:** 219, 1972.

49. Goodman, R. M., W. S. Smith, and C. J. Migeon, *Nature* **216:** 942, 1967.

50. Hudson, B., H. Burger, S. Wiener, G. Sutherland, and A. A. Bartholomew, *Lancet* **2:** 699, 1969.

51. Price, W. H. and H. J. Van Der Molen, *J Endocrinol* **47**: 117, 1970.

52. Santen, R. J., D. M. De Krester, C. A. Paulsen, and J. Vorhees, *Lancet* **2**: 371, 1970.

53. Griffiths, A. W., V. Marks, D. Fry, G. Morley, and G. Lewis, *Br J Psychiat* **121**: 365, 1972.

54. Wakeling, A., A. Haq, F. Naftolin, M. P. Neill, and R. Horton, *Psychol Med* **3**: 28, 1973.

55. Benezech, M. M., G. Robert, J. M. Luciani, and B. Noël, *Bord Med* **4**: 3013, 1971.

56. Welch, J. P., D. S. Borgaonkar, and H. M. Herr, *Nature* **214**: 500, 1967.

57. Wiener, S., G. Sutherland, A. A. Bartholomew, and B. Hudson, *Lancet* **1**: 150, 1968.

58. Alam, M. T., R. Deschamps, E. Gaba, S. S. Kasatiya, and W. F. Grant, *Clin Genet* **3**: 162, 1972.

59. Marcus, A. M. and G. Richmond, *Can Psychiatr Ass J* **15**: 389, 1970.

60. Shapiro, L. R., *Lancet* **1**: 623, 1970.

61. Parker, C. E., J. Melnyk, and C. Fish, *Am J Med* **47**: 801, 1969.

62. Nielsen, J. and F. Henriksen, *Acta Psychiatr Scand* **48**: 87, 1972.

63. Ismail, A. A. A., R. A. Harkness, K. E. Kirkham, J. A. Loraine, P. B. Whatmore, and R. P. Brittain, *Lancet* **1**: 220, 1968.

64. Rudd, B. T., O. M. Galal, and M. D. Casey, *J Med Genet* **5**: 286, 1968.

65. Plasse, J. C., M. C. Patricot, M. Giboulet, B. Noël and A. Revol, *Ann Génét* **13**: 90, 1970.

66. Pfeiffer, R. A., G. Riemer, and W. Schneller, *Med Welt* **2**: 75, 1969.

67. Zenzes, M. T., R. Lisker, M. T. Fonseca, and F. De M. Herrera, *Rev Invest Clin* **21**: 85, 1969.

68. Nielsen, J., H. Yde, and K. Johansen, *Metabolism* **18**: 993, 1969.

69. Skakkebaek, N. E., J. Philip, M. Mikkelsen, R. Hammen, J. Nielsen, O. Perboll, and H. Yde, *Fertil Steril* **21**: 645, 1970.

70. Nielsen, J., A. L. Christensen, J. Schultz-Larsen, and H. Yde, *Acta Psychiatr Scand* **49**: 156, 1973.

71. Lundberg, P. I. and J. Wahlstrom, *Lancet* **2**: 1133, 1970.

72. Skakkebaek, N. E., M. Hultén, P. Jacobsen, and M. Mikkelsen, *J Reprod Fertil* **32**: 391, 1973.

73. Parker, C. E., *Lancet* **1**: 1101, 1969.

74. Parker, C. E., J. Mavalwala, P. Weise, R. Kock, A. Hatashita, and S. Cibilich, *Am J Ment Defic* **74**: 660, 1970.

75. Papanicolaou, A. D., K. E. Kirkham, and J. A. Lorraine, *Lancet* **2**: 608, 1968.

76. Gustavson, K. H. and J. Verneholt, *Hereditas* **60**: 264, 1968.

77. Balodimos, M., H. Lisco, I. Irwin, W. Merrill, and J. F. Dingman, *J Clin Endocrinol* **26**: 443, 1966.

78. Tettenborn, U., E. Schwinger, and A. Gropp, *Dtsch Med Wochenschr* **95**: 158, 1970.

79. Nielsen, J. and S. G. Johnsen, *Acta Endocrinol* **72**: 191, 1973.

80. Cowling, D. C., S. Rigo, and F. I. R. Martin, *Med J Aust* **2**: 443, 1969.

81. Hashi, N., S. Tsutsumi, K. Tsuda, R. Wake, and M. Kitahara, *Jap J Hum Genet* **14**: 34, 1969.

82. Persson, T., *J Ment Defic Res* **11**: 239, 1967.

83. Friedrich, U., E. B. Erling, and J. Nielsen, *Z Rechtsmed* **68**: 138, 1971.

84. Mark, V. H. and F. R. Ervin, *Violence and the Brain*, Harper & Row, New York, 1970.

85. Monroe, R. R., *Episodic Behavioral Disorders*, Harvard University Press, Cambridge, Mass., 1970.

86. Valentine, G. H., M. A. McClelland, and F. R. Sergovich, *Pediatrics* **48**: 583, 1971.

87. Barlow, P., *Humangenetik* **17**: 105, 1973.

88. Hook, E. B. and D. S. Kim, *Science* **172**: 284, 1971.

89. Robinson, A. and T. T. Puck, *Am J Hum Genet* **19**: 112, 1967.

90. Hollingshead, A. B., *Two Factor Index of Social Position*, privately printed, New Haven, Conn., 1957.

CHAPTER 23

Reproductive Hormones, Moods, and the Menstrual Cycle

HAROLD PERSKY

Department of Psychiatry
University of Pennsylvania and the
Philadelphia General Hospital
Philadelphia, Pennsylvania

Association of mood level and endocrine function constitutes one of the principal areas of investigation in the field of psychoendocrinology. Unraveling the relationship between feelings of anxiety and adrenocortical function in human subjects and patients constituted one of the earliest and most fascinating chapters in the history of this fairly young field. In approximately a decade, this relationship was examined in close detail by many investigators active in the area of psychosomatic medicine. Studies of the anxiety–adrenocortical relationship ranged from demonstration of an association between a crude clinical index of anxiety and plasma cortisol level in a variety of emotionally disturbed patients (1, 2), to attempts to manipulate either the anxiety or cortisol level in order to alter the partner variable in normal subjects (3, 4), to obtaining a linear

455

relation between cortisol production rate and a complex, total anxiety rating based on a multicomponent questionnaire (5).

The cited efforts, as well as many others, have led to exploration of the role of the limbic system both with respect to the cerebral cortex and the endocrine system—studies that seem to promise much for a rational, psychopharmacologic approach to the psychotherapy of the affective disorders.

In addition to examining the anxiety–adrenocortical relationship, other psychoendocrine systems have been investigated with profitable results. Some studies have involved psychological parameters other than affects (e.g., defenses and cognitive processes). To document all of these studies is beyond the scope of this chapter.

An important factor in all of these studies has been the availability of reliable endocrine techniques, a product of the explosion in endocrine chemistry since the end of World War II. Likewise, considerable improvement in methodology has also occurred with respect to psychological and sociological factors of importance to such psychoendocrine studies. Here again, documentation would require far more space than is available.

The origins of the present report go back to a study I reported with two of my colleagues, K. D. Smith and G. K. Basu, over 3 years ago. We obtained a highly significant relationship between several measures of aggression and both plasma testosterone level and testosterone production rate for a group of healthy young men (6). To my knowledge, this was the first demonstration of such a quantitative relationship in the area of human reproductive biology. The work reported here is an extension of that initial study to female reproductive psychobiology. Hopefully, the data I shall present for plasma testosterone levels should bear some relevance to the central topic of this volume—sex differences in behavior. It represents a collaborative effort involving my co-workers. and myself, and is concerned with the relation of plasma testosterone and progesterone levels to aggression and depression, respectively, in a group of healthy young women during the course of a single menstrual cycle.* I shall also briefly describe some of our ongoing work that attempts to explore these findings in greater depth.

SUBJECTS, EXPERIMENTAL DESIGN, AND METHODS

Twenty-nine female volunteers, students at a local college, constituted the subject sample of the present report. They were obtained through an

* My co-workers in this study were C. P. O'Brien, C. R. Garcia, Z. Hoch, M. A. Khan, P. Schneider, and T. J. Sheehan.

advertisement in the school newspaper. All subjects were fully informed of the nature of the study and were paid for their participation. They were selected from a much larger group after a rigorous screening procedure; rejectees were also paid on a proportionate basis. Screening of subjects involved three distinct stages: (1) a small psychological test battery intended to elicit some information about their feelings of anxiety, depression, and hostility/aggression, as well as their reliability in reporting such feelings; (2) a brief psychiatric interview intended to screen out individuals who were psychotic, severely neurotic, or had a recent history of illnesses deemed to be psychosomatic and to obtain clinical ratings for depression, hostility/aggression, and sex drive; and (3) a medical history intended to rule out individuals with serious medical problems plus a gynecologic examination in order to assess adequacy of reproductive function.

The psychological test battery contained the manifest anxiety, depression, and lie scales from the Minnesota Multiphasic Personality Inventory (MMPI-MAS, MMPI-D, and MMPI-L, respectively) (7) and the Buss–Durkee Hostility Inventory (B–D-ΣH) (8). The latter instrument yields two factor scores purporting to assess negative hostile feelings and aggressive feelings respectively.

Psychiatric clinical ratings were made by the psychiatrist on the basis of the interview alone and without prior knowledge of the psychological test score results. Close agreement was obtained between the psychiatrist's clinical rating for hostility/aggression and the B–D-ΣH and B–D factor II scores ($p<.01$ and .001, respectively), and between the clinical rating for depression and the MMPI-D scores ($p<.005$).

The 29 selected candidates included 21 subjects who were not currently using a contraceptive steroid preparation nor had used one in the preceding 6 months and 8 subjects who were using such a preparation and had been using it for the preceding 6 months.

Some important physical, psychological, and educational information about these two subgroups, obtained prior to endocrine assessment, are shown in Table 1. These two groups did not differ with respect to age, weight, height, any of the psychological or psychiatric selection variables, or educational level. Perhaps even more interesting, they did not differ with respect to the psychological or educational variables from a group of male student volunteers from the same institution used in the previously cited study (9).

The 29 accepted female volunteers were each tested on three separate occasions during the course of a single menstrual cycle. For the 21 nonusers of the pill, these occasions occurred between days 1 and 4 of their cycles (test I), days 14 and 18 (test II), and days 24 and 28 (test III), cor-

Table 1   Some Characteristics of the Subject Sample[a]

Variable	Nonusers of the Pill (N=21)	Pill Users (N=8)
Age (years)	21.6±0.6	22.1±0.7
Weight (lb.)	136±4	125±5
Height (in.)	66±0.7	66±1
Schooling (years)	15±0.5	16±0.6
MMPI-MAS	12.6±1.5	12.2±3.7
MMPI-D	19.2±1.1	20.0±1.7
B–D–ΣH	20.8±0.4	22.1±3.6
MMPI–L	2.8±1.4	2.6±0.6

[a] Means ± S.E.

responding roughly to the early follicular, ovulatory peak, and late luteal phases of a normal cycle. The eight pill users were tested at the same points in time with respect to onset of their menses. Subjects were tested individually and at almost identical times of day on each occasion.

The testing procedure on each occasion was identical and is given in Table 2. A total of 85 ml of blood was drawn from each subject on each of the three testing occasions. Blood samples were centrifuged immediately, the plasma was removed and stored at −25°C for subsequent chemical analysis. All plasma samples obtained from a single subject on all three occasions were analyzed simultaneously for a single constituent in order to minimize intraindividual variability. Plasma samples 1, 4, and 6 were each analyzed for testosterone, progesterone, and estradiol levels. The purpose of three samples was to provide an estimate of the variability in level of the individual hormones.

Administration of ^{14}C-progesterone and ^{3}H-estradiol was necessary for determining the respective hormone production rates. Plasma samples 2, 3, and 4 were analyzed for progesterone specific activities; samples 4, 5, and 6 were analyzed for estradiol specific activities. These specific activities are necessary for calculating the respective production rates. Production-rate data will be reported elsewhere.

At the conclusion of hormone-level and production-rate assessment, the subject is freed from all infusion equipment and indwelling catheters, and permitted to relax for a few minutes, after which a psychological test battery was administered on each occasion. This test battery included the instruments used during the initial psychological screening procedure as well as Zuckerman's Multiple Affect Adjective Check List (MAACL) (10), Beck's Depression Inventory (B-DI) (II), and Moos' Menstrual Distress

Table 2   Subject Testing Procedure

Time	Elapsed Time (minutes)	Procedure
9:00 A.M.	−5	Subject arrives and voids (sample discarded)
9:03	−2	Blood sample 1 drawn and intravenous catheter inserted
9:05– 9:07	0	Priming dose of ^{14}C-progesterone and ^{3}H-estradiol administered in opposite arm, intravenously
9:27	20	Constant infusion of ^{14}C-progesterone and ^{3}H-estradiol started in opposite arm, intravenously
10:28	83	Blood sample 2 drawn through intravenous catheter
10:38	93	Blood sample 3 drawn
10:48	103	Blood sample 4 drawn
11:03	118	Blood sample 5 drawn
11:18	133	Blood sample 6 drawn
11:19– 11:20	135	Infusion terminated and catheter removed
11:25– 12:15 P.M.	190	Psychological test battery administered

Questionnaire (MDQ) (12). The MAACL contains three scales purporting to measure state feelings of anxiety (A), depression (D), and hostility (H). The MDQ contains eight scales tapping a variety of physiological and behavioral symptoms commonly associated with the menstrual cycle.

All three hormones were determined by radioimmunoassay techniques: testosterone by the method of Furuyama et al. (13), progesterone by the method of Furuyama and Nugent (14), and estradiol by the method of Wu and Lundy (15). All samples were run in duplicate. Results were corrected for loss during processing on the basis of individual sample radioisotope recovery. Duplicate samples of the same specimen yielded an average variation for each hormone of about 5%.

RESULTS

Testosterone Levels

The mean testosterone levels and their standard errors for the 21 non-users of the pill and the 8 users on each of the three occasions of testing are given in Table 3. The values given are those obtained from the

Table 3   Plasma Testosterone Level During the Menstrual Cycle[a]

	Phase[b]			
Group	I	II	III	*F*
Nonusers of pill				
(N=21)	22.4±4.3	32.3±4.1	29.0±4.0	7.80**
Pill users				
(N=8)	20.5±4.5	23.0±4.0	16.9±3.9	
All subjects				
(N=29)	21.8±4.0	29.6±4.1	25.4±4.1	

[a] Quantities in ng%; means±S.E.
[b] Key: I, early follicular phase; II, around the ovulatory peak; III, late luteal phase.
** Significant beyond the 1% level.

samples collected at 9:00 A.M. (blood sample 1). An almost identical set of values were obtained for the fourth and sixth blood samples. The mean hormone levels on the three occasions differed significantly among themselves ($F = 7.80$, $p < .01$), with the ovulatory peak value (test II) being significantly greater than the values obtained in tests I and III. The mean testosterone level around the ovulatory peak was 44% higher than during the early follicular phase, with the elevation in level tending to persist into the late luteal phase. Testosterone level in test III was 29% above that obtained in test I ($F = 6.48$, $p < .05$).

The pattern of testosterone response obtained agrees closely with those reported by two other laboratories (16, 17), as given in Table 4.

Although the pattern of testosterone response in the eight subjects using contraceptive steroids resembled that obtained for the nonusers of the pill, comparison was not attempted because of the small size of the pill group. However, the two groups were pooled for subsequent analyses.

Inspection of individual subject levels during their cycles indicated that almost all of the nonusers of the pill exhibited an increased testosterone level at the time of their ovulatory peak (18 out of 21). A representative case illustrates the group effect: L.W., a 20-year-old female with a 29-day menstrual cycle, exhibited a temperature rise of 1°F 15 days prior to her second onset of menses. The temperature rise was sustained to the second day prior to onset. The temperature pattern was taken to indicate that a normal ovulation had occurred. Plasma testosterone levels obtained on days 3 and 16 of the cycle under consideration indicated an increment of 80%, with the higher value persisting on day 26 (third occasion of testing). While anticipating some of the subsequent material of the present report, her progesterone level doubled by day 16 and reached 1707 ng% by day 26 of her cycle.

Table 4   Plasma Testosterone Levels During the Menstrual Cycle: Comparison with Others

| Investigators | Method[b] | N | Phase[a] | | |
			I	II	III
Judd and Yen (16)	RIA	6[c]	28.9±12	34.2±15	25.2±13
Lobotsky et al. (17)	DID	9[d]	27.0	41.0	
Present study	RIA	21	22.4±4	32.3±4	29.0±4

[a] See Table 3 for description.
[b] Abbreviations: RIA, radioimmunoassay; DID, double isotope derivative.
[c] Average of three to six cycles per subject.
[d] Average of two to seven cycles per subject, with values corrected for water blank.

No attempt was systematically made to exclude subjects with anovulatory cycles since it was unknown what effect an anovulatory cycle had on plasma testosterone level, and only two subjects of the 21 not on the pill evinced basal temperature patterns suggestive of such cycles.

Psychological Measures

Mean test scores and their standard errors are given in Table 5 for the psychological variables assessed on the three occasions of testing. Remarkably little change occurred across the three occasions of testing for either state measures (manifest affects) or trait measures (more stable measures of mood). One-way analyses of variance were carried out for six of these variables deemed to be more likely to be related to plasma testosterone level; in each instance, no significant difference was obtained.

Correlations

Because of the number of variables and conditions involved, it was deemed inadvisable to attempt to interpret the results obtained in a matrix of correlation coefficients. Rather, an attempt was made to see whether a relationship similar to that previously obtained for male subjects between testosterone level and hostility/aggression measures might also be obtained for female subjects. In the male instance, the multiple-regression relationship obtained between the testosterone production rate (PR_T) and four psychological variables indicative of feelings of hostility and aggression yielded a multiple correlation coefficient (R) of .90. A similar relationship for Pl_T was also obtained albeit with a somewhat smaller value of R (.73). The four psychological variables and their contributions to the cumulative variance in PR_T were B–D factor II (38.6%), IPAT-Q_4 (24.2%), MAACL-H (16.7%) and B–D factor I (0.1%). The B–D factors

Table 5   Psychological Test Scores During the Menstrual Cycle[a]

Variable	Phase[b]		
	I	II	III
Multiple Affect Adjective Check List:			
Aggression[c]	8.0	7.5	6.8
Depression[c]	14.0	14.9	14.4
Hostility[c]	7.8	8.9	8.2
Beck's Depression Inventory	4.0	3.6	3.0
Minnesota Multiphasic Personality Inventory:			
Manifest anxiety	12.4	12.4	10.9
Depression[c]	20.0	19.2	18.8
Buss–Durkee Hostility Inventory	22.2	22.5	22.2
Moos' Menstrual Distress Questionnaire:			
Pain	11.4	8.2	8.2
Concentration	9.8	10.4	10.0
Behavioral	7.0	7.2	6.4
Autonomic	5.0	4.8	4.6
Water retention	7.8	5.0	7.0
Negative affect[c]	13.0	11.3	12.2
Arousal	10.2	10.0	9.3
Control	6.2	6.5	6.2

[a] Means of 21 nonusers of steroid contraceptives.
[b] See Table 3 for description.
[c] Variable tested by one-way analysis of variance.

I and II are factor scores derived from the B–D-ΣH; IPAT-Q_4 is a subscale purporting to assess aggression due to sexual frustration derived from the IPAT anxiety scale (18).

Although we have not completed analysis of the regression data, some of the initial results are worth reporting. A multiple correlation R of .68 has been obtained between the four psychological variables and Pl_T for the 21 nonusers of oral contraceptives during the early follicular phase (I). Analysis of variance indicates that the relation is significantly linear and that the contribution of the independent variables is significant (i.e., the t-tests for the significance of their regression coefficients are beyond the 5% level). When the eight pill users were included in the multiple-regression analyses, the multiple correlation was reduced, at least for the analyses attempted to date.

Multiple-regression analyses of similar variables for the late luteal phase (test III) and ovulatory peak (test II) have tended to yield lower values of R (for test III, .45, $p < .05$; for test II, not significant).

Progesterone Levels

The mean progesterone levels and their standard errors are given for all subjects in Table 6. Values are for the 9.00 A.M. sample; samples 4 and 6 are almost identical. The mean hormone levels are obviously significantly different over the three stages of the menstrual cycle. The mean values agree closely with results reported from two other laboratories (18, 19).

Table 6   Plasma Progesterone Level During the Menstrual Cycle[a]

	Phase[b]		
Group	I	II	III
Nonusers of pill ($N = 21$)	57.1 ± 8.6	255.5 ± 68.8	802.5 ± 119.8
Pill users ($N = 8$)	21.2 ± 7.7	96.1 ± 55.1	113.0 ± 74.4
All subjects ($N = 29$)	48.1 ± 7.3	215.7 ± 54.8	630.1 ± 131.4

[a] Quantities in ng%; means ± S.E.
[b] See Table 3 for description.

Correlations

The correlation data for progesterone and psychological indices of depression are even scantier than those for the relationship between testosterone and hostility/aggression. However, work is now in progress to evaluate the results obtained in the present study.

No mention of the estradiol data will be made inasmuch as the samples have not yet been completely analyzed.

DISCUSSION

Because of the relatively incomplete chemical and psychological data analysis, discussion of the results obtained in the present study is not readily feasible. A number of the findings are, however, quite straightforward and deserve some comment. The present study has provided reliable data on the testosterone and progesterone levels for a group of healthy young women at three points in their menstrual cycles. These young women averaged about 22 years in age, had no obvious reproductive disabilities, and had normal menstrual cycles of about 29 days. Of great importance for psychosomatic evaluation, they were not even moderately disturbed individuals from an emotional standpoint. This is an important point, because so often in the popular newspaper reports (and often in what purports to be the scientific literature), mood variation during the menstrual cycle is taken as commonplace. In fact, we found remarkably little change in negative moods (anxiety, depression, hostility) across 29 menstrual cycles of healthy young women. Whether mood fluctuation during the cycle is a product of emotional illness, rather than a specific response to biochemical fluctuation, remains a moot point. Undoubtedly, investigation is warranted on mood fluctuation during the cycles of emotionally disturbed women.

Not only was mood fluctuation slight in this group of young women, the average values for the psychological variables assessed closely resembled those obtained for a group of male classmates of these young women in another study (6). Both male and female students gave values somewhat below that obtained from a larger population, again reflecting the good emotional health of the group.

By contrast with the lack of fluctuation in emotional measures, the plasma testosterone levels obtained showed a marked elevation at midcycle. The origin of this variation has been commented on in both the endocrine and psychoanalytic literature with little real proof in either case. Perhaps when all of our endocrine data are available, we may make some intelligent guesses concerning the origin of the androgen response pattern in menstruating women. One significant failure was noted in this study: the lack of more frequent estimates of testosterone across the cycle. A second study, now in progress, is presently assessing testosterone levels at more frequent intervals (twice weekly) and over three menstrual cycles per subject. It is hoped that these data will provide more accurate information about the pattern of testosterone secretion in the menstruating female.

Another problem that we realized only after initiating this study was that sex drive and sex responsivity might bear some relationship to testosterone level. Gross overall estimates on a three-point scale for subjects' "sex drive" failed to yield any systematic relations to testosterone level. The aforementioned second study is attempting to systematically assess patterns of sex drive and responsivity with the goal of obtaining some correlates with testosterone level.

The actual testosterone levels obtained in this study closely agreed with values reported by other investigators. This agreement suggests that this measure is a quite stable one and may not be the best correlate of psychoendocrine relationship. Perhaps the "free" testosterone level more adequately reflects functional testosterone activity in both the female as well as the male and should be used in future studies.

The finding that relationships between testosterone and aggression persisted at testosterone levels that are approximately 25 times lower than those found in males of comparable age is quite interesting. It is tempting to speculate that the absence of a servoregulatory control for testosterone in women may result in greater end-organ responsivity than occurs in men, despite the lower plasma level.

Few conclusions can be drawn from the progesterone data because of the lack so far of systematic analysis. The tentative hypothesis of our group has been that progesterone secretion is associated with dysphoric feelings whereas estradiol secretion is associated with euphoric feelings and that the position of an individual along a mood continuum would be determined by some function of her progesterone and estradiol secretion. Acceptance or rejection of that assumption must await further data analysis.

SUMMARY

The subject sample of a group in which relationships between reproductive hormones and mood were to be assessed is described. The 29 young women were found to be both mentally and physically healthy, with 21 using mechanical or no modalities of contraception and 8 using contraceptive steroid preparations. These subjects were tested on three occasions during their menstrual cycles: early follicular, ovulatory peak, and late luteal phases. Their plasma testosterone and progesterone levels were determined at these points as well as some selected psychological indices of mood state. Some efforts (preliminary) were made to relate testosterone levels to indices of hostility and aggression.

ACKNOWLEDGMENTS

The work reported here was supported by a grant (MH-21044) from the National Institute of Mental Health, U.S. Public Health Service, and I am the recipient of a Research Scientist Award (MH-18,374) from the same institution.

I wish to thank Mr. Miftah A. Khan and Mr. Timothy J. Sheehan for technical assistance with the hormone assays; Mr. Gopal K. Basu for aid in carrying out the production-rate assessments; and Mr. Paul Schneider, who helped in several ways while pursuing an independent study program in my laboratory.

REFERENCES

1. Bliss, E. L., C. Migeon, C. H. Branch, and L. T. Samuels, *Psychosom Med* **18**: 56, 1956.
2. Persky, H., R. R. Grinker, D. A. Hamburg, M. A. Sabshin, S. J. Korchin, H. Basowitz, and J. A. Chevalier, *AMA Arch Neurol Psychiatry* **76**: 549, 1956.
3. Price, D. B., M. Thaler and J. W. Mason, *AMA Arch Neurol Psychiatry* **77**: 646, 1957.
4. Weiner, S., D. Dorman, H. Persky, T. W. Stach, J. Norton, and E. E. Levitt, *Psychosom Med* **25**: 69, 1963.
5. Sachar, E. J., L. Hellman, D. K. Fukushima, and T. F. Gallagher, *Arch Gen Psychiatry* **23**: 289, 1970.
6. Persky, H., K. D. Smith and G. K. Basu, *Psychosom Med* **33**: 265, 1971.
7. Dahlstrom, W. G. and G. C. Welsh, *An MMPI Handbook*, University of Minnesota Press, Minneapolis, 1960.
8. Buss, A. H. and A. Durkee, *J. Consult Psychol* **21**: 343, 1957.
9. Persky, H., unpublished data.
10. Zuckerman, M. and B. Lubin, *Manual for the Multiple Affect Adjective Check List*, Educational and Industrial Testing Service, San Diego, Calif., 1965.
11. Beck, A. T., C. H. Ward, M. Mendelson, J. Mock, and J. Erbaugh, *Arch Gen Psychiatry* **4**: 561, 1961.
12. Moos, R. H., *Menstrual Distress Questionnaire, Preliminary Manual*, 1969.
13. Furuyama, S., D. Mayes, and C. A. Nugent, *Steroids* **16**: 415, 1970.
14. Furuyama, S. and C. A. Nugent, *Steroids* **17**: 663, 1971.
15. Wu, C. and L. Lundy, *Steroids* **18**: 91, 1971.
16. Judd, H. L. and S. S. C. Yen, *J Clin Endocrinol Metab* **36**: 475, 1973.
17. Lobotsky, J., H. I. Wyss, E. J. Segre, and C. W. Lloyd, *J Clin Endocrinol Metab* **24**: 1261, 1964.
18. Abraham, G. E., W. D. Odell, R. S. Swerdloff, and K. Hopper, *J Clin Endocrinol Metab* **34**: 312, 1972.
19. Lin, T. J., R. B. Billiar, and B. Little, *J Clin Endocrinol Metab* **35**: 879, 1972.

CHAPTER 24

Sexual Differentiation:
Models, Methods, and Mechanisms

RICHARD E. WHALEN

Department of Psychobiology
University of California
Irvine, California

The study of the sexual differentiation process has come in waves. There was a minor wave initiated in the late 1930s by Pfeiffer's classic study of pituitary differentiation (1) and by the work of Greene, Burrill, and Ivy (2, 3) on the hormonal control of somatic development. An enduring wave of study of somatic sex differentiation was initiated in the late 1940s by Jost (4); it continues today. A third and major wave was initiated by Barraclough and Leathem (5), who showed that a single injection of testosterone given to newborn rats would cause permanent sterility. These and other waves and eddies have led to our current concepts of the role of hormones in the sexual differentiation of pituitary function.

On a different intellectual shore were waves of research, exemplified by the work of Wilson, Young and Hamilton (6, 7), which suggested that the development of behavior may also be under hormonal control. This wave, however, did not mature until 1959, when Phoenix and co-workers (8) published their important paper suggesting that the presence of gonadal hormones during early stages of maturation "organize" or differentiate the tissues that mediate mating behavior. This paper and the study by Harris and Levine (9) shortly thereafter formed the basis for the voluminous literature that has developed during the last 15 years on the hormonal control of the sexual differentiation of behavior.

This is not the place to attempt to review the multitude of research findings that have appeared since 1959. Pertinent material can be found in several sources (10–13). Rather I shall discuss three areas where I believe there remain critical issues in the hormonal control of sexual differentiation. These issues deal with models, methods, and mechanisms.

MODELS OF SEXUAL DIFFERENTIATION

In 1959, Phoenix et al. (8) reported that the female offspring of guinea pigs administered the synthetic androgen testosterone propionate (TP) were less likely to display female-type sexual responses and were more likely to display male-type sexual responses in adulthood than were control animals when both were administered the appropriate hormones. Although not so stated by the authors, these findings suggested what appears to be a widespread belief that masculinity and femininity are opposite ends of the same continuum. That is, the guinea pig that shows a high probability and frequency of mounting behavior and a low probability and frequency of lordosis (the behavior characteristic of the receptive female) is considered masculine. Similarly, the guinea pig that shows lordosis, but not mounting, is considered feminine. The prenatally androgenized genetic female guinea pig shows increased mounting and decreased lordosis behavior and is therefore considered to be masculinized.

Another way of conceptualizing the change brought about by early androgen treatment is to say that the androgen treatment defeminizes. Of course, one can say that defeminization is just a different, but still sexist, view of differentiation. This would be true if masculinity and femininity were different ends of the same continuum. Early work in our laboratory, however, led me to the view that masculinization and feminization are not different sexist attitudes, but represent fundamental differences in the nature of the hormonal control of differentiation. I call this the orthogonal model of differentiation to contrast it to the linear model. I believe this to be a critical issue because I believe that our model of the sexual system colors the observations we make, the experiments we do, and our interpretations of research findings.

The Orthogonal Model

The orthogonal model states that masculinity and femininity are not unitary processes, but reflect many behavioral dimensions that can be independent. The model further states that during development hormones can defeminize without masculinizing and masculinize without defeminizing, and that hormones can defeminize one behavioral system (e.g., mating) while masculinizing another system.

To make this concept clearer consider the following studies. Edwards and I (14) gonadectomized male and female rats within 12 hours of birth. Some of these animals were administered TP at the same time. When adult, these animals were administered appropriate hormones and were tested for the display of masculine and feminine sexual behavior. When tested for male behavior, all of these animals showed mounting responses at approximately equivalent levels. Thus the presence or absence of postnatal androgen stimulation failed to alter the probability of responses that are usually considered masculine. When these same animals were tested for lordosis, a typically female response, both males and females gonadectomized at birth showed intense lordosis responses, whereas those gonadectomized and treated with TP at birth did not show lordosis. Control females gonadectomized as adults showed lordosis while control males did not. Because the presence of male hormone after birth did not enhance the display of masculine behavior in adulthood, but did inhibit the display of feminine behavior, we concluded that postnatal androgen stimulation defeminized, but did not masculinize. This means that masculinity and femininity need not be opposite ends of the same dimension, but rather can be orthogonal or independent dimensions of the organism's sexuality.

A similar separation of the dimensions "masculine" and "feminine" can be seen from studies of the hamster. The sexual differentiation of hamsters is unlike that found in rats and guinea pigs. In the latter two species, if the adult male is castrated and administered female hormones, he is unlikely to show female-type behavior. If the adult female rat or guinea pig is ovariectomized and treated with male hormones, she is very likely to display male-type mounting responses. The opposite is true for the hamster. The adult female hamster rarely shows male-type mounting responses even if administered large amounts of testosterone (15), whereas the male hamster will show lordosis if given ovarian hormones (16), although the duration of lordosis in males is generally shorter than in females. Thus the female hamster appears to be demasculinized during development. But the male develops the potential to show both masculine and feminine type of responses.

This separation of masculine and feminine dimensions in the hamster is further illustrated by some recent work from my laboratory with J. DeBold. We administered various doses of TP to female hamsters 24 hours after birth. When adult, the animals were given estrogen and progesterone, and were tested for the display of lordosis. They were then given TP and tested for mounting behavior. The results are illustrated in Figure 1. We see that even the smallest dose of TP given in infancy completely established the potential of the animal to show mounting behavior. That same dose had no effect on lordosis behavior. Substantially more androgen was needed to inhibit the potential for lordosis. Thus separate masculine and feminine control systems seem to exist in the hamster—systems that have different sensitivities to hormone stimulation.

A third example of a dissociation between masculine and feminine systems comes from Beach's (17) studies of dogs. Beach and his colleagues studied the masculine and feminine mating behavior of six groups of dogs:

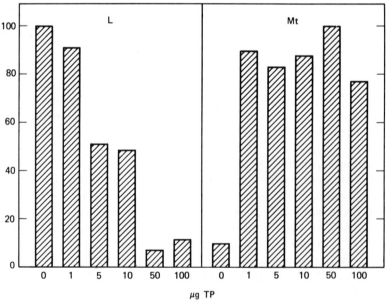

Figure 1   Sexual behavior of adult female hamsters administered oil or testosterone propionate (TP) 24 hours after birth. The left panel shows the duration of lordosis relative to oil-treated controls. All animals were administered estrogen and progesterone in adulthood. The right panel shows the percentage of animals showing mounting behavior when administered testosterone in adulthood. Low doses of hormone given in infancy facilitated mounting behavior but had little effect on lordosis behavior.

1. Males castrated in adulthood (MCA).
2. Females ovariectomized in adulthood (FOA).
3. Males castrated at birth (MCB).
4. Females treated with testosterone shortly after birth (FTI).
5. The female offspring of females treated with testosterone during pregnancy (FTU).
6. Females treated with testosterone both before and after birth (FTUI).

These animals were treated with the appropriate hormones in adulthood and tested for the display of mating responses. The results are illustrated in Figure 2. Males castrated in adulthood mounted females when given testosterone, but they were not mounted by other males when given fe-

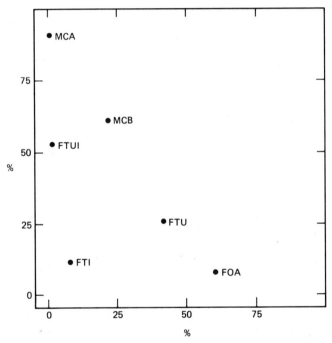

Figure 2 Sexual behavior of adult dogs following perinatal androgen treatment. The ordinate shows the percentage of animals showing mounting behavior when given androgen in adulthood. The abscissa shows the percentage of the same animals accepting mounts in adulthood after estrogen treatment. Key: MCA, males castrated in adulthood; MCB, males castrated shortly after birth; FTUI, females administered androgen both before birth and shortly after birth; FTI, females administered androgen in infancy; FTU, females administered androgen in utero; FOA, females ovariectomized in adulthood. Data from Beach et al. (17). Note that androgen treatment in infancy (FTI) defeminized, but did not masculinize the females.

472 Sexual Differentiation: Models, Methods, Mechanisms

male hormones. Females ovariectomized in adulthood were mounted by males, but never mounted males when given testosterone. Thus, in dogs that mature normally, males are masculine, but not feminine, whereas females are feminine, but not masculine.

Most of the male dogs castrated at birth mounted females when given male hormone, and about 20% of these males permitted other males to mount them while they were receiving female hormones.

The females that were given testosterone in infancy did not mount, and few were mounted.

About 25% of the females that received testosterone prenatally mounted, and about 45% of these females were mounted.

Over 50% of the females that received androgen both before and after birth mounted, but these females were never mounted while receiving female hormone.

These data do not fall on a straight line as would be predicted by a linear model of masculinity–femininity. Particularly striking in this regard is the observation that androgen treatment shortly after birth almost completely suppressed the potential of the bitch to show feminine behavior without altering its potential to show masculine behavior. These data and the data cited earlier have led me to the orthogonal model of masculinity–femininity, that is, that masculinity and femininity are independent parameters of behavioral potential.

METHODS

The orthogonal model of sex differences in behavior forces us to evaluate the possibility that for any given species or for any given behavior pattern genetic males and females may be similar or different. This leads to some methodological considerations. First we must define the behavior in question and determine how best to measure it. For example, Goy and Goldfoot (13) have recently pointed out the importance of the stimulus conditions used for the assessment of sex differences in behavior. They note that apparent contradictions have appeared in the literature because investigators have studied sex differences without holding stimulus conditions constant, for example, by testing experimental males with stimulus males while testing experimental females with stimulus females. A proper assessment of male–female differences in behavior, they point out, should involve the testing of both sexes against the same stimulus partners. This particular problem has been more apparent in studies of sex differences in aggressive behavior than in studies of sexual behavior.

Studies of sexual behavior have suffered by being less quantitative than is desirable. To illustrate, in assessing the potential for lordosis, some investigators have been willing to accept the presence or absence of the lordotic response as an adequate measure of feminine behavior. A more sophisticated approach, one used by many investigators, involves determining the probability (or duration) of lordosis. Using this measure, most studies have shown that female rats and male rats castrated shortly after birth readily show lordosis in adulthood, whereas male rats castrated in adulthood or female rats administered TP at birth rarely show lordosis in adulthood. This measure, however, does have some deficiencies that can influence our interpretation of the nature of sex differences in behavior. For example, in most of the early studies of lordosis behavior in male and female rats, adult gonadectomized animals were tested after treatment with estrogen and progesterone. Combined hormone treatment was used because it has been known for some time that the combined treatment is more effective than is estrogen alone in inducing lordosis in female rats (18, 19). Because combined treatment was used, it was not possible to determine whether the males were less responsive than females to estrogen, to progesterone, or to both steroids. In 1969, two independent studies (20, 21) suggested that neonatal androgen stimulation might differentiate males from females by suppressing responsiveness to progesterone, but not to estrogen. To obtain more information on this problem, we (22) treated with estrogen male rats castrated at birth or in adulthood and females injected with TP or oil at birth and gonadectomized in adulthood. In this study, we measured both intense and weak lordosis responses to obtain a finer grain measure of the lordosis behavior. We found, as before, that neonatal androgenization inhibited intense lordosis behavior: it was rarely shown by males castrated in adulthood or by neonatally androgenized females. However, we also found that "lordosis" occurred with a moderate frequency when we included weak or partial lordosis responses in our analysis. We concluded that postnatal androgen stimulation does indeed suppress responsiveness to etrogen stimulation in adulthood. But we were also led to believe that one's conclusion about the presence or absence of lordosis depends to an important degree on what an investigator will accept as the occurrence of a lordosis response.

Differences in interpretation of the differentiation of the potential for lordosis might have been avoided if investigators, including ourselves, had utilized a sensitive analysis of the lordosis response, such as that utilized by Hardy and DeBold (23), in which the intensity of each lordosis response was assessed. The point of emphasis here is that our understanding of the psychobiology of sex differences depends as much on a sophisticated analysis of behavior as it does on a thorough biological analysis.

A second area where we have been somewhat remiss is in the pharmacology of sexual differentiation. A classical pharmacological analysis involves an assessment of both dose–response and time–response relationships. Systematic studies of this nature, with some notable exceptions, are far too rare. Many investigators have settled on fixed dose and time treatment combinations, which, though effective, provide limited information.

The value of determining time–response relationships for the action of hormones on sexual differentiation can be illustrated as follows. It has been a common observation that female rats administered testosterone in adulthood show male-type mounting responses, on occasion show intromission-type responses, but rarely show ejaculation-type responses (25). However, if female rats are treated with androgen perinatally, they will readily display the complete masculine pattern of sexual behavior, the frequency and patterning of the responses being almost identical with those shown by males (26–28). This masculinization of behavior is dramatic. The interpretation of the observation, however, has not been simple. Perinatal androgenization not only alters behavior in the masculine direction but also facilitates penile growth. The question has been raised whether enhanced masculine behavior reflects a masculinization of the central nervous system or simply the masculinization of the peripheral genital apparatus. To help answer this question, Beach, Noble, and Orndoff (28) castrated male rats at birth and either administered no hormone or gave androgen at various times up to 2 weeks after birth. When the animals were adult, they were again administered androgen, tested for masculine mating responses, and studied for penile development. The correlation between the probability of intromission responses and penis weight was striking and suggested that the ability of the animal to display masculine-type sexual responses is indeed influenced by a peripheral action of the androgens. Although these data have by no means resolved the controversy (13), this interesting hypothesis would not have been viable without the systematic time–response analysis that was carried out.

Time–response analyses have not been uncommon in the recent studies of hormone-induced differentiation of sexual behavior since it became quite clear early in the history of these studies that the organisms involved go through sensitive developmental phases. For example, prenatal androgen treatment of the female rat can cause major changes in genital morphology without altering the potential to show lordosis behavior. Postnatal androgen stimulation can cause the opposite effects. Dose–response studies have been somewhat less common. Our own study of the effects of various doses of TP in infancy on the development of masculine and feminine behavior in hamsters (Fig. 1) illustrates one such study. It has been of great interest to workers in the field why the male hamster can display both masculine and feminine responses. Our data would suggest that the male hamster secretes rather little androgen during the sensitive period. The small amount secreted would be sufficient to develop the potential for masculine behavior, but not sufficient to completely inhibit lordosis behavior. Thus the dose–response analysis suggests an interpretation for what appears to be an unusual pattern of sexual differentiation.

The above are only two of several studies that illustrate the potential value of careful pharmacological studies in our analysis of the hormonal control of sexual differentiation.

MECHANISMS

Since the work of Phoenix et al. (8) in 1959, we have made a great deal of progress toward understanding the behavioral effects of removing and administering gonadal hormones during development. The same cannot be said about our understanding of the mechanisms by which the presence of gonadal hormones during development alter the neural or even the peripheral genital systems that underlie and regulate sexuality.

Within this context there are two questions that are of great interest currently. First, a number of investigators are asking which hormones indeed regulate the differentiation process. Resko, Feder, and Goy (29) have reported that the major plasma androgen in the newborn rat is testosterone. Androstenedione can be found in the testes at that time, but not in the plasma. This finding would suggest that testosterone is the active agent. However, it should be noted that androstenedione administered to neonatal rats is capable of inhibiting the later display of lordosis. D. Rezek and I subcutaneously implanted Silastic capsules containing testosterone, androstenedione, or dihydrotestosterone into newborn rats. The capsules were removed 10 days later. When the females were adult, they were administered estrogen and progesterone, and tested for lordosis behavior. The results are shown in Figure 3. Androstenedione during the neonatal period, like testosterone, suppressed lordosis behavior in adulthood. Thus the possibility exists that low levels of androstenedione normally supplement the secreted testosterone in the control of sexual differentiation.

Thus study also shows that dihydrotestosterone is ineffective in suppressing lordosis. This is interesting in light of the findings of Wilson and Lasnitzki (30) that the urogenital sinus and tubercle of the rat fetus readily convert testosterone to dihydrotestosterone, presumably as part

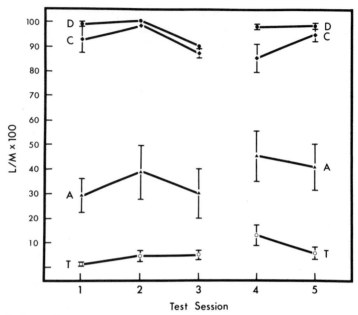

Figure 3   Sexual behavior of adult female rats treated with cholesterol (C), dihydro-testosterone (D), androstenedione (A), or testosterone (T) in infancy. The animals were given estrogen and progesterone in adulthood. Testosterone and androstenedione treatments inhibited the display of lordosis. L/M = lordosis frequency/mount frequency.

of the mechanism of action of the androgen. Consistent with this was our finding that the dihydrotestosterone implants, like the testosterone implants, significantly enhanced penile growth. Taken together, these data lead to the hypothesis that during the differentiation period secreted testosterone (and possibly androstenedione) differentiates the neural structures that control sexual behavior, while dihydrotestosterone metabolized from secreted testosterone differentiates the genital structures involved in copulatory activity.

These findings are, however, subject to an alternative interpretation. Naftolin and colleagues (31, 32) have demonstrated that central nervous system tissues are capable of aromatizing androstenedione to estrone. They have taken these findings to suggest that androgens function only after being aromatized to estrogens. This hypothesis is intriguing because it has been known since our early work that the administration of estrogen to newborn female rats will work like testosterone to inhibit the later display of lordosis behavior (33).

The strength of the aromatization hypothesis comes not simply from the fact that the effects of neonatal estrogen treatment parallel the effects of neonatal androgen treatment but also from the fact that dihydrotestosterone, which is ineffective in inducing differentiation (Fig. 3), is a nonaromatizable androgen that is not metabolically converted to an estrogen.

Of course, these findings in no way prove that sexual differentiation is controlled by an estrogen. The data are cited to raise the critical issue of the role of steroid metabolism in the differentiation process.

The second question of current interest regarding mechanisms of sexual differentiation concerns the detection of sex differences in brain morphology or function. Within this context I shall focus on one aspect of differentiation: the difference between the male and female rat in their response to estrogens. Estrogen can readily induce lordosis behavior in adult female rats, but not in male rats (or in neonatally androgenized rats). This finding leads us to believe that there must be some detectable difference between the brains of males and females that regulates this difference in response to estrogen. Since there is a great deal of evidence that estrogens are selectively accumulated in restricted brain regions in the female rat (34–37), investigators hypothesized that males and females may differ in their ability to accumulate and retain estrogen in the brain. At least 18 studies since 1966 have examined this hypothesis by comparing the accumulation of radiolabeled estrogen in selected regions of the brains of male, female, and neonatally androgenized rats. Maurer (38) has recently reviewed these studies. Although these studies differ in methodological details, which could have influenced the results, the general survey indicates that, in 10 of these studies, neonatal androgenization, endogenous or exogenous, reduced the uptake or retention of estrogen in the anterior hypothalamic–preoptic area of the brain. In the other eight studies, investigators reported that there were no striking sex differences in the brain accumulation of estrogen. All studies reported that the brain of the male (or androgenized female) is capable of accumulating estrogen. In our own laboratory, we have found no sex differences in the uptake of estrogen in the brain (30, 40) nor in the regional distribution of estrogenic metabolites in the brain after estradiol administration (41). Thus the evidence is not convincing that males and females differ in any meaningful way in their ability to concentrate estrogen in brain tissue.

The failure to consistently find large differences between males and females in the tissue accumulation of estrogen does not eliminate the possibility that there are sex differences in the cellular response to estrogen. The general model of estrogen action widely accepted today, and based on studies of estrogen effects on the uterus (42), holds that estrogen enters the cell, where it is bound to a cytoplasmic protein receptor. The estrogen–receptor complex transfers the hormone to the nucleus of the cell, where the hormone is bound to a nuclear protein receptor. This estrogen–receptor complex interacts with the genetic material to regulate cell function (43). This model has been applied to the brain with some success. For example, cytoplasmic estradiol binding has been demonstrated in the hypothalamus of rats (44, 45) and it has been shown that hypothalamic nuclei selectively accumulate and retain estradiol (46).

It is possible that males and females differ either in cytoplasmic or nuclear binding, a difference that is masked in the study of whole tissues. Two recent studies are pertinent to this point. Maurer (38) examined the cytoplasmic binding of estradiol in male, female, and androgenized female rats. His results are shown in Figure 4. Selective cytoplasmic binding was found in the anterior hypothalamic–preoptic area and in the median eminence area, but not in the cortex of all of the animals. Thus male–female differences in response to estrogen are probably not mediated by sex differences in cytoplasmic receptors.

In our own laboratory, we have looked for sex differences in the cytoplasmic and nuclear retention of estradiol. No sex differences were found in the retention of estrogen in the cytosol fraction as would be suggested by Maurer's data. Male–female differences were, however, found in the retention of estrogen by hypothalamic nuclei. Nuclei from females retained more than did nuclei from males, but the magnitude of the difference was not striking. Although possible, it seems unlikely that the small difference in nuclear retention that we have found can account for the large differences existing between males and females in their behavioral response to estrogen.

Thus, after a great deal of research, we are still left with a question about the nature of the cellular differences that presumably exist between males and females and account for their differential response to hormone. Of course it is possible that during differentiation hormones act on the brain not to alter biochemical mechanism, but to alter growth and thereby neural connectivity. The recent work of Raisman and Field (47) is consistent with this possibility. These workers have reported that the synaptic connections in the preoptic area differ between males and females, females having more dendritic spine connections than males. Spine connections are at female levels in males castrated within 12 hours of birth and in females given androgen 16 days after birth; spine connections are at the male level in males castrated 1 week after birth and in females given androgen 4 days after birth. Thus those animals capable of showing lordosis have a different pattern of synaptic connectivity than animals that have a limited capacity for lordosis. Further study of these sex differences in brain morphology may provide important insights into the nature of the biological basis of sex differences in behavior.

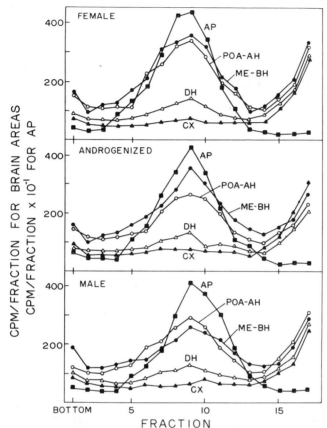

Figure 4 Sucrose-density-gradient analysis of cytoplasmic hormone receptors in the brain of adult male, female, and neonatally androgen-treated female rats. The animals were administered radiolabeled estrogen as adults, and tissues were taken to determine the ability of each tissue to concentrate hormone. Ordinate indicates relative radioactivity levels. Key: AP, anterior pituitary; POA–AH, preoptic–anterior hypothalamic region; ME–BH, median eminence-basal hypothalamus; DH, dorsal hypothalamus; CX, cortex. The figure indicates that the cytoplasm of hypothalamic, but not cortical, brain cells concentrates estrogen and that males, females, and neonatally androgenized females do not differ in this regard. Data from Maurer (38).

SUMMARY

From the psychobiologist's point of view we have made progress toward understanding the hormonal control of sexual differentiation. We have learned a great deal about the kinds of manipulation that will alter the display of sexually differentiated behavior in adult animals. We still need to know more about which hormones are normally effective in bringing about differentiation and about the mechanisms by which they work. To achieve this end, we need experimentation in which careful attention is paid not only to the nature of the hormonal treatments but also the measurement of behavioral differences.

REFERENCES

1. Pfeiffer, C. A., *Am J Anat* **58**: 195, 1936.
2. Greene, R. R., M. W. Burrill, and A. C. Ivy, *Am J Anat* **65**: 415, 1939.
3. Greene, R. R., M. W. Burrill, and A. C. Ivy, *Am J Anat* **67**: 305, 1940.
4. Jost, A., *Arch Anat Micr Morphol Exp* **36**: 271, 1947.
5. Barraclough, C. A. and J. H. Leathem, *Proc Soc Exp Biol Med* **85**: 673, 1954.
6. Wilson, J. G., W. C. Young, and J. B. Hamilton, *Yale J Biol Med* **13**: 189, 1940.
7. Wilson, J. G., J. B. Hamilton, and W. C. Young, *Endocrinology* **29**: 784, 1941.
8. Phoenix, C. H., R. W. Goy, A. A. Gerall, and W. C. Young, *Endocrinology* **65**: 369, 1959.
9. Harris, G. W. and S. Levine, *J. Physiol (London)* **163**: 42P, 1962.
10. Young, W. C., R. W. Goy, and C. H. Phoenix, *Science* **143**: 212, 1964.
11. Whalen, R. E., In Diamond, M. (ed.), *Perspectives in Reproduction and Sexual Behavior*, Indiana University Press, Bloomington, 1968, p. 303.
12. Beach, F. A., in Tobach, E., L. R. Aronson, and E. Shaw (eds.), *The Biopsychology of Development*, Academic Press, New York, 1971, p. 249.
13. Goy, R. W. and D. A. Goldfoot, in Greep, R. O. and E. B. Astwood (eds.), *Handbook of Physiology: Endocrinology II*, American Physiological Society, Washington, D.C., in press.
14. Whalen, R. E. and D. A. Edwards, *Anat Rec* **157**: 173, 1967.
15. Tiefer, L., *Horm Behav* **1**: 189, 1971.
16. Swanson, H. H. and D. A. Crossley, in Hamburgh, M. and E. J. W. Barrington (eds.), *Hormones in Development*, Appleton, New York, 1971.
17. Beach, F. A., R. E. Kuehn, R. H. Sprague, and J. J. Anisko, *Horm Behav* **3**: 143, 1972.
18. Beach, F. A., *Proc Soc Exp Biol Med* **51**: 369, 1942.
19. Boling, J. L. and R. J. Blandau, *Endocrinology* **25**: 359, 1939.
20. Clemens, L. G., M. Hiroi, and R. A. Gorski, *Endocrinology* **84**: 1430, 1969.
21. Davidson, J. M. and S. Levine, *J Endocrinol* **44**: 129, 1969.
22. Whalen, R. E., W. G. Luttge, and B. B. Gorzalka, *Horm Behav* **2**: 83, 1971.
23. Hardy, D. F. and J. F. DeBold, *J Comp Physiol Psychol* **78**: 400, 1972.
24. Whalen, R. E., in McGaugh, J. L. (ed.), *The Chemistry of Mood, Motivation and Memory*, Plenum Press, New York, 1972.
25. Whalen, R. E. and R. T. Robertson, *Psychonom Sci* **11**: 319, 1968.
26. Ward, I. L., *Horm Behav* **1**: 25, 1969.

27. Sachs, B. D., E. I. Pollak, M. S. Krieger, and R. J. Barfield, *Science* **181**: 770, 1973.
28. Beach, F. A., R. G. Noble, and R. K. Orndoff, *J Comp Physiol Psychol* **68**: 490, 1969.
29. Resko, J. A., H. H. Feder, and R. W. Goy, *J Endocrinol* **40**: 485, 1968.
30. Wilson, J. D. and I. Lasnitzki, *Endocrinology* **89**: 659, 1971.
31. Naftolin, F., K. J. Ryan, and Z. Petro, *Endocrinology* **90**: 295, 1972.
32. Reddy, V. V. R., F. Naftolin, and K. J. Ryan, *Endocrinology* **92**: 589, 1973.
33. Whalen, R. E. and R. D. Nadler, *Science* **141**: 273, 1963.
34. Pfaff, D. W., *Science* **161**: 1355, 1968.
35. Pfaff, D. W., in Segal, S. J., R. Crozier, P. A. Corfman, and P. G. Condliffe (eds.), *The Regulation of Mammalian Reproduction*, Thomas, Springfield, Ill., 1973.
36. Stumpf, W. E., *Science* **162**: 1001, 1968.
37. Luttge, W. G. and R. E. Whalen, *J Endocrinol* **52**: 379, 1972.
38. Maurer, R. A., unpublished Ph.D. thesis, University of California, Davis, 1973.
39. Green, R., W. G. Luttge, and R. E. Whalen, *Endocrinology* **85**: 373, 1969.
40. Whalen, R. E. and W. G. Luttge, *Neuroendocrinology* **6**: 255, 1970.
41. Luttge, W. G. and R. E. Whalen, *Steroids* **15**: 605, 1970.
42. Jensen, E. V., T Suzuki, T. Kawashima, W. E. Stumpf, P. W. Jungblut, and E. R. DeSombre, *Proc Natl Acad Sci, US*, **59**: 632, 1968.
43. McKerns, K. W., *The Sex Steroids*, Appleton-Century-Crofts, New York, 1971.
44. Kato, J., *Acta Endocrinol* **72**: 663, 1973.
45. Vertes, M. and R. J. B. King, in *Recent Developments of Neurobiology in Hungary*, Akademiai Kiado, Budapest, 1973.
46. Zigmond, R. E. and B. S. McEwen, *J Neurochem* **17**: 889, 1970.
47. Raisman, G. and P. M. Field, *Brain Res* **54**: 1, 1973.

Discussion: Perspectives on Psychoendocrine Differences

ANKE A. EHRHARDT, Moderator

RICHARD C. FRIEDMAN, Rapporteur

Dr. Ehrhardt asked for discussion on Dr. Doering's presentation on plasma testosterone levels and male behavior patterns.

Dr. Friedman observed that, since the day-to-day plasma testosterone variability is great, studies that have correlated behavior to a single plasma testosterone level are of questionable validity. He felt that the relationship of testosterone to homosexuality, depression, and schizophrenia should be reevaluated. Dr. Doering noted that large-amplitude changes in testosterone level may occur within hours and agreed with the need to reassess single-sample studies.

Dr. Friedman asked whether mental status was evaluated at the time of blood sampling and was informed that it had been within about 15 minutes of the sampling.

Dr. Phoenix pointed out that, in many species, testosterone-related behaviors frequently persist long after plasma testosterone level has fallen following castration. Dr. Doering concurred and also emphasized the importance of testosterone in the early life of the organism. He suggested that the testosterone-influenced behaviors of adults may have been shaped during embryonic or postnatal life and merely have to be activated by adequate levels of testosterone in the adult.

Dr. Whalen observed that the lowest levels of testosterone reported in this study might still be above those needed to influence various behaviors. Dr. Doering agreed and further commented that, since 98% of

plasma testoterone is protein bound and only 2% is free, total testosterone levels that are quite low might still contain enough free testosterone
to affect behavior.

Dr. Meyer-Bahlburg remarked that many subjects may fluctuate in
their motivation to respond to different scales of the Multiple Affect
Adjective Check List and was informed by Dr. Doering that no attempt
had been made to control for this variable in the study reported.

Dr. Meyer-Bahlburg commented on the marked changeability in day-to-
day testosterone levels of one of Dr. Doering's subjects (PH). He asked
whether the coefficient of variation for plasma testosterone was above
25% in other subjects. Dr. Doering answered that the coefficient of variation of most subjects was about 20% (median of all 20 subjects was 21%;
range, 14.4–42.2). For subject PH the coefficient of variation was 42%
and thus was unusually labile. There were five other subjects with coefficients above 25% of their mean plasma levels. Dr. Meyer-Bahlburg noted
that the great day-to-day fluctuation in plasma testosterone levels necessitated the use of multiple-sampling techniques in studies correlating testosterone with behavior.

Dr. Hunt remarked that certain behaviors might be influenced by
changes in blood testosterone levels after considerable delay. He asked
whether correlates were made between testosterone change and delayed
behavioral change. Dr. Doering replied that the results were computer
analyzed. Correlations were run offset by plus or minus 2 days and by
plus or minus 4 days, but no significant new relationships between testosterone and behavior could be found. The largest number of correlation
coefficients were still on same-day comparisons. When affect measured
2 days before blood sampling was compared with plasma testosterone
level, significant correlation coefficients virtually vanished.

Dr. Stern suggested that turnover rate might be more important to
measure than blood testosterone levels. Dr. Doering noted that in the
future his group planned to measure the ratios of free to bound testosterone.

Dr. Friedman commented that, if correlations had been found, the
importance of higher centers controlling testosterone production would
still have to be kept in mind. Altered plasma testosterone levels might
be the effect as well as the cause of altered psychic states. Recent work
relating luteotrophic releasing hormone to mating behavior in rats was
cited to illustrate the complexity of the possible correlations: a behavior
known to be influenced by sex steroids was shown to be directly affected
by a centrally acting hormone that also influences testosterone secretion.

Dr. Doering said that his group tended to hypothesize that testosterone
is a cause of behavior, rather than an effect, although Dr. Friedman's
suggestion was certainly to be considered.

Dr. Meyer-Bahlburg observed that strenuous exercise has recently been shown to produce elevation of blood testosterone levels. He inquired whether this was controlled for by a rest period prior to blood sampling. Dr. Doering replied that, although most subjects did not engage in exercise before sampling, no special effort was made to rigorously control for this variable. Remarking on a report by C. A. Fox that testosterone is elevated by intercourse, but not by masturbation, Dr. Meyer-Bahlburg suggested that an exercise effect may have been demonstrated, rather than an effect specifically related to sexual behavior.

Dr. Rosenblum opened the discussion on the relationship of aggression and androgens to the XYY syndrome. He asked whether any other parameters equalled or exceeded the high incidence of XYY in the prison population as compared with the general population. He explained that the purpose of his question was to emphasize the social significance of screening studies. He mentioned birth order as a specific example of another type of parameter that might be abnormal in a prison population. Dr. Meyer-Bahlburg observed that psychopathology is increased in a prison population and that most of the inmates are of low socioeconomic status. He did not have data available to respond in more detail to Dr. Rosenblum.

Dr. Ehrhardt commented that although levels of testosterone in adulthood might be the same for XYY males and normal males, there is still the chance that differential thresholds of receptor responsivity to the hormone exist. Such differential receptor sensitivities might reflect disparate prenatal levels of testosterone. There were no findings as to the possibility of differential receptor responsivity in these patients, and prenatal androgen levels were not known.

Dr. Rosenblum wondered whether the differential threshold hypothesis might not be experimentally investigated.

Dr. Ehrhardt suggested that castration studies (or observation of adults who had been accidentally castrated) would allow for the construction of dose–response curves for testosterone-related behaviors that might shed light on this question.

Dr. Rosenblum asked whether nonsurgical experiments utilizing cyproterone might be tried on humans. A testosterone antagonist threshold could then be established. Dr. Ehrhardt replied that since the mechanism of action in cyproterone is not known, such experiments would not be useful.

Dr. Whalen commented that it is not yet known whether it is possible to get an assay of tissue response to testosterone. Dr. Green mentioned that a recent project in London comparing the uptake of tritiated testosterone in scrotal skin in transsexuals and normals revealed no differences.

Dr. Whalen emphasized that peripheral tissue and central nervous system tissue cannot be assumed to have similar sensitivities to the hormone. Brain differentiation and peripheral tissue differentiation under the influence of testosterone occur at separate times. An individual could have normal brain differentiation, cease secreting the hormone, and then have abnormal peripheral tissue differentiation. Scrotal skin biopsies, therefore, whether normal or abnormal in terms of the uptake of tritiated testosterone, might be irrelevant with respect to the status of the central nervous system.

Dr. Ehrhardt then asked for discussion of Dr. Whalen's paper concerning hormonal control of differentiation.

Dr. Phoenix commented on the need to be precise with regard to understanding the concepts of masculinity and femininity. These names are given to categories of behavior. Frequently both males and females engage in cross-gender behaviors, and what is "masculine" or "feminine" refers to the frequency of specific types of behaviors rather than to their presence or absence. For example, both male and female rats mount, but since mounting is more common in males, it is defined as "masculine."

He continued by saying that it is incorrect to think of masculinity as an "all-or-nothing trait." Alterations in hormone levels may increase or decrease the frequencies of specific behaviors. For example, a rat castrated on the day of birth will mount. If the presence or absence of mounting behavior is taken as the index of masculinity, a castrated rat will be considered masculine. If, on the other hand, intromission or frequency of ejaculation is taken as the masculinity index, the behavior might be considered demasculinized. It would be more precise to relate the hormones to specific types of behavior, rather than to masculinity or femininity *per se.*

Dr. Whalen suggested that notions of masculinity and femininity could be understood within the context of the description of specific behaviors.

Dr. Doering stated that hormones function through protein receptors and that, in order for a substance to be a hormone, a protein receptor site for it must exist. Sex differences, then, might be related to the presence of receptors for certain molecules in one sex, but not in the other sex.

Dr. Whalen disagreed. Apologizing for being "a little old-fashioned," he stated that he accepted the definition of hormones as secretory products of glands. He noted that, although no receptor site for testosterone has been found in the rat, he still accepts testosterone as a hormone. Furthermore, all hormones may not work on protein receptors; some may chiefly affect membranes. He mentioned progesterone as an example of a steroid hormone that may not primarily function via protein receptors.

Dr. Rosenblum asked Dr. Whalen to speculate on the mechanism by which experience may alter thresholds of the physiological systems described. Dr. Whalen believed that the question really addressed itself to the biochemistry and physiology of learning. He felt that the number of systems was too great, and the possible interactions too intricate, to justify speculation.

Dr. Green commented on the complexities inherent in attempting to understand sex differences in behavior. For example, males masturbate more frequently than females. This difference in sexual behavior might be related to social learning, central nervous system differences between the sexes, or differences in genital anatomy and physiology. With regard to homosexuality, he continued, the only biochemical anomaly whose observation has been replicated is reversal of androsterone–etiocholanolone ratios in homosexuals as compared with heterosexuals. However, these ratios were also reversed in heterosexuals who had various types of medical illnesses, so that the data were difficult to interpret.

Dr. Whalen stressed the need to avoid premature acceptance of hypotheses in view of the complexity of metabolic pathways and our lack of knowledge as to what the active hormones are that may be correlated with various behaviors.

Dr. Sachar noted that a bell-shaped curve exists for the distribution of many biological phenomena. Whether an individual is on a particular part of the bell curve for a given variable could be an accident of fate, yet such fortuitous circumstances might determine behavior. He cited Phyllis Greenacre as having conjectured that clitoral size, for example, might affect personality development. Dr. Ehrhardt related clitoral size to prenatal steroid hormone environment, which may have affected personality functioning rather than clitoral size by itself.

Dr. Phoenix briefly reviewed his work with prenatal hormones in guinea pigs. Small amounts of prenatal androgen stimulation produced no modification in female external genitalia. The lordosis response, however, was reduced when adult females were given estrogen and progesterone. If such females were administered testosterone, they would mount more than untreated females. In the rat, early use of dihydrotestosterone produced increased penile size, but not increased masculine behavior in adults.

Dr. Whalen agreed that both peripheral and central factors were of importance in regulating behavior. During differentiation, a hormone might affect peripheral tissues and also central tissues, each of which might then influence behavior.

Dr. Rosenblum discussed the importance of the environment in fostering sexual differentiation and particularly emphasized the significance of the female as an individual in eliciting sexual behaviors in males. He cited studies performed in his laboratory, where male macaques of 2, 3, 4, or 5 years of age were placed in a sexual situation with an estrogen-primed fully grown female and with an estrogen-primed 2-year-old female. The 4- and 5-year-old males mated with either female effectively. The 2-year-old males showed *no* sexual behavior with the adult female. The 3-year-old males showed much fighting with the adult female and also manifested some sexual behavior. However, 2-year-old monkeys mated effectively with 2-year-old females.

Continuing, Dr. Rosenblum pointed out that dominance–submission factors affect mating behavior, since the 2-year-old male monkeys are less dominant than the adult female, but more dominant than the 2-year-old female. The 3-year-old males are about equal to the adult females and fighting emerges to determine dominance. The older males are dominant over all females.

Dr. Rosenblum concluded by noting that, since dominance behavior is a function of communal interactions, laboratory investigation utilizing dyadic situations might not reflect natural sexual behavior. In the wild, for example, a 1-year-old male monkey might mate with an adult female if his mother is present and is the dominant female. In the laboratory, a 1-year-old male left alone with an adult female would be too frightened to mate.

Dr. Phoenix noted that even in adult normal animals, such as monkeys or dogs, individual sexual preferences might determine behavior. A male that is sexually active with a given female might not respond to a different female.

Dr. Whalen said that he had observed the same phenomenon in *cats* and that, for reasons unknown at present, individual differences in partner preference are important determinants of adult mammalian sexual behavior.

INDEX

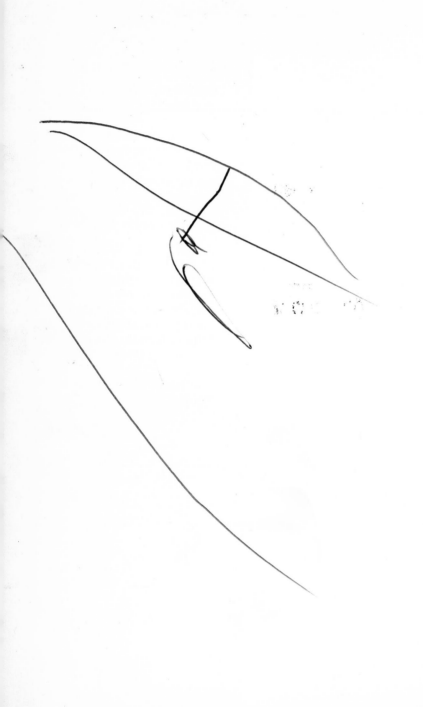